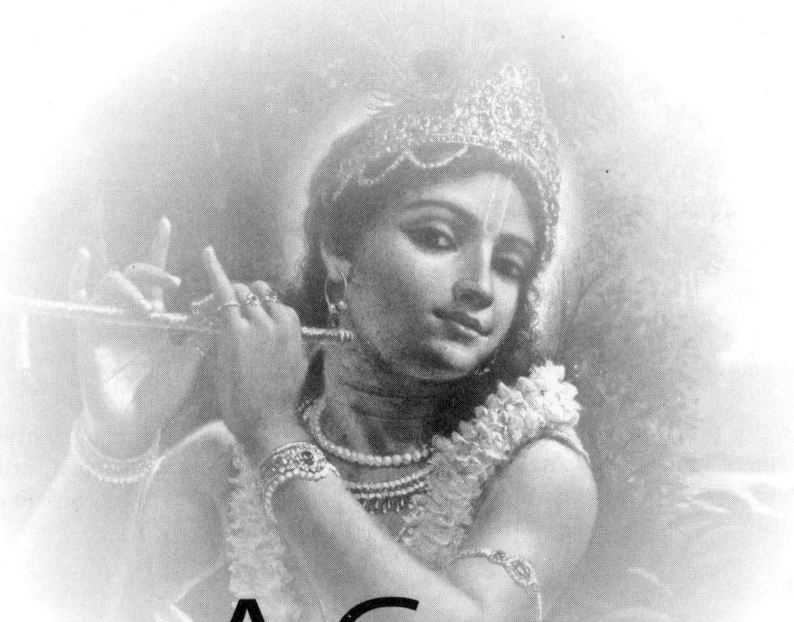

A God Who Dances

Krishna for You

"If they want me to believe in their God
they'll have to sing me better songs . . .
I could only believe in a God who dances."
– ***Friedrich Nietzsche***

By Carl Woodham

Torchlight Publishing
Badger California

Interior design by Jahnudvip dasa & Manideep

Printed in India

Published simultaneously in the United States of America and Canada by Torchlight Publishing, Inc.

ISBN 978-0-9817273-6-3

Torchlight Publishing, Inc.
P. O. Box 52, Badger, CA 93603
1-800-HIDDEN-1 (1-800-443-3361)
email: torchlightpublishing@yahoo.com
web: www.torchlight.com

Readers interested in the subject of this book are invited to contact the author at
carlwoodham@gmail.com
http://agodwhodances.com/book/

CONTENTS

Reader Advisory

Dear Friend,

This book contains information that, if understood, will dramatically change your life. If you want to keep things as they are, put down this book and do something else.

If you read and understand this book, you could lose some friends. Some family members may become disappointed with you. Reading this book could also shrink your net worth.

Why? Because if you catch on, the contents of this book will pulverize the present framework of your reality. It's like the red pill in the film *The Matrix:* once you take it and see what's really going on, you can't go back.

Here are some other reasons to let this book go:

- Seeking truth is hard. Why struggle when you can just let the flow take you where it goes?

- Life is short. Enjoy it. If you pursue spirituality now you could miss out on other things you enjoy. You can always come back to spiritual life later, when you're old and slow.

- Do you need to know who God is? You've got your religion and you'll go to heaven. Or you are spiritual but not religious. You also have friends who are spiritually OK. It's good enough for them. Who are you to want more?

If none of this fazes you—if you are that one-in-many-thousands who wants above all else to know the truth—then read on.

--cw

Part One

Krishna for You

For the Love of a Stranger

Suppose you're at a crowded party. You meet a man who says, "I came with my wife. She's the love of my life."

Looking around the room you ask, "Which one is your wife? Is she blonde or brunette?"

"I'm not sure."

"Well, is she short or tall?"

"I don't know."

"White or black? Fat or thin? Brown or blue eyes?"

"I have no idea. But I really love her."

"How can you love someone you don't even know?"

Now, if someone asked you who God is, would you fare any better?

If we are honest, most of us will admit that our understanding of God is vague, no matter how much we profess our love. No wonder Nietzsche famously asked for a better God than a blustering old man or a nameless nothing. How do you love an unseen some One or some Thing?

The same impersonal notion of God that drove Nietzsche to frustration still prevails in this high-tech age. As a result, we have been cheated of the blissful love of God that is our birthright.

Love of God ought to allow us to live in harmony with ourselves, with others and with the Earth. But even if we ask a nominal authority who God is, we are usually presented with a most unlovable picture. We are told that God is everywhere but we cannot see Him. We are warned that God is watching so we better be good. We are fed some saccharine platitudes about God being love. We are assaulted with sentimental hocus-pocus that says we are all one and together we comprise God.

All of this distracts us from a simple truth: to love someone, we must know them.

Since God created personable, lovable, vivacious people, He must have some of the same stuff. Otherwise, where did our attractive qualities originate? If God had no personality, how could anyone be attracted to Him? If He wasn't attractive, how could anyone love Him?

This book will introduce you to Krishna. Krishna means, 'the all-attractive Person.' Knowing Krishna brings a windfall of new spiritual wealth.

Krishna surpasses everyone, historical or fictional. You're about to meet a person who is stronger than Superman, wiser than Lincoln, richer than Gates, greater than Alexander, more beautiful than (insert your favorite movie star), and—in spite of all that—more renounced than Mother Teresa.

When you meet someone, their personality makes an impression that can lead to a relationship. In this book, you'll learn about Krishna's personality. You'll discover that God has friends, a family, hobbies, adventures and much, much more. And every word you'll read is drawn from authentic sources, not from anyone's imagination.

What does God do for fun? What does He eat? With whom does He hang out? With whom does He dance? In the answers to these questions lies God's personality and the chance for us to build a most valuable relationship.

Now, is Krishna for you? If you're completely content with your idea of God (and your life), then you may not be interested in seeking Him any further. On the other hand, if you're unclear about God and ready to learn, welcome. All you need is an open mind and willingness to listen and to reflect.

As a warm-up, we'll discuss an easy and safe way to approach Krishna. Then I'll tell you my story with Krishna. We'll also discuss some side benefits of knowing Krishna and examine some of the hang-ups people have about Krishna.

Ready? Meet Krishna. You'll never again be embarrassed by not knowing a Person you supposedly love.

The Krishna Experiment

When performing an experiment, a scientist who values the truth keeps an open mind. Great, unexpected scientific discoveries generally come only when the scientist acts objectively and examines the results without bias.

You can look at the life and teachings of Krishna as myths or you can look at them as reality. That's the Krishna experiment: theoretically, take Krishna as a real person who spoke a real book (*Bhagavad-gītā*) thousands of years ago. Take Krishna's memorable activities as things God might actually do. (After all, wouldn't one expect God to be a bit out of the ordinary?).

By *theoretically* accepting that Krishna *might* be God, you will experience how Krishna affects your life in unexpected ways. Then you can objectively decide whether you prefer life with or without Him.

In other words, at this point, whether or not you believe in Krishna makes no difference. When you experience Krishna, you'll see what has thrilled people for millennia. It's simple; ask yourself, if I don't know who God is, can I say for sure that He is not Krishna? Can I set aside any preconceived notions long enough to hear about Krishna?

My Dance with Krishna

Even in 1970 it was a little strange for a sixteen-year-old to voluntarily get up at dawn and do yoga stretches, but that was me—a little strange. I loved the spiritual undertones of Jethro Tull and the Moody Blues and devoured books by Hesse, Ram Dass and Krishnamurti. Something in all the quasi-spirituality drew me in, but I could never catch it. Some friends shared an interest, but they didn't seem to get it either.

In 1972, when I came of age, I decided to defer college. Frustration and curiosity with worldly life drove me to choose the freedom of a spiritual quest, a freedom that did not appear to be part of a liberal arts education. So I took a simple job delivering office supplies in downtown Portland, Oregon, rented an apartment and learned to cook vegetarian meals. After work I was free to read and to meet spiritual teachers.

Freedom, though, was also frustrating. Months of books, church services and seminars left me feeling no more enlightened. Expanding my search, I came upon the *Bhagavad-gītā*. There I found the following story about another confused person.

Arjuna, a powerful warrior, faces a terrible decision: fight in the ensuing battle and kill his beloved teacher and relatives, or leave the battlefield in shame.

Speaking to Krishna, his friend and charioteer, Arjuna lists reason after reason to give up the fight. So many men will die at his hand. Their widows will go unprotected and society will suffer. The battle's prize, the throne of the world, does not justify its miserable cost. In this case, Arjuna argues, to quit is nobler than to fight:

O Krishna, although these men, their hearts overtaken by greed, see no fault in killing one's family or quarreling with friends, why should we, who can see the crime in destroying a family, engage in these acts of sin? (Bg 1.37-38)

It is the Vietnam era. Arjuna's non-violent arguments all strike me as valid.

Krishna, though, taking the role of Arjuna's teacher, urges him to fight. Krishna explains that Arjuna can kill only the bodies of his enemies, not their souls. He urges him to do his duty without attachment:

Do thou fight for the sake of fighting, without considering happiness or distress, loss or gain, victory or defeat—and by so doing you shall never incur sin. (Bg 2.38)

After this, Krishna proceeds to answer Arjuna's questions about uniting with God through yoga and about himself.

At that point I again became lost. Who was this Krishna? I consulted several *Bhagavad-gītās* trying to understand. One translator said that Krishna was a symbolic fictional character. Another said Krishna was a perfected person whom we could emulate. Another avoided the issue by stopping his translation a third of the way through the *Gītā*. Another said that Krishna was God, and by following Him, we could become God, too.

Emulate Krishna? Become God? To me, all of this made no sense. Krishna said such bombastic things as,

I am the source of all spiritual and material worlds. Everything emanates from Me. The wise who perfectly know this engage in My devotional service and worship Me with all their hearts. (Bg 10.8).

Considering my rather inconsequential station in life, future creations seemed unlikely to emanate from me.

Then I came across the *Bhagavad-gītā As It Is* by A.C. Bhaktivedanta Swami (Śrīla) Prabhupāda. Merely by its appearance—thick and colorful and nearly a thousand pages—it stood apart from any other *Bhagavad-gītā* I'd seen. The difference in content was even more striking. Here was a scholarly case for Krishna as the one, monotheistic God, backed by extensive references and detailed word-for-word English translations of each of the *Gīta's* seven hundred Sanskrit texts.

In his commentary, Śrīla Prabhupāda explained that no, we will never *be* Krishna. However, we can resume a long-neglected, loving relationship with Him through *bhakti yoga,* the path of devotion. And, he stressed, to do so is to live the essence of the *Bhagavad-gītā.*

I felt challenged. Krishna seemed quite specific, and devotion to him limited. If I worshipped Krishna as God, could I still pursue other paths? Enlightenment, yes; but through exclusive devotion to one Person? That sounded fanatic.

Still, I was curious enough to poke my toes in the ocean of devotion. What happened next astonished me.

While continuing to read the *Bhagavad-gita As It Is*, I began chanting Krishna's names, as Śrīla Prabhupāda recommended. Day by day I began to feel more energized and alive than I'd felt since childhood. This *Bhagavad-gīta's* guidance to serve God in devotion was intuitive and easy to grasp.

Far from feeling trapped in one path, for the first time in my life I felt free to choose. I could choose to serve Krishna or to not serve Krishna. I could read about Krishna or someone else. And I soon discovered that whenever I chose Krishna, my mood, my attitude—my whole perspective changed. And for me it was a stunningly happy and liberating change.

My encounter with *bhakti* differed sharply from the wispy, vaguely spiritual experiences I'd had to that point. Serving Krishna was rock-solid spirituality, without the guesswork, prerequisite fanaticism or moody ups and downs.

Finally, I got it: all along I was trying to see to my own enlightenment, my own happiness. When instead I turned my meager efforts to bringing God a bit of happiness, my own joy appeared alongside as a by-product.

Prabhupāda explained the same phenomenon in the *Bhagavad-gītā As It Is*. Krishna told Arjuna to fight because it would please Him. For Arjuna, the battle was his service to Krishna, who wanted to relieve the world of the evil embodied by Arjuna's enemies. As such, Arjuna would find his peace only in the battle. And the battles of my life would also make sense only if I fought them for the higher purpose of pleasing God. And God, Srila Prabhupada insisted, "is Krishna."

Under Śrīla Prabhupāda's written guidance, I began serving Krishna in simple ways such as chanting and offering fruits and flowers. One service led to another, each one more blissful, until I found myself losing interest in bad habits out of sheer purpose and joy.

In time I met Śrīla Prabhupāda and accepted him as my spiritual guide. Over the years, with his teachings as a spiritual GPS, I developed two satisfying careers and raised a family for Krishna.

To this day, serving Krishna brings me pleasure surpassing any other, an underlying peace that sustains me through the pressures of life. Now, as a fifty-something grandfather, I offer you the same Krishna in my own words.

What's In It For You?

This book will help you understand these basics of the *Bhagavad-gītā*:

- *each of us is an eternal soul, not our body;*
- *God is a most remarkable person;*
- *we have the right to enjoy a loving relationship with Him;*
- *we will be satisfied only when we awaken that dormant relationship.*

Suppose you apply these basics and evolve from thinking Krishna may be God to loving Krishna. How will you change?

In 1968, a engineering graduate from Ohio State University named James Kohr discovered Krishna and became a much-loved practitioner of *Bhagavad-gita*, widely respected for his remarkable compassion and humility. Years later, after he passed away, a friend found his answer to this question scrawled on the inside cover of one of his dog-eared books:

- *You will quickly experience a new realm of mental poise and experience an inner happiness even in the midst of the most trying circumstances.*

- You will worry less and enjoy more. Your powers of concentration, memory, understanding and creativity will increase.

- You will work more energetically, more confidently and more efficiently, and you will better relate to people.

- You will succeed more easily at whatever you do.

- At night you will fall asleep immediately and in the morning you will awaken thoroughly refreshed, even with less hours of sleep than you normally need.

- You will understand the real purpose of your life and your unique role in creation.

For decades I have been amazed to see Krishna bring these benefits, and more, to thousands of people, from all countries and walks of life.

You needn't change your external life much if you reconnect with Krishna. You may adjust your diet. You may learn to value the early morning hours. You may enter a circle of remarkable new friends, centered on Krishna. While most of your externals remain the same, within yourself you'll learn to act as soul, not a body, and quickly progress in your inner life.

Krishna and Gurus

If we wanted to meet a celebrity, what would we do? We might stalk and try to catch them for a passing moment at a restaurant or on the street. But if we wanted a civil meeting, a chance to actually get to know them, we would approach their secretary for an appointment. From the secretary we might also gain useful advice about the celebrity's likes and dislikes.

An authentic guru is a spiritual guide who acts as a secretary for Krishna. To understand Krishna we need to go through someone who already knows Him and can introduce us. And, unlike many celebrities, Krishna looks forward to speaking with us, when we approach Him in this way.

At first, the idea of accepting a guru might threaten our sense of independence. For many, the word 'guru' has become a cliche. Accepting a guru is for the weak-minded. And it's dangerous; many cheaters show up in the guise of teachers. Can't we avoid the risk and figure out spirituality on our own?

Well, to learn anything quickly and accurately, we need a qualified teacher. No sane person would try to teach themselves brain surgery. Yet on spiritual matters, those most essential for happiness in life, many people decide to be their own guru. Such people are said to have a fool as a disciple, for if we could, we would have enlightened ourselves long ago.

A simple, honest admission of need and request for help, even to an unknown God, brings real help in the form of a genuine guru. To a sincere soul, God brings a guru and then, in turn, the guru brings God.

If we seek help from a guru, won't we be vulnerable? How will we prevent someone from taking advantage of us? How can we identify a genuine guru?

Krishna explains that we can learn to discriminate and check a guru's credentials.

A genuine guru:

• Says the same thing Krishna says, without change or embellishment;

• Teaches by example;

• Serves a guru, who serves a guru, who serves a guru. (Unlike self-appointed upstarts, real gurus have a pedigree, a lineage).

Beyond these basics, we can look for one more trait. John Lennon of the Beatles once asked Śrīla Prabhupāda, "So many people claim to be gurus. How do you tell the right one?"

Śrīla Prabhupāda replied, "Just find the one most addicted to Krishna."

Do we need any special qualification to understand Krishna through a guru? In *Bhagavad-gītā*, Krishna says:

Just try to learn the truth by approaching a spiritual master. Inquire from him submissively and render service unto him. The self-realized souls can impart knowledge unto you because they have seen the truth. (Bg 4.34).

If we don't yet understand Krishna, we need enough humility to listen carefully to someone who does—a truly qualified teacher—and ask meaningful questions. Relevant questions are essential, for without them Krishna remains unknown, even to those who try to follow Him blindly. Our sincere, honest questions, however foolish they may seem, show introspection and help us advance. That is our part in the guru-student relationship.

In this book I will pose some basic questions that you may have about Krishna, and then answer them from the *Bhagavad-gītā* and other sources. If you like what you find, Krishna will in turn lead you to more in-depth sources and, eventually, to your own personal guru.

While reading the right books is a great place to start, it takes a face-to-face guru to answer personal, detailed questions about how to best please Krishna. In addition to books and a guru, the exemplary lives and teachings of other enlightened people, past and present, provide a third point of reference. They help us evaluate what we read and what we hear from a guru.

What is the difference between guru and God?

Exemplary teachers who advocate loving God are gurus, regardless of their spiritual tradition. A guru, though, is not God; a guru represents God as an ambassador represents a country. A guru is one with God in intent, but not in extent. For example, a drop of seawater tastes as salty as the ocean, but it cannot float a battleship. Similarly, a guru is one with God in knowledge and purpose, but far different from God in power.

If gurus are thus both one and different from God, are they one with each other?

Great gurus of the past, such as Christ, Moses and Mohammed, taught and demonstrated love of God. In this sense, all genuine gurus share a oneness. However, they differ enough in culture and style of presentation to have invoked horrific conflicts in God's name, leading many to abandon any systematic approach to God.

An old story illustrates this conundrum: the sons of a beloved father all want to bring him relief and pleasure with a massage. However, after the first soothing strokes and squeezes, they begin to argue over who gets to massage what part of the father's body. Instead of massaging, suddenly they are striking each other. Instead of pleasing their father, they break his heart.

What does one do if one wants spirituality without religious conflict?

The *Bhāgavat Purana* (a Sanskrit text known as the 'post-graduate study of *Bhagavad-gītā*') offers this non-sectarian synopsis:

The supreme occupation for all humanity is that by which one can attain to loving devotional service unto the transcendent Lord. Such devotional service must be unmotivated and uninterrupted to completely satisfy the self. (BP 1.2.6).

In other words, when we please God, we become satisfied. To be satisfied ourselves, we simply need to see to God's satisfaction. All genuine gurus therefore advocate His loving service according to their cultural setting. Their lives exemplify loving service to God.

What if a guru claims to be God?

Such a person is cheating. A real guru always seeks to serve God, not to take over His position. Some people fall for promises that a God-guru can make the student God, too. This is a great marketing idea, but be sure to get a money-back guarantee in case you can't spin out a galaxy, or at least a planet or two, at the end of the course.

Is Krishna a guru?

Yes, and more. Krishna's book, the *Bhagavad-gītā*, advocates loving God, as do other scriptures. Yet unlike other genuine spiritual leaders, in the *Bhagavad-gītā*, Krishna defines Himself as God. For example:

O conqueror of wealth, there is no truth superior to Me. Everything rests upon Me, as pearls are strung on a thread. (Bg.7.7).

A person in full consciousness of Me, knowing Me to be the ultimate beneficiary of all sacrifices and austerities, the Supreme Lord of all planets and demigods, and the benefactor and well-wisher of all living entities, attains peace from the pangs of material miseries. (Bg. 5.29)

After hearing Krishna's teachings, His student, Arjuna, concludes:

You are the Supreme Personality of Godhead, the ultimate abode, the purest, the Absolute Truth. You are the eternal, transcendental, original person, the unborn, the greatest. All the great sages such as Nārada, Asita, Devala and Vyāsa confirm this truth about You, and now You Yourself are declaring it to me. (Bg. 10.12-13).

While others speak of the Father, Krishna claims directly to be the Father:

It should be understood that all species of life are made possible by birth in this material nature, and that I am the seed-giving father. (Bg. 14.4).

Among all the speakers in all the great world scriptures, only Krishna directly says, "I am God."

Why don't other scriptures define God as Krishna?

If people have problems with idolatry or basic morality, their teachers may withhold detailed knowledge of God. A math teacher would not present calculus to third-graders. Yet, math is math. The serious student will eventually reach calculus.

There are degrees of knowing a person. Anyone may read about the powers of the President of the United States and know him in that way. A rare few enter his personal retinue and address him as "Mr. President." But his family members know him as "Dad" or "Dear." They know his powers, but they also know him in person.

In the same way, full knowledge of God includes knowing His personality. This is the great gift of Krishna. If you meet someone else more qualified to be God than Krishna, please let me know.

If past gurus loved God, why not just learn from them?

Regardless of their level of teaching, we can learn much from great gurus of the past. However, to love God today, now, in full, we also need a face-to-face genuine guru to help us apply their teachings and confront our own flaws.

Connecting With Krishna

Is it always beneficial to have a guru between us and Krishna?

Yes. by practical and personal example, our guru will show us what it means to tune in to Krishna. In time, with our guru's help and our own practice, we can perfect our relationship with Krishna. Yet even now, Krishna sits in our hearts, speaking to us through intuition and instinct.

I am seated in everyone's heart, and from Me come knowledge, remembrance and forgetfulness. (Bg. 15.15).

According to the *Bhagavad-gītā*, we and Krishna go way back. We are eternal souls, living pieces of Krishna's spiritual energy. We inhabit physical bodies, just as a driver inhabits a car. When the car breaks down, the driver gets another one to drive to the next stop. In the same way, when our bodies die, we move on to a new body. Krishna always rides beside us, life after life, body after body, encouraging us to try something less grueling.

The living entities in this conditioned world are My eternal fragmental parts. Due to conditioned life, they are struggling very hard with the six senses, which include the mind. (Bg. 15.7).

Yet in this body there is another, a transcendental enjoyer, who is the Lord, the supreme proprietor, who exists as the overseer and permitter, and who is known as the Supersoul. (Bg. 13.23).

One who sees the Supersoul accompanying the individual soul in all bodies, and who understands that neither the soul nor the Supersoul within the destructible body is ever destroyed, actually sees. (Bg. 13.28).

Up to this point, we have refused to listen to Krishna, who is known as the Supersoul in our hearts.

Reincarnating is no fun, and without resetting our priorities, we can't stop it. Against our wishes, our bodies die. Then, as deathless souls, we are forced to move on to another body. According to Krishna's explanation in the *Bhagavad-gītā*, we face this stark choice: embrace the painful illusion of, "I am this body," or gradually realize we are, in fact, *not* these frail and doomed material bodies.

Why would a kind, all-powerful God serve up this difficult choice?

Because God wants our love, and love can only be given voluntarily. It's *our* choice, not His. We can love our body or love its creator. We can live as a temporary body or live as an eternal spiritual being—a soul. We've been making the wrong choice for a long time. Does that make God cruel for giving us a choice in the first place?

The body is meant for eating, sleeping, mating and self-preservation. The soul is meant for loving God. Body or soul? The choice is ours.

When we choose to act in our better interest, God's smile looks sweeter.

How about choosing neither body nor soul?

Sorry. The *Gīta* declares that everyone born in this world identifies with their bodies. Although we are deathless living beings stuck in this body temporarily, we think we are male, female, white, black, old, young, American, Indian, African or German. Doing nothing means keeping things that way.

O Arjuna, all living entities are born into delusion, bewildered by dualities arisen from desire and hate. (Bg. 7.27).

Living as if we were our bodies while neglecting the needs of the soul is like polishing a fancy bird cage while allowing the bird within to starve. Yes, we can care well for both body and soul, but the soul is more important, just as care for the cage is meaningless without care for the bird.

The science of *bhakti yoga* teaches us how to transfer the object of our love from man to God, from matter to spirit. When we love God first, we automatically love His creations. Trying to love God by loving His creation is another mistake, like trying to water each leaf of a tree instead of pouring water on the root.

Have you ever seen a bumper sticker saying, "I Love God"? For me and countless others, discovering Krishna has given a profound new meaning to 'loving God.' When God's identity becomes clear, loving Him becomes a personal affair. And that relationship changes everything.

Krishna, The gods, and Avatars

Isn't Krishna just one of the many gods of Hinduism?

First, the word 'Hindu' does not appear in the *Bhagavad-gītā* or any Sanskrit text. 'Hindu' is a relatively modern, secular word derived from the Persian word for the people of the Indus, a river in India.

The religion known as Hinduism is a diverse conglomeration of beliefs, with many patterns of worship centered loosely on various parts of the huge body of Sanskrit wisdom literature. If anything unites the world's billion Hindus, it is a strong reverence for the *Bhagavad-gītā*. Yet reverence does not equate to understanding; many Hindus respect *Bhagavad-gītā* while having no clear idea what it says.

The *Bhagavad-gītā* urges one to love God in devotion above all else:

Abandon all varieties of religion and just surrender unto Me. I shall deliver you from all sinful reactions. Do not fear. (18.66)

Other parts of the Sanskrit texts direct those seeking money and worldly blessings to bow to various *devas* (gods). Śiva, the god of destruction, is known for making his followers powerful. Lakṣmī, goddess of fortune, brings wealth. Sarasvatī is the goddess of education. Ganesh, Durgā, Brahmā, Indra—there are thirty-three million *devas*, all of them far more powerful and opulent than any human can imagine. And all of them adore Krishna as the supreme, because the *Gīta's* essential message of love of God applies to them as well as to human beings.

Those who are devotees of other gods and who worship them with faith actually worship only Me, but they do so in a wrong way. (B.g 9.23)

According to the *Gīta* and other Vedic sources, the *devas* control the forces of nature under Krishna's supreme direction.

How has Krishna become relegated to just one of the many?

Here's one reason: for the past three centuries, most of what is known of Krishna in the West has filtered down from certain European scholars bent on discrediting Hinduism and establishing Christianity. Many biased scholars deemed Krishna mythological, another Hindu god born of the quaint imagination of aborigines. Despite the strong monotheistic words of *Bhagavad-gītā*, the missionary/scholars did not connect Krishna as the God of their Bible. Instead, they conveniently tossed Him in with the other Hindu gods.

Any idea of Krishna you may have now has likely been tainted by these Euro-centric sources. As we have seen, the tradition itself describes Krishna much differently. Can you now take a fresh look? If so, you will find the company of this charming cowherd boy far more relevant and enjoyable than any character of myth.

The authentic Sanskrit texts comprise by far the world's most exhaustive, consistent and comprehensive scriptural tradition. Although they describe many gods, these ancient texts clearly identify Krishna as the one supreme God, *deva-deva*, the God of gods.

In the revealed scriptures, the ultimate object of knowledge is Śrī Krishna, the Personality of Godhead. The purpose of performing sacrifice is to please Him. Yoga is for realizing Him. All fruitive activities are ultimately rewarded by Him only. He is supreme knowledge, and all severe austerities are performed to know Him. Religion [dharma] is rendering loving service unto Him. He is the supreme goal of life. (Bhāgavat Purana, 1.2.28, 29).

Isn't Krishna known as an avatar of Vishnu?

Though some Western dictionaries say otherwise, the Sanskrit scriptures explain that Visnu comes from Krishna, who is *svayam bhagavan*, the original Person. According to the original, unfiltered texts, both the gods and Krishna's various expansions (*avatars*, or incarnations) assist Him. *Avatars* of Krishna, such as Viṣṇu, possess most but not all of Krishna's power; the *devas*, even less. Still, *avatars* and *devas* all come from Krishna.

In Krishna's pastimes, the gods often play supporting roles, sometimes as the antagonists. Brahmā kidnaps Krishna's friends. Indra hurls thunderbolts on Krishna's village. Śiva battles Krishna face to face. Although the *devas* sometimes fight with their boss, they always end up on the right side, and Krishna remains undefeated.

If you seek the highest spiritual experience, remember that the tradition known as Hinduism is, at its core, deeply monotheistic. Set aside the biased accounts of polytheistic paganism. Keep the *devas* in proper perspective. And even if you can't help but see the gods as mythological, look at what they represent (money, beauty, nature, etc.) and ask yourself: are these things more important than their creator?

Krishna means God with a capital "G".

Krishna and the Devil

Is God stressed about some wicked enemy fighting Him? No; everyone comes from God, even the competition.

The Vedic literature explains that Krishna directly interacts with those who are in love with Him. Everyone else interacts with *māyā*—Krishna's power of illusion. Krishna creates *māyā* to cast a spell over endless souls that makes them think they are temporary flesh and blood. *Māyā* further entices us confused souls to look for happiness through the material body and to invest our love in the things and people of this world rather than Krishna.

Still, *māyā* does not compete with Krishna; she serves Him. Krishna creates *māyā* because He fulfills everyone's desires, even those who seek happiness without Him. Thanks to *māyā*, most of us chase material happiness with great conviction through countless painful reincarnations.

These points deserve review. In summary, *māyā* works like this:

Some souls, misusing their free will, decide to try life without Krishna.

Krishna, fulfilling these souls' desire, creates *māyā* so they can believe He isn't around.

Māyā bewilders the souls into identifying with matter and seeking happiness through material things (materialism).

Faith in materialism forces the soul to stay in this world birth after birth in a futile search for happiness without God.

The *Bhagavad-gītā* describes this process in chapter 15, verse 7: *The living entities in this conditioned world are My eternal fragmental parts. Due to conditioned life, they are struggling very hard with the six senses, which include the mind.*

If maya is serving Krishna, what about people who are serving maya? Aren't they serving Krishna indirectly?

Through *māyā*, Krishna is fulfilling our desire to forget Him. If we choose *māyā*, we are serving our desire, not His.

The *Gīta* and other Sanskrit texts describe those committed to materialism as *asuras*, usually translated as 'demons'. Certainly many people ignorant of the soul have good intentions. Still, materialism breeds heartlessness, greed, pride and other demonic qualities. Thus, demons are not trident-wielding agents of the devil, but forgetful souls suffering under the illusions of *māyā*.

Krishna's pastimes (described later in this book) feature vigorous materialists guised as fearsome brutes. As you'll read, sometimes Krishna's servants also take such roles. These demons terrify everyone else, but Krishna dispenses of them very easily as part of His divine play. Sometimes He literally dances on their heads. By fighting the demons, Śrīla Prabhupāda says, Krishna gets some exercise.

Are there demons today, in the 21st century?

These days, lesser but equally devilish materialists compete with Krishna by brainwashing nearly everyone to believe that life is a material phenomenon. One of the unimagined benefits of studying Krishna is a healthy skepticism towards this all but universally accepted materialistic view. How? The *Bhagavad-gītā* and the *Bhāgavat Purana* elevate the topic of spirit from the realm of religious dogma to that of true science.

As a brief example, here the *Gīta* elaborates on the nature of the soul and its byproduct, consciousness:

The sky, due to its subtle nature, does not mix with anything, although it is all-pervading. Similarly, the soul situated in spiritual vision does not mix with the body, though situated in that body. As the sun alone illuminates this entire universe, so does the living entity, one within the body, illuminate the entire body by consciousness. (13.33,34)

We cannot see the soul, but we can detect its presence by its symptom of consciousness. To fail to objectively consider the possibility that an anti-material energy animates the body shows bias, not science. What we can observe is this: unlike reductionist, materialistic science, understanding the presence of the soul frees one from self-destructive habits and brings one to sustainable happiness.

This knowledge is the king of education, the most secret of all secrets. It is the purest knowledge, and because it gives direct perception of the self by realization, it is the perfection of religion. It is everlasting, and it is joyfully performed. (Bg. 9.2).

The *Gīta* thus challenges the reader to subjectively compare the happiness, insight and satisfaction derived from approaching life as a body or as a soul.

Modern science makes no such challenge; it simply demands blind faith. For example, although scientists have, for many years, isolated all the chemical components of a living cell, they cannot replicate even the simplest form of life in the lab. Still, they insist that they eventually will create life. To them, matter is all that matters; life is merely an accidental byproduct of chemical interaction.

Covertly or overtly, such people deny the presence of an eternal living soul in the human body. If *they* can't make a non-material living entity, they think, no God could either. This too is a demonic mentality—full-on materialism veiled as objective scientific research.

Science and religion are opposites. How can you equate them?

The scientific method—hypothesis, experiment, conclusion—also applies to spiritual life. The hypothesis is this: Krishna is God, and by serving Him you'll nourish your soul and be much happier. Is it scientific to avoid this experiment by dismissing Krishna as mythology or the soul as mere belief?

In the chapter entitled, "The Divine and Demoniac Natures," the *Gīta* describes this mentality:

They say that this world is unreal, with no foundation, no God in control. They say it is produced of sex desire and has no cause other than lust. Following such conclusions, the demoniac, who are lost to themselves and who have no intelligence, engage in unbeneficial, horrible works meant to destroy the world. Taking shelter of insatiable lust and absorbed in the conceit of pride and false prestige, the demoniac, thus illusioned, are always sworn to unclean work, attracted by the impermanent. (Bg. 16.8-10).

By testing and understanding the subtle materialistic hypotheses of life we swallowed whole in science class, we are free to experiment with Krishna and draw our own conclusions.

Now we've met 'the devil' in the form of Krishna's own illusory power, His sparring partners, modern materialists and atheistic science.

Krishna and Idolatry

Isn't it idolatry to think of God as a person and bow to statues?

Throughout the world, hundreds of millions of devotees worship Krishna in the Deity form. Uninformed people compare Deity worship to the idolatry condemned in the Bible and the Koran. Idolatry means to designate something as God and worship it—the Hebrews' golden calf, for example. These days, money, the things money can buy, or people who have money, become idols to millions who may not say so or even realize it.

A Deity, however, differs from some imagined divinity. Though made of material elements such as stone, metal or wood, a Deity of Krishna represents Krishna's eternal, blissful form. When used for this spiritual purpose, such material elements themselves become spiritual, as iron becomes like fire when placed in fire. If a Deity is made to accurately portray Krishna, whom the sacred Sanskrit texts describe in great detail, how can He be a product of someone's imagination about who or what is God?

The Deity of Krishna incorporates Krishna's charming smile, His flute, His pose, His dress—in short, everything about Krishna as described in authoritative sources such as the *Brahmā-samhita* (5.30), which says:

I worship Govinda[1]*, the primeval Lord, who is adept in playing on His flute, with blooming eyes like lotus petals with head decked with peacock's feather, with the figure of beauty tinged with the hue of blue clouds, and His unique loveliness charming millions of Cupids.*

Śrīla Prabhupāda used this example: suppose someone makes their own letterbox, paints it red and blue and labels it USPS. If someone puts a letter in such a box, no one will pick it up for delivery. However, the same letter put in the authorized mailbox will go straight to its destination. In the same way, God, being absolute, receives and accepts the loving offerings that devotees present to His authorized Deity.

---

1 *Krishna, who pleases the cows and pleases one's senses.*

To worship a deity of Krishna, does one have to abandon reason for blind faith?

No. Anyone who simply offers fruits, flowers or water to a Deity (or even a picture) of Krishna at once experiences Krishna's loving reciprocation. Even a small child can quickly grasp the idea and enjoy serving Krishna's Deity.

The spiritual science is simple: Krishna makes fruits and flowers, for no one else can make them in a lab or factory. Thus, offering fruits and flowers back to their Creator in an authorized way pleases Him and, by association, pleases us.

By serving the Deity of Krishna we savor a simple, selfless reciprocation in loving relationship with God, an experience quite distinct from fearfully groveling before an imaginary protector.

Krishna and the Evironment

Is Krishna relevant to today's world?

Yes. by learning about Krishna one does more good for Mother Earth than just about anything else one can do. Why? When we learn to find inner happiness whenever and wherever we want it, the pressure to find external happiness subsides. Unlike materialism, the perpetual struggle for external enjoyment, spiritual happiness is sustainable, renewable and carbon-neutral.

Materialism, so wasteful and abusive, still fails to satisfy. Consider America; according to Earthtrends, in 2004 Americans constituted 4.6% of Earth's population and yet accounted for 33% of mankind's consumption. Is this unsurpassed level of consumption making Americans happy? Apparently not. In 2007, people in America took more antidepressants than any other category of drug.

Why doesn't materialism make people happy?

For one thing, materialism is based on an illusion. During our lifetime, we collect possessions, land and money, thinking them ours. Then we die and leave them all behind. If we cannot keep something, was it ever really ours? Or were we merely operating under the illusion that it was ours?

How does adding Krishna to one's life improve the environment?

Here's one example: a person in the material, bodily conception of life usually subsists, without a second thought, on the physical bodies of other living beings, given quite unwillingly. Such a meat-based diet requires dozens of times more water and land than a vegetarian diet. A 2006 University of Chicago study found that by switching to a meat-free diet, a person saves one and a half tons of greenhouse gas emissions per year. By contrast, switching from an internal-combustion car to a hybrid saves just one ton per year.

On a wider scale, a recent United Nations study tagged the meat industry with eighteen percent of greenhouse gas production; all of mankind's transportation *combined* account for only sixteen percent.

A person who becomes aware of Krishna automatically becomes a vegetarian. That is because Krishna is a vegetarian. However, even if one is not a vegetarian, by finishing the illusory quest for high-octane material satisfaction one redirects time and energy to a natural inner awakening. Krishna makes this possible for anyone.

The first verse of the ancient text *Śrī Isopanisad* sums it up:

Everything animate or inanimate that is within the universe is controlled and owned by the Lord. One should therefore accept only those things necessary for himself, which are set aside as his quota, and one should not accept other things, knowing well to whom they belong.

We discussed the joys and benefits of serving Krishna. We plowed through idolatry, mythology, polytheism, materialism, sectarianism and every other excuse I can imagine to avoid Krishna (except lethargy, for if you were spiritually lazy, you wouldn't have read this far anyway). Shall we proceed? Here are three steps to meeting Krishna.

The primary texts describing Krishna are the *Bhagavad-gītā* and the *Bhāgavat Purana*. The *Bhagavad-gītā* contains Krishna's basic teachings in eighteen chapters; the *Bhāgavat Purana* describes Krishna's life and advanced teachings in over three hundred chapters divided into twelve cantos.

A God Who Dances summarizes both texts. They appear in three sections. First you'll find a highly condensed version of the *Bhagavad-gītā*. Next are key excerpts of the first nine cantos of the *Bhāgavat Purana*. And last is a verse-for-verse rendition of the famous Tenth Canto of the *Bhāgavat Purana*, the detailed narration of Krishna's life. The last two cantos of *Bhāgavat Purana*, containing the denouement of the text, make up an Epilogue.

If you are new to Krishna, you will need to go through sections one and two in order to understand section three.

To better prepare you to understand Krishna's life in the Tenth Canto, I've added short explanations after each section of the *Bhagavad-gītā* and the introductory cantos of the *Bhāgavat-Purana.*

We've finished our orientation. Allow me to introduce the chief guest. Meet *A God Who Dances*. Thereafter, *krishne matir astu*—may you always think of Krishna.

Part Two

Three Steps to Meeting A God Who Dances

Notes About Sanskrit Pronunciation

The Sanskrit words in this book are adapted from the original script in English characters with standard marks (diacritics) that indicate pronunciation. This allows the reader new to the language to read and pronounce the original words with reasonable accuracy. Below is a pronunciation guide for this introductory book. Please note that this is *not* a full and academically accurate Sanskrit pronunciation guide.

VOWELS

The vowel e is pronounced as the e in *they*.
The vowel a is pronounced as the u in *but*.
The long a, written ā, is pronounced as the a in *far*.
The vowel i is pronounced as the i in *pin*.
The long i, written ī, is pronounced as the i in *unique*.
The short u is pronounced as the u in *pull*.
The long u, written ū, is pronounced as the u as in *rule*.
The vowel o is pronounced as the o in *go*.
The vowel ṛ is pronounced as the ri in *rim*.
The vowel ai is pronounced as in *aisle*.
The vowel au is pronounced like the *ow* in *how*.

CONSONANTS

The consonant c is pronounced as the ch in *chair*.

The consonants ś, ṣ, and s are pronounced, respectively, as in the German word *sprechen* and the English words *shine* and *sun*.

Consonants followed by an 'h' produce a combined sound such as ph in *uphill*, bh in *rub hard*, and jh in *hedgehog*.

The consonant ñ is pronounced as in *canyon*.

The letter ṁ, which is a pure nasal, is pronounced like the n in the French word *bon*.

With subtle exceptions that exceed the scope of this book, most other consonants are pronounced like their English counterparts.

Note: since the name Krishna is used so often, it is spelled phonetically (Krishna) rather than with diacritics (Kṛṣṇa).

Step I
Bhagavad-gita Summarized

The *Bhagavad-gita's* Basics for Dancing with Krishna

1. The soul (you) is not the body (your vehicle).

2. Acting as if we are our bodies (materialism) creates *karma*, material reactions.

3. Karma, good or bad, forces us to continually reincarnate in new material bodies.

4. As long as we have material bodies, we will suffer birth, disease, old age and death.

5. Our material bodies, material things, feelings, actions and decisions—all are influenced and controlled by nature's three qualities of goodness, passion and ignorance.

6. As souls, we naturally exist above the three qualities, free of karma.

7. In our natural state, we love and serve God. Such service creates no karma.

8. To love God we must know who God is (Krishna).

9. Krishna loves us and longs for us to detach our loving power from materialism and turn it to Him.

10. Despite Krishna's longing for us, because love is always voluntary, we have free will to choose between Krishna and materialism.

The *Bhagavad-gita* Summarized

1. Action

Arjuna pointed at the thin no-man's-land separating two massive armies arrayed across a vast, flat battlefield. "Krishna, drive my chariot there," he commanded. "I want to see which followers of that criminal Duryodhana have come here to fight."

Krishna obediently steered the golden chariot straight through the corridor. On either side, for miles ahead, countless soldiers cheered, flexed and seethed, ready for battle, taunting their enemies. With a smile and a grand gesture, Krishna said, "Just see, cousin, all the great warriors assembled here."

Arjuna gasped at the sight of several generals among his enemies.

"Krishna, I can't fight these dear relatives," he cried. "Look at them! How can I kill my teacher? My elders? My whole family will be destroyed. Countless wives will become widows. Think of it: rogues will seduce them and breed a generation of bastards. Krishna, I'd rather die than fight. I'd rather scrounge for a living than do this!"

Krishna smiled and stopped the chariot between the two armies. "Why do you degrade yourself, Arjuna? Warriors need strong hearts. Get up and fight."

"You're right, Krishna," said Arjuna, "but I respect these men. Should I kill them just because they've chosen the wrong side? Even if I win, their blood would stain my hands. Killing them would ruin my life."

Slumping in his seat, Arjuna paused for a moment. Choking back tears he looked up and begged, "Krishna, what should I do?"

With a grave expression, Krishna replied, "You're agonizing over some doomed flesh. You forget that these men are eternal souls, not short-lived bodies. Your arrows can kill their bodies, Arjuna, but nothing can kill their souls. As a person puts on fresh clothes and drops the used ones, the eternal soul occupies a new body at death. Why get so upset about the old one?

"Besides, you're a warrior. If you quit, everyone will call you a coward. Imagine the shame! You must fight, but not necessarily for yourself. Dedicate your fight to the Supreme, and act as the eternal soul you truly are. Fight off your materialistic concepts. Then you'll be a *yogī*."

Listening closely, Arjuna asked, "How do *yogīs* act?"

"Like everyone else, except they're detached. While most people slavishly serve their minds and senses, *yogīs* master them. *Yogīs* enjoy an inner freedom and happiness that ordinary people never know."

Arjuna looked skeptical. "How can I be happy within and fight at the same time? That's a contradiction."

Smiling again, Krishna replied, "Arjuna, just to survive you have to do *something*. Instead of sitting idly or acting selfishly, turn your work into a sacrifice for the Supreme. Then you'll be happy."

"What is this power pushing me to act selfishly?" asked Arjuna.

"Lust, Arjuna, born of festering desire. Lust clouds your mind. Because lust can never be satisfied, it leaves you frustrated, angry and disturbed. If you want to be happy, you must fight and conquer every kind of lust."

Krishna paused for a moment to let Arjuna digest these words, and then continued in a kind tone. "For a long time I've been teaching people how to act in yoga and subdue lust. At the dawn of creation I taught the Sun-god, who taught his son, who in turn started a long chain of teachers. Somehow, though, time has obscured this art. Today, dear friend, I'll teach it again for you."

Arjuna raised an eyebrow. "How could You have taught the Sun-god, who's so much older than You?"

"My body is spiritual and never ages or dies," Krishna replied. "From time to time I appear in this world to help the good people and vanquish those who act out of lust and greed. Good people shed their lust and act out of love for Me. Good or bad, though, I respond to everyone individually.

"For your own good, Arjuna, act for My sake. When you do, everything involved—your work, your weaponry, your knowledge—becomes part of a blissful offering for the Supreme. Since there are many ways to turn action into an offering to God, get personal direction from a truly enlightened guru. You'll learn the most sublime sort of knowledge from a genuine guru."

Arjuna paused for a moment and asked, "You say I should act with detachment and that I should act for You. Which is better?"

"Acting without attachment and acting for Me are both forms of yoga. However, by acting for Me you automatically act with detachment. I'm your friend. I own everything. All action is meant for Me. Just knowing this brings you endless peace and allows you to act in perfect yoga, or union with Me. The art of yoga and meditation allows you to work without attachment."

Arjuna winced. "Meditation? It's easier to stop the wind than to make my mind sit still."

"Yes, it's hard, but it is possible with constant practice and detachment."

"But what if I try and fail? Then I'm a loser, materially and spiritually."

"If you do the right thing, how can you lose? At least you'll be better off in your next life. Rather than meditation, though, if you simply serve Me with loving devotion, at death you'll leave this painful world and come to Me."

Insights From Action

Decisions, decisions. Work or school? Move or stay put? Take a risk or play it safe?

How do you decide what to do? What's most important to you?

In the *Gīta*, Krishna says to reach for more than money or pride—things related to the body. Materialists think they *are* their bodies. Things related to the body go up in smoke, yet materialists chase them to death.

Arjuna decided to quit his imperial ambitions, but Krishna wouldn't let him. He told Arjuna to fight, but to fight for God instead of for a profit. Remaining true to his nature while serving a higher purpose would make Arjuna happy and solve his dilemma.

What does this mean for you and me?

Doing what you do best, and doing it for God, allows you to live in harmony with yourself and with others, with a unique inner peace. That kind of work, supplemented with meditation, study and proper association, comprises a basic God-conscious life. But for big decisions, how do you know what God wants? "For that," Krishna says, "you need a genuine guru."

How do you tell who's genuine? Among other things, real gurus:

- come in a chain of recognized gurus;
- confirm what they say from scripture;
- demonstrate a happy life of service for God.

Arjuna and Krishna then discuss detachment and yoga. "But all of that," concludes Krishna, "is contained in working for God—and I *am* God."

2. Devotion

Krishna continued, "Listen, Arjuna. You are one of the rare souls who seeks the highest truth. There is no truth superior to Me. Everything rests on Me as pearls are strung on a thread.

"Four kinds of people turn to Me: the curious, the desperate, the sad and the wise. Four other kinds of people ignore Me: the materialistic, the dull-headed, the arrogant, and the armchair scholars."

"Some overly clever men think I'm just a mouthpiece for *brahman*, the formless spirit. They never get to know Me personally. However, the truly wise who simply serve Me come to Me when they die."

Arjuna, intrigued, blurted out a series of questions.

"Tell me more about this formless spirit, please."

"*Brahman* is my spiritual aura, an eternal light. It's like the sunshine which is a by-product of the sun, yet is neither the sun nor the sun-god."

"What about the gods?"

"I create them to manage this material world."

"What is the soul?"

"A spark of *brahman*, an eternal spiritual individual whom I also create."

"Why do souls suffer *karma*?"

"They're made to serve Me, but if they prefer to serve themselves, I give them karma so they can try to enjoy material bodies one after the next."

"Do you remain in the heart of every soul?"

"Yes. We'll discuss that later."

"How can I know You when I leave this body?"

"Practice thinking of Me now, even as you fight. Think of Me as both ancient and fresh, as huge and tiny, but always as a person, shining like the sun. Thinking of Me brings you all you might achieve from any sort of study, charity, or religion."

Arjuna's questions answered for the moment, Krishna spoke on.

"Because you have some faith in Me, you can understand Me. I create the universe and everything in it, yet I remain an individual, untouched by My creation. Fools see Me as an ordinary man, but great souls bow to Me and serve Me with love.

"Some people offer fancy gifts to the gods in exchange for material enjoyment. Yet I am pleased with simple, loving offerings of flowers, fruit or water. Even if you make a mistake, I'll still accept you, for I'm equal to everyone but partial to one who loves Me. So be My devotee, Arjuna, and I promise that you'll come to Me.

"Here is the essence: I create everything. Always serve and speak about Me and you'll be happy, for I, sitting in your heart, will destroy your ignorance with the shining lamp of knowledge.

Very pleased, Arjuna asked, "I love listening to You, Krishna. It seems that only You can truly know Yourself. How can I know You?"

"When you see the best of anything—the shark among the fish, or lion among beasts, for example—think of Me. At the same time, remember: anything wonderful you see in this world is just a spark of My true splendor."

"Krishna, how kind of You to scatter my illusions!" cried Arjuna. Then, a bit more timidly, he said, "I have one request: if You think I can bear it, please show me that form in which You are the universe and everything in it."

Immediately, Krishna complied. "Yes, Arjuna. You now have divine eyes. Behold My universal form."

Though no one else on the battlefield could see what he was seeing, Arjuna stood, spellbound. "Krishna, I see huge gods with weapons and jewels. They stand on every planet, dazzling with every imaginable color. The blazing glory of it all surrounds and blinds me!

"And yet the gods bow in fear before You. Truly You are everything, Krishna! You see everything with Your eyes, the sun and moon.

Suddenly Arjuna's voice cracked with terror. "Krishna! Now I see You crushing everyone with Your sharp, terrible teeth. My relatives, my enemies—everyone is rushing into Your mouth and being killed! Why are You doing this?"

In a grave, unearthly voice, Krishna demanded, "I am time, the death of all. All the warriors surrounding us are already as good as dead, Arjuna. Now fight! Be My weapon and win your fame!"

Trembling, Arjuna fell to his knees. "Almighty Lord, I bow to You from every side. Everyone should simply praise You, God of gods, but fool that I am I treated You as a familiar friend. Please forgive me, as a father forgives a son or a husband forgives a wife. And please, let me see You again as Krishna."

Still grave, Krishna said, "My universal form has frightened you, Arjuna. Be calm. Now see My true form, which you hold so dear."

Krishna, appearing again in His original form, said, "My dear Arjuna, even if you did every kind of good deed, you would not see Me like this, as I am, as Krishna. Only one blessed with loving devotion can truly see Me."

Recomposing himself, Arjuna asked, "My Lord, should I contemplate You as Krishna, or as *brahman*, the infinite, formless spirit?"

Said Krishna, "Those who meditate on Me as *brahman* may eventually reach Me, but only after much trouble. Those who simply think of Me, however, I swiftly rescue from the sea of birth and death."

Krishna then gave a generous list of further options.

"If you can't always think of Me, then hear and chant about Me. That's called *bhakti*, or devotional yoga. If you can't do that, then work for Me. If you can't do that, then work for charity, because practical work with detachment will bring you more peace than mere theoretical knowledge.

"Those who think of Me in devotion are called devotees. Due to their wonderful qualities of kindness, tolerance and determination, they are dear to everyone and everyone is dear to them. They love Me, and I love them."

Insights From Devotion

What sort of questions would you ask if you suddenly understood that you were face to face with God?

Arjuna asked Krishna to explain why the soul suffers karma. Understanding that, he asked more: "How can I always think of You?" and "How can I remember You when I die so that I can come to You?"

Arjuna also gave in to the urge to see something miraculous—Krishna's universal form. Afterwards, terrified, he asked to see Krishna again as his familiar friend.

Still shaken by this experience, Arjuna then asked Krishna whether meditating on His formless aspect was better than on Him personally.

Formless meditation is so popular these days that it practically defines 'meditation'. Yet Krishna describes it as *kleśa*, needlessly difficult, while thinking of Him is direct and easy.

Thinking of Krishna means to read His instructions (*Bhagavad-gītā*) and His activities (*Bhāgavat Purana*). It also means to meditate on Krishna in the heart.

Thinking of Krishna transforms one's heart and character, making one a sublime, beloved person. Hearing and speaking about Krishna feeds and refreshes the soul. When you, the soul, are nourished, you become as happy as your body does when it's fed. And when thinking of someone makes you happy, love for that person naturally follows.

This powerful yoga process known as devotion (*bhakti*) works only when done voluntarily and lovingly. After all, God is a person, not a machine.

It is easy to be mindful of Krishna. Still, if one can't do it, instead of threatening damnation Krishna graciously offers several subordinate yet progressive options.

3. Spiritual Knowledge

Eager to know more, Arjuna asked, "Krishna, what is the relationship between the body and the soul?"

Krishna replied, "The body is a field of action for the soul. An ordinary soul gratifies the senses and become deeply attached to the body. A wise soul becomes detached from the material body. Such a person is humble, poised and truly independent.

"As the Supersoul in the heart, I advise everyone, wise or unwise. Each soul can choose between My advice and materialism. Those who choose materialism suffer repeated birth and death in different species. Those who choose Me come to see the whole situation—the compassionate Supersoul and the plight of a spiritual being attached to dull matter.

"Let me tell you more about matter. It comes in three varieties, or modes: goodness, passion, and ignorance. As the seed-giving father, I bring dead matter to life by implanting the soul. Then the modes take over.

"Goodness raises the soul to happiness. Passion drives the soul to intense desire. Ignorance dumps the soul in delusion. These three modes always compete for supremacy, knocking you, the eternal soul, from one material situation to the next. Only when you are free of their control can you taste real happiness.

Arjuna asked, "How do you rise above the three modes, and what happens when you do?"

"To conquer the modes and be free of karma, simply love and serve Me in every circumstance. Then, as the modes come and go, you'll observe them without loving or hating them. At that point you'll be unshakably calm and treat everyone equally.

"Imagine this world," Krishna continued, "as a great, ancient banyan tree with branches that grow down to become roots and new trunks. A single such tree can expand for acres, and no one can figure out where it begins or ends. If you want to escape this entangling tree, you must cut it down. Then you can enter My self-illumined abode, where there is no need of sunlight or electricity. I assure you, when you go there, you will not miss the mortal banyan tree.

"I want everyone to come to My abode, so I sit in every heart as the Supersoul, offering guidance. I also write the Vedic literature so that people can understand Me. I am that Person beyond both the materialist and the enlightened soul. If you know Me, you'll be wise and everything you do will be perfect.

"I've told you something about godly souls; they're honest, pure, self-controlled, and detached. You are such a person, Arjuna. Now listen as I describe the materialistic, atheistic demons.

"Demons don't know what to do or what not to do. They're unclean, dishonest and preoccupied with sex. Thinking My creation to be their personal property, they build costly, destructive weapons and feel powerful and proud. Their occasional pretenses of religion or charity are meaningless, for in fact, lust enslaves them. Chained to materialism by greed and anger, they die and are reborn as animals or less.

"Although the Vedic scriptures could save them from such a fate," Krishna concluded, "demons take no interest."

Arjuna asked, "What becomes of religious people who *don't* refer to the scriptures but make up their own ways of worship?"

With a look of mock disgust, Krishna shook His head and replied, "Religion by imagination is a product of the three modes. Religious pretenders influenced by goodness worship the gods, by passion powerful demons, and by ignorance, ghosts."

"You see, Arjuna," Krishna went on, "the three modes affect everything, even your food. Juicy, fatty, wholesome foods are in goodness, Bitter, salty, pungent foods are in passion, and stale, putrid foods are in ignorance.

"The modes also influence what kind of charity you give and what kind of discipline you impose on yourself. Still, you should never renounce charity or self-discipline."

Puzzled, Arjuna asked, "Well, then what does it mean for one to be renounced?"

Smiling again, Krishna explained, "Renunciation means detachment from the fruits of your work. One in goodness works dutifully but renounces the result. One in passion renounces work when it grows troublesome. One in ignorance renounces work because he's lazy."

"Those who work in goodness, or *brāhmaṇas*, often become judges, teachers, or priests. *Kṣatriyas*, those who work in passion, often become administrators, police or soldiers. Passion and ignorance combine to produce *vaiśyas*, businesspeople or farmers. And those largely in ignorance are called *śūdras*. They work as artisans, laborers or servants.

"Regardless of the kind of work that suits you, doing it for Me turns it to yoga and enlightens you. For that reason it's better to do your own kind of work imperfectly than someone else's perfectly. Whatever your career inclination may be, you can renounce this world by dedicating your work to Me. Then you'll be happy."

Krishna paused, raised an eyebrow and scrutinized Arjuna. Then He said, "I'm going to tell you something even more confidential. Serve Me and you will learn to act and live in simple wisdom. You will conquer your mind and senses and renounce the fruits of your work. Soon you will enjoy peace and insight as you achieve unprecedented happiness. You will appreciate everyone you meet. In such a state of mind you will attain My abode.

"Think about Me and stay with My devotees; I will clear every obstacle from your path. If you grow proud and imagine you can make it on your own, you'll be lost.

Glancing around the battlefield, Krishna continued. "You're a warrior, Arjuna. It's your nature to fight, and you'll fight no matter what. Fight for Me and you'll return to your original home in My abode."

With a note of detachment, Krishna concluded, "Now I've told you the secrets of perfection, Arjuna. Think over what I've said and then do as you please."

Krishna then paused and added softly, "Since I love you so much, I shall summarize. Think about Me always. Become My devotee. Worship Me and give Me homage, and you will return to Me. Give up all other duties, Arjuna, and submit yourself to Me. Don't worry; I'll free you from the results of any past mistakes."

Leaning a little closer, Krishna went on. "Please, repeat these words of Mine, but only to honest people. No one is dearer to Me than one who shares this message. And even if someone doesn't believe or understand what you say, just by listening with an open mind, they will rise to heaven and enjoy like a god."

Smiling kindly, Krishna asked, "Arjuna, do you understand?"

Without hesitating Arjuna declared, "Yes! Infallible Krishna, You have smashed my illusions. By your kindness I remember who I really am. Yes, now I will fight!"

Insights From Spiritual Knowledge

Knowledge without spirituality is dry mental calisthenics. On the other hand, spirituality without knowledge is flowery sentiment or religious fanaticism. What is the proper balance?

In this section of *Bhagavad-gītā*, Krishna provides the philosophical basis for Arjuna's spiritual awakening. He brings together the concepts of yoga, duty and detachment introduced earlier in the text. He also introduces the three modes of nature and explains their impact on every aspect of our lives.

Having done all this, Krishna ends the discussion with a heartfelt personal appeal to Arjuna.

Here, in summary, is the philosophy of *Bhagavad-gītā*.

Misusing our free will, we embodied souls long ago chose to reject Krishna for materialism, and we have our troublesome material bodies to show for it. Misidentifying ourselves with our bodies, we suffer the endless turmoil imposed by the three modes of material nature.

Krishna tries to reach us within and without. He advises us within as the Supersoul (intuition) and, for our external vision, personally descends and sends gurus. He tries everything because He dearly wants us to give up our misery and to turn back to His loving care.

If Krishna is God, why doesn't He force us? That wouldn't be love. Thus, at every moment, Krishna leaves the choice to us. In the *Bhagavad-gītā* He implores us to make the right choice for our own good.

Step II

Excerpts From the Bhagavat Purana

Cantos One - Nine

Introduction

In addition to the *Bhagavad-gītā*, the *Bhāgavat Purana* stands among the most loved of Sanskrit literature. One of eighteen *Puranas* (histories), *Bhāgavat Purana* is known as *amala*, spotless, due to its utter focus on Krishna and the reader's spiritual growth.

Bhāgavat Purana consists of some eighteen thousand verses in twelve cantos. The famous Tenth Canto describes Krishna's life. To understand and properly appreciate the Tenth Canto, one is advised to grasp the first nine, for they explain Krishna-theology in exquisite detail. They clearly demonstrate the deep and well-reasoned philosophy behind one's dance with Krishna.

The following summarized excerpts from Cantos One through Nine provide some key background for understanding the Tenth Canto. They are not meant to replace but to encourage a future reading of the complete text.

Canto One

A Death Sentence

King Viṣṇurāta surveyed the banks of the holy Ganges river where thousands of sages sat looking back at him. As he watched, more sages arrived, many from remote places. They had come to watch him die.

The King was ready. Life had given him all he wanted. His empire spanned the Earth, and his beloved son was ready to take the throne. His family affairs were settled. Only one final, monumental task remained: to meet his imminent death in the proper state of mind. Knowing this, great luminaries continued to arrive, one after another, to join the large assembly and study the profound event.

As the esteemed guests settled in and waited quietly, the King rose and, in a loud, strong voice, said, "Thank you for coming. Death awaits us all, but my death is due in just seven days. What should I do to prepare?"

The King's death sentence had come just a few days earlier. Over a misunderstanding, an inexperienced young priest had cursed King Viṣṇurāta to die in a week. Although he had the power to do so, Viṣṇurāta refused to contest the powerful curse. Instead, he accepted his fate as God's will. Before dying he wanted only one thing: to clearly understand the ultimate, highest truth of life.

Many sages offered their opinions, but none seemed conclusive.

Suddenly a striking young man came on the scene. The handsome, swarthy, well-built youth appeared to be bright and well-educated, though his possessions—and his clothing—were all but non-existent.

A crowd of children followed him, pointing and giggling. The assembled sages, however, immediately recognized him as a highly enlightened soul. They ushered the newcomer directly to a small raised platform directly in front of the King. Seeing this, the children abruptly stopped teasing him and shrunk back into the crowd.

His name was Śukadev. Everyone knew his father, Vyās, the foremost writer of the day. The handsome young man, gracious and unaffected, smiled at King Viṣṇurāta expectantly. Speaking more softly, the King again asked, "My dear sir, please tell me the duty of one who is about to die."

Śukadev's eyes lit up as he answered. "Your question is wonderful, dear King. Although everyone has suffered through countless births and deaths, very few ask why. Most people are too busy making money all day and having sex and sleeping at night. Each dawn brings such people one day closer to an unwanted death. Wiser people, who ask about and discuss the highest purpose of life, find in each dawn another step towards a sublime and permanent end to reincarnation."

His voice rising a bit, Śukadev continued, "Any sane person should ask about the purpose of life. Whether it's through yoga, action or education, to think of Krishna at death completes a perfect life. One who thinks of Krishna goes to Krishna and has no further need for miserable material bodies."

"My dear King, as you await death, I shall help you think of Krishna by reciting the *Bhāgavat Purana*, the history of Krishna, just as I heard it from my father."

The truth and gravity of Śukadev's words rang throughout the assembly of smiling sages.

"Thank you," said Viṣṇurāta, who relaxed as he sat back to listen.

Closing his eyes for a moment, Śukadev took a deep breath and began. "When this universe was created . . ."

Insights

Be prepared: death is both a pop quiz and a final exam.

Bhāgavat Purana reverses the commonly accepted idea of human history. At the time of its writing (indicated in the text itself as five thousand years ago), humans were not crude brutes living in caves. In fact, according to the *Bhāgavat Purana*, people in those days were smarter, happier and longer-lived. (The Bible's account of Christ's family lineage reflects the same decrease in human life-span over the centuries as does the *Bhagavat Purana*).

Technology? No one needed it. Although they had the Sanskrit language, everyone had such sharp memories that no one bothered to put things in writing. One hearing was sufficient for a lifetime.

In those happy days, farmers earned a year's income in three months. The more educated people harnessed the subtle but incredible power of sound vibrations, contained in *mantras*, to create or, sometimes, to destroy. Administrators were wise, just and powerful. People possessed and valued honesty, generosity, kindness and self-control.

The author, Śrī Vyāsadeva, wrote *Bhāgavat Purana* just as an age of quarrel and darkness, Kali-yuga, descended on the world. Of the four cyclical universal ages, or *yugas*—Satyā, Treta, Dwapara and Kali—Kali is notorious for degrading humanity. Because people were suffering diminishing memories and life-spans, Vyāsadeva saw the need to preserve essential spiritual information in writing.

The *Bhāgavat Purana* thus begins with this most obvious of thoughtful questions. "I'm going to die," says the King. "How should I prepare?" Most of us prefer to postpone this topic. Others cling to faith that, whatever happens, they will be saved. The *Bhāgavat Purana* relies on neither diversion nor blind faith; it insists that a reasoned answer to the question of death opens the door to a blissful life.

Śukadeva's answer to King Viṣṇurāta's question extends for thousands of verses, a tapestry of fascinating events and personalities. The King periodically interjects questions, and Śukadev frequently quotes other past conversations in reply, but their discussion on a riverbank forms the basic structure of the *Bhāgavat Purana*.

Canto Two

Creation

Brahmā awoke in blackness so complete it made no difference whether he opened or closed his eyes. Silence answered his straining ears.

"Where am I," he thought. "*Who* am I?" Terror and curiosity competed for his attention.

A faint light crept over his immediate surroundings. Dim blurs appeared, gathering clarity until it dawned on Brahmā that he was sitting on the whorl of a giant lotus flower. He walked to the edge and looked down between the huge fluffy petals. An enormous winding stem vanished in the darkness below.

Brahmā flexed his muscles. He felt strong and eager to see the origin of this lotus. Leaning over the whorl's edge, he saw he could get solid handholds along the edge of an adjoining petal all the way to the stem. He grabbed on and slipped his legs off the whorl and into space. Then he pulled himself, hand over hand, until he could wrap his dangling legs around the thick stem. After releasing the petal and grasping the stem, one arm at a time, he began to shimmy down.

As Brahmā descended into the gloom, a booming voice with no visible source sang out two syllables: "*TA- PA*." Clutching the stem, Brahmā stopped his descent. He somehow knew the meaning of these two syllables, and it bubbled to his throat.

"Austerity," he said aloud to himself. "I must perform austerity."

Scrambling back to his lotus platform, Brahmā sat down, crossed his legs, and began to focus his mind. Refusing to submit to fear, curiosity or any other emotion, he concentrated with all his might. There was nothing else to do.

As Brahmā persisted in deep mediation, his sense of time melted away. Through half-closed eyes he peered on and on at the tip of his nose. So intent was his concentration that he almost stopped breathing and blinking. His vigilant mind, fresh and undistracted, grew strong and focused.

Thousands of years passed.

All at once, without any warning, Brahmā found himself surrounded by a breathtaking kingdom. Shocked, Brahmā broke his meditation, stood awkwardly and looked around.

In each direction, palatial dwellings, studded with shimmering jewels, rose from verdant grounds rich with fruit-laden trees and bushes dressed in flowers so fragrant he could savor their sweetness even from a great distance. People passed by here and there, dressed in radiant silks and priceless ornaments. Many smiled blissfully at him as they walked or flew about on airplanes with flapping wings that appeared alive as they floated through the sky.

Turning, Brahmā realized he was in the presence of Krishna, the Lord of all. His gorgeous features seemed to embody the incredible beauty surrounding Him. Without formality, Krishna reached over and shook Brahmā's hand. Smiling, He said:

"Before creation, I was there, and nothing else but Me—
including lifeless matter, My restrictive energy.
As you create your universe, I'll witness your affairs;
and when it all turns back to dust, I'll still be standing there.

If something seems of value but is not attached to Me,
it surely is produced of My deceptive energy.
Do not desire such objects or invest them with affection;
they come not from the light of truth but from its dark reflection.

Components of creation—earth and water and the rest—
at once appear before us, yet remain unmanifest.
I likewise live in everything, unseen by common eyes,
while keeping My identity, as you must realize.

In every circumstance, in every place and every time,
by personal experience or guesswork of the mind,
a seeker of the highest truth must come to know at last
that I am God in person, never equaled or surpassed."

Brahmā felt these words enter his heart. At once he knew exactly who he was and what he was to do. Having qualified himself through austerity, he was now empowered by Krishna to fill up the vacant material universe into which he had appeared.

Thus began the history of the universe, including the human race, which multiplied rapidly under Brahmā's direction.

Insights

The mythology of believing the senses.

The lotus on which Brahmā finds himself comes from the navel of Lord Viṣṇu, an expansion of Lord Krishna charged with providing forgetful souls with a field of activities. Lord Viṣṇu's instruction to his lotus-born son, "*tapa*," indicates that austerity and self-control enable one to escape this entangling material creation. Brahmā understood this message and successfully controlled his mind until he came to see Krishna Himself.

In addition to filling up the universe, Brahmā began a line of teachers to make this spiritual knowledge available to everyone. This distinguished line, known as the *Brahma-Madhva-Gaudiya-sampradaya*, continues to this day.

You may well find this all quite fantastic and far removed from the realities of your own life. What relevance does what many would call the Hindu myth of creation have to you? The answer determines how much you will gain from reading the *Bhāgavat Purana*.

Let's first acknowledge a simple fact: if God exists at all, He exists beyond the reach of our present set of senses. Is that a limitation of God or of our senses?

What is the scope of our senses? Most of us have never been to Antarctica. Do we believe it exists? Why should we if we've never seen it?

We believe Antarctica exists because we've heard about it from people we trust who have been there. "Seeing is believing" has its moments, but it would be foolish to limit what we believe to what we see, taste or touch. However, by *hearing*, we share experiences far beyond our own.

Learning by hearing from trusted authorities is called *descending* knowledge. Learning by personal experience or guesswork is called *ascending* knowledge. To *ascend* the ladder of wisdom means to rely on a very faulty set of senses and a fickle mind. For subtle, spiritual matters, the *descending* method is easy and solid; we can quickly grasp spiritual experience in the company of those who have it.

These descriptions of *Bhāgavat Purana* are far beyond our power to see. The narrow-minded dismiss them as myths. If we can be open minded enough to simply hear them, we find that authentic spiritual sound has amazing power to improve our lives.

We may have yet to fully experience God, but if we know the symptoms of those who have, we will recognize the ecstasy, the compassion, the wisdom and the satisfaction God-conscious people display. Then we can hear from and emulate them. As Brahmā found out, hearing from authorities ends confusion and fear.

Through a simple spiritual sound, Brahmā discovered Krishna and found his destiny in His service. What about those who fight Krishna?

Canto Three

The Demons Arrive

As the years passed, Brahmā filled the universe with descendents. His first four sons, however, known as the four Kumaras, remained celibate mystics and refused to marry. These four brilliant sages used the power gained from austerity and meditation to maintain their bodies as five-year old cherubs. They also possessed the power to travel anywhere, a gift that suited them well, since curious children are allowed through nearly any door.

Having heard of their father's meeting with Krishna, the Kumaras decided to visit the Lord's abode. As they approached the gates to that transcendent realm, two radiant, muscular gatekeepers, Jaya and Vijaya, stepped forward. They placed the heads of their heavy clubs to the ground, forming an "X" that blocked the children's way.

"You children cannot come in here," said Jaya.

"The kingdom of God is for mature, realized souls," said Vijaya.

The saintly Kumaras, eager to see Krishna, became frustrated. Didn't these ignorant gatekeepers know that they were Brahmā's first sons?

"There is no disharmony in the kingdom of God," one Kumara said, "because Krishna is the center. Everyone here loves Krishna and Krishna's devotees, regardless of their age or appearance."

Another Kumara, trembling with anger, stepped forward and said, "Apparently you two are imposters who belong not here but in the material world. We curse you to go there."

Shocked to hear such potent words from the lips of children, Jaya and Vijaya realized their terrible mistake. The material world? Birth, disease, old age and death? Forgetting Krishna? The mere thought of life without Krishna sickened them. A stunned dismay paled their faces and they dropped their clubs. Strong as they were, they could not reverse the curse of these powerful sages.

Terrified, the trembling guards fell before the Kumaras and begged, "If we must leave Krishna's abode, please grant us the ability to remember Him."

At once the Lord appeared. Everyone turned to Him and offered respects.

Addressing the Kumaras, the Lord said, "I approve of this curse.

An offense to My devotee is an offense to Me. If My arm somehow became hostile towards you, I would cut it off. However, My dear Kumaras, as a favor to Me, please allow these two servants to return as soon as possible."

Seeing the Lord's concern for the gatekeepers, the Kumaras became contrite. They said, "Our Lord, we now understand these guards are Your servants and therefore faultless."

"Your curse is approved by Me," the Lord repeated. The Kumaras nodded. Very pleased to see the Lord, they worshipped Him and left.

Turning to the trembling Jaya and Vijaya, the Lord said, "Do not fear. You will remember Me, but in a different way. And you will return here very soon."

Meanwhile, on Earth . . .

Kasyapa already had twelve other wives; still, the lovely Diti had chosen the powerful sage as her husband. She respected him and they got along well. Being the newest, however, Diti had no children. One evening, impelled by desire, she begged Kasyapa to interrupt his evening prayers and lay with her.

"This is a most inauspicious time," the sage warned. But Diti persisted and he gave in.

Diti became pregnant and, in time, gave birth to stout twin sons, Hiranyaksa and Hiraṇyakaśipu. Earthquakes, fires, eclipses, comets and thunderbolts heralded their birth. Taking the first of three births as the most ferocious of demons, Jaya and Vijaya, the two offending gatekeepers, had arrived.

Insights

What happens when we leave Krishna?

Most of the countless individual souls, each one Krishna's beloved part and parcel, choose to stay with Him in the kingdom of God. There, every word is a song, every step is a dance and time is conspicuous by its absence. Countless spiritual planets provide each unique soul with all they need for their blissful, selfless service to Krishna.

Still, some souls choose to try life without Krishna. Three levels of material planets await them: heavenly, earthly and hellish. Heavenly planets shelter the gods, refined souls who live opulent lives and postpone death for many thousands of years. Hellish planets take in entangled souls being forced to transfer material bodies. As will be described in the Fifth Canto, such souls suffer reactions to past misdeeds and become conditioned for their next physical bodies.

Earthly planets (such as ours) are both heavenly and hellish. Here, according to their individual karma, souls have higher or lower situations. Among the millions of species on Earth, human life itself is rare good karma, for only human beings can probe the mystery of their existence. Yet even for human beings enjoying good karma (such as nature, art, wealth, family, and love), the four miseries of material life—birth, disease, old age and death—are only slightly hidden and never far away.

Thus for the most part, Earth is hellish, except for wise human beings who use their brief lives to seek the Absolute Truth. To help them, Krishna Himself descends to Earth to display His pastimes and attract all interested souls back to His eternal, loving service.

The case of the two gatekeepers was different. They came to Earth as part of Krishna's divine play. Jaya and Vijay, deported from the spiritual world, begged only for the ability to keep their priorities straight and avoid attachment to the material world by remembering Krishna.

Canto Four

Misplaced Priorities

King Uttanapada hugged his young son Uttama, who sat on his lap. Seeing this, Dhruva, the King's five-year-old son by another wife, scrambled up the throne to join his half-brother.

"Stop!" demanded Suruci, Uttama's mother, who sat beside the King. "My dear child, you don't deserve to sit on the King's lap. Only *my* children are qualified. If you're pious and you worship God, in your next life perhaps you will have a chance to be born from *my* womb."

The King started to say something, thought better of it and silently looked at the floor. Dhruva bit his lip. Breathing heavily, he stomped out of the room. As soon as the door closed behind him, he ran to his mother, crying.

When she heard the story from her sobbing son, Dhruva's mother, Suniti, feeling her eyes swell with tears, gathered her son into her arms. "It is true," she said. "You have been born to an unfortunate woman. I am nothing to the King."

After a few moments she managed to smile at Dhruva.

"Suruci is right. Give up your envy and serve Krishna," she said. "Krishna is very kind. By worshiping Krishna, your great-grandfather Brahmā gained his exalted post as the engineer of the universe. If you always think of Krishna in the core of your heart, you can shed your anger and serve Him in happiness."

Wiping the tears from Dhruva's face with her thumbs, Suniti looked at him sweetly and caught the attention of his reddened eyes. "Only Krishna can ease your heart," she said.

Dhruva's eyes opened a little wider. His tears stopped, and he pursed his lips.

Later that day, unseen by anyone, Dhruva slipped out of the palace. He walked through the town unrecognized and made his way to the nearby forest. As he entered the forest path, he saw the famous sage Nārada Muni walking nearby.

Nārada took stock of the lad and said, "What are you doing here?"

"I've come to find Krishna," Dhruva replied.

"Finding Krishna can be very difficult, especially for a small boy," said Nārada, somewhat surprised. "First you must learn to tolerate the inevitable ups and downs of life. Then you can meditate with a peaceful mind. Better stay at home for now."

Dhruva replied, "Sir, your advice is good for those aspiring to be saints, free of material desires. However, I am a prince, not a monk. I want something else. I want a kingdom larger than my father's. Can you tell me how to get that?"

"Such a determined boy," Nārada thought. Smiling, he said,

"Dhruva, your mother gave you good advice. Meditate on Krishna, even though you have a material desire. Krishna is beautiful. It's a pleasure to meditate on Him."

Nārada proceeded to describe Krishna's beauty in detail, from His lotus-like eyes down to His golden ankle bells.

"Krishna is also very kind," Nārada concluded. "He will help you in every respect. Even if your reason for approaching Krishna is wrong, by meditating on Him, you're still doing the right thing."

Nārada then taught Dhruva how to meditate on Krishna. He blessed the boy and gathered his few possessions. Dhruva circumambulated the sage and bowed as his teacher departed.

Dhruva did all that Nārada had told him. After finding a secluded spot by a sacred river, he began thinking of Krishna with a vigilant, intense meditation. In the process, Dhruva mastered his breathing and, step by step, stopped eating and sleeping. As Dhruva fixed his mind on Krishna, even the gods took note of his powerful austerity.

As Dhruva's trance came into utter focus, he suddenly saw Krishna, looking exactly as Nārada described Him. Dhruva, ecstatic, prostrated before the Lord. He then stared up at the Lord as if he were drinking Him with his eyes. Smiling, the Lord touched Dhruva's head with a conch shell. This simple act seemed to enlighten Dhruva far beyond his years, for he began reciting exquisite prayers, ripe with scriptural conclusions.

The Lord listened for some time. Then, in a grave voice, He said, "I know your desire, Dhruva. I bestow on you dominion of the pole star, an entire planet that far exceeds any kingdom on Earth."

For a moment, Dhruva felt overjoyed. Then he looked at the ground and said, "O my Lord, because I was seeking an opulent material position, I was performing severe austerities. Now I have gotten You, who are very difficult to attain, even for the gods, saints or kings. I was searching after a piece of glass, but instead I have found a most valuable jewel. After seeing You, I don't want any kingdom. I don't want anything but You."

Without another word, the Lord left Dhruva. Freed of his material desire and rapt with love for Krishna, Dhruva returned to the palace. Even Suruci had been saddened by his long absence. Now she, his mother, and King Uttanapada became overjoyed with his return.

Insights

Chewing the chewed

Our position in heaven, Earth, hell or the kingdom of God depends on our desires. Krishna is neutral; He loves us, and He supplies whatever we most desire.

We have countless ways to fulfill ordinary desires. The problem is that most of our desires circumvent God, and without Him, we have only His inferior, material energy. In this material realm, even if we get what we want, we can't keep it.

Thus the power to adjust and control our desires is the power to become happy. No external circumstance can dictate our desires; we choose them. To get ahead, we can try to squelch our base desires, as Dhruva did, at first. However, it's much easier to add Krishna to our lives and gradually become attracted to Him. When Krishna attracts us, our material desires go away.

Krishna is beautiful, kind and blissful. The more we desire to link up with Him, the less we desire the illusion of material happiness. Once we taste the joy of Krishna, material happiness becomes like a previously chewed piece of sugar cane: a hint of sweetness may remain, but it's cold, repulsive and mostly chewed out. In other words, temporary material happiness is available, but it's not worth the trouble.

Nonetheless, out of ignorance, habit and laziness, most people choose to chew the chewed—a choice leading to most unwanted consequences.

Canto Five

A Tour of Hell

After hearing about Brahmā, Jaya and Vijaya, and Dhruva, King Viṣṇurāta asked, "Why are different souls put in different situations?"

"Because the three material modes of nature force everyone to act differently," Śukadev replied. "Their different actions then influence them to reincarnate in different places.

"Goodness *(sattva)* makes people religious and happy, leading them to higher, heavenly planets in their next lives. Passion *(rajas)* causes people to experience mixed pleasure and pain, pushing them to reincarnate on middle planets such as Earth. Ignorance *(tamas)* leads people to live like animals, so they fall to hellish planets where they prepare for their next birth as animals.

"These hellish planets lie at the lowest end of the universe. The ruler of these planets of hell, known as Yamarāj, dispatches assistants called Yamaduttas to catch godless souls throughout the universe the moment their bodies expire. Based on the type and severity of their karma, Yamarāj assigns sinful souls to endure various reactions. Their suffering occurs not in their gross physical bodies but as a sort of endless nightmare. Once they get used to inhuman suffering, the sinful are prepared to be born in subhuman species.

"Each hellish planet accommodates particular types of sins. For example:

Those who appropriate another's spouse or money go to Tāmishra, where Yamadutas beat and starve them to the point of fainting.

Those who maintain themselves and their families by committing violence against others go to Raurava, where all those they tormented appear as fierce *ruru* beasts who bite them incessantly.

Those who cook defenseless animals and birds go to Kumbhīpāka, where they are themselves cooked in boiling oil.

A government agent who unjustly punishes an innocent person goes to Sūkharamuka and is squeezed exactly as sugarcane is crushed for its juice.

A person who lies while doing business goes to Avīcimat, which means waterless. What appears to be an ocean there is really made of stone. The Yamadutas repeatedly throw the sinner from a high mountain into that ocean of stone. Although his body is broken again and again, he does not die.

Snake-like people who are always angry and giving pain to others go to Dandaśūka, where multi-headed serpents eat them like mice.

A rich person who prides himself in his wealth and maintains it by sinful actions goes to Sūcīmukha. There, the Yamadutas stitch thread through his entire body, just as weavers manufacture cloth.

"My dear King, Yamarāj rules hundreds and thousands of hellish planets for various kinds of impious people. Those who are pious may go to heavenly worlds for a life of incredible opulence. Eventually, though, they exhaust their pious credits and return to Earth where again they risk going to hell.

"Everywhere—heaven, Earth or hell—souls forget Krishna and suffer reincarnation. All of this creation is just a wonderful facet of the Lord's external energy for the sake of those souls who choose to enjoy without Krishna."

Insights

No need to go anywhere.

In London, a reporter once asked Śrīla Prabhupāda, "Do you have a concept of hell in your religion?"

"Yes," Prabhupāda replied. "London is hell."

There was stunned silence. Prabhupāda continued, "Of course, it is a credit to the British people that they have created such a great civilization in such a hellish climate."

The irony of an Indian-born swami saying this in the British capital was lost to no one. However, only a few present understood the deeper meaning of Prabhupāda's statement: without Krishna, everywhere is hell.

Why? Because we are caged in a deteriorating body, and despite our body's painful limitations, we have become attached to it. Soon we will be forcibly removed from it and thrown into another one. While trapped in this relentless pain we may delude ourselves into enjoying money or beauty or prestige. Then that illusion fizzles and we start again. The whole ordeal is thoroughly hellish, and without Krishna, there's no end to it.

Going to hell prepares us to transition from one body to the next. This idea is not just a myth or dogma; it is an experience from our own lives. When we undergo trauma, such as a long hike on a hot day, it blunts our senses and reduces our aspirations to base animal needs (*I don't care about the stupid scenery, I'm thirsty!*). That is how and why the extreme suffering of hell acts to reduce the consciousness of a human to that of an animal. To be an animal is the natural *karma* for a human whose interests resemble those of an animal.

Hell is not God's revenge on the wayward. Nor does Yamarāj, hell's ruler, battle with God over our fate. Rather, with Yamarāj's assistance, God kindly reciprocates with those who want to forget Him by sending them to hell for training in their quest. God is neutral; He fulfills everyone's desire.

Coming from someone on death's door, King Viṣṇurāta's next question shows his great compassion.

Canto Six

Rescue

The kind-hearted Viṣṇurāta asked, "How can people be spared the torment of hell?"

In reply, Śukadev described the life of Ajāmila.

Ajāmila, a studious lad, always served his guru and God in accord with the scriptures he loved to read. However, one day, while running an errand for his guru, he saw a low-class man embracing and kissing a prostitute in public.

Ajāmila at once looked away and left. Later, he tried to forget what he had seen, but the memory lingered. The vision of the beautiful prostitute began to consume him.

At last Ajāmila could no longer resist. Abandoning his religious young wife, he located the prostitute, brought her to his house and began enjoying sex with her. In time they had many children. Soon Ajāmila turned to crime to support his brood. Everyone in town despised him.

Even as an old man, Ajāmila continued siring children. At age 88 he had a young toddler whom he named Nārāyaṇa, a name of Krishna. Ajāmila grew so fond of Nārāyaṇa that the old man spent his days eating, drinking and playing with his infant son.

Before long, Ajāmila became deathly ill and could not rise from bed. His life was ending. One day as he woke from a shadowy sleep, he saw three hairy, iron-muscled men converging on him. Ajāmila tried to move but was paralyzed. These mystical intruders bound the helpless Ajāmila, preparing to take him away.

These were the Yamaduttas, agents of Yamarāj, the lord of death, coming to take Ajāmila's departing soul to hell to compensate for his long record of evil. Confused and terrified, Ajāmila cried for his son, "Nārāyaṇa! Nārāyaṇa!"

At that moment three radiant beings appeared. With fine blue skin, golden crowns and other features, the three resembled Lord Viṣṇu. These were the Viṣṇuduttas, agents of the Supreme Lord. Their commanding presence interrupted the Yamaduttas. With clubs raised, they held out their open palms and said, "Stop! This man will not go to hell. He has repeated a name of God, and that has removed all his sins."

"This man? He has sinned terribly!" the Yamadutas shot back.

The leader of the Viṣṇuduttas replied, "This man has atoned for all his sins by chanting the name of God. Although he did not chant purely, he chanted without offense. His sins have all been erased."

Citing sacred texts praising the name of God, the Viṣṇuduttas persuaded the Yamaduttas, who were defeated with higher knowledge, to leave Ajāmila to them.

Ajāmila stared, open-mouthed, as his captors and his rescuers debated his fate. Then, they all disappeared, leaving him to contemplate what he had seen.

Ajāmila recovered his health. Remembering the piety of his youth, he used all his remaining time to cultivate love for Krishna.

Insights

"Hallowed be Thy name."

Nearly every religious tradition reveres the name of God; the science of Krishna explains exactly *why* it is sacred, and *how* God lets us take advantage.

When something agitates air molecules, they ripple through the air like waves on a pond. Our ears pick up the vibration and we recognize a sound. How can the material phenomenon of sound lead us to the pure spiritual presence of God?

Sound vibration describing God affects more than the auditory nerve; it stimulates the soul. You've likely experienced this yourself, hearing a choir sing Handel's *Messiah* in a cathedral, a congregation belting out a spirited hymn in an AME church, or the piercing, amplified voice of an imam calling the faithful to prayer from a minaret.

So powerful and accessible is the name of God that God Himself advises us to repeat it constantly: "One should chant the holy name in a humble state of mind, feeling oneself lower than the straw in the street, more tolerant than the tree, and ready to offer all respect to others. In such a state of mind, one can constantly chant the holy name." (Śrī Caitanya).

Śrī Caitanya (1486-1534 A.D.) popularized the chanting of Krishna's name, a joyful practice that continues to this day all over the world. It is an entirely non-sectarian process; saying any of God's countless names creates a transcendent sound vibration. It is far easier to meditate by filling the mind with sacred sound than trying to coerce the restless mind into silence.

What's different about the sound of God's name? In this world, a thing is not its name. Repeating, "Water, water," does nothing for our thirst. God, however, is not of this world. Everything about Him *is* Him. Thus, to say His name is to be in His presence. So powerful is God's name that saying it once wipes clean the karma for all the sins we have ever committed. And if we have genuine remorse and want to learn from our mistakes, we will repeat His names over and over again.

Canto Seven explains the aim—and the result—of meditating on the names of Krishna.

Canto Seven

Krishna Protects His Devotee

Hiraṇyakaśipu was furious, but he couldn't show it—yet. Krishna, in the form of Varaha, had killed his brother, Hiranyaksha, and now he had to console his brother's family, including his own mother, Diti.

Hiraṇyakaśipu explained to his weeping mother a philosophy he understood but did not accept. Hiding his anger beneath a soothing voice, he said, "You're lamenting over a lost loved one. But his body is right here. If you can't see your loved one now, you couldn't see him before, either. That's because he is an eternal soul, and not this temporary body that has died. In illusion, we think ourselves the body, just as a householder becomes irrationally attached to his house. The dwelling becomes an extension of himself, but he cannot live in it forever, and thus his attachment will cause him to suffer. By seeing the reality, you can break your attachment to the body of our beloved Hiranyaksha."

When this unpleasant task was done, Hiraṇyakaśipu left his relatives in his palatial home and turned his attention to gaining the power he needed to kill Krishna. Proceeding deep into the wild, he found a remote, desolate mountain. "Perfect," he thought.

Hiraṇyakaśipu began standing on his toes, arms stretched to the sky. Years passed and still he remained unflinching in that awkward position. He did not move at all, even when insects began to eat his flesh.

Through the intense power of his penance, Hiraṇyakaśipu at last forced Brahmā himself to appear on the scene. "What do you want?" said the senior god.

"Make me immortal!" demanded Hiraṇyakaśipu.

"How can I do that? Even I have to die." Hoping to pacify Hiraṇyakaśipu, Brahmā sprinkled him with celestial water. The dazzling liquid at once made what was left of his body fit and whole. But Hiraṇyakaśipu was far from satisfied.

"If you can't make me immortal, grant me that I cannot be killed by man, god or beast!"

"Granted."

"And that I can't be killed inside or outside of any dwelling."
"Granted."
"In the day or in the night."
"Granted."
"In the land, water or sky."
"Granted."
"Or by any weapon."
"Granted."

Hiraṇyakaśipu shouted, "Now I am immortal!" His lustful laughter echoed as Brahmā flew away.

At once Hiraṇyakaśipu left the desolate mountain and began using his extended powers to conquer everyone else in the universe, even the gods. Soon he was able to sit proudly on his uncontested throne. Krishna was nowhere in sight. He had stopped the worship of Krishna throughout his kingdom. "Now," he thought, "that pest is gone. Absolute, endless power in mine!"

* * * * * * * *

One day, the two teachers of Hiraṇyakaśipu's five-year-old son Prahlad entered his room with an urgent report.

"It's your son, sir. He keeps talking to his playmates about Krishna."

Hiraṇyakaśipu could not believe his ears. Calling Prahlad, he lovingly described the joys of demonhood. Somehow, though, Prahlad had learned of Krishna. He listened respectfully to his father, but his heart was unchanged.

Prahlad then reminded his father of the eternal soul and the temporary body, as Hiraṇyakaśipu had described to his mother so many years ago. Prahlad went so far as to encourage his father to chant Krishna's names.

Hiraṇyakaśipu turned red. Sending his son away, he called for his trusted assistants. "Kill my son," he hissed. "He has sided with the enemy."

Hiraṇyakaśipu's obedient assistants tried, but they could not kill Prahlad. They struck him with weapons; Krishna made Prahlad impervious to their blows. They threw him in a pit of poisonous snakes; the snakes slithered harmlessly over the calm and fearless boy. They threw Prahlad from a cliff; Krishna mystically caught him and gently lowered him to the ground. They fed him poisoned food; Prahlad offered it to Krishna and ate it unharmed.

The frightened assistants gave up and reported to their master. "We cannot kill him," they whimpered. "Something protects him every time we try."

"Bring him to me!" roared Hiraṇyakaśipu. The sun was beginning to set, and he stepped onto the palace porch to await his son. When Prahlad arrived, he spoke with false affection. "Such a good boy. Where do you get your power?"

Prahlad replied, "The same place as you do, father—from Krishna."

Hiraṇyakaśipu scoffed. "Krishna. Where is your Krishna?"

"Everywhere, father."

Mockingly, the demon replied, "Oh! Is Krishna in this pillar?" Hiraṇyakaśipu drew his sword and rammed it against a pillar supporting the palace porch roof.

Much to his shock, from the crumbling pillar emerged Lord Nrishimhadev, Krishna's form as a half-man/half-lion. Lifting Hiraṇyakaśipu onto his lap, the Lord used His sharp nails to rip him to shreds.

Hiraṇyakaśipu died on the lap of Lord Nrishimhadev—neither in the sky nor on the land. It was dusk, between day and night, on the palace porch—neither inside nor outside. Lord Nrishimhadev was neither man, god nor beast, and no weapon was used—just the Lord's nails. He thus killed Hiraṇyakaśipu without breaking any of Brahmā's boons.

So angry was Lord Nrishimhadeva that the gods who had gathered to watch were afraid to approach Him. However, Prahlad fearlessly approach his Lord and bowed.

"My dear Prahlad, ask for a boon," said the fierce Nrishimhadev.

"I want nothing, my Lord," he replied. "My love for you does not depend on any reward."

The Lord again asked him to take a boon, so the obedient Prahlad asked the Lord to free his cruel father from suffering in the material world. The Lord replied that a devotee's family, dating backwards and forwards many generations, would automatically be so blessed. "Ask something else," he urged Prahlad.

"Then let everyone in this world be liberated, and let me stay here and suffer the reactions of their sins."

Lord Nrishimhadev, now pacified, agreed to Prahlad's supremely selfless request. He then assured Prahlad that, at death, he too would be forever freed from this painful world.

Insights

There must be some mistake . . .

If a disaster cracks our heads we wonder, "Why has God allowed this, especially to a good person like me?"

Such a question ignores our own fingerprints on the situation, for we have chosen material life, and material life means one disaster after another. Why blame God? He would prefer us to join Him, but we're holding out, and He obliges.

We may not be as ambitious as Hiraṇyakaśipu, but in a tiny way our intent to enjoy this world resembles his. We think, "Let me work around God," or perhaps, "God is on my side in my material quest." In that case, if things go well, we become smug and humbly claim that God has helped us. If things go badly we feel that God has cheated or abandoned us. Rarely do we ask, "What does God want, and what can I do for Him?"

We treat God this way because we have forgotten that He, too, is a person. Understanding Krishna restores our memory and allows us a more balanced, fulfilling relationship.

Does one devoted to Krishna suffer in this world? Yes, as does everyone. However, due to clear spiritual understanding, for a devotee that suffering becomes an impetus to call out to God and to give up materialism.

When sorrow and pain appear, enlightened souls understand it is due to their own past misdeeds. They also know that nothing happens in spite of or unbeknownst to God. For countless lifetimes we have been hanging around, trying to enjoy our soon-to-be-dead material bodies. If God permits us to receive the natural result, it is His will and even His kindness to wake us up.

Receiving suffering in that way, a devotee of Krishna, like Prahlad, accepts difficulties with folded palms and without pointing a finger skyward. Unburdened by confusion and resentment, a devotee remembers Krishna through the pain and perseveres toward a better life.

Canto Eight

Krishna Bewilders the Demons

The demons and gods were battling for control of the universe. At one point, Indra, King of the gods, made a disastrous mistake. As he was riding on the back of his celestial elephant, Airāvata, Indra encountered Durvasa Muni, the powerful sage. Durvasa, pleased to see Indra, offered him a flower garland from his own neck. The proud Indra accepted the garland and placed it on his elephant, who dropped it to the ground and trampled it.

Durvasa scrunched his face, trembling with anger. "I curse you to lose all your wealth," he said to Indra. Then he was gone.

As a result of Durvasa's curse, the gods began to lose battles to the demons. When they stood on the brink of losing everything, they rushed to the abode of Lord Viṣṇu, Lord Krishna's incarnation for the maintenance of the material world. They offered heartfelt prayers, and Lord Viṣṇu was pleased to advise them:

"In this situation you must placate your enemies and make a truce."

He advised the gods to use the logic of the snake and the mouse. Once a snake and a mouse were captured and imprisoned in a wicker basket. The snake thought of eating the mouse, but he would have still been stuck in the basket. So instead, he asked the mouse to gnaw a hole in the basket through which they could escape, although his intention was to eat the mouse as soon as the hole had been opened.

As an incentive to the demons, the Lord advised the gods on how they and the demons could churn the ocean of milk to produce *amrita*, the nectar of immortality. Anyone who drinks *amrita* becomes free of old age, disease, invalidity and death.

The demons agreed. Together with the gods, they began the arduous task under Lord Viṣṇu's directions. Many obstacles ensued, but in time they succeeded in producing a single pitcher full of *amrita*. At that point they began to argue: who would get the first drink of *amrita*—the gods or the demons?

As they argued, a most lovely woman appeared. She had low, full hips, breasts like water jugs and the most enchanting face and smile anyone had ever seen. Immediately the demons surrounded her and peppered her with questions:

"Who are you? We've never seen such a beauty as you. Have you come here to find a husband?"

Many of the demons were eager to apply.

"Providence has sent you," they continued. "Although we and the gods are descendents of Kasyapa, we are fighting over this pitcher of nectar. Lovely lady, please settle our dispute."

"I am just a prostitute," the woman replied, "wandering here and there." In fact She was Lord Krishna appearing as Mohini-murti, the bewildering form of the Lord.

"Why would you put so much faith in me?" She continued. "Learned scholars say that one should never befriend an independent woman."

This only made the demons more confident in their decision. With the gods' assent, they handed the nectar over to Mohini-murti and asked her to distribute it as she saw fit.

"Will you accept whatever decision I make?" She said sweetly.

The infatuated demon commanders immediately agreed.

The demons and the gods then bathed and performed all the rituals needed to properly receive nectar. When they finished, Mohini-murti sat the two groups in a long row. Holding the pitcher high, She sauntered over to the demons. With graceful feminine gestures, She looked even more enchanting than before.

Because She approached them first, the demons felt proud and honored. Instead of pouring nectar, though, She poured sweet words through her lips.

"These gods are so impatient," She said. "They are not heroes like you. Let me just give them their share of the nectar first."

The demons, remembering their promise, did not want to appear weak and compromise their relationship with Mohini-murti. So they sat in silence as she poured goblets of nectar for the gods.

The clever demon Rahu, suspecting a plot, had disguised himself as a god and sat among them. He waited with his goblet, anxious but undetected. The smiling Mohini-murti came by, filled his goblet and moved on. At that point the sun-good and moon-god recognized Rahu and cried out, "He's a demon!"

Mohini-murti promptly turned and sliced off Rahu's head with Her disc weapon. The nectar, however, had already touched Rahu's lips. His head, still alive, flew in the air, destined to ever harass the sun and moon in the form of eclipses.

As Rahu's head flew by, everyone could see the power of the nectar. Everyone also recognized that Krishna had cheated the demons and given all the nectar to the gods.

Said Śukadev, "The demons and gods shared the same place, time, cause, activity and ambition, Yet the gods achieved one result and the demons another. Because the gods always turn to Krishna, they easily drank the nectar and got its result. The demons, however, having failed to seek shelter in Krishna, could not get what they desired."

Insights

How the mighty fall.

Commemorated even in carvings on Cambodia's ancient Ankor Wat temple, this incident makes a well-known point: for a powerful man, what can be more alluring than an exquisitely beautiful woman? As Mohini-murti, Krishna confused and manipulated the mightiest gods and demons.

Everyone knows the sensation of powerful sexual attraction. How does it fit into spiritual life?

Before we address that question, let's consider these words by Dr. William Deadwyler, who begins his essay *Immortal Longings* with this disclaimer:

No one likes to be the bearer of bad news. Not only is it unpleasant; it can be dangerous. Kings routinely used to kill on the spot hapless messengers bringing word of defeat. Even so, most people still acknowledge that truth, however unpalatable, is preferable to illusion, however cheering.

You have probably gathered that I have some fairly unpleasant things to say.

Once one has food, clothes and shelter, the sexual urge steps to the head of the line.

"Sex is good for you," its advocates say. "It is fun, relaxing and natural." Few would object. Yet here is the nub of the issue: whatever else it is, sex *is* material. It is a rare and brief pleasant function of a misery-laden physical body. If you want sex, you must accept the rest of the package.

Spiritual life means to act as the soul you are. That means putting sex in its place.

And what place is that?

In the *Bhagavad-gītā*, Krishna says that sex within marriage for procreation is Godly; otherwise, it is a profoundly deep expression of our desire to enjoy matter. He further explains that no one can give up something enjoyable unless they replace it with something even more enjoyable.

Forgoing sex gives one far more energy and saves tons of trouble, money and anxiety. More than that, the joy of dancing with Krishna far surpasses the joy of sex. Many find that hard to imagine. However, an experience of Krishna through chanting, study and realization makes it possible, even easy, to become free of illusion's most alluring power.

Canto Nine

The *Ramayana* Summarized

After telling of the demons' defeat, Śukadev Goswami began to speak of the dynasty of the sun and its best known king, Lord Rāmacandra. Lord Rāma is an incarnation of Krishna described in the world-renowned epic *Rāmāyana*. Because this older text had already described Lord Rāma's life in detail, Śukadev offered just a brief account.

Prince Rāma was the beloved heir to King Daśarath. All the citizens shared the King's appreciation for the young Prince's wisdom, strength and humility. Through palace intrigue, Rāma, His wife Sītā and His brother Lakṣmaṇa were compelled to leave their beloved father and his kingdom of Ayodhyā. Shortly after Rama went into exile in the forest, Daśarath, the victim of the intrigue, died of a broken heart.

Despite their apparent misfortune, Lakṣmaṇa, Rāma and Sītā enjoyed life in the forest. Then, one day, the deceptive and wicked Rāvaṇa kidnapped Sītā. Desiring to make her his queen, Rāvaṇa forced Sītā to accompany him to his kingdom, the golden island of Laṇkā.

Forging an alliance with Sugrīva, king of the monkeys, and Hanumān, his minister, Rāma assembled an army and brought it to the shore opposite Ravana's island. The ocean between bore the weight of stones thrown in by the monkeys, and thus the army built a bridge and assaulted Laṇkā. There his army battled Rāvaṇa's hideous man-eating soldiers. After annihilating Rāvaṇa's army, Rāma personally killed Rāvaṇa with a shaft to the heart. Sītā, freed from captivity, proved her chastity and returned with Rāma to Ayodhyā to rule exactly in accord with spiritual principles.

Ayodhyā prospered under Rāma's direction. The forests, rivers, fields and mountains gave the citizens everything they needed, without much hard work. Disease, sorrow, fear, fatigue and death itself diminished and disappeared. Everyone faithfully served Rāma according to his or her nature and capacity, living in peace and tranquility. This state of affairs became known as *Rāma-rājya*, the kingdom of God on Earth.

Śukadev thus summarized Rāma's life. He then described the dynasty of the moon, a lineage of kings including Lord Krishna.

Having learned of creation, demons, Godly leadership and the importance of remembering Krishna, King Viṣṇurāta was at last ready to hear Krishna's pastimes.

Insights

How does a God-centered society work?

When Rāma, the ideal king, ruled Ayodhyā, nature fell into harmony with society. The citizens, all honest and kind, easily supported themselves by the renewable gifts of nature. Members of such a God-centered society can enjoy a happy, sustainable life.

In a God-centered society, the enlightened citizens understand and ascribe to four divisions of human labor. A small number of people (*brāhmaṇas*) work with their minds and lead highly principled lives. A somewhat larger number (*kṣatriyas*) tend to take charge of things, protecting and leading the citizens. A still larger number (*vaiśyas*) prefer trading and making money through business. And the majority (*śūdras*) simply want to be guided, employed and cared for by *brāhmaṇas, kṣatriyas* and *vaiśyas*.

Though virtually unrecognized these days, these four divisions naturally appear in all societies, God-centered or not. Do you like to work for others or work for yourself? Are you attracted to law enforcement or to teaching? Can you read for days on end or do you prefer to work with your hands?

To know our strengths and pursue a career accordingly helps minimize stress, freeing us to understand and remember that we are not our material bodies.

When people fail to understand these divisions, society becomes distorted. *Sūdras* go to war or to college. Because they have money, *vaiśyas* become elevated to leadership roles where they buy and sell corrupt *kṣatriyas* and *brāhmaṇas*.

One can still find in India the remnants of a society in which everyone worked according to their nature, but it too has become perverted. In some cases, sons and daughters of *brāhmaṇas* claim automatic status as *brāhmaṇas*, though they actually work as *śūdras*. In other cases, sons and daughters of *śūdras* are labeled as such and relegated to menial jobs, though they may be capable of more.

In a God-centered society, one's work is ascribed by inclination, not by birth. Moreover, anyone, from any situation, can understand Krishna and perfect their lives.

Now, as you listen in, Viṣṇurāta, the *kṣatriya* king, will hear all about Krishna from Ṣukadev, the itinerant *brāhmana*.

Step III

A God Who Dances

Bhagavat Purana, Canto Ten

Introduction

What hero, historical or fictional, can rival Krishna?

Not only is Krishna God the Almighty, Supreme Lord of all; to His intimate devotees Krishna is a good friend and peer, an adorable child or an unpredictable paramour.

Yet in the midst of this familiarity, Krishna displays unimaginable superhuman qualities.

Strength? Even as a child, Krishna destroys huge monsters. Intelligence? Krishna argues any side of a question most persuasively.

Charm? Any woman who sees Krishna can't forget the sight. (Krishna, though, is sufficiently composed to vanish in the middle of the night from an assembly of gorgeous young ladies).

Fame? Centuries ago, in less than an hour, Krishna extemporaneously spoke the renowned *Bhagavad-gītā*. Generations of philosophers throughout the world have studied it ever since.

Krishna's powers, wealth, beauty and brilliance defy superlatives. Once you discover Krishna, you'll realize you've never heard of anyone even remotely comparable.

A God Who Dances will introduce to you and help you contemplate this most extraordinary person.

The better-known *Bhagavad-gītā* contains pure philosophy with little biography. The Krishna-centered *Bhāgavat Purana* contains both philosophy and biography. For example, in the context of Krishna's life story we find a host of persons reflecting in the midst of dramatic situations:

To prevent a murder, Vasudev, Krishna's father, thoughtfully appeals to the shameless king Kaṁsa about the fleeting quality of life.

When Krishna's village elders prepare a ritual offering to a god, Krishna points out their more important relationship with nature.

The sage Nārada describes the advantages of poverty to two drunken, wealthy young gods.

The damsels of Vṛndāvan sneak out at night and discuss intricate affairs of the heart with Krishna.

Because of its graceful combination of pastime and philosophy, scholars regard *Bhāgavat Purana* as the post-graduate study of *Bhagavad-gītā*, and the Tenth Canto as its essence. Why is it presented here in poetry?

The text was, originally, composed and repeated orally in carefully metered Sanskrit. The medium of rhyming, metered poetry aims to recreate, in English, the experience of hearing the Sanskrit original. The rhyming medium also calls for more careful word selection to maintain the flow while capturing the nuances of meaning. Nearly every one of the 3932 verses in the Tenth Canto have been poeticized for this edition. Comments from important translators are woven into the poeticized text.

All this allows you to experience the *Bhāgavat Purana* as if you were a *yogī* sitting by the side of the Ganges and meditatively hearing it in an assembly of other saints. The subtle pleasure of hearing about Krishna grows into a profound experience that clears the path to complete spiritual freedom though realization, taste and devotion.

A Sample Verse

Here, as an example, is how one of the Tenth Canto's 3932 Sanskrit verses proceeds to one of 2160 English quatrains in this work. It is text 60 from Chapter 13, as translated to English by Srila Prabhupada, describing Krishna's abode of Vrindavan:

Original Sanskrit:

यत्र नैसर्गदुर्वैराः
सहासन्नृमृगादयः
मित्राणीवाजितावास-
द्रुतरुट्तर्षकादिकम्

Romanized Transliteration:

yatra naisarga-durvairāḥ
sahāsan nṛ-mṛgādayaḥ
mitrāṇīvājitāvāsa-
druta-ruṭ-tarṣakādikam

English Synonyms:

yatra—where; naisarga—by nature; durvairāḥ—living in enmity; saha āsan—live together; nṛ—human beings; mṛga-ādayaḥ—and animals; mitrāṇi—friends; iva—like; ajita—of Lord Śrī Kṛṣṇa; āvāsa—residence; druta—gone away; ruṭ—anger; tarṣaka-ādikam—thirst and so on.

English Translation:

Vṛndāvana is the transcendental abode of the Lord, where there is no hunger, anger or thirst. Though naturally inimical, both human beings and fierce animals live there together in transcendental friendship.

English verse:

Vṛndāvan, that enchanting place where Krishna's always first,
is free of all such agonies as hunger, hate and thirst.
The tigers, chimps and other beasts who threaten common men
live side by side with humans there as transcendental friends.

A Few Details

There are many Sanskrit names in the text. To pronounce them correctly, see the *Notes About Sanskrit Pronunciation* on page 33. In some of the Sanskrit names, for the sake of the meter the soft 'a' at the end is dropped (as often done in Hindi).

Most of the text appears in the familiar *iambic heptameter* meter (also known as 'Fourteener'). However, when the Sanskrit meter changes in the original, usually to accent a change of speaker or subject, our meter changes accordingly. To follow the meters for these occasional changes, check the little guides above the text. The vertical dash [|] represents a strong beat, and the horizontal [-] represents a soft beat. In other words, "-|-|-|" represents a meter than sounds like "da-Da-da-Da-da-Da".

Sanskrit is a very precise language, and these occasional alternative meters all have specific names. You can learn about them elsewhere, but these and other linguistic details are unnecessary for this introductory book. One exception: when it appears, the *Brahmā Samhita* meter is indicated for the sake of readers who are already familiar with that particular rhythm.

You'll find footnotes explaining possibly unfamiliar references in the poem.

Parts of the text, such as the very first verses, appear in *italics*. Other parts appear with or without quotation marks. All this has to do with who is speaking. As explained in the summary of the First Canto, the story of Krishna's life is told by Śukadev Goswami to Viṣṇurāta. The main conversation in the Tenth Canto runs between Śukadev and Viṣṇurāta, as is described by an omniscient narrator (Vyās, the author). Whenever Vyās speaks, the text is in italics, and he speaks only when he is citing Viṣṇurata's questions.

Viṣṇurāta asks questions of Śukadev seventeen times in these thirty-one chapters, including a flood of questions at the outset of their discussion. Everything else is spoken by Śukadev, or the person he is quoting. Since he is the exclusive sub-narrator, whatever Śukadev says *does not* appear in quotation marks. Śukadev often quotes other speakers, and whatever they say *does* appear in quotation marks.

Technicalities aside, I invite you to simply read the poetry as best you can and enjoy the pleasure pastimes of the Supreme Personality of Godhead. The beauty and majesty therein are indigenous to the original and the faults in this presentation entirely mine.

Are you ready to dance?

Devaki and Vasudev

The Overburdened Earth

1) Said Viṣṇurāta, "Śukadev, you've now described for me
the moon-god and the sun-god and their splendid dynasties.
The moon-god's line, great sage, includes the Yadu family,
the dynasty of Krishna. Would you speak about Him, please?

2) Who wouldn't want to hear about these pastimes of the Lord?
Just those, I think, bewildered, broken-hearted or so bored
they choose to merge into the void, committing suicide,
or spend their lives as butchers, selling gristle, flesh and hide.

3) Lord Krishna saved my grandfather, Arjuna, in the war.
Lord Krishna saved my mother and allowed me to be born.
Lord Krishna is the universe, yet lives within our hearts.
I have so many questions about Krishna. Where to start?

4) Why did the Lord leave Vasudev and live in Nanda's home?
Why did He kill King Kaṁsa and usurp Mathurā's throne,
when Kaṁsa, after all, was Krishna's king and relative.
And why did Krishna later shift to Dvārakā to live?

5) Lord Krishna has a form of endless bliss, I understand,
yet He lived with His family like any common man.
Did He live long in Dvārakā, an often-wedded groom?
Why was His brother born out of another mother's womb?

6) O master, you know everything of Krishna, do you not?
Please, clarify these mysteries, and others I forgot.
My vow to fast from food and drink will surely make me weak
unless I drink the Krishna-nectar flowing as you speak."

Śukadev Goswami replied:
7) Your urge to hear of Krishna has made you the best of kings.
Just as the touch of Ganges water purifies all things,
the person who inquires of Krishna cleans the atmosphere
for he who gives the answers and for everyone who hears.

8) At one time Mother Earth was overburdened by the weight
of armies ruled by godless kings who thrived on greed and hate.
So Earth assumed the body of a cow in desperation
and told the senior god, Brahmā, about her situation.

9) Brahmā, Śiva, and other gods, distressed by Earth's report,
at once went off to Viṣṇu's world, their ultimate resort.
Arriving at the milk-ocean whereon the Lord resides,
they worshipped Him with heartfelt hymns until the Lord replied,

10-11) "I've been aware of Earth's misfortune. Listen well to Me:
Lord Krishna soon shall grace Earth's famous Yadu dynasty.
His older brother Balarām shall join the Lord as well,
and all you gods, and all your wives, should do the same yourselves.
My power to bewilder, Yogamāyā, who can cast
a spell of deep illusion over all who cross her path,
shall also join the entourage of Krishna when He comes.
Now go, prepare yourselves for birth among the Yadu sons."

12) Brahmā returned to his abode, and all the gods began
establishing themselves as members of the Yadu clan.
The capital of Yadu's kingdom, Mathurā by name,
Had flourished with its current king, the pious Ugrasen.

Kamsa Seizes Power

13) In honor of her marriage, Kaṁsa, son of Ugrasen,
took up his sister Devakī's fine chariot and reins.
With Vasudev, her husband, at her side, the royal maid
prepared to ride with Kaṁsa in her wedding day parade.

14) Her dowry featured elephants with garlands made of gold.
Four hundred soldiers riding golden chariots patrolled.
Two hundred lovely bridesmaids, fifteen thousand jeweled steeds—
with pride, all tried to please the bride and satisfy her needs.

15) Sweet music filled the air as Kaṁsa drove the bride and groom.
Then, suddenly, an unembodied voice proclaimed his doom:
"You foolish Kaṁsa! Though today you serve this man and wife,
the eighth child born to Devakī will someday take your life!"

16) The wicked Kaṁsa turned to Devakī with shock and dread.
His sword in hand, he snatched her hair and roared, "Off with her head!"
The tactful Vasudev saw this and, holding Kaṁsa's arm,
addressed his angry in-law without showing his alarm:

17-22) "You are your family's pride, dear Kaṁsa. Heroes sing your praise.
How could someone as great as you behave in such a way?
To kill a girl—indeed, your sister—on her wedding day
will surely stain your reputation. What will people say?

Now think this through, great hero. From the moment of your birth,
your body inexorably returns back into earth.
By one means or another, be it now or decades hence,
your death is surely coming. It is simply common sense.

And when your body turns to dust, your soul again acquires
another earthly body formed to suit your own desires.
As when you walk, you shift your weight from back foot to the fore,
you'll change your body after death and leave the one before.

As one asleep is certain that the life he dreams is real,
the soul believes in everything his body does or feels.

The fleeting, artificial body keeps the soul engaged
while making him forget that he is living in a cage.

As wind distorts reflections of the moon upon a lake,
illusion makes the spirit think, "I'm flesh!"—a big mistake.
Since sinful actions cause the soul to stay in this condition,
why not consider carefully, and then make your decision.

Your younger sister Devakī is like your very child.
She so deserves your loving shelter. Please be reconciled,
for you are very merciful. Do not cut off her head,
but give her love and treat her as a father would instead."

23) Because of his demonic nature, Kaṁsa felt disdain
about the tax for sinful acts that Vasudev explained.
As Vasudev saw Kaṁsa pulling back his sister's head,
he came up with another plan. Within himself he said,

24) "When circumstances threaten one's existence or one's wife,
one must use any method to avoid the loss of life.
Perhaps he will die first, so if I promise now to give
my future sons to Kaṁsa, at least Devakī may live."

25) The anxious Vasudev knew well what panic might invoke,
so with respect he smiled at Kaṁsa, cleared his throat and spoke:

26) "Great soul, why are you frightened by an unembodied voice?
Your sister will not harm you, just, perhaps, her future boys.
You have my word, dear brother: when your sister bears our sons,
I promise to bring each to you to do what must be done."

27) Although he was atrocious, when he heard these gentle words,
cruel Kaṁsa put his sword away, completely reassured.
He fully trusted Vasudev, whose character was such
that Kaṁsa knew he'd keep his word, although he'd pledged so much.

28-29) When Devakī was freed by Kaṁsa, in due time she bore
a shining baby boy whom any parent would adore.

Her husband took the boy away, for though he loved his son,
he would not lie to Kaṁsa, nor indeed, to anyone.
What pain is there for saintly souls devoted to the truth?
What evil is off limits for the low and the uncouth?
And what cannot be given up in service to the Lord
by those who want to please Him and desire nothing more?

30) When Kaṁsa saw that Vasudev had brought the newborn child
exactly as he promised, he examined him and smiled.
"Take back your son, dear Vasudev," said Kaṁsa with good cheer.
"The omen said your eighth child is the one that I must fear."

31) Returning with his baby boy, wise Vasudev perceived
that Kaṁsa was impulsive and could never be believed.
Now, at that time, saint Nārada, the ever-roaming sage,
decided to speed Krishna's birth by prompting Kaṁsa's rage.

32) Said Nārada to Kaṁsa, "Sir, have you been made aware
the gods are here as Yadus and surround you everywhere?
Their presence in your neighborhood should lead you to assess
that Viṣṇu will be coming soon to ease the Earth's distress."

33) The words of Nārada left Kaṁsa thoroughly provoked
and made him tremble angrily. Again the mystic spoke:
"In your last life you also practiced wickedness and sin.
Lord Viṣṇu killed you then and now, it seems, He will again."

34) As Nārada departed, Kaṁsa fumed and set his mind.
"Just see!" he thought, "what happens when a man tries to be kind."
He killed Devakī's baby and, along with Ugrasen,
put her and Vasudev in jail and hailed his new domain.

35) Now Vasudev and Devakī could see their only hope
would come as the eighth child foretold in Kaṁsa's horoscope.
Thus, suffering in prison after Kaṁsa killed their boy,
each year they bore another child for Kaṁsa to destroy.

36) What crime is too outrageous for a person who intends
to please his flesh while caring less for family or friends?

He'll even kill to have a thrill or fill a selfish whim.
King Kaṁsa ruled with terror, and the people bowed to him.

Devaki's Eighth Preganancy

37) As Kaṁsa gathered power he was nearly unopposed,
for many other demons helped him terrorize his foes.
He killed six sons of Devakī. The Yadus fled in fear,
except for some who stayed and prayed for Krishna to appear.

38) Her seventh pregnancy brought Devakī both joy and gloom.
She didn't know the Lord's expansion lived within her womb.
Lord Krishna, elsewhere, summoned Yogamāyā to request
that she protect His devotees through these clandestine steps:

39-42) "My brother Balarām waits in the womb of Devakī,
but He will leave as soon as it has been prepared for Me.
Take Balarām to Rohiṇī, co-wife of Devakī;
King Nanda guards her during Vasudev's captivity.

King Nanda rules Gokula, that enchanting rural land.
Now enter Yaśodā, his wife, and execute this plan:
reside within Queen Yaśodā throughout her pregnancy.
when Balarām has left I'll fill the womb of Devakī.

First Balarām will take His birth and be Rohiṇī's son.
His charm and strength shall be unmatched, delighting everyone.
When Yaśodā delivers you, then I shall join the act:
the eighth-born son of Devakī, My opulence intact.

O Yogamāyā, go now and accomplish all these tasks.
I bless you to bewilder all and finish what I've asked.
Henceforward, using sacrifice and all that it requires,
some people will entreat you to fulfill their sense desires."

43) Obediently, Yogamāyā bowed before the Lord
and left for Srī Gokula. Soon, exactly in accord
with Krishna's order, Balarām departed Devakī
and entered His new home within the womb of Rohiṇī.

44) When Devakī miscarried Balarām, the people said,
"Since Kaṁsa kills her children, she aborted it instead."
At that time Krishna, God Himself, who vanquishes all fear,
went in the mind of Vasudev and readied to appear.

45) While bearing Krishna, Vasudev appeared just like the sun,
his glow so bright the shining light astonished everyone.
When he placed Krishna in the mind of Devakī one day,
her visage bloomed, a waxing moon in opulent display.

46) To bear the Lord while trapped in jail by Kaṁsa's wicked plot
made Devakī seem like a fire kept within a pot,
or like a man enlightened, wise and thoroughly refined
who fails to share his wisdom for the good of humankind.

47-48) As Devakī grew jubilant, King Kaṁsa grew concerned.
"This Viṣṇu killed me once," he thought, "and now He has returned
to kill me once again. Yet killing Devakī today
will only bring me trouble in a different sort of way.

To kill a pregnant relative would cost me all respect.
My opulence would vanish and my subjects would defect.
My health and life and legacy would all die out as well.
A wicked man is just a corpse descending into hell."

49) Deliberating in this way, King Kaṁsa chose to wait
to let the child be born and then administer its fate.
While on his throne or in his bed, King Kaṁsa stayed absorbed
in thoughts about his enemy, the all-pervading Lord.

The gods Pray

50) At that time Lord Brahmā, Lord Śiva, Nārada and Vyās
and other gods and sages grew invisible and crossed
the prison grounds till they found Devakī within her room.
They then recited heartfelt hymns for Krishna in her womb:

(Meter: -|- -|- -|- -|)
51-57) "Lord Krishna, we've come to fulfill Your command.
Your birth in this prison is just what You planned.
You always stay true to Your own perfect vow,
for who could prevent anything You allow?

You're there when the universe comes into place;
You're there when it all disappears without trace.
You favor the person who's honest like You
but never the hypocrite, cheater or fool.

You fill the desires of Your devotees
who conquer the ocean of death and disease.
They use the safe boat of Your soft lotus feet,
then leave it for others, their journey complete.

And what of those nondevotees who aspire
to lift themselves out of this worldly mire?
Imagining they have been freed, they perform
the same mundane actions they meant to reform.

But if a devotee who loves You falls prey
to mundane attraction, he won't go away,
for You will protect him so well, it is said
he'll fearlessly walk on his enemies' heads.

Your lessons apply to each time and each place.
You're equal to all, every species and race.
You are the beginning of all that is true.
Please care for us Lord; we surrender to You.

O Devakī, by your good fortune and ours
Lord Krishna has come here with all of His powers.
Your family is blessed now that this has occurred.
You need not fear Kaṁsa; his death is assured."

(iambic heptameter)
58) Thus having come to Devakī to eulogize and pray,
the many gods and sages went invisibly away.
Lord Krishna can do anything, so all of them were pleased
to see Him be the child of His most faithful devotees.

The Birth of Lord Krishna

(59-61)
One pleasant evening, Earth seemed bathed in happiness and love.
The sacred constellation Rohiṇī appeared above,
with other stars and planets, twinkling in the cloudless sky.
The universe itself seemed pleasing, still and satisfied.

The moonlit Mother Earth displayed her pastures, mines and towns.
In fragrant trees, the birds and bees sang out their pleasing sounds.
The rivers poured clear water into reservoirs and lakes
where lotuses and lilies bloomed, appearing wide awake.

The brāhmans rose before the dawn, took bath and set alight
their sacrificial fires in accord with Vedic rites.
Across the lakes and pastures, silky, fragrant breezes came;
they pleased the brāhmans tending fires but didn't spoil the flames.

The brāhmans, who had suffered much from Kaṁsa and his men,
began to feel tranquility pervade their hearts again.
The higher worlds resounded with the sounds of kettledrums
as gods peered down at Earth, expecting Krishna soon would come.
While gods threw flowers, danced and sang in heavenly enclaves,
assembling clouds made thundering sounds like gentle ocean waves.

62-64)
Then Viṣṇu –He who dwells within the hearts of you and me–
appeared, as if a full moon, from the heart of Devakī.
In His four hands, the child held lotus, *cakra*[1], conch and club.
His bangled arms and jeweled ears and helmet placed above
His scattered hair set off His yellow silks and blue-black skin.
And there around His neck was hung the famed Kaustubha gem.

[1]*Krishna's razor-sharp disc.*

65) As Vasudev beheld the child, he thought his eyes had failed.
How could the Lord, so nicely dressed, be born inside a jail?
The father could not celebrate, though he was much inclined,
so he gave out ten thousand cows within his joyous mind.

66) On seeing how the child's effulgence lit the dismal cell,
the awestruck Vasudev felt peace, his worries all dispelled.
He joined his palms and bowed his head and then, though it seemed strange,
began, with wife and newborn son, the following exchange:

Vasudev: (Meter: -|- -|- -|- -|)
67-69) Primeval, transcendent, ubiquitous Lord,
I see Your position as never before.
You made the creation, and yet, as its God,
You're here as our son by Your sweet facade.

Your powers create everything that we see,
yet they are distinct and complete potencies.
You too are distinct from this world You have made,
yet my confused eyes see You clearly today.

My Lord, You're adored in the finest of rooms;
why come in a jail through a prisoner's womb?
O Master of all, I can safely presume:
since You have arrived, cruel Kaṁsa is doomed."

Devakī:
70-73) "Dear almighty Lord, now at last You have come
within Your creation, as bright as the sun.
The Vedas exalt You and all You arrange.
No one can divorce You or force You to change.

The common man longs for the heavenly skies
and freedom from illness, old age and demise.
But when You appear, death itself runs away,
and we all feel peaceful, no longer afraid.

As Kaṁsa still persecutes good people, please,
defeat all the fears of sincere devotees

and cover this form, much adored by the wise,
from envious, evil, material eyes.

Your four-handed form doesn't fit in this world.
I should have a two-handed boy or a girl.
No one will think Viṣṇu could come from my womb.
Please change and I'll hide You; the guards will come soon."

Viṣṇu: (meter: |-|--|-|)
74-78) "My dear mother, now please be blessed;
among chaste women, you are best.
Let Me now put your mind at rest;
let your heart fill with happiness.

Long ago, in a former life,
you were still Vasudeva's wife.
Though Brahmā said to procreate,
you first sat down to meditate.

Both of you sat through heat and cold,
hearts made perfect by self-control.
I was pleased, so I asked you to
say what you wanted Me to do.

All you wanted, you said humbly,
was the boon of a son like Me.
Twice I came as your son back then;
here, today, I have come again.

Had I come as a normal boy,
would your faith have been unalloyed?
Still, I'm yours, and since you love Me,
when you die you will come to Me."

(iambic heptameter)
79) Lord Viṣṇu then fell silent, and before His parents' eyes,
His figure changed from Viṣṇu to a child of normal size.
Reclining in His legendary, transcendental form,
He showed Himself as baby Krishna, smiling, bright and warm.

80) Then Yogamāyā took her birth, just as Lord Krishna planned,
across the river Yamunā, in Nanda's rural land.
When Yaśodā, King Nanda's wife, gave birth that mystic night,
exhausted from her labor, she slept on, her eyes shut tight.

81) By Yogamāyā's influence, the guards in Kaṁsa's jail,
not hearing sounds of childbirth—not a whimper, sob or wail—
fell fast asleep as well and could not see nor hear a sound.
At this, the gates swung open and their locks fell to the ground.

82) When thund'ring clouds let out their rain as gently as they could,
A mystic serpant sheltered man and son with many hoods.
As Vasudev, the huge white snake and babe of blackish blue
snuck quickly past the sleeping guards, King Kaṁsa slept on, too.

83) The swirling river Yamunā, made deeper by the showers,
came to a halt and made a path (by Yogamāyā's powers).
The river welcomed Vasudev, lest Krishna should be lost,
just as the Indian Ocean once allowed Lord Rām to cross.

84) When Vasudev reached Nanda's house, where everybody slept,
he found the room of Yaśodā and pondered his next step.
In hopes that even Kaṁsa would not kill a newborn daughter,
he switched the babes and ran at once back through the swirling waters.

85) Back past the sleeping guards he slipped, through every open door.
He chained himself and Devakī in shackles as before.
He placed the girl by Devakī, who looked at her and smiled,
while Yaśodā, asleep, knew not the gender of her child.

2

Kamsa

A Brief Remorse

1) By Yogamāyā's influence, the prison doors shut tight.
The guards awoke and heard a newborn crying in the night.
They ran to Kaṁsa shouting, "Devakī has had her child!"
As Kaṁsa bolted out of bed, his scattered hair hung wild.

2) While rushing to the cell of Vasudev and his poor wife,
King Kaṁsa thought, "Now cruel time has come to take my life!"
He burst in to the prison cell, eyes wide in great alarm,
and saw his helpless sister, baby daughter in her arms.

3) Said Devakī, "My brother! May good fortune fill your days.
Great honor will attend you if you show this girl your grace.
You've killed my seven children due to force of destiny,
but kindly spare this harmless girl. She'll be your gift to me."

4) She clutched Yaśodā's child and wept, but even as she begged,
King Kaṁsa snatched the baby girl and gripped her tiny legs.
Collapsing to his knees, he raised the girl above his head
and braced himself to smash her on the floor till she was dead.

5) The child, however, slipped away and rose up in the air,
transforming to an eight-armed goddess. Kaṁsa gasped and stared.
Bedecked in jewels, silks and blooms, as angels sang her praise,
she held eight deadly weapons, such as trident, sword and mace.

6) The goddess Yogamāyā (who was soon to gather fame
as Durgā, Devī, Kali and a host of other names
from avaricious people asking blessings of their choice)
addressed the frightened Kaṁsa in a firm, impassioned voice:

7) "You foolish Kaṁsa! What will be the use of killing me
when God Himself, Lord Krishna, is in fact your enemy?
He's taken birth already in a secret, distant place.
Do not kill babies needlessly and add to your disgrace!"

8-9) To see this fearsome goddess and to hear her reprimand
left Kaṁsa very humble, and he issued a command
to free the blameless couple. Then he turned to them and said,
"Because of my most wicked sins, your seven sons are dead.
Because of me, dear relatives, your pain has been immense.
Now what will be my destiny for such a great offense?
The unembodied voice we heard misled us all and lied,
but I believed it anyway, and all your children died."

10-12) Though Kaṁsa blamed himself, poor Devakī felt no relief,
so he spoke some philosophy to try to ease her grief.
"Your sons had their own karma, which they've finished in this birth.
The body's just an earthen doll that soon returns to earth.

The soul, however, never dies, and those who know this truth
stay unattached to worldly things and seek the Absolute.
Our family and social situations never last.
I now see this quite clearly—though I haven't in the past.

Dear brother and dear sister, you are both as good as saints.
I've treated you so terribly, yet you've shown such restraint.
Can you forgive a heartless wretch, so foolish and inept?"
With this King Kaṁsa fell before his prisoners and wept.

13) When Devakī saw Kaṁsa so repentant and sincere,
her anger at his sinful deeds completely disappeared.
Then Vasudev, who saw that Krishna's plan was taking place,
was also freed from anger and affirmed, with poise and grace:

14-15) "O noble King, what you have said is perfectly correct.
Due only to their ignorance do foolish men accept
their bodies as themselves. As such, they simply think in terms
of all that they possess today and all they long to earn.

The soul immersed in ignorance cannot be satisfied.
When things go well he dances and when things go wrong, he cries.
He always sees some problem or immediate reward,
and never sees the all-controlling presence of the Lord."

16) As all agreed upon these points of shared philosophy,
King Kaṁsa took the chains off Vasudev and Devakī.
Much pleased by this conclusion, Kaṁsa took his sister's leave
and entered his own palace, his anxiety relieved.

17) The next day, though, King Kaṁsa called his ministers to see
what they would think of goddess Yogamāyā's prophecy
that he who would kill Kaṁsa had been born, but somewhere else.
The ministers, great demons all, discussed among themselves.

18) Emerging from their conference, their spokesman said, with pride,
"If this is true, King Kaṁsa, we must use infanticide.
So let us kill each child who has been born ten days before
and save your precious life, O King. Oh, yes. And what is more:

(Meter: -|- -|- -|- -|)
19-22) The gods run in fear at the sound of your bow.
Your arrows harass them wherever they go.
Their weapons abandoned, their fighting all through,
they either escape or surrender to you.

Lord Viṣṇu finds *yogīs* and hides in their hearts.
Lord Śiva takes off for some forested parts.

Brahmā's meditating and Indra's withdrawn;
The danger to you from the gods is all gone.

And yet like the smoldering ashes of fire
the gods may return to obstruct your desire.
Destroy them this time and your worries are through,
and we shall suggest what your Highness should do.

The powerful Viṣṇu must first be controlled;
He only survives where brahminical souls
perform sacrifices and care for the cows.
Great King, you must start persecuting them now!"

23) King Kaṁsa listened carefully to what the demons said
and felt his pride returning as their statements filled his head.
His humbleness and sorrow for his errors slipped away.
He shouted, "Let the persecution start this very day."

24) The mystic demons cheered the chance to plunder, kill and rape.
They started to transform themselves to vicious, fearful shapes.
They thought that killing Vaiṣṇavas would save King Kaṁsa's head,
not knowing that their own destruction waited just ahead.

Joy In Gokula

25) Nearby in Śrī Gokula, where the cows and cowherds lived,
the gentle Nanda Mahārāj was chief executive.
Upon receiving word about his newborn baby boy,
he bathed and dressed and gave out precious gifts in utter joy.

26) He gave two million cows, adorned with gems, to *brāhman* priests,
along with hills of produce, golden cloth and lovely feasts.
Such charity to *brāhmans* made the kingdom purified;
the *brāhmans* chanted Vedic hymns, and all were satisfied.

27) Gokula's happy residents cleaned every nook and crag
and decked the streets with mango leaves, perfumes, festoons and flags.
They mixed up oil and tumeric to make a golden salve
and used it, with some peacock plumes, to dress the cows and calves.

28) The cowherd men put on their jeweled turbans, coats and silks
that proved enormous opulence exists in cows and milk.
Their wives, the *gopīs*, all endowed with lovely hips and breasts,
wore *kuṇkum*[1] and vermillion and were also nicely dressed.

[1]*A festive red powder made of saffron or turmeric.*

29) The citizens, ecstatic at the news of Krishna's birth,
brought gifts of gems and gold and other products of the earth.
They blessed the heir apparent with fine oils and shouted out,
"This child will rule our kingdom long and well, without a doubt!"

30) As drums and trumpets filled the air and festive spirits rose,
the guests splashed milk and liquid *ghee*[2] on one another's clothes.
To satisfy Lord Viṣṇu through His servants, as required,
King Nanda gave to all the guests the gifts they most desired.

[2]*Boiled and filtered butter.*

31) Another wife of Vasudev, Rohiṇī, had remained
within the care of Nanda while her husband was detained.
She felt so pleased for Yaśodā, she donned her finest dress
and wandered through the gathering to welcome every guest.

32) The atmosphere in Nanda's home was naturally endowed
with happiness and opulence derived from tending cows.
But when Lord Krishna came within King Nanda's loving care,
good fortune's goddess, Lakṣmī, also made her dwelling there.

Nanda Meets Vasudev

33) Soon Nanda closed the festival, but he could not relax,
for he was due in Mathurā to pay his yearly tax.
When Vasudev, his stepbrother, learned Nanda had arrived,
he went at once to tell him how his wife and he survived.

34) As Nanda greeted Vasudev, embracing him with love,
he felt he had regained his life and thanked the stars above.
The younger Vasudev showed his respects, and then began
discreetly asking questions on the state of Krishna's plan:

35-37) "Dear Nanda, at your age you'd lost all hope of having sons.
It surely is good fortune that your heir has finally come.
Good fortune also granted me the chance to see you here,
for in this world it's often hard to see those you hold dear.

The river's current brings together floating sticks and leaves
then spreads them quite indifferently by whirlpools, thrusts and heaves.
So too, we come together due to bodily relation
then lose each other's company through time and complication.

How are Gokula's fertile lands, so blessed with grass and trees?
How are the cows you raise so well? I hope there's no disease.
How is my wife Rohiṇī, whom you kindly shelter there?
Is Balarām, our son, still doing well within your care?"

38) "They're fine," said Nanda, "but that wicked Kaṁsa killed your boys.
At least your daughter reached the gods and could not be destroyed.
By destiny your children came and then were taken back.
Dear friend, our fate rules everything. Take comfort in this fact."

39) On hearing this, wise Vasudev could clearly understand
that Nanda had no inkling of Lord Krishna's clever plan.
He said, "You are so wise and kind. Now, since you've paid your tax,
before some danger hits Gokula, please, my friend, go back."

40) So Nanda hugged his stepbrother, and, thanking him again,
prepared to go to Gokula with all the cowherd men.
They yoked their bulls to bullock carts, as was their simple way,
and drove from Mathurā back to the country right away.

41) While contemplating Vasudev and all that he had said,
King Nanda journeyed home with an increasing sense of dread.
Within his heart he offered God sincere and fervent prayers
to save his son, and everyone, from danger and despair.

Putana

42) And danger was indeed upon Gokula at that time,
from Pūtanā, a giant witch, adept at every crime.
Her master, Kaṁsa, sent her to destroy the newly born,
so through her power she assumed a human woman's form.

43) Her breasts were large and firm and seemed to overtax her waist.
A fragrant garland dressed her hair, which framed her lovely face.
She looked like goddess Lakṣmī with a smile in her eyes,
enlivened by her husband, Viṣṇu. Such was her disguise.

44) Enchanted by her beauty, Yaśodā and Rohiṇī
allowed the lovely visitor in Krishna's nursery.
She smiled at Krishna tenderly and held Him to her chest,
preparing Him to sit and suck her poison-covered breast.

45) Now, Pūtanā had murdered many children in her day.
She looked at baby Krishna, but He looked the other way.
And then she placed Him on her lap—a terrible mistake—
as one might think he holds a rope while handling a snake.

46) So motherly was Pūtanā, with wicked heart beneath,
that she was like a deadly sword within a silken sheath.
She pushed her breast in Krishna's mouth. Aware of all her sins,
He sucked the poison—and her life—so she'd not kill again.

47) The demon screamed out, "Leave me! Leave me! Suck my breast no more!"
but as she thrashed, Lord Krishna sucked her harder than before.
So forceful was her screaming that, through heaven, Earth and space,
both men and gods thought hurricanes were surely taking place.

48) She dashed out of the nursery with Krishna at her breast
and tried to flee the village in her terminal distress.
Her human cover vanished with her final shrieking sound,
and when she fell she shook the earth a dozen miles around.

49) The cowherd women ran to see who made the awful screams
and found a giant, ugly corpse, like something from a dream.

The demon's mouth hung open, showing teeth the size of plows,
while eye sockets like deep, dark wells appeared beneath her brow.

50) Her nostrils were like gaping caves, her thighs like riverbanks.
Her stomach was as spacious as a public bathing tank.
Her giant arms and legs appeared like bridges in the sky.
On seeing this, the women were upset and terrified.

51) The hideous and evil Pūtanā lay dead and still,
yet something moved upon her breasts, which seemed as large as hills.
The *gopīs*, looking carefully, saw Krishna crawling there.
Like any ordinary child, He played without a care.

52) The *gopīs* cried in happiness and kissed the baby's brow.
At once they held some rituals with products from the cow
designed to save the baby from what dangers might remain.
And then they sang this ancient song, comprised of Viṣṇu's names:

(Brahmā Samhita meter: -| -| -|-| --| -|-)
53-61) May Ajā, He who is unborn, guard the legs of Krishṇa;
May Maṇimān, almighty Lord, guard the knees of Krishna;
May Yajña, Lord of sacrifice, guard the thighs of Krishna;
O Viṣṇu, Lord of everything, please protect this baby.
May Hayagrīva, horse divine, guard the front of Krishna;
May Keśava, He of fine hair, guard the heart of Krishna;
Acyuta, You who cannot fail, guard the waist of Krishna;
O Viṣṇu, Lord of everything, please protect this baby.
May Iśa, He who is complete, guard the chest of Krishna;
May Vivasvān, god of the sun, guard the neck of Krishna;
May Viṣṇu, shelter of us all, guard the arms of Krishna;
O Viṣṇu, Lord of everything, please protect this baby.
May Urukram of giant steps guard the face of Krishna;
May Īśvara, who has control, guard the head of Krishna;
May Srī Hari, who holds a club, guard the back of Krishna;
O Viṣṇu, Lord of everything, please protect this baby.
May Madhuhā, the demon's death, guard the right of Krishna;
May Ajana, who holds a sword, guard the left of Krishna;
May Haladhar, who holds a plow, guard the rest of Krishna.
O Viṣṇu, Lord of everything, please protect this baby.

May Viṣṇu, lord of Śvetadvīp, guard the core of Krishna;
May Hṛṣīkesh, the self-controlled, guard the nerves of Krishna;
Yogeśvara, *yogī* supreme, guard the mind of Krishna;
O Viṣṇu, Lord of everything, please protect this baby.
O Cakrī, holder of the disk, guard before Śrī Krishna;
O Urugāya, with Your conch, guard around Śrī Krishna;
Upendra, You of mighty deeds, guard above Śrī Krishna;
Garuḍa, eagle-feathered friend, guard beneath Śrī Krishna.
May Govinda, who pleases all, guard Him when He's playing.
May Mādhava, the life of all, guard Him when He's sleeping.
May Vaikuṇṭha, the undisturbed, guard Him when he's walking.
May Nārāyaṇ, husband of wealth, guard Him when he's sitting.

The evil witches such as this who attack our babies,
the ghosts and creatures of the night who can make us crazy,
the hostile stars who make us live as we do not wish to,
are vanquished, frightened and repelled by these names of Viṣṇu."

(iambic heptameter)
62) The *gopīs* finished singing and were pleased to see the child
appearing safe and happy, all the danger reconciled.
As Krishna drank His mother's milk, the cowherd men arrived.
When Nanda saw the giant corpse he said, in great surprise,

63) "My friends! We simple cowherd men could not see any threat,
but Vasudev advised us to take care. He was correct!
He must be blessed with mystic skills and paranormal gifts
to understand the threat at hand from demons such as this."

64) Now Vasudev, a *kṣatriya*, well-versed in politics
anticipated Kaṁsa's mood and all his dirty tricks.
King Nanda, on the other hand, a simple *vaiśya* squire,
could not conceive how Vasudev had known what would transpire.

65) The cowherd men brought axes and cut up Pūtanā's frame.
They reasoned, "Snakes are burned at death, and she deserves the same."
By suckling Krishna, Pūtanā had served Him, in a sense,
Thus her burning body smelled as sweet as frankincense.

66) How powerful is Krishna's service! Even with her faults,
this Pūtanā was blessed at death and gained a good result.
If demons who serve Krishna accidentally are restored,
then what to speak of devotees, so pleased to serve the Lord.

67, 68) The fragrant smoke from Pūtanā infused Gokula's air,
attracting distant village folks to see the strange affair.
"How could a child have killed this awful witch!" the people said.
The simple Nanda, meanwhile, held his son and smelled His head.

69) To hear accounts of Pūtanā and Krishna, as have you,
with fondness and devotion and assurance they are true,
attracts one to Lord Krishna's endless pastimes, leading soon
to sweet, ecstatic love of God—the highest human boon.

Trinavarta

69-70) Said Viṣṇurāta, "Master, all the pastimes God displays
in endless incarnations and in countless different ways,
relieve the soul that suffers from illusion's painful touch.
Yet generally, we do not like to hear them very much.

The pastimes of Lord Krishna, though, as you describe so well,
with Kaṁsa and with Pūtanā and all you've yet to tell,
attract my ear like nothing else. Each one is so sublime,
I only wish to hear them all with my remaining time."

71) Said Śukadev, Lord Krishna's mother, Yaśodā, held rites
suggested by the *Vedas* to protect her baby's life.
As demons in disguise planned new attacks upon the child,
His parents just saw Krishna and enjoyed His charming smile.

72) One day, as Yaśodā sat holding Krishna on her lap,
He grew so very heavy that she thought her thigh would snap.
Unable, all at once, to hold the baby by herself,
she put Lord Krishna on the ground and ran to get some help.

73) The wicked Tṛṇāvarta then flew in from Kaṁsa's lair.
Embodied as a whirlwind, he took Krishna in the air.
He spun with fury, lifting up a swirling, dusty cloud
that blinded people on the ground and thundered long and loud.

74) The dust obscured the sun and made the day like dimmest dawn.
When Yaśodā returned with help, her baby boy was gone!
She looked and looked; then others came to look on her behalf.
When all had failed, she wailed, much like a cow who's lost her calf.

75) As all the dust began to clear, the *gopīs* gathered round
and joined the stricken Yaśodā, who wept there on the ground.
Tṛṇāvarta, meanwhile, took Krishna higher than before,
but Krishna grew so heavy that the fiend could rise no more.

76) With Krishna hanging round his neck, Tṛṇāvarta then shrieked,
"This baby feels like chunks of lead, or giant mountain peaks!"
He tried to shake off Krishna but he struggled as he spun,
for Krishna held on tightly and was having lots of fun.

77) As Krishna grasped him by the throat, Tṛṇāvarta was choked.
He could not move his hands or scream in fear or even croak.
Tṛṇāvarta was frantic. Then, with grossly bulging eyes,
he lost his life and started tumbling downward from the sky.

78) Not far from where the cowherd women cried aloud and moaned,
the body of Tṛṇāvarta fell crashing on a stone.
His limbs were all dislocated, but there upon his chest
the *gopīs* found the infant Krishna, calm and self-possessed.

79) As Yaśodā embraced her son, King Nanda soon arrived,
and all the cowherd men and women repossessed their lives.
When Nanda saw Tṛṇāvarta was dead, he felt relieved.
Then, standing with his entourage, he stated, very pleased,

80) "This demon took our child away to eat Him, but instead,
the baby is quite happy and the wicked beast is dead.
Because we've given charity and excavated wells,
our pious acts are all paid back, while he has gone to hell."

81) The simple Nanda grew astonished looking at the sight,
and thought again how Vasudev had been completely right.
"First Pūtanā, now this!" he thought. Then, feeling quite amazed,
he vowed to keep his baby Krishna safely in his gaze.

3

Yashoda and Nanda

Gargamuni Names Krishna

1) When Vasudev, in Mathurā, could see the time had come,
he asked the senior Yadu priest to see his secret son.
The priest, named Gargamuni, who was learned and austere,
surprised and pleased King Nanda when he suddenly appeared.

2-4) King Nanda rose with folded palms for his exalted guest
and gave him food and beverages until he was refreshed.
Then Nanda said, "My Godly friend, so sanctified and wise,
Is there some sort of service I could possibly provide?

You go from place to place through every sort of circumstance,
impelled by your concern to help the common man advance.
You read the stars and understand both past lives and the next,
which helps one live his present life with wisdom and success.

Your visit is most timely, and we're very glad you came.
May I request you, sir, to give my infant sons their names?
Great sage, please use the stars to see the future of my sons.
Conduct the proper rituals and do what must be done."

5, 6) Said Gargamuni, "Dear King Nanda, everybody knows
I am the Yadu family priest. Now, do you not suppose
that Kaṁsa will find out your sons were given names by me
and think your sons the sons of Vasudev and Devakī?
King Kaṁsa is a devil, and he's very sharp as well.
He knows that Devakī's eighth child is living somewhere else;
he also knows your ties with Vasudev extend way back.
Were he to learn I've named your sons, he might launch an attack."

7) Said Nanda, "Gargamuni, naming children is a must.
If Kaṁsa is a danger, we can easily adjust.
Come with me to the cowshed. Chant your mantras soft and low.
Great sage, my very relatives will never even know.

8-11) The sage at once agreed and when the boys were in the shed,
he studied their astrology at length. At last he said,
"The older boy is Bala—strong. He'll also go by Rām,
the one who pleases all. And there's a third name: Saṇkarṣan.

This name means one who brings together different families—
in this case, both King Yadu's and King Nanda's dynasties."
(Though Gargamuni knew that Vasudev had sired this son,
he didn't mention it to Nanda—nor to anyone.)

Your younger son is Krishna. He's appeared in ages past,
in white and red and yellow shades and different social castes.
He was a son of Vasudev, the timeless stars proclaim,
so in this lifetime "Vāsudev" shall also be His name.

Your son will gather countless names by His activities.
He'll keep your subjects happy and prevent calamities.
Lord Viṣṇu comes when gods have failed and evil floods the Earth,
and someone much like Viṣṇu is your son in His new birth."

12) With this, sage Gargamuni smiled and slipped out of the shed.
King Nanda very happily considered what he'd said.
"How fortunate I am," he thought, "To have such special sons.
I must beware of demons or whatever threats may come."

Krishna's Mischief

13) In time the boys began to crawl upon their hands and knees.
They roamed the sands of Nanda's lands and felt themselves quite pleased.
They'd crawl to see a neighbor lady's shining ankle bells,
then crawl back to their mothers, who stood smiling somewhere else.

14) Their mothers held the mud-stained babies tightly to their chests.
Affection filled their hearts as mothers' milk filled up their breasts.
They looked upon their sons who sucked and smiled from underneath,
and happily took count of all their tiny baby teeth.

15) When Balarāṁ and Krishna saw the baby calves walk by,
they'd grab and tug their tails until the calves were terrified.
In fear, the calves would dash about, the babies holding tight,
until the *gopīs* rescued them while laughing in delight.

16) The village women loved the boys and never could relax
for fear they'd suffer injury from monkeys, dogs or cats.
But when the growing boys first walked and later ran and played,
the women, seeing mischief, came to Yaśodā to say:

(Brahmā Samhita meter: -| -| -|-| --| -|-)
17-23) "We go to milk our family cows early in the morning
and find that Krishna let the calves in without a warning.
The cows give nothing, for the calves sucked up every mouthful.
Dear Yaśodā, your son is wrecking our peaceful households!

Have you observed the local beasts growing fat and chunky?
Your Krishna steals our butter pots just to feed the monkeys.
Our husbands catch Him, but He smiles like a little dandy.
Dear Yaśodā, your son is wrecking our peaceful pantries!

Because you cannot chastise Krishna, it seems, or teach Him,
we hide our butter pots where Krishna can never reach them.
In spite He runs into our nurseries to pinch our babies.
Dear Yaśodā, we simply want to be peaceful ladies!

Your Krishna uses lengths of wood for a makeshift ladder
and climbs up to our butter pots hidden in the rafters.
He breaks those butter pots apart, getting what He's after.
Dear Yaśodā, your son's a thief. Kindly stop your laughter!

We think you're taking Krishna's actions a little lightly.
Your son and Balarām wear jewelry that shines so brightly
They find, within our darkened storerooms, the food we're hiding.
Dear Yaśodā, your son's in need of a good chastising.

Our husbands catch your Krishna robbing us in this fashion
And say to Him, "You are a thief!" with a show of passion.
"No, you're a thief!" your son replies. How He disrespects them!
Dear Yaśodā, He is your son. Won't you please correct Him?

Your Krishna fouls our rooms and kitchens and in between them.
He leaves a puddle and a pile every time we clean them.
Just see Him look at you with such innocent expression.
Dear Yaśodā, it's time your son made a full confession!"

Krishna Eats Dirt

(iambic heptameter)

24) One day while Krishna played with all the other cowherd sons,
His playmates told His mother something new that He had done.
"Your son has eaten dirt!" the boys all breathlessly complained,
so Yaśodā picked up her son and anxiously exclaimed,

25) "Dear Krishna, all Your playmates, even Balarām, assert
that You have run off by Yourself to eat a scoop of dirt.
Our house is full of sweets and food conducive for good health.
How is it they are saying You have done this to Yourself?"

26) Lord Krishna said, "Dear Mother, why would I be eating dirt
when you give Me such lovely meals, including nice desserts?
My playmates are conspiring and telling you some lies.
Just look yourself within My mouth and see with your own eyes."

27) When with His parents, Krishna always hides His majesties,
except in certain times and circumstances such as these.
"All right then," Yaśodā replied. "Sit down and open wide."
So Krishna climbed upon her lap and instantly complied.

28) When Yaśodā looked in His mouth, she saw, by Krishna's grace,
the seas and mountains of the Earth, the stars and outer space,
the elements, the modes, the worlds of heaven and of hell,
all bodies, karma, endless time—she even saw herself!

29) "The universe in Krishna's mouth?" thought Yaśodā, in fear.
"Is this a dream? Am I awake? How could this all appear?
Perhaps this is some mystic power Krishna's showing me."
As love receded, Yaśodā could see reality.

30, 31) "This child is God in person! I should simply bow my head.
No one can understand Him, though so many words are said.
He causes this creation and maintains it all as well.
It seems His mystic energy has put me in a spell.
Illusion has me thinking I am Nanda's wife and queen,
that Krishna is our son, and that our lives are as they seem.
I think my subjects, cows and calves obey my every whim;
in fact, I'm Krishna's servant, and my life is meant for Him."

32) As Yaśodā observed the truth, just then, by Krishna's grace,
maternal love returned and she resumed her former place.
Forgetting Krishna's cosmic mouth, she hugged her son once more,
and relished love for Him more deeply than she had before.

33) The *Vedas* and *Upanisads* declare Lord Krishna's fame.
His glories are expounded in more books than I can name.
Yet Krishna wanted Yaśodā to think of Him as one
of many cowherd boys—her naughty, ordinary son.

Krishna Steals Butter

34) One day as all her servants were engaged with other chores,
Lord Krishna's mother saw the butter churn had been ignored.

So she collected yogurt to make butter for the day,
and as she churned she sang a song describing Krishna's play.

35) She loved to make up Krishna-songs to memorize and sing
so she could think of Krishna as she did most anything.
She sang and pulled the churning rope, her yellow sari moist
from breast-milk born of love she felt just thinking of her boy.

36) Her bangles bounced and sang along. Her earrings danced in time.
Her body shook from labor and her temperature climbed.
As beads of perspiration broke across her lovely brow,
the flowers fluttered from her hair like petals from a bough.

37) Into the room Lord Krishna toddled; He'd just woken up.
He snatched His mother's churning rod and tried to interrupt,
for He was feeling hungry after such a lengthy nap.
His mother then embraced the Lord and sat Him on her lap.

38) When Yaśodā saw Krishna's face, milk poured out from her breasts.
Her son desired nursing, and she granted His request.
The two were sitting happily in motherly repose
when Yaśodā remembered she'd left milk upon the stove.

39) She dashed to save the milk. Lord Krishna gave an angry squeal,
upset to be disrupted in the middle of His meal.
He bit His lips with baby teeth, picked up a nearby rock,
and broke apart the butter pot with one well-measured knock.

40) He reached inside for lumps of yellow butter, freshly churned,
and quickly slipped outside before His mother could return.
On seeing all the chaos, Yaśodā was mildly irked,
for she could understand the mess was Krishna's handiwork.

41) While sitting on an upturned mortar meant for grinding spice,
Lord Krishna felt quite satisfied. He easily enticed
delighted village monkeys to eat butter from His hand,
though now and then He'd glance about in fear of reprimand.

42) While Krishna went on feeding all the monkeys for some time,
He did not see His mother creep up softly from behind.
The crows, who'd come to watch the fun, saw trouble on the way.
As Yaśodā drew nearer, they jumped up and flew away.

43) The startled Krishna turned and saw his mother and her stick.
He ran, His butter-laden footsteps falling short and quick.
His mother ran behind and tried to capture God Himself,
though He eludes great *yogīs* and most everybody else.

44) Her heavy breasts were burdensome upon her slender waist,
and as she ran behind her son, her hair fell out of place.
Because she loved her Krishna, Yaśodā did not complain,
and very soon she captured Him and asked Him to explain.

45) Her naughty son at once confessed; He then began to cry.
His tears mixed with the blackish ointment worn beneath His eyes,
creating tainted teardrops that He rubbed across His face.
His mother smiled but held His hand so He could not escape.

46) Absorbed in motherly affection, Yaśodā could not
see God Himself had left behind that broken butter pot.
Observing Krishna's fearful face and all the tears He shed,
she threw away her whipping stick and tied Him up instead.

47) Now Krishna has no start or end, no front or back or side;
He's everywhere and everything—and still personified.
Both time and karma come from Him, so He's beyond their scope,
yet Yaśodā thought she could bind Him with a simple rope.

48) By love alone would Krishna ever let Himself be bound.
When Yaśodā picked up the rope and tried, she quickly found
that it was just a little short. She tied on more, and then
she found the lengthened rope was just a little short again.

49) She added on another rope. Too short. She tried another,
yet Krishna's tiny waist was still too large for His poor mother.
The *gopīs* in the neighborhood all giggled at the fun,
and Yaśodā laughed too, though all this puzzled everyone.

50) While Yaśodā was trying hard to check her naughty son,
her body was perspiring and her hair had come undone.
On seeing that His mother's strength was quickly running down,
Lord Krishna felt compassionate and let Himself be bound.

51) Though Lord Brahmā, Lord Śiva and such great, exalted souls
who rule the very cosmos are in Krishna's full control,
Govinda has a feature that's exceptionally sublime:
He's bound by His devotees' love, as He showed at this time.

52) A million goddesses of fortune dance to Krishna's flute,
yet He steals butter as if He were poor and destitute.
The god of death, the dread of all, fears Krishna's slight command,
yet Krishna fears His mother with a whipping stick in hand.

53) The mercy shown to Yaśodā, whose selfless love was pure,
surpasses all Brahmā, Śiva, or Lakṣmī could secure.
Ascetics, speculators, or the ordinary man
cannot reach God as easily as pure devotees can.

The Sons of Kuvera Freed

54) Bound tightly to the heavy mortar by His mother's hand,
child Krishna took His punishment as bravely as a man.
When Yaśodā went back inside to clean the broken pot,
the Lord saw two *arjuna* trees adjacent to His spot.

55) These trees had quite a history, and Krishna knew it well.
The two were once Kuvera's sons and shared their father's wealth.
One day the youthful brothers played in Śiva's lush estate
by splashing holy Ganges water in their drunken state.

56) Celestial damsels came along, and in that sacred place,
like maddened, drunken elephants, the boys took their embrace.
Intoxicated, laughing, not restrained in any way,
the young gods rolled their drunken eyes and passed their merry day.

57) Just then, by their good fortune, saintly Nārada appeared.
The damsels quickly snatched their clothes and hid themselves in fear.

The two sons of Kuvera, though, were drunk and didn't care,
and stood in front of Nārada with nothing on but air.

58) Surmising in a moment the condition of the youths,
the sage resolved to help them understand a higher truth.
As parents pinch awake a sickly child they need to nurse,
Saint Nārada decided to assign the two a curse.

59-67) Said Nārada, "Material resources, my dear boys,
like beauty, education or the fame you both enjoy,
are all surpassed by money, for it makes men very proud.
The rich drink wine and have more sex than others are allowed.

The rich man, smug and satisfied with all that he's acquired
quite often grows malicious in pursuit of his desires.
To please the mortal flesh he loves and thinks will never die,
he murders helpless creatures just for sport and exercise.

He does not see the suffering he'll bring himself, the fool,
when his fine body ends up ashes, worms, or vulture stool.
He thinks his body durable, long-lived and very strong
and never asks to whom his body actually belongs.

Does one's employer own his body? Does his mother dear?
Or is it a possession of the king or the premier?
At death, one's children put his body on a funeral pyre.
Is it the asset of the eldest son who lights the fire?

Do slave owners possess the body due to bill of sale?
Or is it owned at death by dogs who eat and wag their tails?
In fact, the body comes from sand and goes back into sand,
as anyone who thinks about it surely understands.

Illusion makes the rich try to enjoy what they cannot,
but poor folks, on the other hand, can hardly give a thought
to sense enjoyment, seeking, as they do, a decent meal.
In poverty one learns how other starving people feel.

A hungry person has no extra energy to chase
the sins of wine and meat and needless sexual embrace.
Impoverished people therefore gain the merits of a saint
who lives without such pleasures by deliberate restraint.

Avoiding wealthy sense-enjoyers, saints live with the poor—
another reason destitutes can spiritually mature.
Because you boys are rich and think your bodies are your selves,
your only hope to learn the truth is through some special help.

Your drinking and illicit sex have made your brains so numb
like trees you stand there naked—and so trees you shall become!
One hundred godly years from now, you both shall have the grace
to reacquire your freedom and see Krishna face to face."

68) Saint Nārada then left, and through his mystic energies
the two sons of Kuvera turned into a pair of trees.
They stood there many, many years until that very day
when Krishna dragged a mortar as He slowly crawled their way.

69) Lord Krishna thought, "I have no obligation to this pair,
but Nārada, My dear devotee, took them in his care.
He wanted Me to see them. Let his prophecy now come
so they can rectify what they have previously done."

70) With this the Lord crawled further on His tiny hands and knees.
The heavy mortar wedged between the bases of the trees.
The rope bound to His belly strained, but Krishna seemed to glide;
He crawled a little further and both trees crashed to His sides.

71) Then from the fallen branches, leaves and trunks, began to rise
two brilliant, glowing gods with folded hands and downcast eyes.
Their beauty lit the very Earth, yet as they bowed their heads
before the toddler Krishna, they looked up a bit and said,

(Meter -|- -|- -|- -|)
72-75) O Krishna, the greatest of mystics, our Lord!
O cause of all causes, our lives are restored!
Your dear servant Nārada called You and thus,
transcendent creator, You've sanctified us.

The planets and stars are within Your control;
You are the director of each spirit soul.
You know all the secrets of every heart,
yet fools think of You as remote and apart.

Unless You disclose Yourself, who can perceive
that You are beyond what the mind can conceive?
We won't try to analyze all that You do;
Instead, we most humbly bow down before You.

Since Nārada cursed us and cured our disease,
our hands are now pledged to serve Your devotees.
Without their intrusion our lives were condemned.
May we see them always and serve You through them."

76-77) *(iambic heptameter)*
The two young gods thus prayed as Krishna smiled to hear the sound.
"I freed these two, " He thought, "yet I remain completely bound."
He said to them, "Saint Nārada indeed is very kind;
your mad desire for opulence made both of you go blind.
As darkness disappears before the presence of the sun,
the presence of a saint at once enlightens everyone.
You both fell down from heaven and were born as naked trees;
go back now with My blessings and remain My devotees."

78) The two sons of Kuvera bowed, enormously inspired.
Lord Krishna's gift—devotion—was the wealth they now desired.
Ecstatic with the blessing saintly Nārada bestowed,
they circled round their bound-up Lord and rose to their abode.

4

The Cowherd Boys

Moving to Vrindavan

1) The sound of crashing, giant trees shook everything in town.
The startled cowherd men assumed that lightning brought them down.
Arriving at the scene they found no bolts had struck; instead,
the cowherd boys who witnessed it approached the men and said:

2) "When Krishna dragged the mortar to the base of these two trees
He quickly pulled them down by simply crawling on His knees.
Two glowing men then left the trees and rose up in the skies.
We saw it all 'cause Krishna did it right before our eyes!"

3) Some men believed the cowherd boys were telling them the truth
but others felt the trees too big for Krishna to uproot.
When Nanda saw his son bound up, he smiled and set Him free
and shook his head, bewildered in parental ecstasy.

4) As time passed by, Lord Krishna charmed the villagers each day.
The *gopīs* loved to tease Him; they would clap their hands and say,
"O Krishna, if You dance for us, we'll give you half a sweet."
So Krishna sang and danced for them according to their beat.

5) His mother and her friends sometimes would play another prank;
they'd send young Krishna to retrieve a heavy pot or plank.
As if He could not lift such things, He'd gaze at them at length
and flex His arms to demonstrate He had sufficient strength.

6) Thus Krishna stayed subservient to loving devotees.
He pleased the hearts of everyone by such activities.
Each day Lord Krishna played with Balarām, His elder brother,
till they were called to dine at noon with Nanda and their mothers.

7) One day a humble vendor woman, simple but astute,
set out papayas, mangos, and all kinds of luscious fruit.
"Come buy my fruits!" she called. On hearing this, Lord Krishna ran,
some grains of rice to barter in His tiny toddler hands.

8) Though when the Lord approached her, he had dropped most of the grains,
the woman loaded up His hands with all they could contain.
Because she did this lovingly, without having been told,
her fruit basket at once filled up with precious gems and gold.

9) In this way, life was peaceful. Still, King Nanda was concerned
that danger from King Kaṁsa or his friends would soon return.
He thus convened the elder cowherd men to plan ahead.
His older brother Upānanda thought a while and said:

10-12) "Our Krishna seems in danger due to someone's ill intent.
Tṛṇāvarta and Pūtanā—were they just accidents?
And then those two gigantic trees crashed down where Krishna plays.
It's only by God's mercy that He's still alive today!

For Krishna's safety, and our own, the time has now arrived
to leave our homes in Gokula before we lose our lives.
Vṛndāvan, that enchanting forest, lush with grass and trees,
will be more inconspicuous, yet fill our every need.

If you agree, then I say we should instantly depart.
We simply need to load our household goods on bullock carts
and keep the cows in front of us." The people all concurred,
and packed their things in happiness without another word.

13) The women, kids, and elders climbed aboard the carts to ride,
while younger men with bows and arrows walked on every side.
They blew their bugles made from horns, and as the sound increased,
the caravan began, complete with bullocks, cows and priests.

14) The women shone with gold and saris, *kuṇkum* on their breasts.
They sang of Krishna's pastimes as the caravan progressed.
Both Yaśodā and Rohiṇī delighted everyone
as they rode on the cart they shared with their respective sons.

15) Arriving in Vṛndāvan, everyone was pleased to see
the atmosphere and climate were as pleasant as could be.
By circling their wagons in the shape of half a moon
they made a temporary home that very afternoon.

16) Young Balarām and Krishna looked around and felt quite pleased
to see the hill of Govardhan and feel the river's breeze.
They happily grew up there and, as smart and sturdy boys,
in time were deemed responsible and ready to employ.

More Demons In Vrindavan

17) Despite their high position in a wealthy family,
both Rām and Krishna worked and took responsibility.
With other boys their age, they were assigned to tend the calves,
an everyday experience a cowherd boy must have.

18) The boys just tended calves all day with no need to commute,
their work and play and education all in one pursuit.
Their ankle bells would tinkle as they went about their day,
and in between their duties they had fun in different ways.

19) Sometimes they used a rope to knock the fruits down from the trees,
or, dressed in blankets, fought like bulls upon their hands and knees.
They played a kind of football, kicking fruits across the ground
and imitated peacock calls and other creatures' sounds.

20) One day as they were playing, only Krishna was aware
a demon in disguise had joined the calves within their care.

Pretending not to notice, Krishna strolled across the ground
then captured both the demon's legs and spun him round and round.

21) The demon, Vatsāsura, was completely caught off guard.
Lord Krishna hurled him at a tree and felled it, loud and hard.
Although he lost his life in that astonishing exchange,
because Lord Krishna touched him, Vatsāsura's fate was changed.

22) Though Vatsa's soul was freed, his corpse resumed its normal shape—
a large and ghastly form that caused the cowherd boys to gape.
"Well done! Well done!" exclaimed the boys, as smiling gods above
tossed flowers on Lord Krishna as expressions of their love.

23) Then Rām and Krishna relished breakfast, took the calves and roamed
across the lovely forest they'd adopted as their home.
These topmost personalities, supremacy unseen,
killed demons, guarded cows and kept their everyday routine.

24) One day when drinking water from a pleasant forest lake,
the boys and calves shrunk back in fear. Their youthful bodies quaked.
A demon named Bakāsura, quite awesome in physique,
attacked them as a bird of prey, complete with deadly beak.

25) Bakāsura, within a moment, swallowed Krishna whole.
Astounded, all the boys just screamed and lost their self-control.
Lord Krishna was untroubled, for He knew the antidote:
He made His body burning hot within the demon's throat.

26) Bakāsura then choked and coughed up Krishna in a flash.
He charged the Lord with sword-like beak, designed to pierce and slash.
But Krishna took the top and bottom beaks within His grasp
and ripped the bird in half, as one might split a blade of grass.

27) The gods in heaven cried with joy to see this demon slain.
They pounded kettledrums and praised Lord Krishna's holy name.
The boys observed the demon's death and, hearing godly praise,
they warmly hugged Lord Krishna and discussed His deed all day.

28) Returning home at suppertime, the boys told in detail
about the bird that threatened and how Krishna had prevailed.
The cowherd men and women shook their heads in disbelief
and fixed their gaze on Krishna and their sons in great relief.

29, 30) King Nanda thought, "How fortunate that all these fiends from hell
attack my Krishna viciously, yet end up dead themselves.
They're just like flies attacking flame and dying foolishly.
It must be God protecting Krishna; what else could it be?
How did our Gargamuni know such demons would attack?
Whatever such a mystic says is certainly a fact.
And just discussing what my son has done since we've been here
makes everybody happy. Troubles seem to disappear!"

Watching the Calves

31) The boys continued watching calves for endless, happy weeks,
while imitating monkeys and enjoying hide-and-seek.
One morning Krishna thought, "Let's have our breakfast in the woods."
He blew His bugle-horn and all His playmates understood.

32, 33) They came with their own bugles, flutes and lunch bags full of food
and steered their calves down forest paths in joyful attitude.
Although the mothers of the boys had dressed their darling sons
with conch shells, jewels, pearls and gold—enough for anyone—
the boys adorned themselves still more as they began to play
with flowers, peacock feathers, forest leaves and colored clay.
Sometimes the boys would steal a lunch and hide it, unconcerned.
But if the owner came to tears, the bag would be returned.

34) When Krishna sometimes wandered off, without being coerced
the boys, as one, would rush to Him and try to touch Him first.
Some cowherd boys played flutes and bugles, raising pleasant sounds,
while others chased the shadows soaring birds cast on the ground.

35) Some boys behaved like ducks or swans that swam the lake with ease,
while others clucked like cuckoo birds or buzzed like bumblebees.
Some pranced like dancing peacocks; others donned a monkey face
and chased their fellow monkeys as they swung from place to place.

36) Some boys ran to the waterfall and jumped in froggish style,
while some watched their reflections in the water and just smiled.
Some boys would loudly shout and hear the echoes bounce away;
in every case, Lord Krishna stayed the center of their play.

37, 38) Impersonal to some, but not to loving devotees,
Lord Krishna joined these lucky boys in their activities.
A *yogī* strives for many lives to overcome his mind,
and yet when all is said and done he never seems to find
a speck of love for Krishna. Yet, these simple, daily joys
were shared in love, like hand in glove, by Krishna and the boys.

Aghasura

39) Dear King, Aghāsura, a demon, watched the boys at play
and made a plot to kill the lot right there, that very day.
His siblings, both Bakāsura and Pūtanā, had died,
so Kaṁsa sent their younger brother for this homicide.

40) Aghāsura thought, "Since my siblings died, I must somehow
avenge them both by killing Krishna and His friends right now.
To kill these boys also destroys Vṛndāvan as a whole;
the village will collapse as if a corpse without a soul."

41) With that, Aghāsura assumed a mystical disguise:
his body took a python shape of monumental size.
He lay across the forest path, his snake-jaws opened wide,
and waited for the cowherd boys to make their way inside.

42) His lips were spread, the upper stretching high into the air.
His mouth became a deep, dark cave, his tongue a thoroughfare.
He breathed the humid stench of fleshy corpses in decay.
His eyes shone bright as blazing lights while watching for his prey.

43) On seeing the colossal python, some boys stopped and cried,
"Let's run! Let's run! A demon's come! He wants us all to die!"
But other boys said, "It's a statue, just a big display
that someone has installed here to enhance our fun today."

44) Deliberating further in the stinking python breath,
the boys agreed the python meant to lure them to their death.
But then they looked at Krishna and recalled what had occurred
the other day when He was preyed on by a giant bird.

45) Assured their friend would save them, all the boys danced in the snake.
Aghāsura sat still and waited, using them as bait.
Expecting Krishna to come running in, the demon lay,
delighted to kill Krishna and His friends this tasty way.

46) When Krishna saw the giant python, He became amazed
at His external energy and its outlandish ways.
Although the Lord remains supreme whenever He descends,
He thought, "If I just smash this snake, I might injure my friends."

47) Reflecting just a moment, Krishna dashed into the beast
and started growing larger, like a dough infused with yeast.
The demon felt his throat fill up, so he too swelled in size,
but he could not keep up, and terror filled his python eyes.

48) When Krishna had gone in Aghāsura, the gods had cried,
while Kaṁsa and his cronies felt their chests swell up with pride.
Then, suddenly, Aghāsura choked up and couldn't breathe.
His body slumped; his soul, however, had no place to leave.

49) Its other exits blocked, its python form now limp and dead,
Aghāsura's eternal soul popped straight out of his head.
Then Krishna saw His friends lay comatose in deadly sleep.
He woke them all and out they marched between the python's teeth.

50) Aghāsura's effulgent spirit drifted in the air,
illuminating all directions, floating here and there.
And then, while singing gods beat drums that made the heavens quake,
that spirit merged with Krishna as He marched out of the snake.

51) Aghāsura, the spirit soul, was freed at once and gained
relief from birth and death as very few great souls attain.
So kind is Krishna, by His touch He'll even grant release
to demons like Aghāsura—a brutal, jealous beast.

52) If Krishna liberates such demons, cruel and unkind,
when schemes and whims for killing Him fill up their wicked minds,
what shall He do for devotees who lovingly embrace
His names and pastimes? Just imagine how they shall be graced!

53) The great commotion in the heavens, stirred up by the gods,
caught Lord Brahmā's attention. He stood up and thought, "It's odd
that everyone makes such a fuss about some cowherd boy
when *I* create this cosmos. This is getting me annoyed!"

54) The people of Vṛndāvan, meanwhile, quite amazed to find
the dried-up, cave-like corpse Aghāsura left behind,
would play and gaze and think of Krishna, growing more inspired,
although it was a year before they learned what had transpired.

*55) "A year?" said Viṣṇurāta, somewhat startled by the phrase,
and speaking for the first time in what seemed like several days.
"Oh great and kindly Śukadev, how did this odd event
stay hidden by the children from the village residents?"*

*56) When Śukadev heard this inquiry, he fell into trance
and, thinking of the Lord, withdrew from outer circumstance.
For some time he sat speechless, rapt on Krishna deep within.
Then, slowly, he recovered and addressed the King again.*

5

Brahma

Lunch with Krishna

1) Said Śukadev, Your question is delightful. I'm impressed.
By now, it seems, you find this Krishna-talk is ever-fresh.
Though pastimes of Lord Krishna are the best thing in this world,
most people tell the pastimes of some common boy or girl.

2,3) Lord Krishna led the boys down to a riverbank and said,
"Let's play in this enchanting spot. Aghāsura is dead.
The fragrant lotus flowers here attract the birds and bees.
The sands are soft and white—just right for our activities.
The calves can drink and eat the grass along the riverside
while we enjoy our lunches. Then we'll all be satisfied."

4) At once the boys sent out the eager calves to drink and graze
while they pulled open lunch bags like some hungry young gourmets.
Lord Krishna sat, surrounded by the boys and looking pleased,
a lotus whorl surrounded by its petals and its leaves.
Each boy sat facing Krishna, hoping He would glance their way.
Thus eating lunch became for them another kind of play.

5) The boys used flowers, leaves or rocks as plates to hold their meal
as, one by one, the items in each lunch bag were revealed.
One boy would taste the dishes that another brought from home.
Devouring half, he'd have a laugh and share half of his own.

6) Almighty Krishna eats the food that's offered day and night
by *pukka*[1] priests in formal feasts with proper Vedic rites.
This time, however, Krishna ate without formality
among His dear associates and loving devotees.

[1]*Precise, cultured.*

7) Lord Krishna sat among His friends and chortled in delight.
His flute hung to His left side and His bugle to His right.
He held a lump of yogurt-rice and fruit in His right hand.
The gods looked on and stood in awe but could not understand.

8) While all the boys enjoyed their lunch, the calves enjoyed theirs too
and wandered off in search of tender foliage to chew.
On noticing the missing calves, the boys were struck with fear,
but Krishna said, "Enjoy your lunch. I'll bring the calves back here."

9) Though Krishna rules creation through assorted agencies,
He gets involved directly when it comes to devotees.
His rice ball still in hand, He left His friends at peace and rose
to seek the calves in fields of grass and fertile forest groves.

Stealing the Boys and Calves

10) From high above, Brahmā had seen Aghāsura's demise
as well as this ensuing lunch. This left him quite surprised.
Deciding to put Krishna to a test, Brahmā came down
and hid away the boys and calves while He was not around.

11) When Krishna soon returned to where the lunch had taken place,
He found no boys or calves at all—just empty, open space.
Although He showed astonishment while looking here and there,
He knew at once Brahmā had hidden all His friends somewhere.

12) Within a moment Krishna chose to answer this new ploy
by mystically expanding to replace each missing boy.
The all-pervading Lord became each boy in full detail,
from lunch bag, bugle, flute, and foot to face and fingernail.

13) The new boys had the old boys' ages, habits, traits and names.
Replacement clothes and ornaments fit each boy just the same.
Once He'd become the boys, the Lord became the calves as well,
so perfectly that even their own mothers couldn't tell.

14) The party danced their way back home with Krishna at the head.
Each boy returned to his own house, each calf to its own shed.
Each mother filled their secret urge for Krishna as a son
by nursing their respective boys, not knowing what He'd done.

15) As Krishna all at once portrayed each missing cowherd boy,
their mothers did their duties with extraordinary joy.
They bathed, massaged and dressed their sons before the evening meal,
surprised to find these routine tasks infused with such appeal.

16) Although the cowherd parents always loved their sons before,
they secretly had loved young Krishna just a little more.
Distinctions between Krishna and their sons now disappeared
and they adored their sons more every day throughout the year.

17) The cows, meanwhile, mooed loudly when their calves came in their sheds
and licked them with maternal love from tail and hoof to head.
Their udders overflowed with milk and didn't seem to shrink
as their respective offspring drank up all that they could drink.

18) A year went by and even Balarām did not catch on,
as He joined Krishna and the boys each day in work and song.
One day on Govardhan, however, He became amazed
to see the older cows charge down that hill on which they grazed.

19) Although these cows had younger calves, their hearts were deeply stirred
with powerful maternal love on seeing Krishna's herd.
They galloped down a rocky trail, their heads and tails erect.
Their four legs worked liked two legs and their humps slid to their necks.

20) The cowherd men, amazed as well, could not hold back the charge,
and soon the cows reached Krishna's calves, their udders full and large.
They nursed and licked these long-weaned calves as if to eat them whole.
The cowherd men, ashamed and angry, struggled for control.

21) They scurried down the rocky slope, but when they reached their sons—
the boys who played with Krishna—their affection left them stunned.
Their own parental feelings swelled. Their shame and anger fled,
as, lovingly, they held their sons and smelled their tender heads.

22) When Balarām saw all of this, He wanted to explore
why everyone's affection had grown stronger than before.
"Some new event is causing all these feelings to arise.
Perhaps these boys and calves are really gods in some disguise.
Could this be Krishna's handiwork? Why, who else could it be?
Yes, only those illusions made by Krishna work on Me."

23, 24) So Balarām asked Krishna, who explained the whole affair,
and both of them remembered, on that day, He'd not been there.
Lord Balarām was absent when Lord Krishna made His clones,
for it had been His birthday and His mother kept Him home.
And when His birthday came again, His mother made Him stay,
so Krishna once again went out without Him for the day.

25) A year to us is to Brahmā a minute's time elapsed,
the time it took to put the boys and calves in mystic naps.
Returning to Vṛndāvan on his swan, he was surprised
to see the stolen calves and boys right there before his eyes.

26) Brahmā exclaimed, "Those boys and calves are safe in hibernation,
yet Krishna is surrounded by some perfect imitations!
Where *have* they come from? Who are they? I cannot understand
how Krishna's friends stayed here all year in spite of all my plans."

27) Brahmā had tried, in mystic pride, to baffle Krishna's mind;
instead he found himself confused, his own plans undermined.
The power of Brahmā, next to Lord Krishna's, fades away,
as brilliant snow grows dull at night, or glowworms pale by day.

28) To show Brahmā the secret truth of what had just occurred,
Lord Krishna let the boys and calves again be who they were.
At once Brahmā saw Krishna at the center of a drove
of monsoon-bluish Viṣṇus clad in yellow silken robes.

29) Each Viṣṇu had four jeweled arms with bracelets on each wrist
and four hands holding lotus flower, conch shell, club and disc.
Kaustubha gems hung from Their necks. Their ornamented feet
and *śrīvatsa* marks on their chests made each Viṣṇu complete.

30, 31) A forest-flower garland reached the sashes round each waist,
and garlands strung from Tulasī were very nicely placed
on each and every portion of Their transcendental forms
by devotees who love to be where *kīrtan*[2] is performed.
Such devotees surrounded every Viṣṇu in the throng
and pleased their Lords respectively with service, dance and song.
Each Viṣṇu smiled as brightly as the moon in ecstasy,
exchanging loving glances with His faithful devotees.

[2]*Congregational chanting of Krishna's names.*

32) Brahmā could see each Viṣṇu had divine authority
to rule the vast creation and its multi-energies.
Their endless, blissful, brilliant forms, beyond the greatest mind,
Brahmā saw both as God and boy, and both at the same time.

33) This vision stunned Brahmā with transcendental ecstasies.
He felt himself a doll before such sacred Deities.
Brahmā, the lord of Sarasvati, queen of education,
could not begin to slightly understand the situation.

34) Brahmā had tried to realize Lord Krishna on his own,
but only through submission is Lord Krishna ever known.
Brahmā was wholly mystified. His purpose now fulfilled,
Lord Krishna showed Brahmā the truth by His transcendent will.

35) Brahmā regained his senses like one rising from the dead
and stared through independent eyes in each of his four heads.
He saw Vṛndāvan's forests and their pleasant atmosphere,
replete with life-sustaining trees that pleased throughout the year.

36) Vṛndāvan, that enchanting place where Krishna's always first,
is free of all such agonies as hunger, hate and thirst.
The tigers, chimps and other beasts who threaten common men
live side by side with humans there as transcendental friends.

37) Brahmā then saw the Absolute, All-Knowing and Most Grand:
a single roaming cowherd boy with rice ball in His hand.
We think a man is ordinary till he makes a move,
but Krishna, as a simple boy, had nothing else to prove.

38) As Krishna wandered here and there, Brahmā jumped off his swan
and fell down like a golden rod, his foolish pride now gone.
Though gods avoid the touch of earth, Brahmā laid on the ground
to bathe Lord Krishna's feet with tears and touch them with his crowns.

39) Remembering what he had seen, his ecstasy complete,
Brahmā stood up and fell again at Krishna's lotus feet.
Again he stood and wiped his eyes, his heads in humble pose,
and said, in heartfelt mantras he instinctively composed:

Brahma Repents

40-60)
"O Krishna, You are God Himself! Who would have know it's You,
a simple child with yellow robes and monsoon-colored hue?
You carry flute and bugle. Peacock feathers dress Your hair.
Your fingers hold a rice ball and Your garland scents the air.

I kidnapped all Your friends and calves—a blunder, I admit—
so You have kindly chastised me for my own benefit.
No one, including me, can estimate Your potencies
nor understand Your happiness or Your activities.

When thoughtful people give up speculating over You
in favor of admiring talks about the things You do,
while filling social duties, doing all that must be done,
they conquer You, Who otherwise can conquer anyone.

But stubborn people still believe the truth lies in their heads.
Abandoning Your loving smile, they speculate instead.
They think and think, but trouble is the only thing they gain,
like one who beats on empty husks of wheat in search of grain.

Some *yogīs*, through devotion, catch a fleeting glimpse of You;
renunciates may see You from tangential points of view;
the wise may count the atoms of the Earth or flakes of snow,
but who can count the transcendental qualities You show?

A person who anticipates Your mercy, all the while
persisting in the face of every obstacle and trial
while offering respects to You within his very core
obtains a claim to Your domain and love forevermore.

My Lord, I'm so uncivilized! Instead of trusting You,
I stole your friends and hid them in my secret rendezvous.
How could I have imagined fooling someone so much higher?
Compared to You, I'm just a spark within a blazing fire.

Though I create the universe, its planets, stars and sky,
my independent spirit has turned out to be a lie.
My arrogance disgraces me; my pride has been betrayed.
Lord Krishna, please forgive me for disturbing You this way!

Yes, I create this universe—a pot that locks me in—
but countless universes pass through pore holes in Your skin
like particles of dust float through a screen on wisps of air.
Can someone seven stretches of his hand in height compare?

Please treat me as a pregnant woman welcomes, with a smile,
the wriggling and kicking of her helpless, unborn child.
A lotus from Your navel gave me birth, Lord, so I pray
that You'll forgive Your child who has offended You today.

You gave me birth then stranded me atop a lotus flower.
I searched for You in vain until You came by Your own power.
But Yaśodā did nothing more than check Your mouth for sand
and You showed her the universe. How can I understand?

I don't create this universe; You make it by Yourself.
You then make me, Lord Viṣṇu and Lord Śiva, just to help.
And then You put us all away. Again, You're on Your own,
just as today You conjured boys, but now You're all alone.

If one mistakes a rope to be a snake, he shakes in fear
but when he sees it's just a rope, his terror disappears.
Without You, Lord, I live like that; whatever I may do,
I'll live in fear of death within this world till I see You.

But when the light of Your association fills the sky,
the darkness of illusion fades and all is pacified.
Can Your devotee suffer everlasting dread or fright?
Can someone living on the sun be touched by day or night?

A person serving You is automatically set free,
while other so-called mystics live a hopeless fantasy.
Imagining they're liberated, rising up in pride,
they miss You and fall down again, their minds unpurified.

These simple boys and calves are far more fortunate than I.
Though I create the universe, they're fully satisfied
to simply play their forest games with You, their dearest friend.
You drink their mothers' breast milk, Lord! How can I comprehend?

Please let me take a future birth within this sacred land!
But if that is impossible, I'll gladly wait and stand,
embodied as a blade of grass in meadows just nearby,
in hopes some cowherd boy will step on me as he runs by.

So very kind are You, my Lord, that You shall never shun
a person giving service, even when it's poorly done.
When Pūtanā, that horrid witch, gave You her poisoned breast,
You took her as Your mother and released her after death.

So how will You pay back the loving service given You
by these Vṛndāvan residents in everything they do?
The sages claim attachment is an anguishing mistake,
but these great souls, attached to You, live only for Your sake.

And fools claim they have realized God! As far as I'm concerned,
to know You, Krishna, takes much more than everything I've learned.
So please excuse this fallen soul and go on to enjoy
more lunchtime pleasures with Your calves and friends, the cowherd boys.

Your sun-like presence brightens all Your friends and family.
Your moon-like smile enriches *brāhmans*, gods, the Earth and seas.
Until the sun globe vanishes, until the planets fall,
please take my humble service. I ask nothing else at all."

61) Brahmā then walked three times around Lord Krishna, bowing low.
Lord Krishna smiled and nodded, indicating he could go.
Then Krishna went back to His friends. Although a year had passed,
the boys, entranced in mystic sleep, thought moments had elapsed.

62) Surprised at Krishna's quick return, the boys at once declared,
"You're back? All right! Let's share this lunch our mothers have prepared."
Lord Krishna grinned, sat down again and joined the lunchtime fun.
They next found all the calves and headed home, their workday done.

63) With bugles, flutes and forest-garlands, dabbed in reddish clay,
each boy resembled Krishna in his own distinctive way.
They danced back to Vṛndāvan with Govinda at the fore,
and everyone who saw the scene loved Krishna even more.

64) Arriving in the village, all the boys cried out in song,
"A giant serpent swallowed us! He stretched out eight miles long!
But Krishna grew so big inside He choked the demon's wind
so we marched out without a scratch and came back home again."

A Question on Love

65) "I see!" said Viṣṇurāta, who'd been sitting very still,
"They didn't know a year had passed since Agha had been killed.
I'm puzzled by a single point: how did the mothers come
to love the Lord's expansions more than they loved their own sons?"

66) Said Śukadev, The living being loves himself much more
than parents, wife or children; they're extensions, nothing more.

This self-love, say the learned, only comes about because
Lord Krishna loves us living beings first, despite our flaws.

67) Since Krishna loves us, even though we're fallen entities,
it's possible for us to love ourselves and feel at ease.
The active force is Krishna. So, the mothers of His friends
feel greater love for Him on whom their own self-love depends.

68) You heard about Lord Krishna and His friends attending cows.
You heard Brahmā's mistake and his remorseful prayers and vows.
By hearing and reciting these events as they transpired,
you soon shall fill your deepest heartfelt spiritual desires.

6

Kaliya

Krishna Praises Balaram

1) As Balarām and Krishna reached the second childhood stage,
pauganda (meant for children ranging six to ten in age)
the cowherd men decided they could now entrust to them
protection of the older cows, with help from all their friends.

2) Each day the happy convoy took Vṛndāvan's forest path.
As Krishna played His flute, the others sang along and laughed.
The woods were packed with vegetables, flowers, birds and bees
and seemed as clean and sacred as the minds of devotees.

3) The crystal lakes had waters that relieved all one's fatigue.
The breezes carried floral scents of pleasure and intrigue.
The fruit- and flower-laden trees, full branches near the ground,
appeared to reach for Krishna's feet by humbly bowing down.

4-7) So Krishna said to Balarām, "Your feet attract these trees.
Just see them offer fruits to You as if on hands and knees.
They pray You'll lift the ignorance that brought them to a birth
where they can't play with us because they're rooted to the earth.

These bees that buzz around You seem to be extremely wise.
They must have been great sages in their recent former lives,
for now they will not leave You as they loudly sing Your praise,
despite Your skillful cover as a cowherd boy at play.

The peacocks step before You as they dance in ecstasy.
The deer, who look like *gopīs*, gaze at You most lovingly.
The cuckoos sing out Vedic hymns to welcome You today,
for great souls welcome great souls to their homes in all these ways.

Your footprints bless Vṛndāvan's soil, Your hands her shrubs and trees.
Your glances leave her rivers, hills and animals quite pleased.
You favor all the *gopīs* with embraces from Your arms
which Lakṣmī, queen of wealth, can't get, despite her matchless charms."

8) Thus Krishna praised His elder brother in a mood of fun
and then began to laugh and joke, amusing everyone.
He said, "These peacocks cannot dance, so watch Me closely now!"
With squeals of joy from all the boys, He tried to show them how.

9) The boys would imitate the humming sounds of bumblebees,
the coos of swans and chattering of parrots in the trees.
Then Krishna called, with thundering voice, the names of all the calves
who'd left the pack and wandered back on nearby forest paths.

10) When Balarām, fatigued from play, desired to take a nap,
He'd lie beneath a tree and place His head on one boy's lap.
Lord Krishna would massage His feet, refresh Him with a fan,
and place a cup of river water near His brother's hand.

11) Lord Krishna, too, would sometimes lie beneath a shady branch
and let the cowherd boys massage His legs. They loved the chance.
Some boys would sing while others fanned, their hearts infused with joy,
as Krishna took their service as a simple cowherd boy.

Dhenukasura

12-14) One day some friends—Śrīdām, Subal, and Stoka Krishna—said,
"Dear Krishna and dear Balarām, a forest just ahead

named Tālavan is full of palms with luscious, fragrant fruits.
Regrettably, it's also home to quite a nasty brute.

The demon Dhenukāsura resides there as an ass,
destroying those who pluck the fruits or take them from the grass.
His demon friends, disguised like him, and equally as strong,
eat men and frighten birds away and lounge there all day long.

No one has even sampled fruits that grow among those trees.
Their fragrance has attracted us. Dear Krishna, if You please,
destroy this jackass demon like the others You have faced.
Then all of us can gather fruits and revel in their taste!"

15) When Balarām and Krishna heard these words, they laughed and said,
"Let's go at once to Tālavan. This ass will soon be dead."
The boys marched to the forest. Seeing no one else around,
Lord Balarām shook trees until their fruits fell to the ground.

16) The sound of falling fruits made Dhenukāsura enraged.
He screamed and rushed at Balarām, and, with his two hind legs,
kicked sharply at Rohiṇī's son and struck Him on the chest.
Still, nothing happened, though the mighty ass had tried his best.

17) The demon brayed and dashed about. Then, turning once again,
he shot his hooves at Balarām with force to kill ten men.
The agile Lord caught both the hooves and spun the ass around
until his braying stopped and he no longer made a sound.

18) The Lord then heaved the lifeless ass into a nearby palm.
It fell and toppled others, like the crashing of a bomb.
On seeing this, the other demons shrieked and bellowed. Then,
they rushed at Balarām, intent on vengeance for their friend.

19) Lord Krishna and his brother grabbed the hooves of every ass
and wheeled them round and round until each one had breathed its last.
Discarding each dead donkey, like their leader, in the trees,
the brothers finished off the pack of ass-devils with ease.

20) Their broken bodies looked like clouds suspended, as they were,
in palm trees high above where the brief scuffle had occurred.
Their bodies, dark like monsoon clouds, their blood of crimson tint,
and heaps of golden fruits became the landscape's ornaments.

21) The gods, in awe of Krishna and the swiftly finished fight,
sang praises and rained flowers down in heavenly delight.
The people came to gather fruits in happiness and peace,
while cows grazed on the forest grass, which grew up to their knees.

22) Their day complete, the boys went home to take some food and rest.
The *gopīs*, in their absence, had been lonely and depressed.
As honey-dripping lotuses appeal to honeybees,
when Krishna came back, all the *gopīs* gazed and felt relieved.

23) Lord Krishna then accepted, as respectful and of worth,
their shy, submissive glances, lightly sweetened by their mirth.
The boys and Krishna all went home, and Yaśodā was pleased
to render service to her son in loving ecstasy.

24) She bathed, massaged and dressed her son in robes of vibrant silk
and fed Him luscious dishes made from produce, grains and milk.
When Yaśodā saw Krishna had been washed and nicely fed,
she tucked Him in for peaceful rest inside His cozy bed.

Poisonous Kaliya

25) One day the Lord and all the boys, their arms in friendly link,
went skipping to the Yamunā to bathe and take a drink.
The sun was hot, the water cool, but as they gulped it down,
the boys and cows all suddenly collapsed upon the ground.

26) The water had been poisoned with a potent toxic brew.
The massacre made Krishna do what only He could do.
His loving glance across the corpses caused them to revive.
The boys stood up and saw, by Krishna's grace, they were alive.

27) Lord Krishna saw the Yamunā, at this bend, was a lake
inhabited by Kāliya, a huge, obnoxious snake.

So toxic was this Kāliya, when birds flew overhead
they'd pass through clouds of venom and then hit the water, dead.

28) The creepers, trees and grass that thrived around the nearby shore
had withered to a crackling brown and could not be restored.
The poison from Kāliya, which made fog above the lake,
drove every living thing away—except his fellow snakes.

29) The hundred-headed Kāliya, of dark and evil hue,
was just the kind of demon Krishna wanted to subdue.
The Lord thus climbed a nearby tree and, readying to fight,
tied back His hair, slapped both His arms and drew His waistband tight.

30) As Krishna dove into the toxic lake, all in a flash,
a tidal wave of poisoned water hit the shore and splashed.
Then Krishna churned and swirled the placid waters round and round,
antagonizing Kāliya when he picked up the sound.

30) The serpent couldn't fathom such a boy in yellow dress
at play within his poisoned lake in utter fearlessness.
The chilly serpent blood of Kāliya began to boil;
He bit the Lord upon His chest and wrapped Him in his coils.

Terror in Vrindavana

32) The residents of Vṛndāvan, who'd run down to the lake,
grew frantic seeing Krishna held by such a deadly snake.
Not knowing Krishna's power and convinced that He was doomed,
they cried and roared upon that shore and fell into a swoon.

33) The bullocks, cows and calves stood still, made numb by shock and fear.
Their eyes, reflecting Krishna, were too stunned for shedding tears.
As meteors fell from the sky and Earth began to quake,
the men all felt the left sides of their bodies start to shake.

34) "These omens indicate the worst!" cried Nanda in despair,
as he and others looked for Krishna, running here and there.
As all the simple villagers lamented on the shore,
Lord Balarām alone was calm. He knew what was in store.

35) Though Krishna's friends and relatives showed great anxiety,
in fact they were experiencing lofty ecstasies,
for every thought and recollection entering their heads
were all the deeds the Lord had done and all the words He'd said.

36) When Nanda and some men saw Krishna under such attack,
they ran into the water. Balarām, though, pulled them back.
The elder *gopīs* spoke of Krishna, shedding tears of pain,
and somehow worked together to keep Yaśodā restrained.

37) For two full hours, Krishna stayed within the serpent's grasp
until He saw His devotees were ready to collapse.
Responding to His parents' and His friends' excessive grief,
Lord Krishna promptly freed Himself, to everyone's relief.

Dancing Krishna

38) The Lord expanded, forcing Kāliya to ease his grip.
With bifurcated tongues the fuming serpent licked his lips.
In fury, he raised all his hoods. His eye slits glared like fire.
His nostrils looked like pots to cook the venom he required.

39) Despite the fearsome sight, Lord Krishna danced around in play.
The evil serpent tried to bite, but Krishna danced away.
Like Garuḍa[1], who plays with snakes before they are devoured,
Lord Krishna played with Kāliya, who slowly lost his power.

[1]*The huge eagle who carries Lord Viṣṇu on his back.*

40) The endless circling left Kāliya's energy in shreds,
and Krishna seized the opening to climb upon his heads.
The master of all arts, Lord Krishna, twirled and danced around,
His feet made red by rubies set within Kāliya's crown.

41) When they saw Krishna dance, the gods assembled and exclaimed,
"Let's bring our wives!" They all, of course, immediately came.
How expertly they played on drums, sang songs and offered prayers
as Krishna danced on Kāliya with great artistic flare.

42) The hundred-headed serpent, who was angry, fierce and proud,
now felt defeat from Krishna's feet, which forced his heads to bow.
Each time the serpent raised a hood to show he disapproved,
the Lord would promptly smash it with another graceful move.

43) Soon Kāliya began to vomit poisoned, bloody mess.
With broken hoods he understood, in absolute distress,
that Krishna is the master of all things that move or sit.
The serpent thought, "I must repent. I even may submit."

The Naga-patnis

44-48) His wives, the Nāga-pātnīs, had been ready, even pleased,
to leave their serpent husband and his foul activities.
But as his dark expression eased, with hopes he'd change his ways,
they spoke to Krishna (though their clothes and hair were disarrayed):

(Meter: -|- -|- -|- -|)
"Dear Lord, You're supreme. It is You that we trust.
Your kicks to our husband are certainly just.
You love everybody, so it's understood
when You punish someone, it's for their own good.

Your punishment drove away all of the sins
our husband has done in his slithery skin.
In some former life did he do something right,
or have You danced on him for Your own delight?

Lord Krishna, the giver of ev'ry decree,
we bow before You and Your pure devotees.
Your faithful devotees are never misled,
unlike one dumb serpent we happened to wed.

A father endures his young children's offense;
a king tolerates when his servant is dense.
Supreme peaceful Soul, You should also forgive
our husband, Kāliya. Oh please, let him live."

Kaliya Repents

(iambic heptameter)
49- 51) By this time Kāliya had fainted. Krishna stepped aside
to let the battered serpent heal his wounds and be revived.
When Kāliya recovered, taking loud and painful breath,
He spoke to Krishna humbly, like a man returned from death:

(Meter: -| -| -- |-|)
When one takes birth as a lowly snake
his rage and envy are hard to shake.
For souls, such bodies are a big mistake;
they seem so real but they're simply fake.

I'm not this snake body; I'm a soul.
My fantasy made me lose control.
My Lord, You know all there is to know;
I'll take the punishment You bestow.

(iambic heptameter)
52, 53) Once Kāliya had finished speaking, Krishna said, in turn,
"You fled your native island; take your family and return.
Though Garuḍa of mighty beak once brought you to your knees,
because My feet have touched your head, he now will let you be.

Now leave these crystal waters for the people and the cows,
and let this holy lake be used for sacred baths and vows.
Go home now with your relatives, your friends and retinue
so all My friends can live their lives, untouched by fear of you."

54) The serpent and his wives were glad to end the deadly fight
so they all worshipped Krishna with respect and great delight.
They offered Krishna necklaces with ornaments and gems
and circumambulated Him again and yet again.

55) The Lord then sent Kāliya, with his children, friends and wives,
back to their distant island to resume their former lives.
The Yamunā grew pure again, and all were overjoyed
by Krishna's pleasing pastimes as a wondrous cowherd boy.

Kaliya's History

56) Said Viṣṇurāta, "Kāliya gave up his island home—
a paradise for serpents—to go out and live alone.
Did Viṣṇu's eagle-servant, Garuḍa, drive him away?
If so, why did he chase the snake, and what role did he play?

57) Said Śukadev, Now, Garuḍa is known to eat reptiles,
especially the serpents who inhabited that isle.
Afraid of sudden, random death, the serpents made a deal
that every month they'd offer him a satisfying meal.

58) This system worked out well enough till Kāliya became
so proud that he devoured the feast before the eagle came.
When Garuḍa, so dear to Viṣṇu, heard about this deed,
He flew at once to Kāliya with unexpected speed.

59) Then Garuḍa found Kāliya and started to attack,
so Kāliya exposed his fangs, prepared to strike him back.
But Garuḍa was swift and strong and smashed the awful snake.
In great distress Kāliya left his island for this lake.

60) He chose this lake in Yamunā with knowledge that his foe
could not pursue him there due to a curse placed long ago
when Sage Saubhari, wanting to protect the local fish
told Garuḍa to eat elsewhere. The bird obeyed his wish.

61) One day, however, very hungry, Garuḍa by chance
ate fish from Yamunā as Sage Saubhari sat in trance.
And when he heard what had occurred, in rage Saubhari said,
"If Garuḍa comes back again, my curse will strike him dead!"
And now you know why Kāliya resided in that lake
until Lord Krishna drove him out for His devotees' sake.

62) When Krishna left the water wearing jeweled, golden dress,
His devotees regained their lives and held Him to their chests.
As Nanda, Yaśodā and others reacquired their breath,
the dried-up trees grew fresh new leaves as they returned from death.

A Forest Fire

63) Lord Balarām embraced His brother, gave a knowing laugh,
and gazed at Krishna's beauty as He kept Him on His lap.
The brāhmans and their wives said, "Nanda, God has saved your son."
The king concurred and gave the word, "My wealth to everyone!"

64) By gifts of gold and cows, he reasoned, Krishna would be safe.
His wife, meanwhile, just held her son in tearful, tight embrace.
Vṛndāvan's frightened citizens were so relieved to see
their dear, beloved Krishna safe, they didn't want to leave.

65) So all of them decided, feeling tired, limp and drained,
to rest there by the river, as such village folk are trained.

66) As all slept on, a giant fire started in the trees.
It seems some friend of Kāliya's was somewhat less than pleased,
or Kaṁsa had sent someone to harass the devotees.
In any case, the fire roused the people with its heat.

67) Surrounded by the searing flames, the people had no choice
except to call for Krishna's help in panic-stricken voice:
"Oh, Krishna of all opulence! Oh, Rām of boundless might!
This fire threatens to destroy us all this very night!

68) We do not fear the hellish smoke, the flames or scorching heat;
we fear that death may separate us from Your lotus feet!"
On hearing His devotees' prayers and knowing their desire,
the Lord at once inhaled the flames, extinguishing the fire.

7

Autumn

Summer in Vrindavan

1) Lord Krishna and Lord Balarām, Their friends and families
returned to village life and day-to-day activities.
The summer season came on them, with blazing sun and all
that made it much less popular than winter, spring or fall.

2) But Krishna's very presence made the summer seem like spring.
It seemed Vṛndāvan's residents were free of suffering.
The pleasant sound of waterfalls was able to usurp
the constant background noise produced by crickets as they chirped.

3) The droplets from these waterfalls bathed trees that lined their pools,
and moistened the refreshing breeze that kept Vṛndāvan cool.
The rivers drenched their muddy banks and nourished fields of grass,
preventing toxic summer sun from turning them to ash.

4) Vṛndāvan is the nicest place that you'll find anywhere.
As dancing peacocks spread their tails, their catcalls fill the air.
The bumblebee's cacophony refreshes night and noon,
while cuckoos thrive and sing in five varieties of tunes.

5) With such a pleasant setting to perform their childhood play,
the boys would daily take the cows and calves to drink and graze.
With flower garlands, feathers and red clay, this boisterous gang
enjoyed their forest pastimes as they wrestled, danced and sang.

6) Sometimes the boys would dance as Krishna showered them with praise,
accompanying them with music many different ways.
They then enhanced Lord Krishna's dance with cymbals, flutes and cries.
These boys, in fact, were gods intact in cowherd boy disguise.

7) They leapt and whirled and slapped and hurled and tugged each other's hair,
played tag with one another and threw fruits high in the air.
They'd put on blindfolds, sing like birds or dress themselves as kings.
They'd jump like toads, make endless jokes and fly on homemade swings.

Pralamba

8) Although They played these common games while roaming through the woods,
one day Lord Krishna saw something that only Krishna could.
One boy stayed home with chores that day, but right there in his place
a demon named Pralamba had assumed his shape and face.

9) Pralamba planned to kidnap Balarām and Krishna, too.
Aware of this, Lord Krishna played while planning what to do.
He gathered all the boys for games, divided them in teams
and set some rules. The demon, fooled, did not know Krishna's scheme.

10) Lord Krishna made a game in which the losers had to pay
by holding winners on their backs and walking round that way.
Pralamba was on Krishna's team, which lost and carried boys,
and Balarām became Pralamba's passenger of choice.

11, 12) Afraid of Krishna's potency, the demon chose to go
away from where the others played with Balarām in tow.
While looking for a quiet place to make a cruel attack,
Pralamba felt the boy become a mountain on his back.
Pralamba felt so burdened that he could no more maintain
his cover as a cowherd boy amidst the crushing pain.

13) His childish features vanished and the form that he resumed
was like a giant storm cloud; Balarām looked like the moon.
The giant demon scowled as he rose up in the sky
and showed his fearsome eyes and teeth, to Balarām's surprise.

14) Upset at being kidnapped by a demon such as this,
Lord Balarām grew furious and struck him with His fist.
With one blow from Lord Balarām, Pralamba's skull was cracked.
Then, vomiting a gush of blood, the demon's form grew slack.
Pralamba crashed upon the ground, producing such a jolt
he seemed to be a mountain crushed by Indra's thunderbolt.

15) The cowherd boys, astonished by Pralamba's ghastly form
and by the great, heroic deed that Balarām performed,
cried, "Sadhu! Sadhu!"[1] praising Him till they ran out of breath
and lovingly embraced Him as if He was back from death.

[1]*Saintly person.*

16) In heaven, all the gods had been observing in suspense
the violence of Pralamba and Lord Balarām's defense.
They felt so pleased with Balarām to see Pralamba dead
they tossed celestial flower garlands round His lovely head.

The Forest Fire

17) One day the boys were playing when the cows all strolled away
to join some goats and buffalo in search of fields to graze.
A great inferno suddenly appeared among the beasts.
In fear they cried out helplessly amid the flames and heat.

18) Soon Krishna, Balarām and all the boys saw their neglect.
At once, in great anxiety, they started to inspect
the forest paths for prints of calves or other signs displayed
that cows would raise if they had grazed on grass along the way.

19) As Krishna called the cows by name, and each one understood,
at last the boys tracked down the cows and steered them from the woods.
Then all at once the forest fire, driven by the wind,
surrounded and impounded them. It seemed to have no end.

20) The blazes shot out fearsome sparks and licked with tongue of flame
the many plants and animals who lived in its domain.
The frightened cows and cowherd boys could only stand and stare.
The boys then turned to Balarām and Krishna and declared,

21) "O Krishna, Krishna, mighty one! O Balarām, most brave!
Should not this deadly blaze be stopped and Your devotees saved?
Our Lords, You both know everything throughout the universe,
so You must also know Your friends will burn if this gets worse."

22) On hearing the alarming statements His companions made,
Lord Krishna said, 'Just close your eyes and do not be afraid.'
As soon as all the boys had done what Krishna had desired,
their dear companion opened wide and swallowed up the fire.

23) And when the boys at last began to open up their eyes
they found themselves in safe surroundings, much to their surprise.
The cows were safely with them, too. The boys, both pleased and awed,
then lovingly decided their friend Krishna was a god.

24) As they returned to Vraja, all the cowherd boys recalled
the wondrous deeds of Krishna to the joy of one and all.
As Krishna played a special flute, the cowherd girls looked on,
relieved of blazing sorrow that had burned while He was gone.

25) Their parents heard the boys explain how Krishna stopped the flames
and Balarām destroyed Pralamba when he spoiled their games.
The elder cowherd men and ladies, stunned to hear of this,
as well concluded these two boys were gods born in their midst.

Description of Autumn

26) At that time summer yielded to seasonal monsoons,
when thunderclouds and lightning fill the sky each afternoon.
The natural effulgence of the sky becomes obscured
as spirit souls are covered up by matter in this world.

27) For months the sun had drunk Earth's moisture, just as kings exact
the money of their citizens through tariffs, tolls and tax.

And as a good king places funds wherever needs arise,
the moisture came again to Earth from storm clouds in the skies.

28) Ablaze with lightning, windswept clouds gave back their stored up rain
as saintly persons give their lives to lessen others' pain.
The Earth, so lean and parched from drought, at once became revived
as *yogīs* use the fruits of their *tapas* to energize.

29) The nighttime autumn skies have clouds, obscuring stars and moon,
but glowworms wriggling in the trees shine brightly through the gloom.
In just that way, the age of Kali covers truthful saints,
but speculators rise to fame by trickery and feint.

30) When thunder sounds, the frogs, who had been silent, croak and squeak,
as student *brāhmans* work in silence till they're told to speak.
The streams fill up with heavy rains and flood themselves off course,
as men who lose their sense control will sin again by force.

31) With fields of green, red ladybugs and mushrooms brilliant white,
the Earth seems like a poor man turning rich, to his delight.
The rain makes wheat fields brim and farmers shout in ecstasy,
though men too proud to farm and blind to God do not agree.

32) The dried-up creatures feel their bodies active, fresh and pleased,
as atheists smile brightly when becoming devotees.
The swollen rivers agitate the oceans where they meet,
like *māyā* bothers *yogīs* whose restraint is incomplete.

33) As devotees with minds absorbed in Krishna stay at peace,
the mountains are unmoved by rain clouds battering their peaks.
The rain, however, floods the roads and makes them hard to find
as scriptures, long neglected, can be lost in course of time.

34) The rain clouds, overhead, befriend the Earth and give her life,
but fickle lightning runs around like someone's unchaste wife.
A rainbow comes, unique indeed—a bow without a string—
as Krishna lives within this world not tied to anything.

35) The common soul is covered, though alive with inner light,
as moonbeams lighten clouds that keep the moon removed from sight.
And when the clouds appear, the peacocks call in ecstasy
as householders, distressed, are pleased to greet a devotee.

36) The brittle trees drink rainwater and thus return to health
as *yogīs* mend their bodies when good karma brings them wealth.
The cranes stayed by the lakeside, though the storms made it a mess
as foolish men remain at home, enduring much distress.

37) The rains brought floods that devastated irrigation dikes
as speculators break down Vedic laws that they dislike.
The winds impel the clouds to let their pent-up moisture fall
as priests instruct the kings to shower charity on all.

38) And when the forest grew resplendent, fit to be enjoyed,
Lord Krishna came with Balarām, the cows and cowherd boys.
When it would rain, they ran to caves and ate bulbs where they grew;
and when it cleared they ran outside and ate their lunches too.

39) The grass-stuffed cows, with bulging udders, gait grown very slow,
would jump and run to Krishna, causing milk to overflow.
Content and tired, they lay down to chew their cuds and rest
as Krishna watched His own creation, full of happiness.

40) The rainy season yielded and autumn time appeared,
with gentle wind and cloudless sky and water crystal clear.
The season brought out lotuses and left the lakes refined,
as *bhakti* yoga purifies the fallen *yogī*'s mind.

41) The autumn cleared the sky of clouds, as students are enhanced
when they progress from basic skills to something more advanced.
Confined by rainstorms, animals were freed, at last, to roam
like householders renouncing their confinement to their homes.

42) Retired in their later years, such householders become
enlightened, just as autumn ends the rainy-season scum.
The autumn makes the muddied ponds and streams as purified
as wise, mature renunciates whose minds are sanctified.

43) Such persons, who have given up material delights,
are delicate as rain-spent autumn clouds of downy white.
These saintly persons speak for days or may not speak at all,
as mountain springs may gush away—or stop—throughout the fall.

44) Receding waters strand some fish on banks of streams and lakes.
Some fools can't see their lives recede and make the same mistake.
Investing all their energy in family affairs,
they fail to waken love for God and die in great despair.

45) As autumn sunshine scorches fish who swim in shallow streams,
the pain of family life bears down on happy household dreams.
As muddy lands dry up and plants grow full and rich in fall,
a sober person goes beyond attachment to it all.

46) With autumn, all the seas and lakes grow peaceful, calm and still,
as sages overcome temptation through their strength of will.
Such sages keep their senses in a state of full withdrawl
as farmers keep the water on their crops with earthen walls.

47) The autumn moon relieves the summer heat, restoring health,
as wisdom uplifts fools who take the body as the self.
When clouds depart, the stars glow brightly through the atmosphere
as if, for them, the meaning of the *Vedas* has grown clear.

48) Vṛndāvan's moon, surrounded by the stars, grows round and pleased
like Krishna in Vṛndāvan with His loving family.
A fragrant, pleasant breeze blows in and troubles soon depart
for all except the *gopīs*, who are struck with broken hearts.

49) The women, cows and female birds grow fertile, drawing mates,
just as, when one serves Krishna, piety accumulates.
The rising sun thrills lotuses, save those that bloom at night
as kings can frighten thieves while bringing honest men delight.

50) The Earth, adorned by Krishna's feet, confers abundant crops.
The grains grow ripe for harvesting and soon begin to drop.
The citizens hold festivals and honor the first grains
by cooking them in sacrifice and tasting the remains.

51) When rainy season ends and autumn breezes fill the air,
the priests go out to travel, merchants leave to sell their wares,
and leaders walk about to manage, study and take tolls—
as death frees *yogīs* to pursue their own respective goals.

8

The Gopis

Krishna's Flute

1) Returning to the forest, Krishna noticed the perfume
that wafted from the crystal lakes where lotus flowers bloomed.
His friends and cows nearby, the Lord heard bees and birds in song,
which prompted Him to grasp His flute and start to play along.

2) The lovely sound of Krishna's flute brought Cupid into play
within the hearts of all the *gopīs* hearing it that day.
They wished to speak of Krishna, who was beautiful and young,
but Cupid overwhelmed their minds and quieted their tongues.

3) They thought of Krishna's *dhotī*[1], like the sunshine's golden rays,
and how His dancing feet blessed Earth as friends sang out His praise.
They thought of Krishna's peacock feather-ornamented head.
And then they heard His flute again. They all embraced and said,

[1]*A simple male garment*

(Brahmā Samhita meter: -| -| -|-| --| -|-)
4-15) My friends, what sight could be more sweet for the eye's perception
than Krishna with His brother leading this nice procession

of cows and boys into the forest in autumn season,
with flute in hand and loving glances on those who please Him?

As Balarām wears blue and Krishna wears silks of yellow
adorned with lotuses and leaves, They sing *a cappella*
and shine in splendor as They dance through Vṛndāvan forest.
Like actors dance across a stage, They appear before us.

What pious deeds has Krishna's flute done to gain His kissing,
the very nectar meant for us and which we are missing?
The bamboo, father of that flute, cries with tears of pleasure.
Its mother, Yamunā, feels joy that cannot be measured.

The peacocks dance to Krishna's flute song with jubilation
while other birds stand still and watch them with admiration.
Vṛndāvan makes the planet Earth known throughout creation,
for Krishna's footprints touch her surface without cessation.

When Krishna, dressed in gorgeous clothes, plays His flute so sweetly
reluctant deer creep up and drop all their fears completely.
The bucks are happy as the does gather round to please Him,
yet our resentful husbands protest when we just see Him.

What woman can remain unmoved when she sees Govinda?
In heaven, even wives of gods, so well-off and splendid,
while flying great celestial airplanes feel such attraction,
the flowers fall out of their hair and their garments slacken.

When Krishna plays His flute, the cows raise their ears and listen.
The calves stop drinking milk and swoon as their eyelids glisten.
The birds just roost in trees with eyes shut and do not call out,
for they are listening, hanging on, trying not to fall out.

When rivers hear the flute, their current becomes abated.
With swirling whirlpools, all their waters grow agitated.
The waves embrace Lord Krishna's feet, holding on for hours,
and bring to them a humble offering of lotus flowers.

Observing Krishna lead the boys in the blazing sunlight,
with cows to care for in the heat till the evening twilight,
the friendly cloud assembles droplets of condensation
to make a great umbrella, shading the congregation.

The aborigines who live in Vṛndāvan's precincts
include young ladies like ourselves, full of lusty instincts.
They satisfy themselves with dust from the One they covet,
turned reddish by His lotus feet touched by His beloveds.

When Krishna leaves our village, Govardhan Hill provides Him
the water, grass and fruits to nourish the cows beside Him,
and caves and vegetables that He and His friends require.
Thus Govardhan is Krishna's servant, and none is higher.

The sound of Krishna's flute is so very sweet and soothing
it stuns all creatures that can move, and they all stop moving,
while trees, immobile, grow ecstatic and start to quiver.
Such wondrous power Krishna's flute and its song deliver!"

(iambic heptameter)
16) The simple *gopīs* talked about Lord Krishna's flute for hours,
and though they lacked an education, affluence or power,
Lord Krishna was exclusively the hub of their desire—
the standard of devotion to which all of us aspire.

The Gopis' Clothes Stolen

17) The *Vedas* call, at end of fall, for special sacrifice,
so unwed maidens eat a simple *khichri*[2] without spice.
They praise Kātyāyanī, a goddess, hoping to obtain
a worthy husband to protect and keep them well maintained.
[2]*A dish of rice and lentils.*

18) The eager *gopīs* hurried to the Yamunā to bathe
and make an image of Kātyāyanī from river clay.
They worshiped her with sandalwood, fresh flowers, nuts and fruits,
as each spoke out this mantra to shed light on their pursuit:

19) "O dear Kātyāyanī, my goddess, now that you're installed,
I worship you as God's own power, reigning over all.
Please make the son of Nanda marry me, and if you do
I will forever offer my obeisances to you."

20) Each day they'd rise and hurry to the Yamunā at dawn
to beg Kātyāyanī for Krishna. Soon, the month was gone.
While singing Krishna's glories they observed a final bath,
undressing on the shoreline near the 'women-only' path.

21) Lord Krishna, who knows everything, could clearly understand
that every single *gopī* prayed for Him to take her hand.
Since He fills every wish and gives whatever one requires,
Lord Krishna crept up silently to fill their heart's desire.

22) The Lord snatched all the *gopīs'* clothes and climbed a nearby tree
and, laughing, held their garments high for all of them to see.
He said, "Now girls, to get your clothes come up here one by one.
I'm serious; you *must* come now. Your sacrifice is done."

23) The *gopīs*, pleased with Krishna's joking, kept themselves immersed.
They laughed in their embarrassment, but none would come out first.
Their honor was protected—one could only see their heads—
but soon the water made them chilly. Shivering, they said,

24) "Dear Krishna, foremost son of Nanda, tease us if You will.
We find Your prank unjust and wrong, and now we're getting chilled!
We are Your humble maidservants; we'll do most anything,
but first You must return our clothes—or we will tell the King!"

25) Said Krishna, "If you are My servants, every one of you
must come and get her garments now. What can King Nanda do?"
On hearing Krishna's statements, so determined and so strong,
the *gopīs* saw they had no option but to go along.

26) While shivering, they all stepped from the river to the land,
while covering their private parts with forearms, wrists and hands.
Though such exposure crushes any girl who's pure and chaste,
the *gopīs* loved the Lord so much they suffered no disgrace.

27) The Lord fulfilled the *gopīs*' prayer to wed Him with this guise,
for chaste women are naked only for their husband's eyes.
When Krishna saw the bashful love the cowherd maids had shown,
He shouldered all their clothing, smiled, and said in loving tones,

28) "By going naked in this sacred river as you bathed,
you all offended Yamunā and Lord Varuṇadev.
To counteract your sin and the reactions that you dread,
you now must join your palms in prayer and touch them to your heads."

29) Although the *gopīs* weren't concerned that *devas* might protest,
they deeply cared for Krishna, so they followed His request.
The simple *gopīs* trusted Krishna so implicitly
their mood of loving service was as deep as it could be.

30) Accepting blame for taking bath with less than full attire,
the *gopīs* raised their hands in prayer as Krishna had required.
They prayed to Him to cleanse their sins and offered humble bows.
Lord Krishna then returned their clothes, rewarding their strict vows.

31) Although their Lord had cheated them and treated them like toys,
the *gopīs* were enchanted by their favorite cowherd boy.
And even if He broke their hearts to satisfy a whim,
the *gopīs* always happily surrendered unto Him.

32) The *gopīs* quickly sorted out their clothing and got dressed.
And still they did not want to leave, for they were all obsessed.
They glanced at Krishna shyly, standing still with covered heads.
The Lord thought of their sacrifice and, smiling at them, said,

33, 34) "O saintly girls, I understand your sacrifice was moved
by nothing more than love for Me. Please know that I approve.
Your love for Me leads not to lust but makes you purified,
as seeds won't sprout once they are cooked or left to dry outside.

My dear pure-hearted *gopīs*, now that you are nicely dressed,
return to your own homes and put your troubled minds to rest.
Your worship of Kātyāyanī has gained for you the right
to dance and have My company through coming moonlit nights."

35) Reluctantly, the *gopīs* left. They thought of nothing more
than Krishna, for they loved Him now more deeply than before.
They hankered for those coming nights when, dancing in the woods,
they'd serve the purpose of their vows, which Krishna understood.

Krishna Praises the Trees

36) Some months after this incident, Lord Krishna and His mates
took out the cows for grazing in a new and distant place.
The sun was very fierce and hot, and when He saw the trees
give shade just like umbrellas, Krishna commented, quite pleased,

37-39) "O Aṁśu, Śrīdhām, Ojasvī, Vṛṣabha and Viśāl,
Varūthapa, Arjuna, Stoka Krishna and Subal,
just see how all these trees endure the sunshine, rain and wind
to shelter and protect all kinds of animals and men.

These trees give of themselves so much so others may survive,
they seem to be like generous persons leading saintly lives.
If anybody asks a tree for something they require
they always leave in pleasure, having filled their heart's desire.

These trees give us their fragrant flowers, foliage and fruits,
their wood for fuel, shade to cool, and ashes, sap and shoots.
They show how everyone should act to benefit mankind
by giving of their resources, their statements and their minds."

40) While sharing these instructions, Krishna strolled among the trees
until He reached the river with His band of devotees.
The waters of the Yamunā, transparent, cool and sweet
relieved the boys and cows alike from weariness and heat.

The Brahmans' Wives

41) The cows went to a nearby field, but as they calmly grazed,
the boys themselves were out of food and soon their hunger raged.
The boys, who thought of Krishna whether happy or distressed,
approached the Lord and Balarām, presenting this request:

42) "O mighty-muscled Rām! O Krishna, evil's greatest foe!
Please tell us where to find some food. Our hunger burns us so."
Though Krishna liked to see the cowherd boys eat well and thrive,
as He replied His thoughts applied to certain *brāhmans*' wives:

43) "Some nearby *brāhmans* wish to reach the planets of the gods.
Just now they're holding sacrifices; ask them for *prasād*.[3]
Say, 'Krishna and His brother have dispatched us all to you,
for we need food and They said you would know what we should do.'"

[3]*Pure food offered in sacrifice.*

44, 45) The boys went as instructed and submitted their request.
With folded hands they fell like sticks and prayed with great respect,
"O *brāhmans*, you are God's extensions walking in our midst.
Our masters, Balarām and Krishna, sent us to ask this:

The two of Them are tending cows nearby and need some food.
Would such a gift, O learned souls, befit your attitude?
We know you're holding sacrifice and should not eat right now,
but giving food to hungry boys can always be allowed."

46) When all the *brāhmans* heard this plea from Krishna (through the boys),
they didn't look at them or speak or even make a noise.
Preoccupied with complicated Vedic rites and prayers,
they went on with their sacrifices, noses in the air.

47) The elements of sacrifice—the mantras, gear and fire,
the gods, the place, the time and the results that one desires—
are simply Krishna's opulence. The *brāhmans*, though, ignored
a personal inquiry from their proudly worshipped Lord.

48, 49) The cowherd boys were disappointed. Slowly they returned
to Balarām and Krishna to report they had been spurned.
When Krishna heard what happened He just laughed and laughed again.
"A beggar often fails," He told the boys. "Forget these men.

Now go and ask the wives of those same *brāhmans* for a meal,
for they are pure devotees, and I know how *they* will feel."

The boys walked past the *brāhmans* and went to their homes instead.
Approaching all their chaste and well-dressed wives, they bowed and said,

50) "Respected ladies, pardon us, and kindly lend an ear.
Lord Krishna and His brother are nearby. They sent us here
to see if you would feed Them. We are tending cows, you see,
and all of us are famished. Have you food for us to eat?"

51) Delighted by this question, all the *brāhmans'* wives agreed
to bring to Balarām and Krishna anything They'd need.
For Krishna they filled pots with food to please the taste and touch,
and ran like rivers to the sea, for they loved Him so much.

52) Their husbands, sons and brothers saw the women. "Stop!" they said.
The wives loved Krishna more than them and ran on straight ahead.
They found Him near the Yamunā amid a grove of trees,
relaxing with His brother and His cowherd devotees.

53) He wore a golden *dhotī*. His complexion, monsoon blue,
was set off by a peacock feather, full of brilliant hues.
With garland, lilies, ointments and long hair hung round His face,
He chatted with His friends and showed a dancer's form and grace.

54) For months and years these ladies had been hearing Krishna's name,
and now that they were seeing Him, their hearts were set aflame.
Embracing Him within their hearts, they satisfied their needs,
as *yogīs* grasp the soul within to conquer lust and greed.

55) Lord Krishna, who knows everyone and every secret thought,
could see these ladies' other plans for life had come to naught.
They set aside their family life to come to Him that day.
His face warm with affection, Krishna smiled and turned to say,

56, 57) "Your families objected but you've come here nonetheless.
Please sit a while and speak to Me. Do you have some request?
Those thoughtful souls whose needs and wants are clearly diagnosed
approach Me out of love, for that will benefit them most.

Affection for one's spouse and children, home and property
can only come from contact with the soul and, thus, from Me.
You love Me, but your husbands are the persons you should serve.
Please help them hold the sacred rites all *brāhmans* must observe."

The wives replied:
(Brahmā Samhita meter: -| -| -|-| --| -|-)
58-60) "Almighty one, do not inflict such harsh words upon us.
Reciprocate with Your devotees as You have promised.
We'll leave our husbands and remain with You in this forest
and wear what garlands You may kick on the ground before us.

Now we've surrendered unto You. Who else will protect us?
Our husbands, fathers, sons and brothers will all reject us.
Chastiser of the wicked, Krishna, our destination,
oh please, we beg You, let us keep Your association."

(iambic heptameter)
61, 62) Said Krishna, "Why should you stay here? You have your families,
and no one will find fault with you for meeting here with Me.
But everyone would be displeased were you to simply stay.
Remain at home and think of Me and build your love that way.

Affection for Me does not come from mere proximity;
it grows in one who hears and chants My pastimes constantly.
While worshipping My Deity, remember Me alone
and you will love Me more and more. Now, go back to your homes."

63) The *brāhman*'s wives obeyed the Lord. Returning to their men,
they helped them with their sacrificial rituals again.
When one wife who had not seen Krishna heard what had transpired,
she grasped the Lord within her heart and instantly expired.

64) Govinda, meanwhile, fed His friends the ladies' tasty food
and then ate some Himself in a triumphant, joyous mood.
Appearing by His will in human bodily attire,
the Lord fulfilled the *gopīs*', cows' and cowherd boys' desires.

65) The *brāhmans*, meanwhile, noted the devotion of their wives.
They thought, 'Now we have missed the greatest prospect of our lives.
We could have shared our offerings with Krishna, but instead
we went on with our rituals!' In agony, they said,

66-70) "To hell with our auspicious birth, our vows and all we've learned!
To hell with all our rituals and honors we have earned!
Because we failed to please Lord Krishna, we are now condemned.
Illusion has bewildered us supposed 'holy men'.

The flawless love for Krishna shown by each and every wife
destroyed the fearsome bond to death that's known as family life.
Our wives have never mastered Vedic rites as we have done,
but they have oceans of ecstatic love, and we have none!
Each part of Vedic sacrifice is Viṣṇu, Lord of all.
He came to us as Krishna; how our pride has made us fall.

Although we have been mesmerized by honor, pride and fame,
we now remember Krishna is the goal we must attain.
He must have wanted to expose how arrogaṇt we were,
for otherwise what purpose would this incident have served?
Since Krishna is the master of Śrī Lakṣmī, queen of wealth,
why else would He send others to beg foodstuffs for Himself?

O Krishna, we are foolish *brāhmans*. Pardon our offense!
Your powers of illusion overwhelmed our common sense.
We'd go to You at once just as our wives did, but You see,
King Kaṁsa might find out and he would surely be displeased."

The Lord stayed with the *brāhmans,* since they had so many doubts
about King Kaṁsa's anger, should they leave and he find out.

9

Indra and Varuna

A Shift In Sacrifice

1) Lord Krishna saw the cowherd men, preparing sacrifice
to offer for Lord Indra, honored King of paradise.
Although the Lord knows everything, he very humbly asked
King Nanda why the cowherd men worked hard at such a task.

2-4) "Dear Father, kindly stop a moment. Tell your loving son
the purpose of your effort and for whom it's being done.
A saint like you will never lie, embellish or pretend;
he speaks straightforward, simple truth to enemy or friend.

But even if you keep the truth from someone you don't trust,
to keep it from your allies or your son would be unjust.
While following tradition, doing what's been done before,
some people practice rituals but don't know what they're for.
Is yours a common ceremony, held with wives and friends,
or is it something sacred which the scriptures recommend?"

5, 6) "We're serving Indra," Nanda beamed. "It's simply protocol.
The clouds, his representatives, give sustenance to all.

So people offer sacrifice like this, with *ghee* and grain,
the products Indra gives us through the agency of rain.

The remnants of the sacrifice, which Indra then dispenses,
allow mankind to prosper, be upright and please the senses.
Tradition says this sacrifice gives joy to heaven's master.
Neglecting it is selfish and would bring us to disaster."

7-16) Lord Krishna, knowing everything, including Indra's pride,
and how to please His family and friends, at once replied,
"My father, it is karma by which one is born and dies.
From karma all our happiness, distress or fear arise.

If we're rewarded for our work by higher deities,
then first of all the gods need *us*, and our activities.
It's karma that determines whether we shall sink or swim.
Lord Indra can do nothing. Why should people worship him?

We all have our own natures, which determine what we do,
and work, in turn, determines the results that we accrue.
Our karma creates bodies, good or bad, as our reward,
so karma is, in fact, our friend, our enemy, our lord.

Good work creates good karma, with prosperity and health.
Instead of Indra-worship, let us worship work itself!
If one influence rules our life, but we revere another,
are we not like a faithless wife attending to her lover?

The *brāhmans* work at teaching and the *kṣatriyas* defend;
the *śūdrās* serve all others, and the *vaiśyas* farm and lend.
Since we, as *vaiśyas*, keep and milk the cows for livelihood,
the object of our rightful worship must be understood.

Of course we need the rain, but is it Indra who supplies?
The clouds produce the rainfall that comes freely from the skies.
The mode of passion fills the world with full variety—
including clouds that squander rain on desert, rocks and sea.

We live on hills with forests – not municipalities.
The hills provide our water, food and all necessities.
Why waste your lovely offerings on unseen figureheads
when you could bring them to a hill like Govardhan instead?

Make cool, delicious sweet rice and hot soups of salty taste.
Make fancy cakes, both baked and fried. Let nothing go to waste.
Assemble *brāhmans*, qualified to light the sacred fire,
and feed and offer cows and gifts to them, as they desire.

Give food to lowly dog-eaters, the dogs, and all who come.
Give fodder to the cows and then embellish everyone
with ornaments and sandal paste and festive silk attire.
Then circumambulate the hill that fills our heart's desires.

You now know My idea, Father. Take it if you please,
for such a sacrifice will satisfy the cows and priests.
Drop Indra from your sacrifice for now, for if you do
the Hill of Govardhan itself will share its wealth with you."

17) When Nanda and the cowherd men took in Lord Krishna's words,
they all appreciated and accepted what they heard.
Because of their pure love for Him, the cowherd men complied
with Krishna's timely plan to reprimand King Indra's pride.

18) The cowherd men, proceeding as Lord Krishna had advised,
prepared to worship Govardhan with all of their supplies.
The *brāhmans* chanted mantras as the cows were fed, and then
they danced around the charming hill again and yet again.

19) The lovely cowherd women, wearing rings and ankle bells
climbed into oxen-driven carts and rode around the hill.
Their songs of Krishna's pastimes mingled with the *brāhmans*' prayers.
Then Krishna, pleased with all of this, smiled broadly and declared:

20) "The hill you know as Govardhan is actually Me!"
With that, the hill exhibited its personality

and started to consume great pots of *sabji*, *dāl*[1] and rice
prepared by Nanda's subjects for the Indra sacrifice.
[1]*Sabji: vegetable dishes. Dāl: bean or lentil soup.*

21, 22) The people bowed before the hill, and Krishna did as well
(although He was, essentially, prostrating to Himself).
"Just see!" the Lord proclaimed, "how Govardhan has now agreed
to come and shower blessings on our whole community!

Since He can take the form of snakes and other deadly shapes,
to fail to worship Govardhan would be a grave mistake."
Festivities completed, all the citizens felt blessed,
and went back to Vṛndāvan with Lord Krishna and took rest.

Indra Attacks

23) When he saw Nanda rearrange the honors meant for him,
Lord Indra grew as angry as a god has ever been.
He called his most destructive cloud (Sāṁvartaka by name),
and, feeling like the king of all, stood smartly and proclaimed:

24-26) "These forest-dwelling bovine-tenders, rich and drunk with pride,
have let their Krishna cast my rightful sacrifice aside.
They're like those fools who try to cross the ocean of distress
in leaky boats of mundane quotes while truth goes unexpressed.

These cowherds dare to anger me so they can idolize
a foolish boy who talks too much and thinks Himself so wise?
They think they can ignore me? How their wealth has made them proud.
Sāṁvartaka! Destroy their cows! This cannot be allowed!

The wind-gods will be helping you rebuke this land of Vraj.
My elephant, Airāvata, will lead the entourage.
Together we shall smash this village! Then we'll see them bow
to he who gives them rain and thus maintains their precious cows."

27) Sāṁvartaka, who saturates the very universe,
began to rain on Vṛndāvan until it was immersed.

The clouds poured water ceaselessly on Nanda's small domain
and frightened all the residents with lightning bolts and rain.

28) Torrential rain in massive columns fell in endless flow.
The high ground could no longer be distinguished from the low.
The cows began to shiver from the rain and freezing wind.
Their hands aloft, Lord Krishna's friends and family cried to Him,

29) "O Krishna, Krishna! No one is as kind and great as You!
Protect our cows from Indra's wrath—and please, protect us too!"
On seeing their distress and reams of storm clouds gone berserk,
Lord Krishna knew the blasting wind and hail was Indra's work.

30) Lord Krishna thought, "My intervention led this god to send
unseasonable rain, fierce wind and hail to harm my friends.
A god like Indra, strong and proud, is prone to such mistakes.
I'll help him keep in mind he's here to give and not to take.

31) This god is meant to act in goodness, not from foolish pride.
I'll humble him. His ego has grown over-magnified.
Since Indra has harassed My friends and brought them to their knees,
I'll save them now, for I have vowed to guard My devotees."

Lifting Govardhan Hill

32, 33) And then, just as a child might pluck a mushroom from the lawn,
Lord Krishna stretched His youthful hand and lifted Govardhan.
"Oh Mother, Father, friends!" He called, "take shelter here for now.
Be safe beneath this gracious hill. And don't forget your cows.

Your rescue from the wind and rain already has been planned.
Fear not, for I will safely hold this hill up with My hand."
Their minds relieved by Krishna's words, the people all conformed
and with their wagons, cows and priests, escaped the deadly storm.

34) As Krishna held the hill aloft the people stared, amazed,
and felt no hunger, sleepiness or thirst for seven days.
They gazed with fascination at the sight of Nanda's son
supporting the gigantic hill and pleasing everyone.

35) King Indra, on the other hand, could not believe his eyes.
He said, "Our rainfall floods the ground, but then, at once, it dries!
Sāṁvartaka, your lightning falls like flowers on that hill.
Stop pushing air—someone down there has greater strength and skill."

36) Lord Krishna saw the tempest stop and sunshine fill the sky.
"It's over," He informed the men. "You'll all be safe and dry.
The river has receded. Let us go on with our lives.
Go home now with your property, your children and your wives."

37) Collecting their respective cows and filling up their carts,
the people under Govardhan got ready to depart.
Soon everybody stepped outside. And then, with strength and grace,
the little son of Nanda put the hill back in its place.

38) The residents of Vṛndāvan, in waves of ecstasy,
came up, by age and rank, to thank the Lord accordingly.
Some blessed Him; some embraced Him; others chose to genuflect.
The women gave Him yogurt and whole grains to show respect.

39) His father, mother, brother and stepmother then appeared
and hugged Lord Krishna feelingly while shedding happy tears.
Completely overwhelmed with bliss, they blessed their darling boy,
while denizens of heaven showered flowers out of joy.

40) While drums and song resounded through the heavens high above,
the cowherd boys, the Lord's dear friends, surrounded Him in love.
The boys left Govardhan and let their cows eat grass and roam.
The *gopīs*, rapt in thoughts of Krishna, ambled to their homes.

The Puzzled Cowherd Men

41-45) The cowherd men, amazed by Krishna, found themselves confused,
so they requested their beloved Nanda for his views.
They said, "Your son lifts mountains and kills demons without fuss.
Since He is our superior, why *does* he stay with us?

Your son is only seven, yet He has tremendous powers.
He picks up hills as elephants might pick up lotus flowers.
In fact, when He was just an infant, yet to cut a tooth,
He sucked the life from Pūtanā as time sucks out one's youth.

At three months, with His toe, He kicked a pushcart to the ground.
And then He rode a whirlwind in the air and brought it down.
Your toddler Krishna then uprooted two arjuna trees.
Can you explain the meaning of your son's activities?

He killed the demon Vatsa masquerading as a calf.
He seized the demon Baka's beaks and tore the rogue in half.
He spun the giant asses round and hurled them into trees
and danced around Kāliya's heads with much dexterity.

With all the feats and superhuman powers He deploys
how can we think of Krishna as a seven-year-old boy?
And Nanda, let us ask you this: now, why is everyone
so caught up in affectionate relations with your son?"

46) King Nanda said, "My friends, my friends, please do not tax your heads.
When Gargamuni studied Krishna's horoscope, he said
that Krishna would do miracles, and that is what He's done.
Let me tell you exactly what he said about my son:

47, 48) "Your Krishna has appeared before in many ages past,
in white and red and yellow shades and sundry social castes.
He was a son of Vasudev, the timeless stars proclaim,
so in this lifetime 'Vāsudev' shall also be his name.

Your son will gather countless names by His activities.
He'll keep your subjects happy and prevent calamities.
Lord Viṣṇu comes when gods have failed and evil floods the Earth,
and your son is like Viṣṇu. Serve Him well in this new birth."

49) Continued Nanda, "I've seen Krishna, ever since that time,
behave so much like Viṣṇu one might think that He's divine."

50) The cowherd men, enlivened and relieved by what they'd heard,
began to worship Krishna with sweet offerings and words.
They saw how Indra pelted them with hail as sharp as knives,
till Krishna simply lifted Govardhan and saved their lives.
The strength and grace and kindness that He showed, as we discussed,
is typical of Krishna. Oh, may He be pleased with us!

Indra Repents

51-57) Accompanied by Surabhi, the foremost mother cow,
King Indra fell before the Lord in full prostrated bow.
The helmet of the king of heaven, brilliant as the sun,
then rose as Indra sang these prayers in praise of Nanda's son:

(Meter: -|- -|- -|- -|)
"This world is a river of anxiety,
stupidity, passion, and false piety.
Its currents don't touch You; You're pure and aloof.
Your body itself is the Absolute Truth.

No lust, greed or anger appear within You
or cause You to fall or affect what You do.
So pure is Your purpose it's well understood:
when You punish someone it's for their own good.

My father, my guru who fully controls
all-powerful time which rebukes fallen souls,
You come to refurbish the lost mental health
of those who would be God instead of Yourself.

You chastised this fool; his conceit is now purged.
Your boldness awakened my spiritual urge.
Engrossed in my power, I made an offense.
Forgive me, My Lord, and protect my good sense.

You free Mother Earth from the warlords and thieves
while serving the welfare of Your devotees.
You live in each atom and in between, too;
O seed of all being, I bow before You.

When worship for me was disrupted, I tried
to rain on Vṛndāvan till everyone died.
You've broken my plans and You've humbled me, too,
so now I have come to surrender to You."

(iambic heptameter)
58-62) Lord Krishna smiled as Indra, finished, joined his palms and bowed.
Then Krishna spoke, His voice so deep it rumbled like a cloud.
"When one becomes too proud I sometimes show a special grace:
I take all of his wealth away and put him in his place.

Though I disturbed your sacrifice and caused anxiety,
you've learned you cannot make decisions independently.
A man intoxicated by his power grows so proud and blind
he does not see Me, stick in hand, awaiting just behind.

I humbled you to help you, not because I am unkind.
I always seek the welfare of the spiritually inclined.
Oh Indra, take your leave now. You may stay as heaven's king
among the gods and goddesses who frolic, dance and sing.
It seems you've learned a lesson now, and if it is applied
you'll do your duty soberly, without so much false pride."

62-65) The foremost cow, Surabhi, then, surrounded by the herd,
began to speak to Krishna with these gentle, humble words:

(Meter: |- |- -|-|)
"Krishna, Krishna, the mystic king,
You're the origin of everything.
You're our master. You never fail.
Indra hurt us, but You prevailed.

Though 'Indra' means 'the lord', it's said,
we want You for our lord instead.
You will care for the cows and priests.
All the gods will be very pleased.

You have saved us from Indra's wrath;
please consent to the sacred bath

marking You as our sovereign lord
now that reason has been restored.

(iambic heptameter)
66) King Indra, quite embarrassed, heard his relatives and friends
persuade him to serve Krishna and to try to make amends.
His elephant Airāvata approached Indra and gave
a trunk of sacred *gaṅgā-jal*[2] so Krishna could be bathed.
Surabhi gave abundant milk to bathe Lord Krishna, too,
and Krishna smiled and said to them, "Do what you wish to do."

[2]*Water of the sacred Ganges river.*

67) The bathing was a coronation, crowning Krishna king
of oceans, Earth and heaven—Lord Supreme of everything.
The gods above sang out in love and danced through heaven's streets.
The cows drenched every part of Earth as milk poured from their teats.

68) The rivers flowed with tasty liquids. Honey poured from trees,
and mountains gave up precious stones in endless quantities.
The fruits and roots and vegetables grew ripe and good to eat
while creatures, kind or wicked, all felt satisfied and sweet.

69) The leading gods threw waves of petals pulled from heaven's flowers
and residents of all the planets sang and danced for hours.

70) Amidst this happy situation, Indra understood
Lord Krishna is almighty God, all-powerful and good.
Again he took the Lord's permission, joined his friends and rode
by mystic grace through cosmic space back to the gods' abode.

Varuna and Beyond

71) Soon after came Ekādaśī, a time to pray and fast.
King Nanda went to bathe quite late, before the night had passed.
In prayerful mood, he entered Yamunā's auspicious waves
without a thought that this was not a proper time to bathe.

72) A servant of Varuṇa (god of water everywhere)
saw Nanda taking bath at night and seized him then and there.

This servant knew the law book. Feeling powerful and proud,
he said, "To use these waters in the dark is not allowed!"

73) The servant took King Nanda to Varuṇa to be tried.
The cowherd men, alarmed when Nanda disappeared, all cried,
"O Krishna, Krishna! Nanda hasn't come back from his bath.
We fear that he has drowned or somehow caused Varuṇa's wrath."

74) Lord Krishna ran and jumped into the water to transport
Himself, by mystic power, promptly to Varuṇa's court.
Varuṇa was ecstatic to see Krishna in his lair.
He offered his respects and fancy worship, then declared,

75, 76) "My body has fulfilled its purpose. Life is now complete!
Material existence dies when one beholds Your feet.
Obeisances to You, my Lord. Your form is absolute.
Illusion orchestrates this world, but You are perfect truth.

My foolish servant took Your father, lacking common sense.
King Nanda sits here on my throne. Forgive our great offense.
You love Your father deeply, Lord. Return him home now, please,
and show Your causeless mercy. We are all Your devotees."

77) Contented with Varuṇa and his pacifying tone,
Lord Krishna took His father and returned him to their home.
The relatives were overjoyed to see his safe return,
but Nanda was astonished and explained what he had learned:

78) "Varuṇa was so opulent. Indeed, he rules the seas,
yet he addressed my son just like a beggar on his knees.
Varuṇa then rebuked his servant who arrested me,
directing all his servants to show Krishna courtesy."

79) On hearing these fantastic dealings told in Nanda's words,
the cowherd men went home and thought of all that had occurred.
"When Indra and Varuṇa bow to Krishna," they surmised,
our Krishna must be God Himself and live in paradise!"

80, 81) Lord Krishna, who knows everything, could very clearly sense
the men all longed to visit His eternal residence.
"The people in this world endure much karma," Krishna mused,
"entrapping them in birth and death and leaving them confused.

The common man ignores My strength and My divinity.
The residents of Vraj ignore them too, but differently.
Their love for Me illusions them, not pride or nature's modes,
and now these loving servants wish to see My own abode."

82) So Krishna took them far away and gave them all the sight
of His divine effulgence, called the *brahmajyoti* light.
And then they went beyond that light, the target of the wise,
and entered in the regions of the spiritual sky.

83) The atmosphere was like Vṛndāvan, something they all knew,
but Krishna, here, was worshiped—something they would never do.
The Vedic texts personified surrounded Nanda's son
and prayed to Him incessantly. The cowherd men were stunned.

10

The Rasa Dance

A Call of Love

1) As fall arrived, the springtime jasmine kissed the evening air
and Krishna schemed, with loving dreams, for His unique affairs.
The moon adorned the eastern sky with soothing garnet rays,
a husband bringing *kuṅkum* to his wife to dress her face.

2) The moonbeams turned vermilion, lit the woods and drew the blooms
of reddish lotus flowers, which in turn shared their perfume.
With pleasure Krishna placed a bamboo flute upon His lips
and played a tune the cowherd girls of Vraj could not resist.

3) These *gopīs*, busy milking cows or tending to their stoves
(with boiling milk pots set on top and baking cakes below),
found Krishna's flute song pulling them away from hearth and home
to search the night with hopes they might find Krishna all alone.

4) Some *gopīs* served out dinner; others changed and nursed their tots;
and others were still getting dressed. Regardless, they all stopped.
As soon as they heard Krishna's charming flute they ran away,
their duties all forgotten and their clothes in disarray.

5) Their husbands, fathers, sons and brothers dashing to their doors,
found out their wives and daughters had departed long before.
Some *gopīs* who could not escape and had to stay behind
shut tight their eyes and thought of Krishna deep within their minds.

6) These prisoners remembered Krishna, feeling great remorse.
They thus wrapped up their karma that had yet to run its course.
Their thoughts of Krishna deepened and ecstatic feelings grew
till they abandoned all respect for Vedic moral rules.

7) Said Viṣṇurāta, "They thought Him their lover and their friend,
not God Himself who crafts the world and brings it to an end.
How could these girls, their minds caught up in nature's ardent swells,
get free of such attachment and its strong, deceptive spells?"

8) The *gopīs*' lust is sacred, unlike that of common souls.
As sages in their former lives, they practiced self-control
and prayed to join with Krishna as His lovers or His mates.
When meant for Krishna, lust—or even hatred—liberates.

9) When Krishna meets the *gopīs* and fulfills their hearts' desire,
He acts from great compassion, not the force of passion's fire.
Since Krishna builds this mortal world in which we *jīvas*[1] fall,
attachments that bewilder us don't bother Him at all.

[1]*Souls.*

10) For us, directing all our feelings straight to Nanda's son—
the friendship, hatred, lust or fear well known to everyone—
will make the thought of Krishna fill our minds quite blissfully.
For love of Him, the *gopīs* left, and risked their chastity.

The Gopis Arrive

11-16) On seeing all the girls appear, Lord Krishna feigned surprise.
"Dear *gopīs*, what has brought you out beneath these moonlit skies?
Are things well in the village? Why on Earth have you come out?
Dear slender-waisted *gopīs*, there are dangerous beasts about.

You're walking through these fearsome woods, with hours yet till dawn.
Your relatives will surely be distressed to find you gone.
Why cause your husbands, sons and parents such anxiety?
Have you left home tonight because of some emergency?

Tonight you've seen the forest full of graceful, moonlit trees
that lean and sway with blossoms in the fragrant, gentle breeze.
Now go back to your husbands, for your calves and children cry.
They wait for you to feed them milk and dry their moistened eyes.
The best pursuit a woman can maintain throughout her life
is service to her husband as a chaste and loyal wife.

Or have you come tonight because you feel a love for Me
that usually slumbers in the living entity?
Regardless, if you care about your futures, I suggest
you serve and please your husbands, even if they aren't the best.

Adultery is horrible. What trouble it creates!
Unfaithfulness may keep your souls from crossing heaven's gates.
So if you're feeling love for Me, just hear and chant My name
while worshiping My deity, as scripture has explained.
To stand beside Me here beneath this evening's starry dome
will not bring You the same results. Now please, go to your homes."

17) On hearing these unpleasant words the *gopīs* grew morose,
for they could neither plead with nor give up their callous host.
Their lips dried up from heavy breathing. Tears rolled down their cheeks.
They hung their heads and toed the ground and could not even speak.

18) Although He had discouraged them, their love remained undimmed,
for they were mad for Krishna and left everything for Him.
They wiped their eyes and stopped their tears. Their simple hearts provoked,
they vowed within to stay with Krishna. Stammering, they spoke:

(Brahmā Samhita meter: -| -| -|-| --| -|-)
19-28) Almighty Krishna, why do You make such mean suggestions?
For You we threw away our husbands and our possessions.
O stubborn Krishna, you should show some reciprocation
as Lord Nārāyaṇ does to one seeking liberation.

You're everybody's dearest relative, friend and spirit,
yet You would send us all back home? We refuse to hear it!
The sages steer their love to You, and we wish to follow.
To live with troublemaking loved ones is hard to swallow.

Until today our household chores kept our concentration.
Now You've distracted us and broken our regulation.
How can we now return to live in that situation?
Our feet refuse to move an inch from their new location.

Your flute and smiling glance have kindled our hearts' desire,
and only nectar from Your lips can put out the fire.
If You refuse, our flesh will smolder in separation,
and we shall have to reach You solely by meditation.

Lakṣmī can rarely touch Your feet, yet You're here before us,
some simple women who reside in Vṛndāvan forests.
And once we touch Your feet and relish that happy feeling,
all other men become repulsive and unappealing.

Lakṣmī resides upon Your chest—a unique position.
Although the gods chase after her for their own provisions,
she shares the dust upon Your feet with Your other servants.
Is our desire to have that dust such a great disturbance?

To worship You we left our homes in a reckless fashion.
O vanquisher of all distress, have You no compassion?
O jewel of men, our hearts ignite by Your loving glances.
We beg to serve Your lotus feet in all circumstances.

Your nectar lips, adorned with smiles that Your glance expresses;
Your face, with dancing earrings, circled with curling tresses;
Your mighty arms and chest, where Lakṣmī enjoys her leisure—
all stir our hankering to serve You and bring You pleasure.

Your gorgeous form has made the three worlds become auspicious.
The cows and birds and even trees find the sight delicious.
And when Your flute pours out such sweet-sounding compositions,
what woman anywhere can salvage her chaste position?

As You appear among the gods to provide protection,
You must have come to please us girls, not to cause dejection.
Your lotus hands should stroke our heads in a calming fashion
and cool our fevered, burning breasts set aflame by passion."

(iambic heptameter)
29) These sweet, enchanting words, all said in humble, helpless style,
incited from the Lord of mystics His most gracious smile.
Though He Himself needs nothing, Krishna saw the *gopīs*' plight
and set His mind to stay with them throughout that moonlit night.

30) He smiled with teeth like jasmine buds. The *gopīs*' faces bloomed,
and they encircled Krishna like the stars surround the moon.
When *gopīs* by the hundreds sang His praise, the Lord replied.
His presence was a garland making all more beautified.

31) They sauntered to the riverbank and sat in cooling sands.
As lotus-perfumed breezes blew, Lord Krishna's playful hands
embraced the *gopīs*, touched their breasts and stroked their hands and hair.
They laughed and joked, invoking Cupid's arrows then and there.

Krishna Disappears

32) The *gopīs* felt so blessed to be with Krishna they could not
avoid becoming somwhat proud. In secret, each one thought,
'Compared to time with Krishna, what is any treasure worth?
Why, I am the most fortunate of women on the Earth!'

33) Lord Krishna sensed the *gopīs*' pride and, thinking it not right,
decided to desert them, so He vanished from their sight.
Now, after all, what better stirs a lovers' tender play
than offering a taste of love—then taking it away?

34) When Krishna left, the *gopīs* felt their joy evaporate.
Tormented like she-elephants who've lost their loving mate,
they visualized the joyous, playful smile of Nanda's son
and madly imitated Him and everything He'd done.

35) In deep affection, unrehearsed, the *gopīs*' bodies each
repeated Krishna's movements, smiling, gestures, steps and speech.
So baffled by the shock of losing Krishna's company,
some *gopīs*, quite immersed in love, asserted, "I am He!"

36) They loudly sang out "Krishna! Krishna!" Rushing through the night,
they madly searched Vṛndāvan's forests, looking left and right.
Aware that Krishna, like the sky, pervades all entities,
the *gopīs* started asking for directions from the trees:

37, 38) "O fig tree, have you seen the son of Nanda pass this way?
O banyan tree, He smiled, stole our hearts and went away.
Aśoka, nāga, campak trees! Has Rāma's brother passed?
His smile removes all vanity a woman could amass.

O *tulasī*, you love our Krishna. Kindest of all trees,
have you seen Him walk by with swarms of nectar-seeking bees?
O jasmine vines, you're bowing down. Did Mādhava, in play,
pass by and gently stroke you and delight you all that way?

(*Brahmā Samhita meter*: -| -| -|-| --| -|-)
39-43) O mango, jackfruit, *bel* and rose-apple trees, please tell us!
You used to give your fruits so freely. Have you grown jealous?
O tiny *arka* plant, abloom in this autumn season,
have you seen Krishna? We are losing our sense of reason.

O Mother Earth, what kind of penance have you accomplished?
Your grassy hairs standing on end make you look astonished.
Is this because Lord Krishna's footsteps tonight have graced you,
like Vaman's footsteps—or Varaha, who once embraced you?

O doe, your widened, joyful eyes show you must have seen them:
Lord Krishna's lovely arms and some lucky girl between them.
We smell His jasmine garland's fragrance throughout the forest
and *kuṅkum* from the breasts of she who found Him before us.

O trees, we see you bowing low with your fruits and flowers.
Did Rāma's brother glance at you with His loving powers,

His hand at rest upon the shoulder of His beloved,
a swarm of bees around His garland, which they so covet?

O creepers, kindly verify our distinct suspicion
that Krishna touched you. We can see it in your condition.
Although you're wrapped around your tree-husbands, you are showing
goose-bumps and quivering where creeper-leaves should be growing."

(iambic heptameter)
44-50) Exhausting their unstable visions, all the *gopīs* sighed,
and feeling quite discouraged, set their frantic search aside.
But then, absorbed in Krishna, they began, impulsively,
to mimic other pastimes He had shown them recently.

One *gopī* played as Pūtanā, the giant demoness;
another played as Krishna and sucked poison from her breast.
Another played the demon who had hidden in a cart;
another, playing Krishna, feigned to kick it all apart.

Another rendered Tṛṇāvarta, swirling round and round
while clinging to a Krishna-*gopī* till they both fell down.
Another *gopī*, thinking Krishna's infancy most sweet,
just crawled about the forest, anklets tinkling on her feet.

Two *gopīs* played as Rām and Krishna; two more girls deployed
as Vatsa (calf) and Baka (crane). In play, both were destroyed.
As some portrayed the flute-play and the sports of Nanda's son,
the others watched and clapped their hands while calling out, "Well done!"

A *gopī* placed her arm around a friend and then declared,
"Now I am graceful Krishna!" as she sauntered here and there.
"And I shall fend off Indra's wind and rain!" another cried,
and raised her shawl like Govardhan so other girls could hide.

One *gopī* climbed another's back and called, "This snake is dead!"
portraying Krishna's dance upon Kāliya's many heads.
"I've come to punish demons!" she announced. Another roared,
"I'll save you from this blazing forest fire. Fear no more!"

One *gopī* stole some butter as a second gave her chase,
then used a flower garland to bind up her slender waist.
She said, “Now I have captured this elusive butter thief!”
The first *gopī* concealed her face and shed mock tears of grief.

Telltale Footprints

51) The *gopīs*, staging dramas and inquiring from the trees,
then came across some footprints and exclaimed excitedly,
“This thunderbolt and lotus bloom and other telltale marks
confirm that Krishna walked this way and passed us in the dark!”

52-56) They followed Krishna’s footprints but were soon disturbed to see
young-lady footprints intermixed. They cried, in agony,
“Some girl and Krishna walked here arm in arm, this indicates,
like elephants who rest their trunks upon their loving mates.

This girl has so pleased Krishna with her love and charming face
that He forsook the rest of us and brought her to this place.
In dust that Śiva, Lakṣmī and Brahmā place on their heads,
these sacred tracks of Krishna’s feet confirm what we have said.

These footprints cause us so much pain! Some girl came here, alone,
to savor our unfailing Krishna’s lips upon her own.
And look! Her footprints disappear! Our Krishna is so sweet,
He must have picked her up because these creepers hurt her feet.

His footprints sink more deeply now. It all seems very clear:
our strong, romantic Krishna must have carried her from here.
And look! That clever boy walked over there and set her down
then reached up for some flowers. See His toe prints in the ground?

Then, after picking flowers, He induced the girl to sit.
And look! He sat behind her, here, so He could bend and fit
those fragrant flowers, one by one, embellishing her hair.
‘I now crown you the goddess of the forest!’ He declared.”

57) The *gopīs* had indeed detected Krishna’s acts of love.
Dear King, you must remember Krishna always stays above

those stale and common acts of lust that merely please the flesh.
He's fully self-contained. His love is selfless, pure and fresh.

58) The *gopīs* grew bewildered as the evidence unfurled
that Krishna had rejected them for one selected girl.
But they did not see pride had also caused *that* girl to fall
when she thought 'He left others just for me. I'm best of all.'

59) Believing herself foremost of the *gopīs*, she'd declared,
"I've walked enough. Please pick me up and carry me somewhere."
So Krishna crouched and touched his shoulder. "Climb aboard, my dear."
In shock, the poor girl shouted out (for He had disappeared),
"O Master! Lover! Dearmost friend! Where are You? Are you here?
O mighty-armed! Your wretched servant prays You'll reappear!"

60) The other *gopīs*, trailing Krishna, found their shaken friend,
her lover's sudden absence far too much to comprehend.

61) She said, "At first He honored me in many different ways,
but I grew proud and then He left!" The *gopīs* were amazed.
Again they followed Krishna's trail in hopes to reunite,
but soon the forest thickened, blocked the moon and hid its light.

62) They acted, thought and talked of Krishna, following His tracks.
The darkness quickly stopped their search and forced them to go back.
Returning to the riverbank, unmindful of their homes,
in love they sang for Krishna in morose but hopeful tones:

Song Of Separation

(Meter: -|- -|- -|- -|)
63-81) "So famed is Vṛndāvan since You have appeared
the Goddess of Fortune herself resides here.
We searched everywhere, yet You hide from our view.
Dear Krishna, please come! Our lives hinge upon You.

The beauty we find in Your glance goes beyond
a full-blooming lotus in still autumn pond.

Your absence will kill us; we'll never adjust.
Is this not the same thing as murdering us?

You saved us when Kāliya poisoned the lake.
You saved us from Agha, that man-eating snake.
You saved us from thunderbolts Indra let fly.
Will You now abandon Your servants to die?

O, heart-dwelling witness within everyone,
You're more than your father and mother's dear son.
You rescued the Yadus at others' request;
Will You now neglect those who love You the best?

When woes of this world drive a soul to Your feet,
Your lotus-like hand makes their fear obsolete.
Your hand holds the Goddess of fortune's, it's said.
Beloved, please lay that same hand on our heads.

Great hero, You free Vraja's people from pain.
Your smile intervenes when Your servants grow vain.
Take us as Your servants and show us the grace
embodied in Your lovely, lotus-like face.

Your lotus feet, Lakṣmī's abode, absorb sins,
yet chase after cows when the herd must go in.
Your feet, which You pressed upon Kāliya's head,
should favor our passionate breasts now instead.

O lotus-eyed Krishna, Your speech is so sweet
it captures the minds of the learned elite.
Your words cause our ethical judgment to slip.
Restore it, dear hero, with Your pleasing lips.

The words that You speak and descriptions of You
will cleanse those who hear till their sins are removed.
Compassionate persons who speak on such themes
are gracious and worthy of endless esteem.

Your smiles and sweet glances, the intimate games
and private discussions we loved to exchange
were pleasing, auspicious and sweet memories.
But now, our dear cheater, they're just miseries.

Our minds grow disturbed when we think how You lead
the cows to the pasture to forage and feed.
Your soft lotus feet must be pricked by the blades
of brambles and bushes that grow on the way.

And when You come home we observe that Your face
is coated with dust that the cow's footsteps raise.
Your lotus-like visage and bluish-black hair
awaken our minds to our loving affairs.

Brahmā serves Your feet, which fulfill all desires.
The jewels of Earth, they are all one requires
to meditate on in a time of distress.
Please place those two soft lotus feet on our breasts.

The sweetness that flows from Your lips feeds our lust
and renders attachment and anguish to dust.
We envy Your flute, so strategically placed.
Bestow on Your servants that nectar-kissed taste.

When we cannot see You, a moment appears
to stretch in duration for thousands of years.
Your loveliness shames the creator,[2] we think,
for he gave us eyelids that force us to blink.

[2] *Here the gopīs refer to Lord Brahmā.*

Infallible Krishna, You know why we've come.
What other deceiver would do what You've done?
You walked out on us, though we gave up our men
to hear Your sweet flute in the night once again.

When we recall pledges You secretly made,
Your glance and Your smile and the love they conveyed,

or think of Your chest, which is Lakṣmī's abode,
our lust leaves us thrust on a dangerous road.

When You walk among us, we're happy and blessed
and every Vrindavanite shed his distress.
A drop of that medicine surely will ease
the tormented hearts of Your pure devotees.

The ground in the forest, with stones and rough sand,
is painful indeed for Your feet to withstand.
Dear Krishna, our breasts are both tender and smooth;
Please rest Your feet there, and we all shall be soothed."

Krishna Returns

(iambic heptameter)

82) The *gopīs*, having filled their ears with songs of touching themes,
burst into tears, for Krishna still was nowhere to be seen.
O King, their sobs for Krishna, loud and long, reflected pain
and eagerness to see Him they no longer could contain.

83) And then Lord Krishna, smiling with a lotus-blossom face,
returned to them, His yellow robes and garland still in place.
So pleased were they to see Him once again that moonlit night
they doubted Cupid, god of love, himself could bear the sight.

84) At once the *gopīs* all stood up, their eyes all blooming wide.
It seemed they had regained their life air after having died.
One girl put Krishna's arm upon her shoulder, leaning near.
Another placed her hands around the hand she so revered.

85) A slender *gopī* joined her palms, in reverential mood,
around discarded *betel* nuts that Krishna had just chewed.
Another *gopī*, burning with the flames of passion's heat,
positioned her excited breasts on Krishna's lotus feet.

86) Beside herself with loving anger, one girl bit her lip
and glared at Krishna crossly, as if striking with a whip.
Another stared insatiably at Krishna's lovely face,
as mystics meditate on Krishna's feet with endless taste.

87) One *gopī* looked at Krishna, took Him in and shut her eyes,
then held Him tight inside her heart, her dreams now realized.
While standing there in ecstasy, the hair rose on her skin,
and she became a *yogī* fixed on Krishna deep within.

88) Each *gopī* felt so pleased with Krishna in her special way
the pain He caused by leaving them appeared to go away.
They acted like those common souls whose miseries abate
as soon as an enlightened person enters through their gate.

89) Encircled by the *gopīs*, Krishna's luster shone so bright,
He seemed to be the Supersoul appearing in the night.
They walked together on the shore, delighting in the breeze,
made sweet with jasmine fragrances that brought in bustling bees.

90) As autumn moonlight quelled the dark, the Yamunā, with hands
of softly rippling river waves, made cushions from the sand.
The *gopīs* placed, upon those cushions, *kuṅkum* covered shawls
to seat their dearest Krishna, scripture's goal and friend to all.

91) The Lord, who sits in every heart, sat too amongst those girls
and gleamed with an attractiveness esteemed throughout the worlds.
The *gopīs* rubbed His hands and feet, yet, miffed with what occurred,
they mixed their playful smiles and looks with these uncertain words:

92) "Some people only love when they are loved by someone else,
while others freely give their love and ask none for themselves.
Still others don't love anyone, regardless of their mood.
Dear Krishna, please explain to us these different attitudes."

93) By making this inquiry, the *gopīs* gave a hint
they felt harassed and could not grasp the evening's incidents.
Why did their lover disappear, inflicting so much pain?
Lord Krishna understood their minds and smiled as He explained:

94-99) "Those friends who show affection but are self-absorbed at heart
are not friends in the truest sense. They simply play a part
in mutual self-interest. They would never show their love
unless there was some profit they could take advantage of.

Oh slender-waisted *gopīs*, others love without concern
for what they have to gain from love or get back in return.
Such people may be parents, friends or saints, but you can tell
that they are truly friendly and wish everybody well.

Still others don't or can't give back the love that they receive.
They don't love friends or family—what to speak of enemies!
Such people might be self-contained, in spirit or in wealth,
ungrateful, or just hateful toward those better than themselves.

Sometimes I too hold back My love from people who love Me,
for that allows their love to build still more intensively.
Like rich men who have lost their wealth can think of nothing else,
My devotees' unanswered love refines their higher self.

Your love for Me makes you detached from mere morality,
the Vedic rules, your schedules, and even family.
I left to make your love for Me increase. Don't be upset.
Did you believe that I could leave without extreme regret?

A lifetime of the gods would pass before I could express
how deeply I appreciate the love that you possess.
Since you've forsaken all for Me, what gift can I give you?
Your glorious devotion in itself will have to do."

The Dance Begins

100) The *gopīs* heard these charming words and, casting off distress,
enjoyed themselves by touching Krishna's ample arms and chest.
Those jewels among women, linking arms in great delight,
began to dance with Krishna in Vṛndāvan's moonlit night.

101) As they began the *rāsa* dance each *gopīs* quickly found
that she was all alone with Krishna, dancing round and round.
On seeing Krishna multiply, His arms around each neck,
the gods and goddesses above flew closer to inspect.

102) Amazed, the gods beat drums and threw down flowers in cascades.
Gandharvas[3] and their wives sang out Lord Krishna's endless praise.

The chimes of bracelets, anklets and the bells strung from their waists
resounded as the *gopīs* danced with Krishna face to face.

[3]*Heavenly singers.*

103) Surrounded by the dancing *gopīs*, Krishna seemed to be
a sapphire set in most exquisite golden jewelry.
The *gopīs* sang of Krishna as they curtsied, twirled and swayed,
their hands in graceful gestures and their smiling eyebrows raised.

104) The *gopīs*' twisting waists propelled their blouses left and right.
Their earrings swung in rhythm, though their braids and belts held tight.
When gentle perspiration broke and glistened on their brows,
they shone like bolts of lightning set in bluish-blackish clouds.

105-107) The *gopīs* throats turned crimson as if tinged with passion's thirst.
At Krishna's touch, their songs of pleasure filled the universe.
One *gopī* sang in harmony and Krishna joined the fun.
And then she deftly changed the beat. The Lord called out, "Well done!"

Her hair and bracelets hanging limp, her energy all gone,
one *gopī* hung on Krishna's arm, which held a dance baton.
Another *gopī*'s shoulder served as Krishna's resting place.
She thrilled to smell His lotus arm, adorned with sandal-paste.

A *gopī* placed her earring-laden cheek next to the Lord's,
and took His *betel*-remnants from His hand as her reward.
Another *gopī*, bracelets tinkling, stopped to take a rest,
and placed Lord Krishna's tender lotus hand upon her breast.

108) Now, everybody knows that goddess Lakṣmī, queen of wealth,
insists that Krishna spend His time with no one but herself.
To find that very Krishna's arms around their necks that night,
the *gopīs* felt quite fortunate and chanted in delight.

109) The perspiration on their cheeks and flowers in their hair
combined to make the *gopīs*' faces sweet beyond compare.
As they danced on, their tinkling bracelets raised a pleasing tune
in harmony with singing bees beneath the lustrous moon.

110) Caressing and embracing them and dancing all the while,
Lord Krishna showed the *gopīs* love with cordial, playful smiles.
Since they are all His energies (as is the queen of wealth),
He frolicked like a child with a reflection of himself.

111) My dear King Viṣṇurāta, by the touch of Nanda's son,
the *gopīs*, overwhelmed with joy, began to come undone.
Their ornaments and garlands seemed to scatter everywhere,
and all their lovely clothes grew as disheveled as their hair.

112) The goddesses in heaven were aroused to watch this dance.
The moon and his associates, the stars, fell in a trance.
Each *gopī* had her Krishna to exclusively possess,
and Krishna, who needs no one, loved each *gopī* nonetheless.

113) When all the *gopīs* tired, Krishna kindly wiped their brows.
His soothing hand induced their smiles, their love still more aroused.
These smiles enhanced their glowing cheeks, their earrings and their hair.
Again, inspired by Krishna's touch, their singing filled the air.

114) Their hugs crushed Krishna's garland and left marks of *kuṅkum* red.
Aware of their exhaustion and their fevered limbs and heads,
Lord Krishna led the *gopīs* to the Yamunā to swim
just like a lordly elephant brings wives to bathe with him.

115) As elephants might trample fields and paddies carelessly,
the *gopīs* and the Lord ignored mundane morality.
While playful *gopīs* splashed Lord Krishna, laughing out of love,
the gods thought Him majestic and rained flowers from above.

116) Refreshed, the Lord emerged into the floral-scented breeze.
Surrounded by an entourage of lovely girls and bees,
He strolled among the forest groves along the riverside
as if a drunken elephant carousing with his wives.

117) Despite the host of gorgeous *gopīs* at His beck and call,
the self-contained Lord Krishna had no lust for them at all.
He went on with His pastimes through that perfect moonlit night,
itself an inspiration of which every poet writes.

118, 119) Astonished by these topics, Viṣṇurāta quickly asked
"Lord Krishna, God Himself, had just descended for the task
of setting Vedic principles to govern human lives.
How could he break a moral law by touching other's wives?

Lord Krishna, the self-satisfied, the Yadu family's jewel,
proclaims, protects and follows every single Vedic rule.
It seems He acted shamefully. Since you are so devout,
please tell us what He had in mind and satisfy our doubt."

120) Transgressions of the Vedic rules that tarnish you or me,
do not taint Krishna—or the gods—with immorality.
The actions of such deities are free of any fault
as fire cleanly burns dry wood and makes no smoke at all.

121) Such great souls come for us to see, but not to imitate.
Their actions far exceed what we can do or contemplate.
Though Śiva drinks a sea of poison, we can't drink a sip.
Can we then dare to mimic Krishna's pure relationships?

122) We need not try to imitate what great devotees do;
we simply need to follow them and hear their words of truth.
How could Lord Krishna's actions bring a consequence to Him
when those who simply follow Krishna cleanse their hearts of sin?

123) The devotees of Krishna, so agreeable and pure,
are wise and potent *yogīs* with no karma to endure.
So how could Krishna, God Himself, who comes at His sweet will,
be less than His devotees or be somehow unfulfilled?

124) What fault is there for Krishna, who resides in every heart,
to take the *gopīs* with Him to the woods to be apart?
Since Krishna has created us, the *gopīs*, and the rest,
what sin occurs should He embrace a *gopī* to His chest?

125) When Krishna comes before us in His true identity,
His pastimes draw devotion from each person that He sees.
Why, even all the *gopīs*' husbands felt quite satisfied,
for Krishna's *māyā* made them think their wives were at their sides.

126) The dance went on a thousand *yugas* till a hint of dawn
at last led Krishna to advise the *gopīs* to move on.
The *gopīs*, leaving Krishna to return to home and hearth,
preserved these secret pastimes in their unpolluted hearts.

127) Now, anyone who faithfully recites or hears these words
of Krishna and the *gopīs* and how everything occurred,
shall gain both love for Krishna and the wisdom of disgust
with ordinary sex affairs that spoil the heart with lust.

A Snake Swallows Nanda

128) When autumn ended, Nanda and the cowherds went away
to certain distant holy sites on *Śivarātri* day.[4]
Arriving at the sacred Sarasvati riverside,
they bathed and bowed to Śiva as the Vedic texts prescribe.

[4]*The appearance day of Lord Śiva.*

129) They gave the *brāhmans* gifts of clothing, honey, gold and cows.
"May Śiva now be pleased with us!" they sang and prayed aloud.
King Nanda and his fellow cowherds, through the fading light,
observed their vows of fasting that continued through the night.

130) When Nanda rested on the ground (as pilgrims often do),
a monstrous snake appeared nearby, his dinner overdue.
He slithered through the thicket and, without a moment's pause,
began to swallow Nanda whole, with giant, unhinged jaws.

131) King Nanda cried out, "Krishna! Krishna! Help me please, dear son!
This serpent will consume me if You don't come now. Please run!
Already he has half of me! My arms are going, too!
Nobody else can save me, son—nobody else but You!"

132) The other cowherds heard his cries and rushed to save their king.
Their forceful blows, with clubs and torches, didn't do a thing.
Then Krishna, their beloved master, came among the men
and placed His lotus foot upon the serpents' scaly skin.

133) The touch of Krishna's lotus foot at once had its effect:
the karma of that sinful snake was gone in all respects.
The spirit soul, abandoning his nasty serpent's dress,
transformed into a god of splendid beauty and finesse.

134) The luster of his body could illuminate the night.
His necklaces of purest gold cast self-effulgent light.
He turned his gaze to Krishna and quite humbly bowed his head.
Desiring to hear him speak, Lord Krishna smiled and said,

135) "My dear effulgent sir, you seem so wonderful and bright.
Your body is celestial. It doesn't quite seem right
that recently you've occupied the body of snake.
Who are you. What has happened? Did you make some grave mistake?"

136-139) The god replied, "I used to be a well-respected soul.
I flew a godly airplane anywhere I chose to go.
Because I was so beautiful—and lacking in restraint—
I once indulged in laughing at a group of ugly saints.

'You find us all so ugly that you laugh?' the saints replied.
'We curse you to become a snake and curb your blatant pride.'
I now can understand they truly blessed me for my sin;
that curse has caused Your lotus feet to touch my scaly skin.

Infallible and dear Lord Krishna, simply by Your sight
the burden of my punishment has ended here tonight.
To see You or to chant Your holy name makes one complete,
so what to speak of one who gets to touch Your lotus feet!

Your lotus feet have set me free and changed my attitude;
My Lord, they make one fearless and create auspicious moods.
I beg to serve them always, like Your perfect devotees.
I'm ready now to go back home to heaven, if You please."

140) The shining god received the Lord's permission to depart.
He circumambulated Krishna, praying from his heart.
The men wrapped up their Śiva *pūjā*,[5] looking rather stunned.
As they rode home they spoke in awe of what the Lord had done.

[5]*Worship.*

Shankhachuda

141) Some weeks went by. Then, Rām and Krishna, dressed in spotless clothes,
went deep in Vraja's forest as the evening moon arose.
Bejeweled, decked and garlanded, they met the *gopīs* there
and watched the bees drink up the breeze of jasmine-scented air.

142) The brothers started singing, blending varied tones to one
and sending happy feelings to the minds of everyone.
The *gopīs*, stunned to hear the sound the singing brothers made,
forgot their clothes were loosened and their hair was disarrayed.

143) As both the brothers sang and laughed, impaired (or so it seemed),
the demon Ṣaṇkhacūda chanced to come upon the scene.
He eyed the *gopīs*, eyed the stars and eyed the singing boys,
then chased the *gopīs* through the woods, expecting to enjoy.

144) The *gopīs* cried out, "Krishna! Rām!" The boys replied, "Don't fear!"
They picked up stones and trailed the wretch as lions hunt a deer.
When Ṣaṇkhacūda saw them, he saw death personified.
Afraid his time was running out, he scurried off to hide.

145) Govinda chased the demon while His brother stayed behind
to safeguard all the *gopīs* and to pacify their minds.
The mighty Krishna captured Ṣaṇkhacūda as he fled
and with a single blow removed the demon's wicked head.

146) This Ṣaṇkhacūda's turban held a gorgeous, precious jewel
that Krishna found too opulent to leave with the late fool.
He couldn't give it to one girl, for others might object,
so He gave it to Balarām to show His deep respect.

Songs of the Flute

147) Whenever Krishna left His home, the *gopīs* ran behind,
though not in the external sense but only in their minds.
Thus, when He took the cows and bulls to pasture every day,
the *gopīs*, sadly stuck at home, expressed themselves this way:

(Meter: -|- -|- -|- -|)
148-162) When Krishna positions His flute to His lips,
and fills up its holes with His soft fingertips,
He rests His left cheek on His arm as He plays,
and both His sweet eyebrows start dancing away.

As Krishna's flute-melodies spread through the sky
the gods in their heavenly planes are surprised.
Their wives become flustered, their minds so seduced
they don't even notice their garments are loose.

The sound of His flute makes the cattle and deer
abandon their chewing and stiffen their ears.
The Yamunā's water grows perfectly still.
Like us, she stands trembling, her arms unfulfilled.

The flute song makes *tulasī's* fragrance intense;
wild flowers and fruits become sweet and immense.
The trees bow their limbs and pour buckets of sap,
their twigs and their leaves standing stiff on their backs.

When bees swarming Krishna delight Him with song,
He blows on His flute and, with thanks, plays along.
The sound draws the minds of the swans and the cranes,
who meditate deeply on every refrain.

When Krishna and Rām, flowers strung in Their hair,
climb hillsides for fun, Krishna's flute fills the air.
As clouds gently thunder and shade them from sun,
the resonant music delights everyone.

O Yaśodā, how has your Krishna compiled
such unheard of flute-playing methods and styles?
Lords Śiva and Brahmā become so perplexed
they bow to the sound to display their respects.

The trampling of cow hooves cause Earth immense grief,
so Krishna steps on her and brings her relief.

Such marvelous markings He leaves on the road—
a thunderbolt, lotus and elephant goad.

As He strolls through Vraj like an elephant king,
His glances at us are as lively as spring.
How quickly we fall under Cupid's attack,
forgetting our garments and hair have grown slack.

Our Krishna counts cows using gems on a string
then hugs all His friends, plays His flute-songs and sings.
The sound attracts she-deer to sit by His side,
their family attachments, like ours, cast aside.

A garland of jasmine enhancing His dress,
our Krishna amuses His friends with a jest.
They walk by the river as sandal scents drift,
and various gods gather round, bearing gifts.

The gods line His path, bowing low to His feet,
till He returns home, His day's labor complete.
The cowherds surround Him and sing out the praise
of He who wears dust many cow hooves have raised.

Lord Krishna, the lifter of Govardhan Hill,
envelops the cows and His friends with good will,
His beauty appears like the brightest of moons
so kindly arisen from Yaśodā's womb.

The full moon of love that comprises His face,
displayed as He walks with an elephant's grace,
has eyes that seem drunken with bliss as He speaks
offset by gold earrings on soft whitish cheeks.

When Krishna returns in His glorious way,
relieving the cows from the heat of the day,
we girls of Vṛndāvan are also relieved
for we nearly die every time that He leaves."

(iambic heptameter)

163) The women of Vṛndāvan sang and passed their time this way,
remembering Lord Krishna when He took the cows away.
By singing of His pastimes in this mood of ecstasy,
they filled the hours—and their hearts—with great festivity.

11

Akrura

Arishta

1) As Krishna was preparing for a *rāsa* dance at dusk,
a demon named Ariṣṭa, who was fearsome, cruel and brusque
descended on Vṛndāvan as a bull of massive size.
His hooves tore ruts in Mother Earth and left her terrorized.

2) With glaring eyes, his tail erect, Ariṣṭa roared and fussed.
His sharpened wildly swinging horns turned levees into dust.
Clouds gathered round his back hump—they mistook it for a peak—
and as he thundered here and there his stool and urine leaked.

3) Ariṣṭa's awful bellowing caused people's hearts to pound.
The pregnant cows and women all miscarried at the sound.
Domesticated animals fled quickly through the fields,
and everyone cried, "Krishna!" with their terror unconcealed.

4) On seeing the community distraught and taking flight,
Lord Krishna called, "Don't be afraid," and dared the bull to fight.
"You fool! You wicked rascal! What do you intend to do
when I am here to take the lives of miscreants like you?"

5) To further agitate the demon, Krishna slapped his arms,
then leaned upon a friend and faced the bull without alarm.
Ariṣṭa pawed the ground, enraged, and raised his tail so high
it passed his hump, attracting all the floating clouds nearby.

6) His head held low, his horns straight out, his rage intensified,
Ariṣṭa glared at Krishna from the rims of bloodshot eyes.
Stampeding straight at Krishna to destroy Him then and there,
the bull shot like the thunderbolt of Indra though the air.

7) The deadly bull closed in on Him, but Krishna didn't mind;
He seized Ariṣṭa's horns and threw him eighteen steps behind.
He looked to be an elephant who tosses on his back
a smaller, rival elephant who foolishly attacks.

8) Repulsed in such degrading terms, Ariṣṭa, with a snort,
stood up and shook his head and charged again in fierce retort.
Sweat pouring from his body, running fast and breathing hard,
Ariṣṭa pounced on Krishna with a reckless disregard.

9) Again Lord Krishna seized his horns and tossed the bull aside.
He thrashed Ariṣṭa like a rag and kicked his scruffy hide.
At last the Lord yanked out Ariṣṭa's horn up to the root
and beat him with it forcefully until he stilled the brute.

10) Ariṣṭa rolled his eyes, retched blood and felt his frame implode.
While passing stool and urine, he was dragged to death's abode.
The gods above, rejoicing with a loud, triumphant sound,
showed honor to Lord Krishna, tossing flowers to the ground.

11) The Lord, who is a festival within the *gopīs*' eyes,
went home with Rām to celebrate the demon bull's demise.
Lord Krishna is so versatile—as every *bhakta*[1] knows—
He's harder than a thunderbolt and softer than a rose.

[1]*A devotee of Krishna; one who practices bhakti-yoga.*

Kamsa's Scheme

12) In Mathurā soon afterwards, Śrī Nārada, the sage,
perceiving that Lord Krishna's life had entered a new stage,
decided to see Kaṁsa, who was evil and misled.
To expedite Lord Krishna's plans, the saintly caller said,

13, 14) "You've lost so many demons in Vṛndāvan recently.
Are you aware that Krishna is the son of Devakī?
Yes, Vasudev exchanged his son for Nanda's baby girl,
deceiving you, her parents and the balance of the world.

A prophecy has stated that your death will come about
from Devakī's eighth son. That son is Krishna. Have no doubt.
His older brother Rām is also Vausdeva's son.
These nephews of King Nanda killed your demons one by one."

15) On hearing this, King Kaṁsa's fury surged within his brain.
He snatched his sword and shouted, "Vasudeva shall be slain!"
But Nārada reminded him, "Think well before you act;
if you kill him, his sons will flee, but later they'll attack."

16) So Kaṁsa sent his soldiers to imprison Devakī,
along with Vasudeva, under tight security.
He thought, "I'll dispatch Keśī to make Krishna disappear,
but if he fails, these foolish boys will seek their parents here."

17-19) King Kaṁsa next assembled all his ministers and said,
"Dear Cāṇūra and Muṣṭika, this Krishna wants me dead.
You both are very famous for your wrestling skill and might;
If Krishna reaches Mathurā, you challenge Him to fight.

Erect a great arena. Let the people come and cheer.
Invite the foremost wrestlers. Make a festive atmosphere.
When Krishna and His brother are attracted to compete,
my elephant will trample Them beneath his massive feet!

Caturdasi is coming soon. Assemble beasts and *ghee*
and hold a Vedic sacrifice so Śiva will be pleased."

Completing his instructions, wicked Kaṁsa then decreed,
"Now bring Akrūra, foremost of our dynasty, to me."

20) Akrūra, highly learned and respected through the land,
appeared the perfect pawn for Kaṁsa's latest wicked plan.
"Akrūra!" he said gushingly, "You generous, brilliant man,
do me a little favor." Kaṁsa smiled and held his hand.

21-24) "As Indra turns to Viṣṇu for the most important tasks,
I need a man like you who can accomplish what I ask.
Proceed now to Vṛndāvan and return with Nanda's sons.
Here, take our finest chariot—the new and shiny one.

The gods, with help from Viṣṇu, sent these boys to murder me.
Bring them to visit Mathurā where, confidentially,
my elephant will trample them. And if they should survive,
my wrestlers will confront them in the ring and take their lives.

When they are dead their father, Vasudeva, shall be next.
And then I'll kill their relatives on this or that pretext.
And when I kill my father, Ugrasena, who shall mourn?
The Earth, my friend, shall then be mine, devoid of any thorns!

My friends-in-arms, Jarasāndha, Dvivida and the rest,
will help me kill remaining kings who fail to acquiesce.
And that's my plan. Now, bring those boys to savor their surprise.
Our city and a wrestling match await their childish eyes."

25, 26) As Kaṁsa chuckled wickedly, the grave Akrūra said,
"You've planned things quite precisely so that you'll come out ahead.
And yet, one must be steady throughout failure or success.
Despite our planning, fate alone determines what comes next.

An ordinary person plans and struggles and aspires,
despite the fact that fate intrudes and stifles his desires.
He gains, but then he loses and he suffers. Nonetheless,
I am your subject, duty-bound to honor your request."

27) The foolish Kaṁsa listened, but he could not understand
Akrūra had, discreetly, laid a curse upon his plans.
King Kaṁsa laughed, dismissed his staff, and strolled off on his own.
Akrūra, thinking deeply, left the palace and went home.

Kesi

(Meter: -|- -|- -|- -|)
28) When Keśī arrived in a huge horse's form
he ravaged through Vraj like a thunderous storm.
His snort scared the people. The hairs on his mane
split clouds and shook gods from their heavenly planes.

29) When Krishna saw everyone running in fright,
He challenged the demon to face Him and fight.
Although the beast happily met His request,
his lion-like roar left the Lord unimpressed.

30, 31) Enraged, the beast charged with his mouth open wide,
apparently trying to swallow the sky.
The Lord seized his legs with a marvelous knack
and spun him and threw him a hundred yards back.
The rogue lay unconscious and injured. But then,
he angrily stood and charged Krishna again.

32) Lord Krishna so gracefully parried and faked,
He looked like Garuḍa tormenting a snake.
When Keśī reached Krishna, his mouth open wide,
Lord Krishna propelled His left fist deep inside.

33) It looked like a snake who, on hearing a sound,
goes slithering in to a hole in the ground.
The fist of Lord Krishna took out Keśī's teeth
and made a sensation of terrible heat.
His arm then expanded beyond normal size,
quite like a bare belly that swells when one dies.

34) As Krishna's left fist enlarged deep in his throat,
The demon's breath stopped, and he started to choke.

With sweat and with kicks, rolling eyes in his head,
the demon passed stool, crumpled up and fell dead.

35) As Krishna withdrew His all-powerful arm,
The beast lay where he could no longer cause harm.
Without the least pride in his effortless coup,
Lord Krishna sniffed flowers the demigods threw.

Narada Meets Krishna

(Iambic heptameter)
36) My dear King Viṣṇurāta, after Keśī was erased,
sage Nārada found Krishna in a solitary place.
The sage saw Krishna's pastimes in Gokul were almost through,
and, eagerly, he praised the Lord and forecast what He'd do:

37-40) "Immeasurable Krishna! Perfect mystic! Lord Supreme,
residing in the cave of every heart, and yet unseen
as if You were the fire buried deep within all wood.
For You, all things are organized and fully understood.

You build, maintain, and break apart the planets and the stars.
Your wishes come about at once, no matter what they are.
And yet You've come in person to protect the godly souls
and sport by killing demons such as this gigantic foal.

I see that, in a day or two, you'll kill Mathurā's king,
his elephant and ministers and wrestlers in the ring.
And then, I see, You'll marry many worthy, loyal wives
while tracking down more demons and demolishing their lives.

I see You driving Arjuna in some colossal war,
destroying massive armies so they burden Earth no more.
I thank You, Krishna, perfect, pure and undeluded Lord,
for pastimes such as these that ease humanity's discord."

41) Completing his predictions in a reverential voice,
the foremost of the sages bowed to Krishna and rejoiced.

As Nārada departed, Krishna turned again to tend
His father's many cows with the assistance of His friends.

Vyomasura

42) The cows were grazing happily one day, as all the boys
were busy playing games like those that every child enjoys.
Some boys were thieves, some sheep, and others shepherds in their play.
The thieves would steal the sheep when their protectors looked away.

43) Observing this, Vyomāsura, a demon, hatched a ploy
and changed himself to look just like another cowherd boy.
By acting as a sheep-thief in the context of their play,
He snatched those boys dressed up as sheep and carried them away.

44) Then Vyoma hid his prisoners within a cave nearby
and sealed it with a boulder, cackling out a loud "Goodbye!"
When Vyoma next returned to take still other boys away,
he found himself arrested as if he were lion's prey.

45) This Vyoma's so-called cowherd play was just about to end,
for Krishna had been watching, and He seized the bogus friend.
Resuming his gigantic form, the demon rose to fight
but could not shake off Krishna, whose embrace was much too tight.

46) The gods above intently watched Lord Krishna's swift attack
as instantly the flawless Lord threw Vyoma on his back.
As Vyoma wriggled, struggled, pushed and strained to be released,
Lord Krishna choked his life out like a sacrificial beast.

47) Proceeding to the cave where many boys had been entrapped,
Lord Krishna set them free as all the gods in heaven clapped.
The boys and gods commended Krishna, singing out His praise,
as Krishna ambled home in the most nonchalant of ways.

Akrura's Prayers

48) While Nārada praised Krishna and Vyoma had been killed,
Akrūra drove a chariot to Vraj, as Kaṁsa willed.
While thinking about Krishna in an endless mood of bliss,
Akrūra sped along the road while pondering like this:

49-52) "What pious work have I completed? What austerity?
I can't recall what rituals or gifts of charity
are coming back to me today as this outstanding chance
to see Lord Krishna's lotus feet and gain His soothing glance.

Since I am a materialist, completely self-absorbed,
I think it is as difficult for me to see the Lord
as it would be for *śūdrās*, who are plain and lowly born,
to chant the Vedic mantras in the proper style and form.

But why should I berate myself? Yes, even hearts like mine,
adrift upon the brutal flood of unrelenting time,
can climb out of the torrent to the safety of the shore
by making some arrangement to behold the faultless Lord.

Today my sins have been erased! My life will be complete
when I behold the cherished sight of Krishna's lotus feet.
Indeed, King Kaṁsa favored me, dispatching me this way,
for seeing Krishna's toenails gleam shall make me unafraid.

(Meter: -|- -|- -|- -|)
53-62) Lord Krishna's soft feet and Lord Krishna Himself
are worshipped by gods and the goddess of wealth.
Adorned by the *gopīs* with red *kuṅkum* dust,
those feet carry Krishna from morning till dusk.

The deer on my right are an omen of grace
that soon I'll behold Krishna's beautiful face.
His soft curly hair frames His cheeks and His nose;
His smile sets His lotus-like dark eyes aglow.

Lord Krishna has come to deliver the Earth.
My eyes will embrace Him, perfecting my birth.
His presence dispels every puzzle and shame.
Though everyone feels Him, they don't know His name.

His birth and His actions eliminate sin,
and bless everybody, both women and men.
Descriptions of Krishna are joyfully said;
all others are wasted, like gems on the dead.

He lives in Vṛndāvan, tends cows and just plays,
as gods speak His teachings and sing out His praise.
Today when I come as His driver and guest,
the dawns of my lifetime will all have been blessed.

When I see Lord Krishna, and Balarām, too,
I'll bow to Them both and their whole retinue.
Though Kaṁsa has sent me, the all-knowing Lord
will see that I love Him and wish no discord.

Then Krishna will place His soft hand on my head.
His touch will remove every worry and dread.
That hand made the scent of the *gopīs* its own.
When Balī adored it, he gained Indra's throne.

Infallible Krishna will understand me;
though I must serve Kaṁsa, I'm His devotee.
I'll bow before Him, palms together in prayer.
His smile will relieve me of any despair.

When He sees that I am a kinsman and friend,
He'll hug me and all of my anguish will end.
He'll see how His presence has made me inspired,
and then, like a wish-tree,[2] He'll fill my desires.

[2]*Trees in the spiritual world that give whatever is asked.*

And as I am standing, my head and hands bowed,
Lord Balarām, too, will emerge from the crowd.
He'll greet me with honor, and when we're alone
He'll ask about schemes Kaṁsa dreaṁs from his throne."

Meeting the Vrajavasis

(iambic heptameter)
63) Akrūra, rapt in Krishna, barely noticing the road,
at sunset reached Gokula, his beloved Lord's abode.
"Why, those are Krishna's footprints," said Akrūra as he parked,
"distinguished by a lotus bloom and other well-known marks."

64) The feet that all the gods adore indeed had blessed that ground.
Akrūra, teary-eyed, his hairs on end, at once jumped down
and rolled amid the dust that had been touched by Krishna's feet.
He lost all fear of Kaṁsa's wrath and felt his life complete.

65) Proceeding on as quickly as his chariot allowed,
Akrūra saw Lord Krishna, who had finished tending cows.
Lord Krishna's skin was bluish-black and dressed with yellow silk.
Lord Balarām was with Him, dressed in blue with skin like milk.

66) The brothers strolled like elephants, displaying mighty arms,
Their lovely faces graced with smiles of endless warmth and charm.
They marked the grazing pastures with impressions from Their feet
of goads for steering elephants, festoons and lightning streaks.

67) These two primeval Deities, descended among men,
were freshly bathed and garlanded and decked with precious gems.
They seemed to be two mountains, one of silver laced with white,
the other made from emeralds, effulgent, rich and bright.

68) Akrūra, overwhelmed with love, fell down as if a rod.
His speech impaired and hair on end, in ecstasy he sobbed.
When Krishna recognized Akrūra, feeling very pleased,
He raised him and embraced him as a faithful devotee.

69) Lord Balarām then grasped Akrūra's folded, prayerful hands
and brought him to His residence to learn of Kaṁsa's plans.
He made Akrūra comfortable, asked about his trip,
massaged his feet and brought hot, honeyed milk for him to sip.

70) Both Balarām and Krishna served Akrūra tasty foods
and gave to him a first-rate cow in reverent attitude.
They brought him after-dinner herbs, fresh garlands and the rest,
in perfect Vedic custom for receiving honored guests.

71, 72) Akrūra was quite pleased by his supremely gracious hosts
and listened to the inquiries the gentle Nanda posed:
"My dear Akrūra, how can you survive with Kaṁsa there?
You seem just like a lamb who's trapped within a butcher's care.

That cruel, selfish Kaṁsa snatched his sister's infant sons,
and, right before their mother's eyes, destroyed them, one by one.
Why should we even ask about your health or your well-being
when you live in the realm of such a ruthless, heartless king?"

73) When he heard Nanda speak in this most candid, trusting way,
Akrūra's deep exhaustion from his journey went away.

74) King Nanda and his sons first fed their uninvited guest
then gently asked Akrūra to lay down and take some rest.
When they stepped out to take their meals, Akrūra sat in bed,
amazed at how the Lord complied with every prayer he'd said.

75) What wish could ever go beyond the Lord's capacity,
especially when cherished by a spotless devotee?
A devotee's desire differs from a common whim;
such wishes are for Krishna and for service unto Him.

76-78) Lord Krishna soon returned to ask Akrūra for some news.
He said, "Beloved uncle, may good fortune come to you.
I hope your trip was pleasant and you didn't strain yourself.
Are all My friends in Mathurā content and in good health?
Alas, as long as Kaṁsa lives, what good news can there be?
He's nothing but a cancer on our royal dynasty.

My parents—how they've struggled since the day that they were wed.
They now are both in prison and their seven children dead.
Because of Me—their son, who, prophets said, would kill the king—
my parents have been shackled by incessant suffering.
At least I have the pleasure of your company today.
Please tell Me, dear Akrūra, what has brought you all this way?"

79) Akrūra said, "When Nārada disclosed the secret fact
that you are Vasudeva's son, King Kaṁsa chose to act.
He sent me to convey you to Mathurā right away
for he has plots to murder you in several different ways."

80) On hearing this Lord Krishna (and His brother, who stood by),
guffawed and giggled heartily till tears filled up Their eyes.
When Nanda came and heard all that Akrūra had explained,
he called the village constable who went out and proclaimed,

81) "O cowherd men, now listen to King Nanda's new decree.
The time has come to pay our taxes. Gather all your *ghee*.
Tomorrow we shall travel to Mathurā, give our tithe,
and watch some entertainment that King Kaṁsa shall provide."

The Gopis Stunned

82) The cowherd men were pleased and thrilled, for, coming from small towns,
they loved to see Mathurā's sights and hear its bustling sounds.
Some *gopīs*, on the other hand, quite breathless from distress,
showed pallid, ill complexions amid drooping braids and dress.

83) Some other *gopīs*, realizing that Krishna would depart,
withdrew themselves like *yogīs*, holding Krishna in their hearts.
Still others thought of Krishna's charming speeches, smiles and play.
Remembering His lovely words, they fainted dead away.

84) Would Krishna leave them, even for the briefest span of time?
The *gopīs* could not grasp this most unwelcome paradigm.
They came together, spoke of Krishna, shared their thoughts and fears,
and sang to one another as they shed incessant tears:

(Meter: -|- -|- -|- -|)
85-90) O Providence, you have a merciless heart!
You put friends together and tear them apart.
You gave us our Krishna, His charms and His smiles;
now you take Him back like a petulant child.

You've come as "Akrūra,"[3] but you are so cruel,
you take back your gift like a dishonest fool.
We gambled our futures to join Him in dance,
and now Krishna won't even give us a glance.
[3]*Akrūra means, "One who is not cruel."*

The Mathurā girls soon will greet the sun's rise
with tastes of the nectar that pours from His eyes.
What use will He have for some bumpkins like us
when their honeyed words turn His pledges to dust?

As Krishna rides by, crowds will shout with delight,
and all Mathurā will rejoice with the sight.
This so-called 'Akrūra' won't care who survives
as he chauffeurs Krishna and ruins our lives.

Our elders just watch callous Krishna depart.
Oh, fate! All the men follow Him in their carts.
Let's stop Him ourselves! We have nothing to lose;
our chaste reputations are already through.

We've danced with our Krishna, who smiled with such love
and charmed us with glances, kind words and warm hugs.
We'll die not to see Him at dusk with the cows
or hear His sweet flute—look, He's leaving us now!"

(iambic heptameter)
91) And then the *gopīs* all broke down and cried in great despair,
"Govinda! Damodar! Mukunda!" Wailing filled the air.
Akrūra drove off anyway with both of Nanda's sons.
The cowherd men left too, in carts with milk goods by the ton.

92) The *gopīs* walked behind the fleet and caught Lord Krishna's eye.
They stopped and stared in hopes He'd turn, at least to say goodbye.
When Krishna saw the broken-hearted *gopīs* feeling spurned,
He sent a messenger who said, "He swears that He'll return."

93) The *gopīs* stood as still as figures painted on a wall.
They watched until the chariot could not be seen at all.
Convinced their Lord would not return, they sadly turned away
and started chanting Krishna's pastimes every night and day.

To Mathura

94) Akrūra and the brothers rode as swiftly as the wind.
Arriving at the Yamunā, which washes off all sins,
Akrūra parked the chariot within a grove nearby.
Both Balarām and Krishna drank and felt quite satisfied.

95) Since pious *brāhmans* like Akrūra take three baths a day,
the boys stayed in the chariot and lingered while he bathed.
Immersed in the clear water, chanting prayers with half-closed eyes,
at once Akrūra saw the boys. He thought, in great surprise,

96) "Now, how did my two passengers get here so suddenly?
They must have left the chariot to swim nearby with me."
Akrūra turned and saw the boys still seated, calm and cool.
He turned again and, squinting, looked more deeply in the pool.

97) This time he saw Ananta Śeṣa circled by a throng
of gods and demons, palms together, praising Him in song.
That thousand-headed Lord of snakes, whose skin was snowy white,
resembled a great mountain range with peaks of dazzling height.

98) Upon the giant serpent's lap, Lord Viṣṇu lay at ease.
His dark-blue body had four arms; His reddish eyes looked pleased.
With facial features finely formed and large and lovely limbs,
He showed the transcendental form described in Vedic hymns.

99) His neck was like a conch shell graced with three successive lines.
His monsoon skin was draped in yellow silk that brightly shined.
Between Lord Viṣṇu's massive chest and navel, dark and deep,
His chiseled stomach, sharply ridged, looked like a banyan leaf.

100) His toenails glowed like petals from effulgent lotus blooms.
His two right hands held conch and lotus, ready to give boons.
His two left hands held disk and mace so demons, too, were blessed.
The *śrīvatsa* mark and Kaustubha gem adorned His chest.

101) Around Lord Viṣṇu, faithful servants prayed with all their hearts.
The Earth, *tulasī* plants and other pious souls took part.
His knowledge, wealth, renunciation, beauty, strength and fame,
personified as goddesses, sang out His holy name.

102) To see Lord Viṣṇu so directly brought Akrūra bliss
that overwhelmed his heart with lucid, loving consciousness
and made his eyes turn tearful as it raised his body's hairs.
Akrūra joined his palms, bowed low, and spoke these thoughtful prayers:

103-116) "My Lord, when You appear within the universal void,
Your navel sprouts a lotus where Brahmā is then deployed.
Assembling all the energies that You, my Lord, supply,
He engineers the universe as You have specified.

This universe of matter, though, where You cannot be found,
keeps every soul—even Brahmā—perpetually bound.
Philosophers, ascetics, priests and others all may try,
but devotees alone know You, for they are purified.

When others worship demigods like Śiva and the rest,
they mean to worship You but, somehow, falter and digress.
And yet, as every river moves from mountain range to sea,
such people, by Your kindness, come to You eventually.

The modes of nature—goodness, passion, darkness—ebb and flow
throughout creation, seizing every creature, high and low.
Thus every *deva,* man and beast, bewitched and stupefied,
enjoys and grieves, as You perceive with Your unbiased eye.

Your endless strength and vital air are found within the wind;
The four directions are Your hearing, mighty gods Your limbs;
The fire is Your face, the Earth Your feet, the sun Your eye;
The ocean is Your abdomen; Your navel is the sky.

The trees are hairs upon Your body, clouds Your head of hair.
Your nails and bones are mountain peaks that tower in the air.
Your head itself is heaven, day and night Your blinking eyes,
and semen from Your genitals the rainfall from the skies.

As fish live in the sea or tiny bugs reside in fruit,
the worlds of gods and men alike originate in You.
To end the pain of pious souls who love to chant Your praise,
You come Yourself so willingly in countless different ways:

I pray to You as Matsya, Lord of devastation's seas.
I pray to You as Hayagrīva, killer of the beasts.
I pray to You as Kūrma, holding mountains on Your shell,
and also as Varaha, who supported Earth itself.

You come as Narasiṁha to relieve Your servant's fear.
As Vāmana You step across the universal sphere.
As Lord Paraṣaurām, You slay the fallen royal class.
As Rāma You slay Rāvaṇa, whose strength was unsurpassed.

I bow to You as Buddha, who bewilders foolish men.
I bow to You as Kālkī, bringing Kali-yuga's end.
Lord Vāsudeva, of the Yadus, You are surely best.
Lord Saṇkarṣan, Pradyumna, Aniruddha: my respects.

Dear Lord, in this world every soul becomes illusion's serf
and walks the path of 'pleasure' that concludes in death and birth.
My Lord, I too believe in much that is not as it seems;
my precious family, wealth and fame are simply fleeting dreams.

Mistaking body for the soul and misery for joy,
I've traded endless love of God for things that time destroys.
I'm just a fool who leaves behind a lush, refreshing lake
to chase a desert-born mirage and die from his mistake.

So weak is my intelligence it cannot curb my mind,
the slave of every evil urge my shameless senses find.
Although I can't approach You till my foolishness has ceased,
I pray to think of You and serve Your spotless devotees.

All energy and consciousness, My Lord, arise from You.
Why, even nature cannot change Your body's innate truth.
O Lord of mind and senses, whom all beings live within,
protect me, please! I bow to you again and yet again!"

12

In Mathura

Reaching the City

1) Akrūra spoke with eloquence, yet even as he prayed,
Lord Viṣṇu disappeared just like an actor quits the stage.
Akrūra left the water, packed his gear and shook his head,
and as he reached the chariot Lord Krishna beamed and said,

2) "Have you observed some marvel? The expression on your face
suggests you saw a miracle beside your bathing place."
Replied Akrūra, "All on Earth and heaven and between
exists in You. On seeing You, what sight have I *not* seen?"

3) At that, Akrūra shook the reins, sped off without delay,
and brought the boys to Mathurā before the end of day.
As they passed towns en route Akrūra saw the people stare,
for Balarām and Krishna were sublime beyond compare.

4) The cowherd men and Nanda, who had kept a steady pace,
awaited Krishna's chariot outside the city gates.
The brothers joined the others, but before they moved ahead,
Lord Krishna took Akrūra by the hand and, smiling, said,

5) "Akrūra, take the chariot, go home and spend the night.
Our group will now relax a while and tour the city sights."
Akrūra gently shook his head and said, "That isn't fair.
You never, Lord, abandon Your devotee anywhere.

6) Instead, please bring Your entourage and grace my humble home.
My dwelling, food and family belong to You alone.
Though I'm a *pukka* householder attached to pious deeds,
my rituals are incomplete. Your feet are all I need.

7) King Balī bathed Your lotus feet, acquiring strength and fame,
and in the end attained You in Your own divine domain.
That footwash flowed, as Ganges water, straight to Śiva's hair
and freed the sons of Sagara from hell and great despair."

8) Akrūra prayed for Him to stay, but Krishna gently said,
"I'll come to you when I am through and Kaṁsa's finally dead."
With heavy heart, Akrūra went to Kaṁsa all alone,
reported that the boys had come and lumbered to his home.

9) Lord Krishna, meanwhile, entered Mathurā with all His friends.
They saw a vast and splendid town that seemed to have no end.
Its gates and doors were cut from crystal edged with shining gold.
The brass and copper granaries held all that they could hold.

10) The major roadways, freshly cleansed, festooned with blooms and rice,
had intersections trimmed in gold like those of paradise.
The public parks and gardens were expansive and serene,
while mansions featured pleasure groves where no one could be seen.

11) The common houses, dressed with coral, pearls and precious stones,
had latticework where singing doves and peacocks made their homes.
Each house was graced with water pots on both sides of its doors,
adorned with yogurt, mango leaves, cool sandal paste and more.

12) The womenfolk of Mathurā, who knew of Nanda's son,
at once prepared to see Him upon hearing He had come.
They set aside their bathing, meals or rest to see Him first,
not noticing that, due to haste, their dresses were reversed.

13) Some ladies wore one earring, having left behind its mate,
while others made up one eye and ran off to not be late.
When they saw Krishna, strolling like an elephant with glee,
they held Him in their hearts and fell apart in ecstasy.

14) Their faces flushed, the ladies climbed their roofs and showered flowers.
They said, "Those lucky *gopīs* get to see these boys for hours!"
They watched the priests receive the Lord with garlands, curd and grains,
and other worship-items Vedic etiquette maintains.

Krishna Gets Dressed

15) The Lord then saw a laundryman and, glancing at His dress,
said, "Give us all fresh garments and you surely will be blessed."
The laundryman had Kaṁsa's clothes and sternly shook his head.
He eyed the self-sufficient Lord and arrogantly said,

16) "Impertinent, uncultured boys! You live out in the trees,
yet you request the King's possessions – royal clothes, like these?
You fools! Go home to village life if you wish to survive.
King Kaṁsa dislikes beggars and will rarely spare their lives!"

17) Lord Krishna was dissatisfied with what the man had said,
and, with a simple finger-flick, removed his haughty head.
The man's assistants dropped their bags and scurried all around
as Krishna and His friends picked fine new clothing from the ground.

18) A weaver came to Krishna and His brother, saw Their clothes,
and trimmed and decorated them with ornaments and bows.
The boys soon looked like elephants adorned for a parade,
so Krishna blessed the weaver to be strong and unafraid.

19) The two Lords then proceeded to a garland-maker's home.
That humble man, Sudāma, welcomed them, and, bowing low,
he gave them seats and washed their feet and offered pleasant gifts.
He said, "My home and family are blessed by guests like this!

20) The sages, gods and forefathers are surely pleased with me.
You two Lords of the universe will bring prosperity

upon our realm. I'm overwhelmed! With Your unbiased view,
You're fair to all but still recall us souls who worship You.

21) Please order me, my Master. Is there something I can do?
What blessing could be greater than a service done for You?
Fresh flowers are the trade on which my family depends;
please, take our finest garlands for Yourselves and all Your friends."

22) Sudāma proved to be a servant worthy of the task;
he satisfied his Lord before his Lord could even ask.
His garlands made Lord Krishna and Lord Balarām inspired
to give Sudāma any benediction he desired.

23) Sudāma said, "Devotion to Your feet is my request,
with friendship to devoted souls and mercy for the rest."
Lord Krishna gladly gave all this and other boons as well.
Sudāma bowed and said goodbye, his troubles all dispelled.

24) As Krishna walked the road He saw a woman, hunched and bowed.
Her tray of fragrant ointments made her stand out from the crowd.
"O lovely lady," Krishna asked, "who is this ointment for?
Place some of it on us and you'll be happy evermore."

25, 26) The woman, named Kubjā, looked up, smiled prettily and said,
"I made this for King Kaṁsa—why don't You take it instead."
Attracted by Lord Krishna's sweetness, lovely smiles and charm,
Kubjā spread ointment generously across His face and arms.
Lord Krishna's monsoon-bluish skin took on a yellow hue.
The ointment then turned Balarām's white skin a pleasant blue.

27) The brothers were delighted, and to show His gratitude,
Lord Krishna touched this sweet-faced hunchbacked girl of generous mood.
He placed His feet upon her toes. Then, fingers to her chin,
Lord Krishna raised His hands and made her straight as any pin.
By Krishna's touch, Kubjā became a most attractive girl,
her limbs and breasts made lovely as her twisted back unfurled.

28) Kubjā, now an appealing beauty, pinched Lord Krishna's cloth.
She blinked and smiled and said to Him, her voice abruptly soft,

"O hero, come to my house. I can't bear to leave You here.
O best of males, be kind and make my tensions disappear."

29) Lord Krishna glanced at Balarām and all His cowherd friends.
He laughed and said, "Your house, indeed, is good for homeless men.
A tourist such as me can find protection there in you.
Yes, surely I shall visit when My duties here are through."

30) Continuing along the road, accepting many gifts,
Lord Krishna touched the ladies' hearts and set their minds adrift.
Their bangles, braids and clothing slackened. Standing, stunned and still,
they seemed to turn to painted forms as Cupid worked his will.

Preparing for the Festival

31) The boys then heard the festival tomorrow would include
the worship of a sacred bow of striking magnitude.
They entered the arena where the bow was being viewed.
A squad of guards surrounded it, but Krishna walked right through.

32) To everyone's astonishment, Lord Krishna raised the bow.
He pulled the heavy weapon's string as far as it would go
and snapped it as an elephant might break a sugar cane.
A booming 'CRACK' reached Kaṁsa's palace, rattling his brain.

33) Enraged, the guards cried, "Kill him! Kill him!" Circling the boys,
they closed on them forebodingly with swords and shields deployed.
Then Krishna picked up half the bow and Balarām the other,
and all of Kaṁsa's soldiers there were routed by the brothers.

34) Lord Krishna and His friends strolled out the main arena gates
and carried on their tour before the hour grew too late.
The citizens thought gods had come and marveled at the sight.
At last the boys returned to Nanda's camp to spend the night.

35) The *gopīs* had predicted Mathurā would soon enjoy
a host of benedictions from Yaśodā's charming boy.
The residents indeed saw Krishna's opulence themselves,
a treasure even sought by goddess Lakṣmī, queen of wealth.

36) Lord Krishna and His entourage ate rice and milk and said
goodnight to all their fathers. Then they calmly went to bed.
King Kaṁsa, meanwhile, knowing Krishna's actions, could not find
a moment's rest, for evil omens paralyzed his mind.

37) He could not see his footprints; all the stars appeared in twos.
He could not hear his breath; his shadow showed a hole right through.
He looked at his reflection but his head, somehow, was gone.
With dreams of ghosts and poison, Kaṁsa tossed and turned till dawn.

38) At last King Kaṁsa rose to make arrangements for the day.
He ordered the arena dressed in lively, festive ways.
The crowds sat in the galleries, chief guests in special seats,
and Kaṁsa on the dais—though his heart kept skipping beats.

39) The royal band played loudly with a stirring, martial sound
as muscled wrestlers, finely dressed, marched in and looked around.
Muṣṭika, Cāṇūra and others sat on wrestling mats
as Nanda and the lesser rulers paid their royal tax.

40) King Kaṁsa said, "Dear Nanda, you're my leading village chief.
Did you not visit me because your sons have caused me grief?
Don't worry. Please, be seated." Nanda bowed and glanced around,
and noticed his precocious sons were nowhere to be found.

41) Lord Krishna heard the drumming from the festival and said,
"The time has come for justice to descend on Kaṁsa's head.
We showed our power harmlessly by fracturing his bow,
and still this stubborn tyrant will not let our parents go."

Kuvalayapida

42) As Krishna reached the stadium, intent on Kaṁsa's fate,
the elephant Kuvalayāpīḍa stood in the gate.
His driver glared at Krishna as if wishing He were dead.
The Lord made tight His belt, tied back His hair, looked up and said,

43) "O driver! Driver! Move aside at once and let us pass,
or else today your elephant and you shall breathe your last."

The driver became furious and, riding on its back,
he spurred the angry elephant to rear up and attack.

44) Enraged, the beast charged Krishna, stomping feet as large as kegs.
The Lord pushed off its trunk and slipped from view behind its legs.
That fearsome trunk traced Krishna's scent and seized Him with its tip.
Quite forcefully the Lord struck back and broke its deadly grip.

45) Lord Krishna snatched the monster's tail and, with a playful shake,
He dragged it fifty yards just like Garuḍa drags a snake.
The elephant squirmed left and right. As Krishna pulled away,
His friends recalled Him pulling calves like this in childhood play.

46) The Lord then stopped, ran back and slapped the monster's upper lip.
The monster tried to chase the agile Lord until it tripped.
Returning to its feet, the beast saw Krishna playing dead.
It tried to gore Him with its tusk but stuck the earth instead.

47) The angry Kuvalayāpīḍa raged and raised a din.
The driver, goading frantically, cried, "Charge him once again!"
The livid elephant attacked. Lord Krishna, legs astride,
thought, "I have killed so many beasts," and tossed it on its side.

48) Then, pouncing on the monster, Krishna yanked its tusk about
and used a final, graceful tug to pull the ivory out.
He swung it, struck the driver and smashed in the monster's head
and moments later both of them were obviously dead.

49) Positioning the tusk upon His shoulder, Krishna turned
and entered the arena, to the King's extreme concern.
With drops of blood and perspiration shining on His skin
Lord Krishna seemed quite beautiful as He came strolling in.

Chanura and Mushtika

50, 51) The wrestlers saw this Krishna as a lightning bolt from hell;
the local women saw Him as the god of love himself;
the local men thought Krishna the ideal of every male;
malicious kings saw reckoning and felt their faces pale.

The cowherds saw a relative; His parents saw their child;
the *yogīs* felt their difficult austerities worthwhile;
the fools saw an incompetent; the Vṛṣṇis saw their Lord;
King Kaṁsa saw the god of death and fumbled for his sword.

52) Effulgent in Their garlands, dress and fearless attitude,
Lord Krishna and His brother overwhelmed the multitude.
Their faces flushed, the crowd grew hushed and opened their eyes wide
to drink the lovely vision—but they still weren't satisfied.

53) They seemed to want to lick the Lord and understand His taste,
inhale His pleasing fragrance and enjoy His warm embrace.
Spontaneously, everyone told friends what had occurred—
the elephant, the giant bow, and everything they'd heard.

54, 55) "He's just a boy, but Krishna must be God!" the people said.
"Though Vasudev's His father, Nanda brought Him up instead.
While hidden in Vṛndāvan He has slaughtered fiends galore,
like Pūtanā, Tṛṇāvarta, Keśī and many more.
He saved the cows and cowherds from a snake,
a giant snake and thunderbolts from Indra, who admitted his mistake.
His elder brother Balarām, who's equally sublime,
shall help Him raise the Yadu clan to prominence, in time."

56, 57) King Kaṁsa's strongest wrestler, named Cāṇūra, couldn't bear
to hear such praise of Krishna, so he stood up and declared:
"You two are skillful wrestlers and renowned for mighty feats.
King Kaṁsa is aware of this and called you to compete.
You wrestle in the forest while attending to your calves,
and this explains the skill that You both obviously have.
The King embodies everyone; obey him and be blessed,
for, otherwise, how shall your fame and fortune manifest?"

58) Lord Krishna liked to wrestle, so He graciously replied,
"You're right. We forest-dwellers must make Kaṁsa satisfied.
But boys like us should challenge boys of equal rank and place
if this affair is to be fair and spared from sheer disgrace."

59, 60) Cāṇūra said, "You're not a child who plays the whole day long
and neither is Your brother—You're the strongest of the strong.
For, after all, if You recall, You just destroyed a beast
whose strength was worth another thousand elephants, at least!
You both should therefore wrestle with the best of Kaṁsa's men.
What possibly could be unfair about it? Let's begin.
Muṣṭika and your brother have the same ability,
and, Krishna, there is no one to match You—except for me."

61) Cāṇūra's challenge stirred the boys, and, quickly, they complied.
On climbing in the ring to face what looked like suicide,
each boy locked hands with His opponent, stared them in the eyes,
and matched the potent thrusts and shoves of men five times Their size.

62) The boys and men fought vigorously, eager for success.
Their fists struck fists and knees struck knees and chests crashed into chests.
In turn, each foe knocked down the other, dragged him all around,
and used his mighty arms to crush and pin him to the ground.

63) One fighter lifted his opponent high above his head,
and strained his arms so much he seemed to hurt himself instead.
Cāṇūra and Muṣṭika thought the boys were on the run,
but Balarām and Krishna were, in fact, just having fun.

64-69) However, all the women present, gathering to speak,
considered the event unfair, a match of strong and weak.
Compassion for the boys and an increasing sense of dread
aroused their deep anxiety. Among themselves they said,

"Well, Kaṁsa may enjoy this mismatch. What about the rest?
Will all these men just watch these boys get hurt? I'm not impressed.
Two mountain-sized professionals with limbs like lightning bolts
against two tender boys? A moral person should revolt."

"Morality? There's not a drop in anybody here.
Why, we should simply walk away from such an atmosphere.
Refined and decent people never join with the uncouth,
but if they do by accident, they'll stand and speak the truth."

"See how the face of Krishna, as He darts around His foe,
looks like a lotus kissed with dew when He's perspiring so.
And look at Balarām! His eyes are copper-red with rage.
And still He laughs and bends in half a man four times His age."

"How pious is Vṛndāvan, where the Lord, disguised like this,
enjoys so many pastimes with His friends in constant bliss.
Both Sivaji and Lakṣmī worship these exalted boys—
but here they meet two thugs our useless government employs."

"As they churn milk, thresh wheat, tend cows, cook dinner, nurse or mend,
the women of Vṛndāvan sing of Krishna without end.
How fortunate they are to see Lord Krishna come and go!
He smiles in his kindhearted style, and all their voices choke."

70) The women's words reached Vasudev and Devakī in jail,
and both of Krishna's parents thought their hearts about to fail.
Aware of their anxiety, Lord Krishna finally chose
to expedite the crooked fight and bring it to a close.

71) As Balarām and Muṣṭika fought on, Cāṇūra sensed
his arms and legs were weakening. The fight was too intense.
As Krishna's blows rained down on him like lightning from the sky,
Cāṇūra gathered all his strength to make a final try.

72) With hawk-like speed Cāṇūra struck the Lord with fearsome power,
as one might strike an elephant with nothing more than flowers.
Then Krishna grabbed Cāṇūra's arms and, swinging him around,
dispatched him like a giant statue crashing to the ground.

73) Muṣṭika, meanwhile, hurled his iron fist at Balarām,
who took the blow without a flinch, then slapped him with His palm.
The demon trembled, threw up blood and, knees both caving in,
fell toppling to the ground as if a tree in heavy wind.

74) Another fighter, Kuśa, rose to take Muṣṭika's place.
Lord Balarām dispatched him with a left fist to the face.
Two more—Śala and Tośala—rushed in on his behalf,
but Krishna deftly kicked their heads and tore them both in half.

75) On seeing this, the other wrestlers jumped up in surprise
and ran from Kaṁsa's grand arena just to save their lives.
The cowherd boys joined Balarām and Krishna dancing round,
and as the band played joyful songs, they reveled in the sound.

The Death of Kamsa

76) The audience rejoiced at this extraordinary feat.
"Outstanding work! Outstanding!" cried exalted saints and priests.
King Kaṁsa, on the other hand, his plots all nullified,
said, "Stop the music!" Standing tall, he obstinately cried,

77, 78) "These wicked sons of Vasudev do not deserve to stay.
My soldiers! Quickly! Arm yourselves and drive them far away.
And as for all these cowherd yokels, confiscate their grains.
Impound their carts and tie that foolish Nanda up in chains.
Destroy that wretched Vasudev. His fate is overdue.
And kill my father Urgrasen and all his cohorts, too.
These relatives are traitors who oppose my every move.
Now go with care. Don't stand and stare! We have no time to lose!"

79) While Kaṁsa raved audaciously, Lord Krishna, quite enraged,
ran over and jumped high upon the monarch's royal stage.
As Krishna marched across the stage like death personified,
King Kaṁsa quickly drew the sword that dangled from his side.

80) Prepared to sever Krishna's head, revulsion in his eye,
King Kaṁsa darted sideways like a falcon in the sky.
But Krishna quickly seized the king, despite his thrusts and fakes,
as easily as Garuḍa might pounce on deadly snakes.

81) Lord Krishna grabbed King Kaṁsa's tresses, knocked away his crown,
and tossed him to the wrestling mats still spread across the ground.
He threw Himself on Kaṁsa and, while straddling his chest,
repeatedly struck Kaṁsa till his life force acquiesced.

82) The people, watching breathlessly, thought Kaṁsa was knocked out,
so Krishna dragged the demon's corpse to vanquish any doubt.

He seemed to be a lion pulling prey across the ground.
The crowd made loud, astonished cries that filled the sky with sound.

83) At meals, at work, at rest—in fact, with every living breath,
King Kaṁsa had seen Krishna, and His razor disc of death.
His meditation earned a boon that rarely fate affords:
eternal liberation in a body like the Lord's.

84) The monarch's younger brothers, eight in all, their jaws gone slack,
became enraged and rushed the Lord in foolhardy attack.
Resembling a lion king at play with several cubs,
Lord Balarām dispatched them with a few blows from His club.
The gods so much enjoyed this unexpected circumstance
they showered flowers, praising Krishna, as their spouses danced.

85) The wives of Kaṁsa and his brothers, shocked and paralyzed,
then struck their heads and claimed their dead as tears poured from their eyes.
Embracing their dead husbands on a hero's final bed,
the widows grieved aloud and, through their wails and sobbing, said,

86-88) "O, Masters! Dear ones! Who shall be as kind to us as you?
Your death is also our death, and your homes' and children's, too.
Now Mathurā has lost its beauty. Ours is gone as well.
The happiness and fortune of our past have gone to hell.

When you have been so violent to those you should protect,
what other fate beyond your own today could you expect?
Lord Krishna should be honored, but you showed Him such contempt,
your lives have ended this way despite all your great attempts."
The Lord consoled the widows with some kindly words and then
arranged, on site, the proper rites for funerals to begin.

Reunion

89) Next, Balarām and Krishna set Their tortured parents free,
displaying great respect by bowing down on hands and knees.
Now, Vasudev and Devakī saw past their sons' facade;
they stood with folded palms and could not face embracing God.

90) Since Vasudev and Devakī held back affinity
for their beloved Krishna and His clear divinity,
the Lord invoked his power of illusion to restore
the deep parental love for Him the two had known before.

91-94) "My dearest loving parents," said the Lord respectfully,
"both Balarām and I have caused you such anxiety.
Deprived by fate, we could not spend our childhood in your home
enjoying all the loving care you surely would have shown.

The parents give the body, which accommodates the soul,
and keep this precious vehicle protected, strong and whole.
Though he return a lifetime's service to the partnership,
what man could ever compensate his parents for their gift?

A healthy, wealthy son whose parents starve must realize
the guards of hell will force-feed him his body when he dies.
A man of means who fails to care for parents, guru, wife
or children is a dead man who pretends to harbor life.

For many years we failed to honor both of you because
King Kaṁsa always frightened us and passed unfriendly laws.
Forgive us, Father, Mother, please. King Kaṁsa took away
our freedom to express the love we felt for you each day."

95) To hear their darling Krishna making statements such as these
made Vasudev and Devakī choke up and feel quite pleased.
Parental love for Krishna flooded both their eyes with tears,
and, speechless, they embraced the sons they'd missed for all these years.

96) Lord Krishna gave the throne of Mathurā to Ugrasen.
"We're cursed to never take this throne ourselves," the Lord explained.
"But have no fear; we'll both stay here and join your entourage.
What other kings shall challenge you, O King. Indeed, what gods?"

97) Lord Krishna welcomed family members back from long exile.
They'd fled in fear of Kaṁsa, but could now be reconciled
with friends and loved ones they had left behind some years before.
Appreciating Krishna, they rejoiced at home once more.

98) Protected by Lord Krishna, all these pious refugees
felt safe and pleased in Mathurā with Krishna's devotees.
And watching Krishna smile each day, which they would do at length,
made even elder refugees feel young and full of strength.

99, 100) When Krishna and His brother had seen every need addressed,
they came before King Nanda, hugged him tightly and expressed,
"O Father, you and Yaśodā have cared for us so well,
you loved us more completely than you even loved yourselves.

When parents who give birth cannot fulfill their children's needs,
adoptive parents such as you are true parents indeed.
Return now to Vṛndāvan, Father. We shall see you when
we've given some relief here to our long-tormented friends."

101) Consoling Nanda and his men, Lord Krishna then bestowed
a host of gifts on them, including jewels, tools and clothes.
Lord Krishna's speech made Nanda weep and left him overwhelmed.
He hugged his sons again and, slowly, went back to his realm.

102) Since Vasudev, at last, could do the things he'd never done,
he called for priests to now complete the rites for both his sons.
The boys received their *gāyatrīs,*[1] a person's second birth,
and Vasudev gave everyone donations of great worth.

[1]*An ancient mantra that priests recite daily.*

103) He gave out costly ornaments, like famous kings of old,
along with many cows and calves adorned with cloth and gold.
Released from Kaṁsa's prison, he gave gifts of every kind.
(When both his sons were born he'd done the same thing in his mind).

104) Both Balarām and Krishna seemed like good, submissive boys,
completing all these rituals with gravity and poise.
Approaching Garga Muni, honored guru of their peers,
they vowed to stay as celibates throughout their student years.

At Sandipani's School

105) Although they are the origin of everything that's known,
the Lords next chose to go to school some distance from their home
with Sāndīpani Muni in the town of Avantī.
When they arrived, they chose to hide their true identities.

106-112) The two new students bowed before their teacher with respect
and quickly learned the *Vedas* and the corollary texts.
They learned of warfare, law and philosophical debate;
They learned when they should fight, sit tight, or just accommodate.

They learned both arts and sciences—in total, sixty-four:
Singing; music; dancing; drama; drawing on the floor;
painting (self and canvas); laying floors with ornaments;
gardening and dressing up in earrings, jewels and scents.

Spreading bedsheets; ringing pots of water; making wreaths;
mixing colors; wearing helmets; dressing; tinting teeth;
sleight-of-hand; drink-making; masquerading; jugglery;
weaving; sewing; cooking; playing lute and puppetry.

Writing and resolving puzzles; memorizing verse;
book-reciting; puzzlecraft; to act and to rehearse;
solving enigmatic statements; making bows and shafts;
spinning with a spindle; woodwork; jewel-testing crafts;

Architecture; mineralogy; the use of herbs;
metallurgy; training fighting rams and different birds;
teaching parrots how to answer questions and to talk;
making herbal ointments; reading books and curling locks;

Writing books; constructing shrines; devising sophistry;
learning rural languages; composing poetry;
building carts from flowers; using math to make up games;
using charms; conversing; setting verse in mental frames;

Playing; tinting; gambling; dice; achieving victory;
using mystic power to assert authority,

and waking one's superior at dawn with gentle tones.
The boys, each day, would concentrate and make one skill their own.

113) Thereafter, as is customary, both the grateful Lords
presented to their teacher his selection of rewards.
Considering these students and consulting with his wife,
the learned teacher asked them, "Bring our dead son back to life."

Recovering Sandipani's Son

114) On learning how the boy was lost at sea, the Lords agreed.
They climbed aboard their chariot and drove at lightning speed
directly to the beach that claimed the boy. Upon its sands,
the god of all the oceans came and bowed with folded hands.

115) Said Krishna, "You have claimed my guru's baby in your waves.
We want you to return him to us safely, right away."
Replied the god, "That boy succumbed to one I can't control,
a demon named Pancajaña who preys on blameless souls."

116) The Lord dove in the water and destroyed the guilty beast,
a giant conch who plied the surf enjoying human feasts.
There was no trace of Sāndīpani's son in his remains,
so Krishna went at once to search the Lord of Death's domain.

117) Accompanied by Balarām and carrying the shell
recovered from the beastly conch, the Lord drove straight to hell.
He blew the conch shell loudly; He was not to be ignored.
The denizens of hell all stopped, unsettled by the roar.

118) The razor-leaves fell off the trees. The *ruru* beasts who toil
to punish sinful souls dispersed. And those who boiled in oil
for all their sins felt cool again. Yes, every sinner flew
to Krishna's planet, hell abandoned, when that conch shell blew.

119) And then, before the boys, the Lord of Death himself appeared.
King Yamarāj, that very person everybody fears,

approached Lord Krishna and his brother, humble and serene,
and said, "How can I serve You in Your play as human beings?"

120) "Great king, due to his karmic lot, our guru's son is dead.
He's come to you; now bring him here to Me," Lord Krishna said.
"So be it," answered Yamarāj, returning his young guest.
The three returned to Sāndīpani, meeting his request.

121) Said Krishna to his guru, "Do you have another task?"
Said Sāndīpani, "Dear disciples, what more could I ask?
You have no further obligation. Please go back to home.
In this life and the next, may You be wise and widely known."

122) The boys complied and quickly plied to Mathurā again.
Their chariot, as loud as thunder, swifter than the wind,
returned Them to a city fraught with separation's grief
where only Their arrival brought the citizens relief.

13

Uddhava

Krishna's Envoy

1-4) Lord Krishna had a problem: He had promised to return
to Nanda, Yaśodā and all the *gopīs*, who felt spurned.
And yet He owed more time to Vasudev and Devakī.
He thus requested someone blessed with great diplomacy,
His brilliant cousin Uddhava, a counselor and friend.
He said, "My gentle brother, kindly go to Vraj and mend
the broken hearts of Nanda and our family living there,
and pacify the *gopīs*, who are drowning in despair.

The *gopīs* think of Me with every moment of their lives.
Forsaking pious deeds and joys of ordinary wives,
they love Me with a fervent and unique intensity.
How can I give up those who give up everything for Me?

Dear Uddhava, the *gopīs* cherish Me above all else.
When I am far away, how can they manage by themselves?
Imagine what anxiety they feel when I am gone.
Because I promised to return, they somehow carry on."

5) Uddhava bowed and nodded in a sympathetic way.
Ascending his fine chariot, at once he sped away
for Nanda Mahārāj's lands. When he arrived at dusk,
he came unseen, for cows in streams were walking, raising dust.

6) For miles around he heard the sounds of bulls in playful fight,
the heavy-uddered mothers chasing calves in great delight,
sweet-singing flutes and cow-horn toots and splashing milk in pails
and men and women singing Krishna's deeds in great detail.

7) The people, wearing ornamented silks, were greatly blessed
with homes equipped for worship of the cows, the gods and guests.
Surrounding this quaint village lay the forests of Gokul,
with swarming bees and swans at ease in lotus-covered pools.

Nanda and Yashoda

8) When Uddhava arrived at Nanda's home, the king exclaimed,
"My friend, let me embrace you! I'm so very glad you came."
With first-class food, a foot massage, and all that was required,
King Nanda satisfied his guest, then tactfully inquired,

9-14) "King Kaṁsa and his brothers have been killed due to their sins.
They so hated the Yadus, the most saintly, righteous men.
My wonderful Uddhava, now that Vasudev is free,
is he enjoying peace with all his sons and family?

And Krishna—does He think about his mother and his friends?
Does He recall the cowherds and the cows He used to tend?
Will even once He think of us and come back for a while
and let his shining face embrace us all in lovely smiles?

Why, Krishna staved off forest fires, floods, and angry winds.
He saved us from enormous demons time and time again.
When we recall His deeds and words and playful, smiling glance,
we also smile and disregard our tragic circumstance.

Each time we see our rivers, woods and hills we understand
that Krishna rules our hearts and minds. His footprints grace these lands.

In my view, Balarām and Krishna must be gods engaged
in some great cause, as Gargamuni long ago presaged.

For instance, they killed Kaṁsa, Cāṇūra and Muṣṭika.
They killed the mighty elephant Kuvalayāpīḍa.
For them, these fearsome enemies were merely rats or mice
disposed of by a lion who does not think of them twice.

As easily as elephants can snap a twig in two,
my son snapped Kaṁsa's bow, which was exceptionally huge.
He also held a hill up for a week with just one hand
and killed a slew of demons who descended on our land."

15) Remembering Lord Krishna, Nanda grew extremely tense
as overwhelming love drew him from outer consciousness.
And, shedding tears to hear the themes of Krishna thus addressed,
poor Yaśodā said nothing, though her milk poured out her breasts.

16) Despite the burning agony these parents seemed to show,
Uddhava realized what only devotees could know:
he'd just seen perfect love of God in pure parental mood,
so he replied as follows in a joyful attitude:

(Meter: -|- -|- -|- -|)
17-25) "Dear Nanda and Yaśodā, you should be praised.
What loving devotion your hearts have displayed!
Such love is so potent it even controls
Lord Krishna, the guru of all spirit souls.

If sinners think briefly of Krishna and die,
they gain a new life in the spiritual sky.
Since you're so absorbed in the thought of your son,
what more pious deeds could remain to be done?

Creation itself only comes to a start
when Krishna and Balarām enter each heart.
The killer of Kaṁsa, whose absence so burns,
will please both of you when He shortly returns.

Nobody makes Krishna feel thrilled or appalled,
or greater or lesser, yet He loves us all.
He craves no respect; He respects everyone.
He dwells in each heart, yet you think He's your son.

The Lord has no parents, no children or kin.
No karma imposes a body on Him.
He comes to deliver His pure devotees
and relish His personal activities.

Nārāyaṇ, the parent of all, far exceeds
the three modes of nature, which dictate our deeds.
The good, dark and ardent are in His employ—
His tools to create and His tools to destroy.

A person who's twirling around and around
perceives that what's spinning is really the ground.
In just the same fashion, false ego erodes
our knowledge of how we're controlled by these modes.

Our dance with the modes brings us joy and distress.
The Lord doesn't cause them, as fools may profess.
Past, present or future, no thing, great or small,
exists without Krishna, the soul of it all.

In that sense, dear Nanda, your son never leaves;
He's here in his countless diverse energies.
And if one loves Krishna, like you and your wife,
he's always with Krishna, each day of his life."

The Gopis Rise

(iambic heptameter)

26) As Uddhava and Nanda went on speaking through the night,
the cowherd women rose from bed and set their lamps alight.
When they had done their service for the household Deities,
they started churning yogurt into butter to make *ghee*.

27) While pulling on the churning rope with golden-bangled arms,
their gems reflected lamp-light and illumined all their charms.
Their bosoms, hips and jewels danced with ev'ry dip and peak,
their golden earrings shining on their *kuṅkum*-shaded cheeks.

28) They sang of Krishna as they churned. Combined, these pleasant sounds
dispelled all inauspicious threats that might have lurked around.
When dawn revealed the chariot in front of Nanda's home,
the *gopīs* all discussed it in discreet, sarcastic tones:

29) "Perhaps Akrūra, Kaṁsa's servant, brings us more good news.
Last time he stole our Krishna. Now, perhaps, he's come to use
our very flesh as firewood to burn in Kaṁsa's pyre."
Just then Uddhava stepped outside to fill the Lord's desire.

30) Astonished to behold this handsome stranger in their midst,
the *gopīs* gauged his face and form with this analysis:
"Who is this man? Why, he's dressed up in Krishna's clothes and gems!"
Uddhava, now encircled, prayed to Krishna deep within.

31-35) The *gopīs* duly honored him with shy and pleasant praise.
Aware that he was Krishna's envoy, in a quiet place
the *gopīs* asked him questions using sweet but urgent words:
"Since Krishna sent you here, we can deduce what has occurred:

The darling of the Yadus wants his parents to be pleased.
Why else would He take interest in old farmlands such as these?
The bonds of one's affection for one's family are such
that sages even have them, though they've given up so much.

A friendship is another thing; it only lasts until
the interests of the selfish friend are thoroughly fulfilled.
Relations are as transient outside the family
as women are to scoundrels or as flowers are to bees.

A prostitute abandons one who cannot pay her fee;
the voters change a ruler when he rules improperly;
a student leaves a teacher once he feels he's well-informed,
and priests give up their sponsor once the *yajña* is performed.

A bird gives up a tree when all its fruits have been devoured.
A guest gives up a home when it is past the dinner hour.
The animals abandon woods consumed by forest fire,
and lovers spurn their women once they've satisfied desire."

36) Since they enjoyed this special guest and much preferred to stay,
the *gopīs* all postponed their household duties for the day.
Absorbed in thoughts of Krishna in His childhood and His youth,
they cried, despite the presence of a man they barely knew.

Talks With A Bee

37) A certain *gopī* thought of Krishna so intensively,
she started a discussion with a passing honeybee.
Imagining the insect was a messenger instead,
she thought he'd take a message back to Krishna, so she said:

(Meter: |---|---| --|-||)
38-45) "Do not touch your whiskers to my foot; they have *kuṇkum* on them
from a rival's breasts, for Krishna's garland was crushed upon them.
She can have him! Surely one who sends little envoys like you
always will be ridiculed in Mathurā by the Yadus.

Krishna made us taste his nectar lips for a single hour.
Then He left us like a honeybee tastes and leaves a flower.
Why does Goddess Lakṣmī serve His feet? Does she never realize
Krishna has enchanted her and stolen her mind with His lies?

Why do you sing on about this Krishna to us who lost Him?
We have heard it all; you should perform for the girls who got Him.
Krishna knows their smoldering desires and He gratifies them.
Do not bother us with your requests. Why not go and try them?

Arching eyebrows show off the sweet smile of that charming Krishna.
Women throughout heaven, Earth and hell never can resist Him.
Goddesses of fortune serve the dust in which He is standing.
We have nothing left except His name, which we're always chanting.

Keep your little head off of My feet! I know what you're doing.
Krishna taught diplomacy to you, which you're clearly using.
He abandoned us although for Him we gave up our famlies.
Where's his gratitude? He shall receive no new message from me.

Conquered by his Sītā, he disfigured a lusty lady,
then killed a monkey monarch in a way that was very shady.[1]
After taking everything from Balī, the king, he bound him.
Let's give up this person, even if we must talk about him.
[1]*References to the Ramayana.*

Hearing all these things that Krishna does fills the ears with nectar.
Normal people taste a single drop and become collectors.
Giving up their homes and families, they arrive, quite often,
here to live like wretched, roving birds begging in Vṛndāvan.

Like some foolish deer who trusts the hunter's enchanting singing,
faithfully we trusted Krishna's words, like the ones you're bringing.
Now we feel excruciating lust that his touch created.
Kindly talk no more about your Krishna—we're saturated."

46) As the *gopī* spoke, the honeybee darted from her presence.
When she couldn't see the bee, her anger grew obsolescent.
Fearing that the bee told Krishna how all her words attacked Him,
when the bee returned she tried to soften and then retract them:

47-49) "Friend of my beloved, is it He who has sent your message?
Tell me how to show you due respect. Would you like my blessings?
Why would Krishna, who we can't forget, call us in this fashion?
After all, dear bee, Lakṣmī herself is His staunch companion.

Uddhava! We can't believe that Krishna no longer lives here.
All his friends, His parents and His home—does He still remember?
Does He ever talk about His maidservants in the forest?
When will His *aguru*-scented hand once more touch our foreheads?

Surely Krishna tells the city ladies they cannot please him
as much as we *gopīs* do. And soon He'll get up and leave them.

Coming back to us He will declare, 'All throughout creation
no one has your qualities. I want your association.' "

Krishna's Message

(iambic heptameter)
50) Uddhava, now, was wise enough to easily discern
the *gopīs*' love for Krishna and their ache for his return.
But when he heard a *gopī* in discussion with a bee,
he made this speech to try to breach their great anxiety.

51-57) "The charity they give and the austerities they've done
allow great souls to serve and to remember Nanda's son.
The matchless concentration on the Lord that you've acquired
have made you a success and universally admired.

Since famous sages fail to match it, you may rest assured:
your standard of devotion is unparalleled and pure.
By your great fortune you gave up your husbands, sons and homes
to take a chance in Krishna's dance and think of Him alone.

You rightfully and surely claim the privilege to know
unrivalled love for Krishna, and you've kindly let it show.
To ease your separation I will share your lover's views,
a confidential message that His servant brings to you.

Lord Krishna says, 'How can you ever be apart from Me?
As water, earth and fire are in everything you see,
so I am in the life air, all the senses and the mind.
The elements themselves are also Me, for they are Mine.

'Comprised of only consciousness, the soul is quite distinct
from all that's made of matter and, in time, becomes extinct.
As sleepers wake, yet dwell upon their dreams, we always find
the soul hangs on to matter through the stubborn, reckless mind.

'As every river finds its destination in the sea,
the truth, the sages say, will bring the mind tranquility.

As your beloved, I have stayed away from you, you see,
so you would think and dream of Me so much more easily.

'A woman whose beloved leaves can only think of him.
And since you always think of Me, I'll soon be back again.
Why, some of you could not attend our moonlit autumn dance
yet thought of Me intensively, despite your circumstance.' "

The Gopis Respond

58-71) The *gopīs* were delighted at what Krishna had to say,
and one by one they commented, each one in her own way.

"It's very good that Kaṁsa and his friends have all been killed
and Krishna lives in Mathurā, His loved ones' dreams fulfilled."

"In Mathurā, does He give women love we used to prize
as they display their worship with their shyly smiling eyes?"

"Since Krishna is so expert in His conjugal affairs
how can He not be captured by the charming women there?"

"When Krishna and the city women freely share their minds,
does he discuss the village girls He lately left behind?"

"Does He recall those forest nights beneath the autumn moon
when lotuses shone brightly and the springtime jasmine bloomed?

"Does He recall our dancing, when our chiming ankle bells
played music for His pastimes as we chanted them so well?"

"As Indra brings a forest back to life with generous rain,
His touch will soon relieve our limbs from separation's pain."

"But why would Krishna, now a king, come back to us again?
He's satisfied in Mathurā, surrounded by his friends."

"Why, He possesses everything! He rules the queen of wealth.
Could any girlfriend please Him when He's pleased within Himself?"

"Though Piṅgalā[2] says joy will come when one gives up desire,
can we give up this cowherd boy for whom our hearts aspire?"
[2]*A famed, enlightened prostitute*
"What girl could give up Krishna, who surpasses all the rest?
Why even Srī,[3] whom He ignores, will never leave His chest."
[3]*Another name of Lakṣmī, the goddess of fortune.*

"Uddhava, when our Krishna and His brother roamed these hills,
He loved the forests, cows and flutes. He always seemed fulfilled.
Although He left, we still recall Him well, for ever since
we walk upon this land in which His lotus feet left prints."

"His honeyed words, His generous smile, His restless, darting eyes—
can we forget our Krishna when our hearts are hypnotized?"

"We'd gladly give up Krishna and this vacant, gloomy land
if only our intelligence would follow our commands!"

"O Mādhava, Govinda, you destroy unhappiness.
Lift up your dear Gokula from this ocean of distress!"

Uddhava's Return

72) While speaking of (and to) their Lord, the *gopīs* found relief.
His message and His messenger had eased their burning grief.
Uddhava, who had Krishna's features, wardrobe and physique,
delighted Nanda and the rest by staying on for weeks.

73) Discussing Krishna's pastimes in Vṛndāvan's atmosphere,
Uddhava and the devotees felt time had disappeared.
The *gopīs*' love for Krishna, which disturbed them night and day
so greatly pleased Uddhava that he sang for them this way:

(Brahmā-samhita meter: -|-| -|-| |-| -|-)
74-78) "Of everyone on Earth, you *gopīs* have won perfection,
adoring Krishna with such pure, unalloyed affection.
The sages strive to taste that love, which is so uncommon
it's never found among the gods or the high-class *brāhmans*.

How have you simple forest women, whose reputations
are sullied by a paramour, reached such exultation?
As patients get relief without knowledge of their potions
the simple gain the grace of God if they have devotion.

You *gopīs* gained the Lord's embrace, which is so exclusive
that Lakṣmī and his other wives find it still elusive.
Those loving arms elude the queens of the gods' dominions,
and too, the wishes of this world's most enchanting women.

The husbands, sons and peace of mind that you all have traded
for Krishna, goal of every verse that adorns the *Vedas*,
are hard to leave. Would you great souls come and bless me often
were I a creeper or a bush growing in Vṛndāvan?

Brahmā and Lakṣmī and the gods touch, in meditation,
Lord Krishna's lotus feet. And yet, in infatuation,
you *gopīs* get to touch those feet and embrace them freely.
I bow before you all, who praise Krishna's feet so sweetly."

(iambic heptameter)
79) When months had passed, Uddhava asked King Nanda for consent
to leave. He asked the *gopīs*, too, who added their assent.
As he climbed on his chariot, King Nanda and the rest
approached him bearing presents and this tearful last request:

80, 81) "May all our thoughts be thoughts about Lord Krishna's lotus feet,
descriptions of his deeds the only words that we repeat,
obeisances to him the only posture that we form,
and anything He wants the only service we perform.

Wherever we may wander in this world by Krishna's will,
directed by reactions to our work we must fulfill,
may every deed of piety and charity we do
bestow pure love of Krishna till our mortal lives are through."

82) To hear these loving statements left Uddhava so impressed,
he raced to Mathurā, entered the palace and expressed
to Balarām and Krishna and to Krishna's entourage,
"Ecstatic love for You, my Lord, consumes the land of Vraj!"

14

In Hastinapur

Kubja

1) Lord Krishna, who knows everything, showed interest nonetheless
in what Uddhava said about His kin's unhappiness.
While staying home in Mathurā with duties to address,
within their hearts, He showered love on Nanda and the rest,

2) When Krishna first arrived in Mathurā, He'd made a vow
to see Kubjā, the humble hunchbacked lady, at her house.
When she had offered sandal paste to Krishna selflessly,
the Lord had promptly fixed her back. She now looked heavenly.

3) Kubjā had been consumed by lust for Krishna ever since,
and Krishna did not wish to keep her waiting in suspense.
Her home was furnished lavishly with paintings that could fan
the flames of lust and turn to dust the vows of any man.

4)When Krishna came, Kubjā stood up and welcomed Him with grace.
With great respect she led Him to her finest sitting place.
Uddhava, too, was shown a seat but chose the floor instead,
while Krishna chose an inner room and stretched out on a bed.

5) Kubjā prepared herself with water, oil and fine perfume.
She put on flowers, silks and gems and entered Krishna's room.
Because all this was new to her, Kubjā could only stand,
so Krishna pulled the bashful, lovely woman's bangled hands.

6) The only trace of piety Kubjā had ever shown
was putting sandal paste on some young man she'd never known.
Today she sat beside this man, ablaze with passion's fire,
and Krishna, Lord of everything, fulfilled her heart's desire.

7) The touch and lovely fragrance of Lord Krishna's lotus feet
was all Kubjā required to feel sated and complete.
By holding Krishna to her heart and she vanquished all distress.
This former hunchback, now a beauty, said, "I've one request."

8) "Beloved Krishna, stay with me for just a few more days
and I shall make you satisfied in all delightful ways.
I've waited all this time and now my dreams are realized.
How can I carry on without your smiling lotus eyes?"

9) Lord Krishna then assured Kubjā that she'd feel ever-pleased.
He showed her great respect and, with Uddhava, took her leave.
To meet with Krishna, Lord of lords, is difficult to do,
and if one does, mere sense pleasure is not the boon to choose!

Reunion With Akrura

10) A visit to Akrūra having also been postponed,
Uddhava, Balarām and Krishna next went to his home.
Akrūra rose in ecstasy to see these honored guests
and welcomed them exactly in accord with Vedic texts.

11) Akrūra bowed, embraced his guests and took them to their seats.
He gave them gems and other gifts and washed their lotus feet.
He bowed down to the floor and sprinkled footwash on his head.
Massaging Krishna's feet, in humble tones Akrūra said,

12) "You've blessed us by destroying evil Kaṁsa and his men.
You've vanquished all our misery. We're happy once again.
Yes, everyone and everything is blessed by what You do,
for nothing in the universe exists outside of you.

(Brahmā Samhita meter: -| -| -|-| --| -|-)
13-17) You are the truth, unparalleled in Your whole creation.
The wise can recognize Your limitless incarnations.
As earth and air appear in all forms of living creatures,
You're one and yet You have appeared in Your countless features.

You start the universe and bring it to its conclusion.
Your tools, the modes, can never trap You in their illusions.
Your body *is* Your soul; You need no emancipation,
and anyone who thinks You do lacks discrimination.

You give the *Vedas* so the universe has direction.
When atheists get in the way, You provide protection.
You've stopped these armies steeped in criminal inclinations
and blessed our family with goodness and reputation.

The gods, the forefathers, mankind and the common creatures
are worshipped when we worship You, universal teacher.
Who else but You could be so powerful, kind and pleasing?
You give so fully of Yourself, yet without decreasing.

Your simple presence is a blessing that's so exclusive
the greatest gods and *yogīs* find it remains elusive.
Our friends and families and wealth give us no solutions;
please cut the ropes of our attachments to such illusions."

(iambic heptameter)
18-22) Akrūra's humble prayers always stood him in good stead.
Delighted by his statements, Krishna smiled at him and said,
"Akrūra, Uncle, you're our guru. We are like your sons,
dependent on your empathy, regardless of what comes.

We pray to serve exalted souls like you in all we do.
The gods are always selfish, unlike souls as pure as you.

By sacred baths and *pujas* one may gradually advance,
but saints can purify a soul with just a single glance.

Of all our friends and well-wishers, you're certainly the best.
We pray now, dear Akrūra, that you'll grant us one request.
The Pāndavas are dear to us and dear to you as well.
Have they survived their father's death? Dear Uncle, we can't tell.

They've gone to Hastināpur under Dhṛtarāṣṭra's care
and live in mortal peril though they've taken shelter there.
The sons of Dhṛtarāṣṭra use their father as a toy
and easily could force abuse on Kuntī and her boys.

Please, go and see the Pāndavas, and if you recommend,
we'll quickly make arrangements to protect our treasured friends."

23) Akrūra very happily took Krishna's words to heart;
he called for his best chariot and readied to depart.
Lord Krishna loves His devotees, as these two visits show.
With Balarām and Uddhava, the Lord then went back home.

A Secret Mission

24) Akrūra went to Hastināpur, site of Kuru's throne,
where he had many loved ones and was very widely known.
He greeted all respectfully and asked about their health,
and they in turn asked him for news of family and self.

25) For several months he scrutinized the conduct of the king
whose wicked sons and poor advisors kept him on a string.
Vidura told Akrūra on the side, in great detail,
how Dhṛtarāṣṭra's sons tried killing Pāndu's sons, but failed.

26) He said, "The sons of Pāndu have extraordinary skill.
The citizens adore them, but their cousins want them killed.
Duryodhan gave them poison, though they managed to survive."
Then Kuntī came to see him. She disclosed, with tearful eyes,

27-29) "My dear Akrūra, gentle cousin, does my family
in Mathurā remember my five orphaned sons and me?
Do Krishna, my kind nephew, and his brother Balarām
recall their aunt and cousins now that Pāndu's dead and gone?

My enemies surround me here as wolves surround a doe.
Will Krishna come and speak to us so we may be consoled?
O Krishna, Krishna, our protector, can you hear my call?
Govinda, our predicament has overwhelmed us all!

For those alarmed by birth and death, what shelter is complete
aside from that provided by your sacred lotus feet?
I bow to You, the Lord of all, supremely pure and true.
You know I need Your shelter now, since all is known to You."

30) As Kuntī cried from yearning for her loved ones and her Lord,
Akrūra and Vidura tried to offer her support.
"Remember," said Akrūra, "though you face depressing odds,
your sons can well protect you, for they *are* the sons of gods."

31) King Dhṛtarāṣṭra loved his nasty sons to a degree
that made him treat his brother's sons with crass inequity.
Before he left, Akrūra came to Dhrtarasthra's court
with these words from Lord Krishna (who awaited his report):

32-36) "Enhancer of the Kurus' fame, your state is widely known.
Upon your brother's death you have assumed the royal throne.
By being noble, strong and fair in everything you do,
success, respect and high regard will surely come to you.

However, if you falter, who will ever wish you well?
In this world you will be condemned, and then you'll enter hell.
Be equal, prudent King; thus far, the love that you have shown
is skimpy for your brother's sons and wasted on your own.

In this world who can stay involved with any wife or son?
Our bond with our own body will itself be soon undone.
Alone the soul must take its birth; alone, again, it dies;
alone it takes its karma, be it punishment or prize.

Dependents take away whatever wealth a man might hold,
as offspring from a fish drink up the water in its bowl.
A fool performs a thousand sins to keep his children fed.
His children keep the food and he the sins when he is dead.

Abandoned, blind and ignorant, the fool who fails his soul
discovers that his loved ones fail to pay his *karmic* toll.
To understand your life is but a dream that's bound to cease
will bolster your intelligence and bring you inner peace."

37, 38) Said Dhṛtarāṣṭra, "Gracious soul, I fully understand;
Your words to me are heaven's nectar for a common man.
And yet my heart leans to my sons, so everything you say
remains like lightning in the clouds that flares but doesn't stay.

Lord Krishna comes to bless the Earth and ease its crushing weight.
Who dares defy this dazzling soul whose energies create
a universe, complete with natures' full variety,
that we try to exploit while He observes us patiently?"

39) Akrūra thought about King Dhṛtarāṣṭra's baffled mood,
"He bows to God while clinging to a selfish attitude."
Departing with permission from his relatives and peers,
he brought news of the Pāndavas to Krishna's waiting ears.

15

In Dvaraka

Jarasandha Attacks

1) Asti and Prāpti, Kaṁsa's widows, feeling dispossessed,
left Mathurā and went back to their parents in distress.
Jarasāndha, their father, ruler of Magadha state,
was furious to hear about his daughters' husband's fate.

2) Jarasāndha, a powerful and cruel, wicked man,
announced, "I vow to rid the world of Krishna and his clan."
Then, feeling sure his troops would quickly smash the opposition,
he launched a siege of Mathurā with twenty-three divisions.

3) When they saw this attacking army swelling like a sea,
the citizens of Mathurā felt great anxiety.
Though Krishna saw conditions He could easily adjust,
He comes for certain reasons, so He started thinking thus:

4, 5) "So many soldiers, chariots and elephants have come.
I'm here to lift Earth's burdens, and this force is surely one.
They all shall die, but I shall free Jarasāndha, for then
he'll go away and recreate his army once again.

I save those who are pious and destroy those who are not,
so I shall end this army and the suffering they've wrought.
In other days and other ways, in other sites and climes,
I've vanquished irreligion when it flares from time to time."

6) At once two golden, transcendental chariots appeared,
complete with horses, drivers, shields and military gear.
His *cakra* in His hand and golden helmet on His head,
Lord Krishna called for Balarām and courteously said,

7) "Respected elder brother, Your dependents need Your help.
Your chariot and weapons are awaiting Your good self.
Remove these evil soldiers from this planet, if You please,
for after all, we've come to Earth to save our devotees."

8) Resplendent in Their armor and without a moment's wait,
the brothers and a hundred men rode past the city gates.
Although His force was tiny, Krishna's mighty conch shell blast
alarmed Jarasāndha and the divisions he'd amassed.

9) Jarasāndha looked mockingly at Krishna and declared,
"I will not fight with you, mere boy, for that would be unfair.
You killed your Uncle Kaṁsa! Go away, you craven fool.
Now, Balarām, if You're not scared, I'll fight you in a duel."

10) Said Krishna, "Heroes never boast; they simply show their skill.
You speak deceits like these to ease your fear of being killed."
And then, as dust obscures a flame or clouds obscure the sun,
the army circled Krishna's troops—four thousand men to one.

11) When Krishna was surrounded and, from all appearance, doomed,
the women, looking on from Mathurā, felt faint and swooned.
The archers of Jarasāndha fired arrows by the score,
so Krishna drew His fabled bow, which all the gods adore.

12) Lord Krishna's arrows, razor sharp, became an endless blaze
that slaughtered men on horse and foot who rushed Him from all ways.
The horses, men and elephants fell dead in great surprise
as Krishna's arrows split their heads and sliced their arms and thighs.

13) The severed necks and limbs of man and beast released their blood
which grew into a current that became a crimson flood.
That bloody river's snakes were arms, its turtles severed heads,
and islands formed where elephants lay in that river, dead.

14) The hands and thighs appeared like fish, the human hair like weeds;
abandoned bows were ripples, other weapons brush and reeds.
The floating wheels of chariots revolved like swirling pools;
the gravel in that bloody stream was ornaments and jewels.

15) The flow of blood, which shocked those souls who watched with timid eyes,
aroused a sense of great relief and joy among the wise.
Lord Krishna used His arrows and Lord Balarām His plow,
and neither showed a speck of perspiration on their brows.

16) Why should one be surprised when God annihilates His foes,
for He creates and dictates all, as everybody knows.
Though Krishna has no need to fight, no kingdom to be gained,
His actions can attract lost souls, as sages have explained.

17) Jarasāndha's great army was completely put to death.
Jarasāndha was caught and bound—the only demon left.
But Krishna ordered him released; He had a plan to fill.
So Balarām untied his ropes, obliging Krishna's will.

18) Jarasāndha, once highly honored, trudged away in shame
and pledged himself to penance to restore his tarnished name.
But then his friends persuaded him that he should fight again.
They said, "Your loss is just the cost one pays for former sins."

19) Lord Krishna entered Mathurā; He hadn't lost a man.
The gods tossed fragrant flowers and a festival began.
The people, freed of fearfulness and ready to rejoice,
cheered loud and long as bards raised song in strong, proficient voice.

20) As conches blared and kettledrums laid down a booming beat,
the citizens strung banners and splashed perfume in the streets.
The flutes and vinas sweetly played as priests sang Vedic hymns,
and everyone felt happier than they had ever been.

21) The women gazed at Krishna with affection-laden eyes
and showered Him with garlands, blooms and freshly toasted rice.
The Lord, whose glance had liberated all the slaughtered men,
presented Ugrasen, the king, with piles of captured gems.

22) Again Jarasāndha assembled soldiers by the score,
but Krishna cut down every one, just as He'd done before.
And still, another fifteen times, the fool launched vain attacks.
and as the soldiers fell, the overburdened Earth relaxed.

Constructing Dvaraka

23) As Krishna's plan unfurled and ran precisely on its course,
Jarasāndha began to build another fighting force.
However, Kālayavana, a beast, arrived there first,
with soldiers by the millions to turn Mathurā to dirt.

24, 25) Lord Krishna said to Balarām about this latest threat,
"An ancient curse upon the Yadus has this rogue upset.
Jarasāndha could come while Kālayavana attacks
and steal or kill our relatives behind our very backs.

We must construct a fortress that will keep away these beasts
so everyone in Mathurā again can live in peace,
We'll call this fortress Dvārakā; I'll set it up tonight.
We'll relocate our citizens, then come back here to fight."

26) Lord Balarām agreed in full, so Krishna instantly
produced a fort one hundred miles wide within the sea.
(We couldn't float a single stone, but Krishna's God. As such,
He floats the stars and planets, so for Him, this wasn't much).

27) The fortress, known as Dvārakā stood tall and bright and grand.
Broad avenues surrounded public parks on ample land
that boasted fragrant trees and vines that demigods supplied
along with golden gates and spires that seemed to touch the sky.

28) The houses, too, were made of gold, with emeralds for floors,
fine gem-encrusted crowns and golden pots outside their doors.

The dwellings were luxurious, for every rank and class,
with watchtowers and temple rooms and stables made of brass.

29) Lord Krishna's many palaces lined clean, enormous streets.
The gods each brought a certain gift to make the fort complete.
From heaven, Indra brought a *pārijāta* tree and the
Sudharmā meeting hall, where all gained immortality.

30) Varuṇa offered horses of a most distinctive kind,
with varied hues, both white and blue, and swifter than the mind.
Kuvera gave eight mystic gifts, assuring all of wealth,
and other gods and goddesses gave richly of themselves.

31) The people went to sleep in Mathurā that mystic night
and woke up in their rich new homes, amazed in great delight.
And meanwhile, Balarām and Krishna planned new strategies
to end the threat designed and set by these two enemies.

The Death of Kalayavana

32) That morning, Kālayavana's enormous, brutish force
saw Krishna exit Mathurā without a bow or horse.
They seethed to see that Krishna held them in such low respect
that He would walk outside unarmed, a garland on His neck.

33) When Kālayavana saw Krishna nonchalant and bold,
he noted how his enemy was pleasant to behold.
The Lord's dark blue complexion and His eyes tinged lotus-pink
made Kālayavana look twice, stand still and crudely think,

33) "This Krishna has the mark known as *śrīvatsa* on His chest.
The famed Kaustubha gem hangs on His neck. He has the rest
of Viṣṇu's special qualities as Nārada describes.
But he's insulted me, so I shall tear Him up alive."

35) So Kālayavana threw down his weapons on the spot
and dashed off after Krishna, sure He'd easily be caught.
Lord Krishna turned and ran away, the fiend in hot pursuit,
a fool absorbed in hope to apprehend the Absolute.

36) Remaining just beyond the range of every grasp he gave,
Lord Krishna guided Kālayavana inside a cave.
The fiend cried, "Stop, you coward! Now your reputation's stained!"
but he could not catch Krishna, for his karma still remained.

37) Lord Krishna ran inside the cave, ignoring these remarks.
When Kālayavana ran in, he stumbled in the dark
upon a man who lay at rest and gave him no regard.
"He runs, lies down and hides!" the demon cried, and kicked him hard.

38) The sleeping man was someone else who'd long been resting there.
He lifted heavy eyelids, looked about and grew aware
of Kālayavana, who stood by staring, unabashed.
Those sleepy eyes fell on the demon, burning him to ash.

39) King Viṣṇurāta, listening for hours without a word,
at once put forth this question after hearing what occurred.
"Who was this man who lived in caves and yet was so adept
that he could burn to ashes one who woke him when he slept?"

40, 41) Said Śukadev, This man, named Mucukunda, was renowned
as one who cared for *brāhmans* and who always kept his vow.
He once enjoyed a kingdom, but he set his throne aside
when Indra came to him and begged, "The gods are terrified!

The demons have attacked us, and we fear they may succeed.
Since you're the strongest mortal king and famous for your deeds,
take up your sword and lead our forces. When the war is through,
the gods will do whatever you may wish for them to do."

42-45) He fought for years, till Śiva's son took charge of heaven's troops.
The gods said, "Mucukunda, you have been most resolute.
Since we no longer need you we release you from your vow,
so if you want a benediction, ask it of us now.

You set aside a kingdom that was strong and unopposed
and selflessly took up the heavy task that we proposed.
Because you went to heaven, though, to stop the demon's crimes,
your children, queens and friends have died. They lived on mortal time.

A minute passed in heaven is a year for earthly men,
yet even here, the hand of God, as time, will do us in.
Now, take your choice of boons from us to savor while you live—
except for liberation, which the Lord alone can give."

45, 46) "If that's the case," said Mucukunda, "what could I desire?
My kingdom's gone. I've fought so long, and I've become so tired
that all I can look forward to is long and peaceful rest.
So this, O gods, shall be the benediction I request:

Allow me to remain asleep for days or weeks or years,
as long as I may wish. And if someone should interfere—
let's say, a god in peril who implores me to return—
a glance from my awakened eyes will make that person burn."

47) The gods could understand that Mucukunda wanted peace.
They granted his bizarre request and gave him his release.
So Mucukunda found a place where he would never wake—
till foolish Kālayavana performed his last mistake.

48) Then Krishna, who knew all of this, revealed His splendid form
before King Mucukunda, who was instantly transformed.
Astonished by the beautiful effulgence He displayed,
the pious king stared straight at Krishna, shook his head and prayed,

49) "Who are You? Why have such soft feet traversed this thorny ground?
Are you Lord Indra? Candra? Agni? Someone more renowned?
You must be God Himself, for in this cave as dark as night,
the luster of Your body has filled everything with light."

50) The King explained his story and the vow he undertook
and said, "Your luster stuns me. I can scarcely bear to look.
My Lord, please tell me of Yourself, if that would be allowed."
Lord Krishna, pleased, replied in words as deep as rumbling clouds:

51-54) "Dear King, My births are thousands, and My names the same amount.
In fact, I've had more births and names than I can even count.
If one could count Earth's particles of dust on hands and knees,
he'd still not count My births or names, My deeds or qualities.

Great sages list My present, past and future deeds, dear friend;
despite their patient efforts, they have never reached the end.
Some time ago, Brahmā requested Me to save the Earth
so I became the son of Vasudev and took this birth.

Through Me, Pralamba, Kaṁsa, and their kind met their demise.
Now you've burned Kālayavana, this demon, with your eyes.
Since in the past, repeatedly, you've offered prayers to Me,
I've met you in this cave, for I'm inclined to devotees.

My dear and saintly Mucukunda, take some blessing, please.
I'll give you anything you ask and put your mind at ease.
If someone somehow satisfies and proves himself to Me,
he never need again lament or suffer misery."

55) On hearing this, the king bowed down, his forehead to the ground.
Sage Garga had foretold he'd see the Lord, and now he found
the Lord Himself had come to him in such a perfect way.
Rejoicing in his fortune, Mucukunda gently prayed,

56-64) "My Lord, the men and women of this world are most confused
by Your divine illusion. Thus, they fail to worship You.
Oblivious to their own good, they build up families
that fail to bring them happiness and cause them misery.

A soul who squanders human life forgetting You will dwell
within some mortal home as if a beast trapped in a well.
Intoxicated by my wealth, my wives and my domain,
I thought myself this mortal flesh and suffered endless pain.

I arrogantly raised an army, roamed the Earth and thought
my body was eternal, though it's obviously not.
A greedy fool like me ignores You till You come at last
as death, a hungry snake devouring blind and helpless rats.

A body, riding elephants or chariots of gold,
is called "the king" and flaunted for the public to behold.
And then Your endless form of time renames that royal corpse
as "feces," "worms" or "ashes" when its lifetime runs its course.

I conquered all directions. When my splendid throne was raised,
my former enemies bowed down before me and gave praise.
But when I went to see my queen, my sovereignty was gone
and I became her pet, a helpless beast to be led on.

A king desiring happiness performs austerity
and overcomes his self-important, proud mentality.
When one stops chasing matter, he may meet Your devotee
and gain a realization of Your true supremacy.

To see You here has ended my affection for my throne.
A wise king leaves his empire for the woods and lives alone.
Devotees serve your lotus feet. Please let me do the same.
Why should I ask a boon that brings entanglement and pain?

Henceforward I renounce those things I used to want to do.
Relieved of such attachments, may I now depend on You?
You have no designations; You are undiluted proof
that nature—goodness, darkness, passion—can't obscure the Truth.

My senses can't be satisfied. They'll never give me peace.
I'm trapped and burning in this world and cannot gain release.
Protect me, Lord! This world is just a dangerous masquerade.
To serve Your lotus feet will make me pleased and unafraid."

65-67)
The Lord replied, "Great ruler, you've a clear and potent mind.
You could have taken any boon from me, were you inclined.
I offered you some blessing just to prove that you are pure.
The honor of my unalloyed devotees is secure.

Though *yogīs* master breathing drills, their inner, mental state
remains a site for sensual desire to incubate.
Your mind has no such problem; it is simply fixed on Me.
Now wander where you will with your unfailing loyalty.

Because you were a *kṣatriya*, you've killed both man and beast,
incurring many sins from which you now must be released.

Perform your penance in this life, and surely in the next
you'll come back as a *brāhman* and achieve complete success."

68) King Mucukunda honored Krishna, left the cave and smiled.
Of course, he had not been outside at all in quite a while.
"The Kali age has come!" the monarch quickly realized;
the people, beasts and trees he saw had shrunk in rank and size.

69) The sober king was firm and transcendental. Going forth,
he reached Badarikāśram in the distant, frigid north.
He worshipped Lord Nārāyaṇ and remained there peacefully
in constant thought of Krishna through severe austerity.

16

Rukmini

Satisfying Jarasandha

1) Lord Krishna, meanwhile, went back home to Mathurā and found
the army of Kālayavana near the vacant town.
He thoroughly destroyed the horde of devils by Himself
and traveled on to Dvārakā with their abandoned wealth.

2) As Krishna headed westward with some bullock carts and men,
Jarasāndha (with many new divisions) charged again.
In perfect imitation of two frightened human beings,
Lord Krishna and Lord Balarām turned round and fled the scene.

3) Abandoning their riches, they ran north for many miles.
Jarasāndha laughed loudly as he chased them all the while.
With chariots and infantry, the demon stormed behind
until the Lords, appearing tired, found a peak to climb.

4) Jarasāndha surrounded this great mountain from below
but could not find his quarry despite searching high and low.
The overconfident Jarasāndha remained unfazed
and shouted to his men, "Set all this mountain's trees ablaze."

5) On seeing all this fun, the brothers took a little hop
and gently floated down from the enormous mountaintop.
Jarasāndha saw nothing and was sure his foes were dead.
In fact, they'd gone to Dvārakā, their island home, instead.

A Secret Invitation

6) Lord Balarām, the elder, His maturity attained,
then married Revatī as Lord Brahmā had preordained.
Lord Krishna took the princess Rukminī to be His bride
by overcoming Śiśupāl and those who took his side.

*7) Said Viṣṇurāta, "Why did Krishna marry her by force
instead of by arrangement, or some other normal course?
Please tell me how He beat His foes. I never tire to hear
Lord Krishna's pastimes. Speak on, please, and cleanse the atmosphere."*

8) Said Śukadev, King Bhīṣmaka had five boys and one girl.
The daughter, Rukminī, was a great beauty of the world.
When she heard of Lord Krishna from some sages passing through,
she knew within herself no other man would ever do.

9) Lord Krishna also heard that Rukminī alone comprised
the perfect wife: attractive, chaste, auspicious, young and wise.
Rukmī, her elder brother, hated Krishna, so he said,
"I don't care what you think; you'll marry Śiśupāl instead."

10) Upset with this arrangement, Rukminī implored a priest
to take a note to Krishna with a plea for her release.
The trusted priest reached Dvārakā, discreet and all alone.
The guards brought him to Krishna, who was sitting on His throne.

11) At once the Lord attended to this unexpected guest.
He worshipped him and made arrangements for his food and rest.
The Lord then came to visit and inquire of his task.
Massaging the priest's tired feet, the patient Krishna asked,

12, 13) "Oh best of the exalted *brāhmans,* is your mind at ease?
Are you performing all your sacred rituals in peace?
While some men would be restless even in Lord Indra's house,
a saintly priest like you can thrive on principles and vows.

I bow to you, a faithful soul who cares for others' pain.
I pray your king takes care of you and all in his domain.
Where is your home? What service brings you here across the sea?
How may I serve you? Kindly now disclose your task to Me."

14-20) The priest said nothing in response to Krishna's words. Instead,
he brought out Rukminī's clandestine letter, which he read:
"Descriptions of Your beauty and the wondrous things You do
have pleased my heart, O Krishna, so I've set my mind on You.

In knowledge, youth and character, in influence and wealth,
the only one to equal You, Mukunda,[1] is Yourself.
What well-raised, noble, sober, young and eligible girl
would not select a groom who can enchant and thrill the world?

[1]*Krishna, bestower of liberation.*

Thus I have chosen You to wed. To You I now submit.
Yet I'm betrothed to Śiśupāl, who's totally unfit.
He's like a jackal set to take away a lion's meal.
Almighty one, please come at once, and let our vows be sealed.

If I have served and worshipped God sufficiently till now
by pious duties, sacrifices, charity and vows,
directed to preceptors, priests, and to the gods themselves,
may You accept me, please, not Śiśupāl or someone else.

Invincible Lord Krishna, if I frankly may suggest,
tomorrow you could mingle in our kingdom as a guest.
Before the wedding starts You could approach me on a horse,
defeat the troops of Śiśupāl and take me off by force.

I live inside the palace, so You've probably surmised,
my relatives might try to stop You, fight with You and die.

Instead, before the wedding, I shall dress up as the bride
and go to Durgā's temple. You will find me there, outside.

Great souls like Śiva do away with ignorance and lust
by worshipping Your lotus feet and rolling in their dust.
If I cannot attain You, Krishna, I shall take my life
in hopes that in some future lifetime I may be Your wife."

21) The priest concluded, "Rukminī entrusted this to me
and asked that I deliver it to You exclusively.
And now that I have filled her wish and brought her words to You,
please carefully consider what Your Lordship wants to do."

22-23) Lord Krishna took the *brāhman*'s hand and smilingly replied,
"We want each other. I shall not take rest till she's My bride.
I sense her brother stops our marriage. How I'll thrash his men!
As one pulls flames from wood, I'll rescue Rukminī from them.
O Dāruka! My chariot at once! We must depart
before this bogus, so-called wedding ceremony starts."

24) His driver, Dāruka, yoked Krishna's horses then and there,
one blackish-blue, one green, one gold and one of fine white hair.
Lord Krishna scaled the chariot and helped the priest climb on.
Then Dāruka picked up the reins and urged the steeds, "Ride on!"
The horses ran so swiftly that it seemed they might take flight;
they made the trip of many days within a single night.

Rukmini's Wedding Day

25) King Bhīṣmaka, the father of the bride, who had succumbed
to Śiśupāl's proposal out of fondness for his son,
prepared his kingdom grandly. Every avenue and road
was cleansed, adorned and scented, almost like the gods' abode.

26) Triumphant archways spanned the roads, uplifting every soul,
while multicolored banners fluttered high on bamboo poles.
The citizens left perfumed homes dressed up with flawless taste
in silken garments, garlands, gems and fragrant sandal paste.

27) According to the Vedic codes, King Bhīṣmaka gave heed
to *brāhmans*, gods and forefathers by filling all their needs.
He then requested learned priests assembled at his side
to chant the sacred mantras for protection of the bride.

28) Some priests made gifts to planets, keeping fortune in the fold.
King Bhīṣmaka rewarded all with foodstuffs, cows and gold.
The father of Prince Śiśupāl, King Damaghosh by name,
observed the priests of Bhīṣmaka and had his do the same.

29) Along with priests, King Damaghosh deployed his royal force
of elephants, gold chariots, and men on foot and horse.
Then Bhīṣmaka met Damaghosh to praise him and present
his guest with keys to his fine quarters, built for this event.

30) The friends of Śiśupāl disliked Lord Krishna deep within.
They too arrived with armies packed with thousands of strong men.
"If Krishna tries to steal the bride, we'll kill him," they agreed,
and all their men stood by to see the travesty proceed.

31) When Balarām learned all of this through one means or another
He rushed off with a fighting force to look after His brother.

32) As all the guests and soldiers gathered, Rukminī began
to brush and bathe and dress in fresh new clothes and costly gems.
Her trusted priest had not returned and she grew more distraught.
Not seeing Krishna anywhere, the lovely princess thought,

33, 34) "Alas, the dawn has almost come. By nightfall, I'll be wed.
Lord Krishna hasn't come, nor has the priest I sent ahead.
Perhaps Lord Krishna sees some fault and won't accept my plea.
My priest, in turn, went off somewhere in his despondency.

Brahmā, Durgā and Śiva must have grown displeased with me.
But Krishna still might come in time; I'll have to wait and see."
She then felt some auspicious signs—a twitch in her left eye—
accompanied by twitches in her left forearm and thigh.

35) Just then that learned priest returned, his countenance content.
How purely Rukminī then smiled, aware of what that meant.
The priest confirmed that Krishna had arrived and they'd be wed.
Not finding gifts to thank the priest, the princess bowed her head.

36) King Bhīṣmaka had heard he had two unexpected guests:
Lord Krishna and Lord Balarām. With wonderful finesse,
he greeted them with many gifts. As music filled the air,
he gave them clothing, sweets and other customary fare.

37) The gracious King supplied the Lords, their troops and retinue
with food and drink and rooms for rest, as good hosts always do.
He settled all the wedding guests and welcomed them at length
according to their status, age, prosperity and strength.

38) The citizens saw Krishna's face and could not shift their eyes.
"Why who," they said, "but Rukminī deserves this handsome prize?
And Krishna must become her groom, not any other man.
Please, Krishna, if we've any pious merit, take her hand."

39) Then Rukminī, well guarded, stepped outside the palace gates
and walked to Durgā's temple, as the ritual dictates.
The guards raised swords. Her friends and loved ones walked with Rukminī.
Despite the horns and drums, she thought of Krishna constantly.

40) Behind the bride a thousand women, bearing gifts and food,
sang psalms and prayers from Vedic scriptures, settling the mood.
The singers sang and heralds cried; musicians played their scores,
until the bridal train arrived before the temple doors.

41) The princess washed her hands and feet and took, for purity,
a sip of sacred water. Then, before the deity,
she prayed to goddess Durgā to fulfill her inner hope:
"May Krishna rescue me today, and may we then elope."

42) The elder women guided her through further rituals
involving gifts of incense, clothing, food grains, lamps and jewels.
They offered goddess Durgā food in great variety,
including cane juice, sweetcakes, fruits and many savories.

43) The remnants went to Rukminī to honor as *prasād*.
She bowed to all her elders, to the goddess and the gods.
The ladies blessed the princess, who departed from the shrine,
extending to her maid a hand with rings that seemed to shine.

44) The kings were all enchanted by this beautiful young girl,
who, like the Lord's illusions, put a spell upon this world.
A jewel-studded belt adorned her shapely virgin waist.
Expensive jeweled earrings traced her sweetly smiling face.

45) Her smile revealed a perfect set of jasmine bud-like teeth
between her reddish lips, her budding breasts hid just beneath.
Her eyes seemed apprehensive of her fine, encroaching hair.
Her swan-like gait and tinkling ankle bells attracted stares.

46) Indeed, the kings who saw her felt their hearts give way to lust.
Some fainted from their chariots and lay there in the dust.
Some kings mistook her furtive looks as personal rewards
when Rukminī, in fact, was simply looking for her Lord.

Krishna Steals the Bride

47) And then she saw Him. Krishna saw her too and seized the bride,
who jumped aboard His chariot and gladly took His side.
The kings attacked, but Balarām repelled them right away,
and Krishna, as a lion rebuffs jackals, took His prey.

48) Jarasāndha, a leading guest, screamed out a different view:
"Oh, damn! How could this excellent event have gone askew?
These cowherds kidnapped Rukminī? It seems that rats or mice
have made off with a lion's food. Now they must pay the price!"

49) The royal friends of Śiśupāl, their fury unconfined,
roared off in chase of Krishna with their armies right behind.
Lord Balarām and His divisions, seeing them give chase,
turned sharply round to stand their ground and meet them face to face.

50) On elephants and chariots and horses they arrived.
Their arrows rained on Balarām like storms on mountainsides.

The slender Rukminī saw weapons streaking through the sky
and shyly looked at Krishna's face with terror-stricken eyes.

51) Lord Krishna laughed and said to her, "Dear beauty, lift your chin
and watch this wicked force become demolished by your men."
The Yadu heroes cut the charging chariots in half
and pierced great steeds and elephants with heavy iron shafts.

52) Soon weapons, lifeless limbs and slaughtered beasts lay all around.
Decapitated heads of many soldiers hit the ground.
The kings could not stop Balarām and Krishna, so they said,
"Let's save our men to fight again some other day instead."

53) Though he'd just lost a fiance and not a darling wife,
at this point Śiśupāl looked drained and hopeless for his life.
The kings were sad to see their friend preferring to be dead.
Jarasāndha, their leader, went to Śiśupāl and said,

54-56) "My tiger-like associate, this episode has passed.
The happiness and sadness of this life will never last.
As puppeteers can make their puppets stumble, dance or twirl,
so God imposes ups and downs on all within this world.

Why, Krishna's triumphs over me have come to seventeen.
On only one occasion could I drive him from the scene.
But I do not allow myself to cry or celebrate
for I can see that everything depends on time and fate.

Today we've been defeated by the smaller Yadu force,
and yet you see I don't agree to wallow in remorse.
As circumstance has brought to them an unexpected win,
tomorrow it shall favor us to conquer them again."

Rukmi Persists

57) Persuaded by these statements that their luck had been postponed,
King Śiśupāl and his surviving friends went to their homes.
Rukmī, however, couldn't bear his sister's choice of grooms
and galloped after Krishna with a hundred strong platoons.

58) Enraged, Rukmī had sworn an oath for all the kings to hear:
"I'll either kill this Krishna or forever disappear."
The armor on his mighty chest and arms reflected light
as he sped on to Krishna for a last, decisive fight.

59) Rukmī cried out, "The wicked cowherd somehow got away
with kidnapping my sister on her joyous wedding day.
My arrows shall remove his pride!" With this, the prince attacked
the chariot of Krishna with his sister in the back.

60, 61) "Just stand and fight, you coward!" cried Rukmī, who gave a laugh
and penetrated Krishna with three formidable shafts.
"You've made off with my sister like a crow might steal some *ghee*.
Wherever you may run, you thief, you'll not be rid of me!

Release this girl before my stinging arrows finish you!"
Before Rukmī could shoot again, his bow was sliced in two.
The smiling Krishna's arrows flew in streams without a lag
and struck Rukmī, his horses, driver, chariot and flag.

62) Rukmī was quite heroic, fighting Krishna on his own.
He took a new bow even as Lord Krishna's shafts had flown.
Again he struck Lord Krishna, who again destroyed his bow.
Though he had lost, Rukmī was cross and not prepared to go.

63) He picked up sword and shield, spears and bludgeon in his blitz,
but Krishna's arrows struck each weapon, smashing them to bits.
Rukmī then snatched a sword and dashed at Krishna once again,
appearing like a tiny bird who flies against the wind.

64) Lord Krishna smashed that weapon, too, and taking His sharp sword
prepared to kill this enemy who would not be ignored.
On seeing Krishna set to kill her brother, Rukminī
Bowed down at Krishna's feet and, speaking softly, made this plea:

65) "My mystic Lord, Your endless strength puts You above all others.
O all-auspicious Krishna, please be kind and spare my brother!"
As Rukminī thus spoke, her arms and legs began to shake.
When Krishna saw her choking tears, He held off for her sake.

66) Although Rukmī had tried to thwart his sister's heart's desire,
she showed him such compassion, Krishna did what was required.
As Balarām beat off the troops Rukmī had brought to bear,
Lord Krishna bound Rukmī and cut off sections of his hair.

67) Rukmī looked very comical. His tresses and mustache
were largely scattered at his feet by Krishna's artful slash.
When Balarām returned, He saw Rukmī was mortified.
Untying the embarrassed prince, he spoke up for the bride.

68-75) "My brother, you've defamed us. Have you failed to realize
disfiguring this in-law brings him shame in others' eyes?
An in-law should be banished, never killed, when he has sinned.
Besides, his sin has killed him once. Why kill him once again?

Though Rukminī chose You to be her husband, sight unseen,
Rukmī tried to coerce her to become his comrade's queen.
Conceit and power led him to commit this grave offense,
but he has suffered quite enough. Please, show some common sense.

Dear Rukminī, can you forgive my father's younger son?
Your brother's only suffered the results of what he's done.
According to Brahmā's instructions and the Vedic laws,
a person sometimes kills a loved one for a higher cause.

Besides, why should you waste your tears on some relation who
has threatened your well-being and imposed his whims on you?
Illusion made this fool accept his body as himself
and punish some as enemies while giving others help.

The body ends, as do the things of which it is composed:
its water, earth and fire, all its senses and the modes.
The endless soul who fails to see this fact, remains disguised
by bodies that repeatedly appear, grow sick and die.

Although the soul makes choices that create its poor domain,
it still remains aloof from outward happiness and pain.
The soul is like the sun, whose rays illuminate so much
and yet remains so distant, unaffected and untouched.

The body always changes, but the soul remains the same.
Consider how the shining moon appears to wax and wane.
Though it may seem to shrink and fade away to me and you,
we know the moon remains unchanged; it's just our point of view.

The foolish stay identified with bodily routines
as sleeping people struggle with some action in their dreams.
So do not be affected if your brother seems disgraced.
Dispel your grief with knowledge and restore your smiling face."

77) Enlightened by Lord Balarām, the princess calmed her mind
and saw herself as spirit, as the Lord so well defined.
Rukmī, however, shaven, pallid, weakened and deprived,
constructed a new city there, and stayed to nurse his pride.

Krishna Weds Rukmini

78) His enemies defeated, Krishna brought the princess home
to formal wedding rituals, with garlands, fire and stone.

79) The citizens of Dvārakā rejoiced among themselves
for Krishna was the object of their love, and no one else.
The joyful people, decked in silk and gems (their very best)
gave gifts to Rukminī and Krishna, both superbly dressed.

80) Triumphant arches spanned the streets; their columns seemed to soar.
Auspicious candles, water pots and scents adorned each door.
Intoxicated elephants hosed down the city lanes
and placed in every doorway limbs of betal and plantain.

81) A dozen royal families converged for the affair,
embracing one another as they scurried here and there.
The royal guests, astonished, heard but one thing all day long:
the kidnapping of Rukminī, retold in verse and song.

The goddess of good fortune had herself, it seemed, appeared
to wed her master, Krishna, whom the people so revered.

The Life of Pradyumna

82) The first son of Lord Krishna and His first queen, Rukminī,
received the name Pradyumna. Listen to his history.
He last appeared as Cupid, god of love, divinely blessed,
but broke the trance of Śiva who then burned him to protest.

83) He entered Krishna's body, and his mother's womb was next.
Pradyumna would, in time, show Krishna's strength in all respects.
Alas, a cruel demon named Śambara kidnapped him
and threw him in the ocean because he was Krishna's kin.

84) A fish gulped up the infant and was subsequently caught,
delivered to Śambara's kitchen, weighed, appraised and bought.
The fish was cleaned, his belly sliced. The infant was set free
and given to a nearby kitchen maid, Māyāvati.

85) Māyāvati wrapped up the child, surprised it was alive.
Then, unexpectedly, the prophet Nārada arrived.
"This child was taken from his parents," Nārada explained.
"He stayed with you in other lives, and with you he remains."

86) Māyāvati could then recall that, in a former life,
this child once was Cupid and she Rati, Cupid's wife.
Delighted that her husband had returned to her this way,
Māyāvati took care of him and loved him every day.

87) Pradyumna quickly grew to show the splendor of his youth.
Indeed, no woman who beheld him could remain aloof.
Māyāvati felt natural attraction for the boy
and started making looks and moves a girlfriend might employ.

88) Pradyumna said, "O mother, how your attitude has changed.
You're acting like my lover, which indeed is very strange."
Māyāvati explained herself and what had come to pass.
Aware the boy had Krishna's strength, she thought a bit and asked,

89) "Please kill Śambara. After all, he put you through such hell.
He's daunting, yes, but I shall teach you potent mystic spells.

Your mother lost her darling son and cries on your behalf
exactly like a mother cow who's lost her newborn calf."

90) "Of course." Pradyumna said. Māyāvati then taught him how
to use the mystic weaponry with which she was endowed.
Now well prepared, Pradyumna found Śambara, stood and cried,
"You ugly, foolish monster! Come along, it's time to die."

91) These insults to Śambara were far more than he could take.
With eyes turned red from rage, the demon, hissing like a snake,
picked up his club and spun it round and hurled it with the sound
a thundercloud would make when hurling lightning to the ground.

92) Pradyumna knocked the club away and threw his in reply.
Śambara, though, had vanished. Then, at once, up in the sky,
the demon laughed and launched at him a deadly mystic rain
of axes, clubs and shafts that would leave other rivals slain.

93) Harassed by this incessant rain, Pradyumna cast a spell,
deflecting each demonic weapon even as it fell.
Śambara knew destructive tricks from each demonic race;
Pradyumna's godly powers, though, could never be erased.

94) Surprising the bewildered fiend, Pradyumna flashed his sword,
and cut Śambara's head completely off its spinal cord.
Its red mustache and golden earrings wobbled on the ground.
The gods praised Krishna's son and showered flower petals down.

Pradyumna Returns

95) Māyāvati, Pradyumna's mystic wife, then volunteered
to fly her darling husband back to where he'd disappeared.
He looked like thunderclouds and she like lightening in a squall
as they flew inside Dvārakā's majestic palace hall.

96) On seeing this enchanting man with bluish-blackish skin,
the ladies in Lord Krishna's palace thought it must be Him.
His yellow silken garments, charming smile and curly hair
made all the women bashful, and they scattered here and there.

97) On noting subtle ways in which he differed from the Lord,
some ladies became curious and cautiously came forward.
Queen Rukminī observed the boy and felt so overcome
her breasts began to trickle milk as she recalled her son.

98-100) Queen Rukminī said, "Who is he, this jewel of all men?
If I have ever seen him, I cannot remember when.
Who are those lucky parents who have given him his life?
Who is this lovely woman he has taken as his wife?

If my son, who was kidnapped from his cradle long ago,
came back today, would he display this hero's handsome glow?
How is it he resembles my dear Krishna's limbs and form?
His speech, his pace, his smiling face are just as sweet and warm.

My left arm is now quivering, a sign of some great boon.
I love this youth so much. Could I have borne him from my womb?"
Just then Lord Krishna, Vasudev and Devakī appeared.
The truth was known to Krishna, but it wasn't volunteered.

101) Sage Nārada, as always, coming timely on the scene,
knew everything that happened, so he kindly intervened.
"Some wicked fool," he said, "kidnapped Pradyumna out of spite.
Māyāvati, his long-lost wife, returned him here tonight."

102) As Rukminī embraced the pair, her tears choked up her voice.
Lord Krishna and His parents hugged them too, and all rejoiced.
Pradyumna, gone for years and for whom countless tears were shed,
appeared as someone long revered returning from the dead.

103) The palace women who withdrew when he at first arrived
had thought Pradyumna Krishna, whom they loved, so they were shy.
It's natural, of course, for he was Cupid once himself,
and looked just like his father, who can charm the queen of wealth.

The Syamantaka Jewel

Krishna Defamed

1) My dear king Viṣṇurāta, since you're listening so well,
there is another pastime of Lord Krishna I could tell.
Satrājit once offended Krishna. Then, to make amends,
he gave his daughter and a gem so they could stay as friends.

2) Said Viṣṇurāta, "How did King Satrājit wrong the Lord,
and what gem could he give to Him to serve as a reward?
And why did he present his daughter for the Lord to wed?
Please, kindly add this knowledge to what you've already said."

3) Satrājit served the sun god, Sūrya, both in work and prayer,
so Sūrya gave to him a jewel far beyond compare.
This jewel, Syamantaka, was effulgent and so bright
Satrājit wore it round his neck and hid behind its light.

4) Satrājit entered Dvārakā and went unrecognized.
"The sun god must have come!" some cried, while shielding their eyes.
The people ran to Krishna, bowed, and being quite perplexed,
said, "Sūrya's come to visit you and offer his respects!"

5) The lotus-eyed Lord Krishna found this viewpoint so naive
he smiled and said serenely, "Things are not what you perceive.
The gods may sometimes visit Me, but this time you've been fooled,
for this man is Satrājit with his Syamantaka jewel."

6) The Syamantaka jewel was a marvel to behold.
Each day it generated eighty kilograms of gold.
It kept out famine, serpents, liars, illness and demise.
Satrājit had some priests install and adulate his prize.

7) Lord Krishna thought Satrājit should, in light of everything,
present the gem to Ugrasen, Satrājit's ruling king.
The king is, after all, God's representative on Earth
and should receive such objects of extraordinary worth.

8) However, greed compelled Satrājit to refuse to Lord;
the gem was his to keep and all the gold was his to hoard.
He failed to see his action had comprised a great offense
for wealth had made him arrogant and crushed his common sense.

9) To flaunt his wealth, Satrājit let his brother take the gem,
oblivious to how his greed would soon leave him condemned.
His brother, named Prasena, hung the jewel on his neck
and rode off on a horse to hunt, his head and back erect.

10) A lion killed Prasena and consumed him then and there.
The Syamantaka gem went with the lion to his lair.
The king of the gorillas, Jāmbavān, received this news
and thought, "That shining gem will keep my youngest son amused."

11) So Jāmbavān tracked down the lion, killed him and retrieved
the Syamantaka gem, which pleased his son, as he'd believed.

12) In Dvārakā, meanwhile, Satrājit, full of deep concern,
kept looking for Prasena, who had failed to return.
He said, "This Krishna seems to be so envious of me
that he has killed my brother to acquire my property."
The accusation quickly spread, for everyone who hears
salacious gossip tends to leave it in some other ears.

13) When Krishna heard this rumor, he resolved to end the stain
Satrājit made upon His name throughout His own domain.
He gathered several witnesses who'd speak on his behalf.
Together, they went off to trace the late Prasena's path.

14) They came upon the bodies of Prasena and his horse
and found the killer lion, killed by even greater force.
Lord Krishna told his men to wait. Then, undisturbed and brave,
He walked alone into a nearby dark, forbidding cave.

A Battle with Jambavan

15) The cave belonged to Jāmbavān. When Krishna went inside
He saw a child at play, the precious jewel at his side.
The child's nurse was terrified and shouted out in fear.
The mighty Jāmbavān, alerted, instantly appeared.

16) Completely unaware of Krishna's real identity,
the angry Jāmbavān attacked with great hostility.
Concerned about his son's protection, Jāmbavān could not
perceive it was his own beloved Lord with whom he fought.

17) They battled fiercely on and on, each one intent to win.
They hurled rocks and branches, then they beat each other's skin.
They struggled like two fearsome hawks with talons, wings and beaks
prepared to fight to death to claim a single piece of meat.

18) For twenty-eight unbroken days the two opponents fought.
Their fist-blows fell like lightning bolts, incessant, loud and hot.
Though Jāmbavān had bulging muscles well beyond compare,
his strength began to fail. He wiped his brow and then declared,

19, 20) "You must be God, the life and strength of every entity.
In all my years and travels, no one else defeated me.
Creator of creators, You're the substance of the whole.
Subduer of subduers, You're the Soul of every soul.

Your glance of anger forced the mighty ocean to sustain
a floating bridge to Lanka for your warriors' campaign.

You decimated Rāvaṇa, the multi-headed beast.
It must be You, almighty Rām! I prostrate at your feet."

21) Lord Krishna placed His transcendental hand on Jāmbavān
and spoke in grave, empathic tones, his fighting mood withdrawn:
"Your words are true. This mystic jewel brought Me here, you see,
for it alone can disprove allegations thrown at Me."

22) Said Jāmbavān, "Our enmity, my Lord, is now dispelled.
The gem is Yours. My daughter, Jāmbavatī is, as well."
The lovely maiden Jāmbavatī gladly gave her life
to serve her father's dearest Lord as His beloved wife.

23) Outside the cave the citizens who watched the Lord attack
stood by for twelve long days before they turned and lumbered back.
The tearful people said, "It seems our Lord has met his fate."
His parents and His wife fell in a shocked, despondent state.

24) The other people cursed Satrājit for his greed and lies.
They went to Durgā's temple, praying Krishna would survive.
As Durgā reassured them there was no need for concern,
Lord Krishna and His bride chose that occasion to return.

25) To see the Lord come back with both a jewel and a queen
made everybody jubilant, ecstatic and serene.
Lord Krishna called Satrājit and, before the royal court,
returned the Syamantaka gem and made a full report.

Satrajit Killed

26) Satrājit took the gem and trudged away from everyone,
his head hung in remorse and shame for everything he'd done.
Concerned that his offenses would forever be denounced,
he contemplated deeply, went to Krishna and announced,

27) "To cleanse my shame and save my name in this community,
I offer you the treasures that I love most fervently.
The Syamantaka jewel, Lord, I now present to you.
Please take my lovely, brilliant daughter Satyabhāmā, too."

28) The gem-like Satyabhāmā, who was sought by many men,
inspired the Lord sufficiently to choose to wed again.
(An ordinary king might wed a dozen times or more,
but Krishna far exceeded any king who'd come before).

29) Lord Krishna told Satrājit, "Keep the Syamantaka jewel.
Presented by the sun god as a special gift to you,
it's yours by fate. You adulate the sun-god, after all.
Besides, its very presence here will benefit us all."

30) Thereafter, tragic news arrived that took away one's breath:
the Lord's dear friends the Pāndavas had somehow burned to death.
Omniscient Lord Krishna knew these rumors were untrue,
yet he and Balarām went to the scene, as loved ones do.

31) The so-called deaths took place in Hastināpur. There, the Lords
shed tears with Bhīṣma, he for whom the boys had long been wards.
Vidura, Drona, Kripa and Gandari also cried;
Duryodhana did not, for he had planned the homicide.

32) Just then, in Dvārakā, another plot was underway.
Akrūra and Kṛtavarma were outraged by the way
Satrājit had so arrogantly circulated lies
that Krishna killed Prasena for a jewel he had prized.

33) The plotters called Śatadhanvā and, stuffing him with praise,
said "Let Satrājit join his brother, dead for many days.
He promised Satyabhāmā would be one of ours to wed
and then, neglecting us, let Krishna marry her instead."

34) The evil fool Śatadhanvā, thus thoroughly misled
snuck in and killed Satrājit as he rested in his bed.
Satrājit's family pleaded, but Śatadhanvā was cruel
and killed them too before he stole the Syamantaka jewel.

35) When Satyabhāmā saw her father dead, she was aghast.
She placed his corpse in oil and, before the day elapsed,
rushed off to see her husband, who was in Hastināpur,
to tell Him of this heartbreak that so suddenly occurred.

36) When Balarām and Krishna heard the news, they played the roles
of sad, lamenting relatives, like ordinary souls.
They all returned to Dvārakā. Then, comforting His wife,
the Lord set out to take Śatadhanvā's disgraceful life.

37) The killer, struck with terror, saw Kṛtavarmā and cried,
"You must give me protection!" But Kṛtavarmā replied,
"How could I battle Krishna, who killed Kaṁsa and his men
and overwhelmed Jarasāndha again and yet again?

38, 39) Śatadhanvā then begged Akrūra, "Please come to my aid!"
"How can I," said Akrūra, "fight with Krishna, who has made
the whole created cosmos with a motion of his hand?
He acts in ways the gods themselves can't change or understand.

When he was only seven, Krishna lifted a great hill
as if it were a mushroom. Who can counteract such skill?
I simply offer my respects to Krishna. Please recall,
He is the soul, the source, the very center of us all."

40) The killer said, "Akrūra, keep this gem till I come back."
He found the fastest horse around and, jumping on its back,
dashed off as Balarām and Krishna steadily pursued
with swiftly running chariot and angry attitude.

41) Outside the town of Mithilā, Śatadhanvā's fine steed
collapsed in an exhausted heap. With terror-induced speed,
Śatadhanvā attempted to outrun the peerless Lord
who split him with His *cakra*, which was sharper than a sword.

42, 43) Lord Krishna searched the killer's garments, looking for the jewel.
Not finding it, he said, "Have we destroyed a useless fool?"
Said Balarām, "He clearly left it with somebody else;
I'm sure when you're in Dvārakā you'll find it by yourself.

While you return to Dvārakā and solve this mystery,
I'll stay here, for the king of Mithilā is dear to me."
Lord Balarām indeed received such deep respect and love,
He stayed for years and taught Duryodhana to fight with clubs.

44) Lord Krishna soon arrived at home and told His loving wife
He'd caught her father's murderer and taken his foul life.
He lessened Satyabhāmā's grief with pleasing, gentle words
and firm determination to find out what had occurred.

45) Lord Krishna held the final rites Satrājit now required
and comforted the relatives He'd recently acquired.
Akrūra and Kṛtavarmā, who hatched the fatal plot,
slipped off to other cities out of fear they would be caught.

Akrura Returns

46) Akrūra's absence seemed to bring an unexpected blitz
of natural disturbances and great unhappiness.
When floods and wild creatures put the people in distress,
they wondered what had happened. Then, some frightened elders guessed,

47) "We hear Akrūra now lives in Benares and, we're told,
is offering a sacrifice on altars made of gold.
Has Krishna banned Akrūra from our city out of pride?
Disaster reigns without Akrūra. How will we survive?"

48-50) On hearing these insinuations, Krishna sent out word
Akrūra should return so all could learn what had occurred.
Lord Krishna, knowing all, addressed Akrūra with a smile:
"I'm glad to see you back, my friend. Let all be reconciled.

Śatadhanvā killed poor Satrājit; then he fled our land
and left the Syamantaka jewel safely in your hand.
Satrājit had no son, and now his wives are also dead.
By law the gem should go to Satyabhāmā's sons instead.

However, you may keep it, for with you I am assured
the gold is used astutely and the gem remains secure.
To pacify My relatives, I simply ask that you
display the gem and prove to them that all I've said is true."

51) Ashamed, Akrūra showed the gem he'd hidden in his clothes.
It seemed as if the sun itself was suddenly exposed.
On seeing the enchanting jewel, all of Krishna's peers
accepted they'd been wrong. Thus Krishna's name, again, was cleared.

52) This sweet narration, splendid with descriptions of the Lord,
removes all sins and leaves one cleansed, auspicious and restored.
A person who remembers, speaks or hears of it will find
increasing reputation and unending peace of mind.

18

Krishna's Queens

Kalindi

1) Some time elapsed. The Pāndavas, so cherished by the Lord,
survived the plots against them, and their kingdom was restored.
When they built Indraprastha as the new seat of their throne,
Lord Krishna went to visit them, as He was always prone.

2) When Kuntī's five outstanding sons saw Krishna had arrived,
they rose as if five senses of a lifeless man, revived.
To see His loving face filled them with overwhelming joy.
As they embraced the Lord each felt his problems were destroyed.

3) Lord Krishna paid obeisances, as Vedic texts direct,
to Yudhiṣṭhir and Bhīma, who, as elders, earned respect.
He hugged his equal, Arjuna, His peer and lifelong friend
and took the praise the younger twins were happy to extend.

4) The Pāndavas' Queen Draupadī was chaste beyond reproach.
She dearly loved Lord Krishna, whom she timidly approached.
His traveling companions, meanwhile, took their honored seats.
Queen Kuntī then arrived, and all the greetings were complete.

5) Queen Kuntī loved her nephew, whom she'd longed to see for years.
Emotion choked her throat and filled her eyes with blissful tears.
Since she had lost her husband, life had caused her much distress.
Remembering Lord Krishna's help, she made this short address:

6) "My dear Lord Krishna, in our grief, You've given us such help.
You kindly sent your father and, at last, You've come Yourself.
You're everyone's well-wisher; You treat everyone the same,
and yet You please your devotees and add to their acclaim."

7) Queen Kuntī's son King Yudhiṣṭhir continued on this theme.
"By grace we have Your presence and Your help in our regime.
Though we are fools, please stay with us until the rains have passed."
The Lord complied and, kingdom wide, delight was unsurpassed.

8) Since warriors are allowed to hunt by Vedic moral codes,
Arjuna drove Lord Krishna through the kingdom's forest roads.
His chariot held mystic weapons, useful in pursuit
of rhinos, tigers, boar and deer the pair would stalk and shoot.

9) Arjuna's servants packed the corpses, carried them away
and used them all for sacrifice. So doing, all the prey
gained new and better bodies through the power of the priests
who'd consummate the sacrifice and benefit the beasts.

10) Arjuna, feeling thirsty, saw the Yamunā nearby.
Lord Krishna came and drank with him till both were satisfied.
Just then they saw a lovely girl with charming face and hips.
At Krishna's hint, Arjuna went to question her like this:

11) "Who are you, lovely lady? Is this place your native land?
Your father—is he with you? Are you here by his command?
Who is your father? Do you seek a husband in these woods?
Please help us understand things so we see you as we should."

12, 13) The woman, named Kālindī, said, "My father is the one
that you would know as Sūrya, or the god who rules the sun.
He built for me a mansion in the Yamunā nearby
where I reside and spend my time just as you have implied.

My husband will be Viṣṇu, or I'll have no mate at all.
To satisfy the Lord, with whom I've always been enthralled,
I put myself through penance and divine austerity
in hopes He will be satisfied and someday marry me."

14) This sweet account (which Krishna knew) was all He had to hear.
Kālindī on his chariot, he went to Yudhisthira
in splendid Indraprastha (which the Lord had helped to build
by calling Viśvakarmā,[1] whose construction is most skilled).
[1]*The architect of the gods.*

15) Lord Krishna stayed for weeks until, with matters to attend,
he went back home to Dvārakā with fiance and friends.
And then, when ev'ry planet showed auspicious qualities,
He wed Kālindī lavishly and pleased His devotees.

Satya and More

16) Duryodhana detested all the Pandava's success
and gathered allies who imbibed his poisoned consciousness.
Two brothers named Vindya and Anuvindya held such hate,
but Krishna wed their sister, which they could not tolerate.

17) The sister, Mitravindā, in the classic Vedic way
prepared to choose her husband on her *svayaṁvara*[2] day.
Her heart was set on Krishna, which her brothers found obscene,
but when the Lord rode off with her they could not intervene.
[2]*A princess' ceremonial selection of a husband from a pool of suitors.*

18) Then Krishna heard that Nagnajit of Kauśalya decreed
Satyā, his lovely daughter, would be his who could succeed
in taming seven vicious bulls. Forever discontent,
these bulls had blades for horns and couldn't stand a warrior's scent.

19) Lord Krishna knew King Nagnajit and, with a massive force,
went promptly to his friend to meet this challenge at its source.
King Nagnajit, delighted to see Krishna, left his throne
and gave Lord Krishna more respect than he had ever shown.

20, 21) Lord Krishna offered his respects. Satyā, the lovely maid,
observed her latest suitor and immediately prayed,
"As I have kept my vows as well as any woman can,
may Providence arrange that, somehow, I may wed this man.

If goddess Lakṣmī, Lord Brahmā, Lord Śiva and the rest
of all the gods and goddesses were here, they would request
the dust of Krishna's lotus feet. To save humanity,
He incarnates Himself like this. May He be pleased with me!"

22) King Nagnajit first worshiped Krishna, seated Him and said,
"What can I do for You, my Lord, but simply bow my head?"
Lord Krishna, smiling from the royal throne he'd been allowed,
addressed the king in pleasing words that rumbled like a cloud:

23) "The sages say that kings like you and me, with men and land,
should not engage in begging nor extend an empty hand.
And yet, to build our friendship, if the match can be arranged,
I ask to wed your daughter—though I've nothing to exchange."

24) The King replied, "My Lord, to see she'd wed a man like You,
I've bound her to a hero's task I'm certain You can do.
These seven wild bulls have broken many suitor's bones;
defeat them and my daughter shall belong to You alone."

25) The Lord then pulled his belt and seven Krishnas came in view.
Each one fought with a bull until the beasts were all subdued.
As Krishna coalesced again and tied the bulls with ease,
Satyā saw how, despite His other wives, she could be pleased.

26) King Nagnajit then gave Satyā to Krishna with delight
and held a wedding festival with joyful Vedic rites.
Satyā, her mother and the court were filled with ecstasy,
and common people shared the mood of great festivity.

27) The mighty Nagnajit bestowed a dowry for the bride
that reached such great proportions it could not be quantified.
The multitudes of maidens, cows and elephants surpassed
its hordes of men and chariots, which in themselves were vast.

28) The King sent this beloved couple off, with much remorse,
aboard a royal chariot amidst a mighty force.
This proved to be prescient, for on the road, in fact,
a slew of jealous, disappointed rival kings attacked.

29) Before, the seven vicious bulls had overwhelmed these kings;
now Arjuna and other soldiers managed the same thing.
They parried every king's attack with fortitude and skill
as lions drive off jackals who attempt to steal their kill.

30) Lord Krishna, who ruled Dvārakā and all the Yadu clan
returned with His new bride and her vast dowry to His land.
As citizens applauded them with boundless happiness,
Satyā and Krishna entered their palatial home in bliss.

31) But Krishna wasn't finished; He had many wives to wed,
for He expands in countless forms, as we've already said.
Bhadrā came as a gift, then Lakṣmanā by strength of force;
and Krishna married sixteen thousand others in due course.

Sixteen Thousand Queens

32) "Said Viṣṇurāta, "How did He wed sixteen thousand queens?
I've heard that Bhauma kidnapped and imprisoned them, unseen,
when they were only princesses. Please, tell me what occurred
when Krishna killed that scoundrel and released the captive girls.

33) The villain Bhauma stole King Indra's mother's jeweled rings,
umbrellas of Varuna, and still other godly things.
When Indra asked Lord Krishna for assistance, He replied
that He would go at once, with Satyabhāmā at His side.

34) Aloft on Garuḍa, Lord Krishna and his fearless wife
flew off to see to Bhauma, who was causing all this strife.
They found his kingdom fully ringed by sharply slicing wire,
a slew of deadly weapons and a moat of blazing fire.

35) Lord Krishna's spinning disc broke up the moat and doused the fire;
Lord Krishna's shining sword sliced through the labyrinth of wire.

Lord Krishna's arrows caused the demon's weaponry to fall,
allowing Krishna's club to smash the daunting fortress walls.

36) When Krishna blew His vict'ry conch, He broke the magic spell
protecting Bhauma's fort and all his soldier's hearts as well.
It also roused a sleeping beast of five ferocious heads
named Mura, who had made the fortress moat his water bed.

(Meter: -|- -|- -|-|-|)
37) The horrible Mura blazed brighter than the sun
His five massive mouths roared and frightened everyone.
Like venom some poisonous snake reared back and spat,
his trident flew straight at Garuḍa's feathered back.

38) Lord Krishna's first arrows broke up the trident's flight.
His next arrows struck Mura's faces, left and right.
The furious demon then hurled his deadly club
expecting to leave his foe crushed and streaming blood.

39) Lord Krishna threw His club, abruptly smashing both.
Then Mura, upset, raised his arms and screamed an oath.
He rushed at his foe to destroy him with his fists,
but Krishna lopped off his five heads with His sharp disc.

40) Deprived of its heads, Mura's corpse splashed in the moat
as hilltops are felled by Lord Indra's thunderbolt.
His seven sons joined in their father's failed assault
till Krishna's sharp arrows brought that fight to a halt.

41) On seeing his guardians thoroughly destroyed
the demon Bhauma, furious, instantly deployed
his elephants, soldiers, and all his entourage
to bury their foe in an unrestrained barrage.

42, 43) Garuḍa flew Krishna and Satyabhāmā high.
They looked like a cloudbank with lightning in the sky.
Lord Krishna rained arrows on Bhauma's vicious troops;
their pierced limbs and mounts made the field a bloody soup.

Garuḍa swooped down on the elephant array
and, using his talons, drove all of them away.

44) His elephant army destroyed and overthrown,
The demon Bhauma stood before Krishna all alone.
Then Bhauma's sharp spear struck Garuda harmlessly,
who looked like an elephant tickled by a flea.

45) As frustrated Bhauma prepared his trident next,
Lord Krishna's sharp *cakra* went sailing through his neck.
The gem-studded head of the demon hit the ground.
The gods showered flowers and made triumphant sounds.
The goddess of Earth, Bhumi, brought the stolen goods,
gave gifts and said prayers to Lord Krishna as she stood:

(iambic heptameter)
46-50) "Respects to You, my Lord, who dwells in every single heart.
You bring Your disc to help like this. You play so many parts!
Primeval, all pervading one, Creator absolute,
my boundless Lord, I offer my obeisances to You.

The lotus-like depression on Your abdomen adorns
the lovely lotus garland, Krishna, draped about Your form.
Your cooling lotus glances make the imagery complete,
including all the lotus marks embellishing Your feet.

You craft the mode of passion when you bring about creation
and then the mode of ignorance when you want devastation.
As everything's maintainer and enjoyer you are linked
to all of your creation—yet, you're separate and distinct.

Illusion makes us think that fire, water, earth and air,
the mind and senses, gods, and all of which we are aware,
are independent, separate units, standing on their own.
In fact, they are within you and belong to you alone.

I gave birth to this Bhauma, yet his sins disgusted me.
My Lord, here is his son, who has been frightened terribly.

Please place your lotus hand, which conquers sin, upon his head.
Protect him, please, for you can shelter those beset with dread."

51) Content with Bhumi's humble prayers, Krishna blessed the boy.
He then entered the palace evil Bhauma had enjoyed.
Besides the demon's treasures, jewels, silks and other things
were many kidnapped maidens, all the daughters of great kings.

52) These sixteen thousand and one hundred princesses concurred:
the handsome man who freed them was the one they wished to serve.
"May Providence allow this man to marry me," they prayed
as each one thought of Krishna in her own distinctive way.

53) The Lord provided every princess spotless new attire
and sent them all to Dvārakā to fill their heart's desire.
He also sent off horses, treasure, elephants and such
that Bhauma had collected, and indeed, he'd stolen much.

54) With this encounter finished, Krishna took his wife and left
to take back to the heavens all the gods had lost to theft.
When Satyabhāmā asked Him for a *pārijāta* tree
that Indra grew in heaven, Krishna instantly agreed.

55) The most exquisite flowers issue from this famous tree.
But Indra cried, "It's mine!" So Krishna took it forcefully.
Although he'd gained Lord Krishna's help and bowed to Him as well,
this Indra was ungrateful. May his riches go to hell!

56) Lord Krishna, back in Dvārakā, assumed a separate form
for each and every princess. When their weddings were performed,
each one had her own palace, too. What ordinary man
could even dream of doing things that God, Lord Krishna, can?

57) Extraordinary Krishna, who cannot be understood,
led household life with every wife as any husband would.
His smiling, joking wives exchanged with Him a mood of love
that left Brahmā and other gods bewildered up above.

58) A hundred servants waited, but the queens had such a taste
to rub their husband's feet or cool His head with sandal paste
or dress His hair or bring Him garlands, gifts and *pan* to chew,
that all the servants had to find some other work to do.

Rukmini Faints

59) One evening Krishna lay, relaxed, on Rukminī's soft bed.
Her maidservants stood waiting as she fanned His handsome head.
This calm domestic scene obscured the cause of every cause,
the universal Lord who plays along with human laws.

60) Effulgent gems lit up the room, as did the ruddy moon.
The lattice windows let in light and scents from fragrant blooms.
Fresh jasmine garlands in the room drew swarms of humming bees.
Lord Krishna lay on milk-white pillows, seeming quite at ease.

61) Queen Rukminī served Krishna with a jeweled yak-tail fan
that made a gentle breeze while in her graceful, bangled hand.
Her ankle bracelets tinkled and the necklace on her chest
grew reddened by the *kuṇkum* from her sari-covered breasts.

62) Lord Krishna knew that goddess Lakṣmī, ruler of all wealth,
had taken this enchanting form to serve her lord herself.
Her jewels and the gently curling hair upon her head
adorned a joyous, brilliant face. Lord Krishna smiled and said,

63-68) "So many kings sought you, my dear, each one a god on Earth
endowed with power, kindness, beauty, strength and huge net worth.
Your brother brought such kings, like Śiśupāl, for your review;
why did you choose a minion such as Me to marry you?

In fear of all these kings, O lovely one, I left my throne
to hide here in the sea where enemies leave Me alone.
A woman often suffers when she stays with men like Me
who act in some unstable way and flaunt society.

I own nothing material, nor do My devotees.
The wealthy rarely find a good excuse to follow Me.

Moreover, equals wed each other; that's how it should be.
When greaters marry lessers, though, they live in misery.

Because you failed to realize this, you chose to marry Me,
a person praised by beggars who misjudge His qualities.
You need a first class, royal husband, capable and blessed
to help you realize happiness in this life and the next.

Jarasāndha and Śiśupāl and Śālva dislike Me,
as does Rukmī, your elder brother. Clearly you can see,
I carried you away to set them down a notch or two.
humiliating bullies as I always love to do.

A man like Me cares nothing for his children, wives or wealth,
for he is always satisfied, complete within himself.
I don't do much externally; like some unnoticed light,
I quietly observe and witness all within my sight."

69) Because she was accompanied and cared for by the Lord,
Queen Rukminī had thought herself especially adored.
These statements from Lord Krishna, though, shut down her subtle pride.
She'd never heard such words from Him; her heart shook and she cried.

70) The stricken Rukminī choked up and couldn't make a sound.
Her tears were stained with makeup and her toenail scratched the ground.
Her fan abruptly clattered as she fainted to the floor
as if she were a plantain tree sent sprawling by a storm.

71) Lord Krishna joked with Rukminī to stir her loving wrath
but her great love invoked this unexpected aftermath.
Displaying his four-handed form, the Lord picked up His mate,
caressed her lovely face and set her scattered tresses straight.

72) Lord Krishna's wife misread His jokes, for she was deeply chaste.
He wiped her eyes and tear-stained breast and, warmly, they embraced.
Compassionate for Rukminī and her bewildered mind,
the expert Krishna spoke again, His tone supremely kind:

73, 74) "You need not be displeased with Me for speaking in this way;
I spoke in jest to test your love and see what you would say.
I longed to see the corners of your smiling lips turn down,
your eyes shoot angry glances and your forehead knit a frown.

The greatest pleasure one enjoys in worldly household life
is spending time and making jokes with his beloved wife.
O timid, temperamental Love, despite My best attempt,
I couldn't bring about your rage nor stir your harsh contempt."

75) At this point Rukminī grew calm and clearly understood
this joking Krishna wouldn't leave her as she feared He would.
Her glances at her husband's face affectionate and shy,
the charming, lovely Rukminī extended this reply:

(Brahmā Samhita meter: -| -| -|-| --| -|-*)*
76-82) You've spoken nothing but the truth, lotus-eyed beloved;
I *am* unsuitable for you, the almighty Godhead.
You rule the demigods who start and complete creation,
while fools treat common girls like me to their admiration.

Since *māyā* rules this world, you lay down within the ocean
of every living heart, awaiting their lost devotion.
You left the throne of Mathurā, for, in my opinion,
You and your servants do not care for mundane dominion.

It's true you flaunt society, for it simply stands on
the beastly joys that You and your devotees abandon.
It's true that You own nothing; everything is within you.
The gods obey and follow you, yet the rich resent You.

It's true the ordinary man wants a perfect marriage
and its accouterments that your devotees disparage.
A couple locked in common lust must enjoy and suffer;
the wise give up that life and seek You above all others.

Some see Your devotees as beggars who have no money.
In fact, You've made their former lives appear unbecoming.

The best of kings go to the woods, giving up their empires,
and never feel they could desert You for someone higher.

I married You instead of Indra and other highbrows
whose plans lay crushed by time itself, which comes from your eyebrows.
You do not fear my other suitors; in fact, they fear You.
Like jackals flee before a lion, they won't come near You.

The fragrance of Your lotus feet offers liberation,
a scent that shows all other men as mere imitations.
When death awaits and fills the heart with a sense of terror,
to disregard Your feet would be a colossal error.

You suit me perfectly and fill all my heart's desires.
You give this vagrant soul the shelter that she requires.
Those other kings can wed a girl who neglects Your splendor
and live like oxen, slaves or donkeys as they attend her.

Such kings are simply living corpses with fleshy covers,
a frame with whiskers, nails and hairs someone calls their lover.
These foolish women hug a bag full of bile and feces,
the mucus, air and bloody bones of the human species.

You're pleased within Yourself, so Your glances rarely grace me
yet loving You will surely save and resuscitate me.
Despite my arguments against all that You were saying,
I am a woman, after all, and could end up straying."

(iambic heptameter)
86, 87) Lord Krishna then exclaimed, "My saintly princess, all My words
were spoken to elicit the expressions I just heard.
You'll surely gain the blessings that will set your spirit free
for you are ever faithful and My spotless devotee.

My sinless wife, you've shown such love and perfect chastity
that even My disturbing words fell off you harmlessly.
Some people pray to Me for better family situations
despite the fact that I can give them endless liberation.

(Brahmā-samhita meter: -|-| -|-| |-| -|-)

88-91) Dear Love, those people who attain me are quite ill-fated
if they choose riches when they could have been liberated.
Such worldly gains are found in hell, which is surely fitting,
for hell, indeed, is where such people will end up sitting.

While wicked, selfish women pander to each temptation,
your faithful service has assured you of liberation.
I should have known My teasing words never could deceive you;
in all My other palaces, no wife supersedes you.

By simply hearing news of Me, who had never met you,
you disregarded other kings trying hard to wed you.
Courageously, you sent a note through your trusted sources
requesting Me to rescue you on My fastest horses.

When I did not respond at once, you were so dejected
you planned to kill the body so many kings requested.
Such great devotion surely merits reciprocation,
yet what have I to offer you but appreciation?"

(iambic heptameter)

92) The self-contained Lord Krishna thus enjoyed a repartee
by joking with His wife in an extraordinary way.
He mimicked, in this palace, common men in household spell—
and in His sixteen thousand other palaces as well.

The Death of Rukmi

93) Each one of Krishna's many queens thought she was His most dear,
for Krishna stayed with her all day—or so it would appear.
And every youthful queen bore Him ten sons in course of time,
each one as handsome as the Lord and equally sublime.

94) Enchanted by Lord Krishna's features, charming words and thoughts,
each gorgeous wife would try to stir His passion, but could not.
Their intimacy ever-fresh, their glances ripe with love,
each wife enjoyed a husband who eludes the gods above.

95) A hundred servants waited, but the queens had such a taste
to rub their husband's feet and cool His brow with sandal paste
and make His bed and set His hairstyle, garlands, dress and jewels
that all the servants had to find some other work to do.

96) Lord Krishna and Rukminī had a grandson, Aniruddha,
King Rukmī's daughter's son by Krishna's eldest son, Pradyumna.
Why did, you ask, Rukmī allow his hated rival's son
to wed his daughter? Listen, I'll explain why this was done.

97) The daughter, named Rukmavatī, was sought by many men.
Her secret choice Pradyumna, though, defeated all of them.
Rukmī gave his approval, though reluctantly, because
his love for Rukminī surpassed his hate for his in-laws.

98) The couple wed and celebrated in Rukmī's domain.
Obliged by etiquette, both Balarām and Krishna came.
Rukmī's puffed-up associates gave him this bad advice:
"Why not embarrass Balarām by beating him at dice?"

99) The match began with wagers of ten thousand coins of gold.
Rukmī prevailed, and all his wicked friends could not withhold
their pleasure seeing Balarām subjected to this grief.
Kaliṅga's King laughed long and hard, exposing all his teeth.

100) Rukmī then bet one hundred thousand coins to up the fun.
Lord Balarām accepted, and this time his numbers won.
Rukmī, however, cheated; he picked up the dice and cried,
"Ah ha, I've won again! Good luck is surely on my side.

101) Lord Balarām was trembling like the sea on full-moon day.
He bet one hundred million coins and dared Rukmī to play.
When Balarām again prevailed, Rukmī up stood and screamed,
"I won! Let all these witnesses confirm what they have seen."

102) The witnesses, Rukmī's dishonest friends, of course, all lied.
Then, suddenly, an unembodied voice rang through the sky:
"Rukmī has lied, for Balarām has fairly won this match."
Though destiny was calling him, Rukmī was too attached.

103) Rukmī ignored the voice. He laughed at Balarām and said,
"You forest-people can't play dice. Go tend your cows instead.
The sports of dice and archery and other things we do
are meant for kings like us and not for cowherds such as you."

104) Insulted and defrauded by Rukmī, Lord Balarām,
provoked enough to set aside his usual aplomb,
surrounded by the wedding guests in festive moods of love,
struck dead the thieving Rukmī with his swift, unerring club.

105) Rukmī's companions, warriors all, abruptly lost their nerve
and fled in all directions when they saw what had occurred.
Lord Balarām's ferocious club left them in bloody grief.
Kaliṇga's King—the one who laughed—was struck and lost his teeth.

106) Lord Krishna neither cheered nor raged at Balarām's assault;
He knew Rukminī loved Rukmī, despite his many faults.
The Lord had bonds of love with both He did not want to risk,
so He observed, without a word, His face expressionless.

107) Lord Balarām sat Aniruddha and Rukmavatī
aboard a fine new chariot. Lord Krishna's family
did not lament as they all went to Dvārakā, their home,
for malice to their Lord was all Rukmī had ever shown.

19

Shiva

Bana Brags to Shiva

1) Said Viṣṇurāta, "Aniruddha somehow wed a girl
and caused a war with Śiva, almost burning up the world.
Her father, Bāṇāsura, Balī's son—could he not see
arresting Krishna's grandson would conclude his vanity?"

2) Although his father once presented Krishna with the Earth,
this Bāna was a devotee of Śiva from his birth.
He used his thousand arms to beat a drum as Śiva danced,
and Śiva gave his blessings, making Bāna quite advanced.

3) The gods themselves were serving Bāna. Śiva took the task
of giving Bāna's city the protection Bāna asked.
Puffed-up with power, Bāna one day meekly laid his head
at Śiva's lotus feet and, being falsely humble, said,

4, 5) "I bow to you, controller of the worlds. You are the tree
fulfilling every wish of your aspiring devotee.
The thousand arms you've given me are just a useless weight
because, my lord, I want to fight some worthy candidate.
Aside from you, no one at all can give me a good fight.

The elephants who rule the four directions all took flight
when I stepped up and challenged them, for in my battle lust
I'd smashed the mountains on the way to heaps of stone and dust."

6) When Śiva heard these haughty words he angrily replied,
"When you confront my equal he shall devastate your pride."
The foolish Bāṇāsura was delighted by this news,
for he imagined anyone he fought was sure to lose.

Usha and Aniruddha

7) At that time, Bāna's daughter, Ūṣā, resting with some friends,
experienced the kind of dream in which the dreamer spends
an amorous few hours in a lover's warm embrace.
Her lover was a stranger, though she clearly saw his face.

8) The young man's face then disappeared and Ūṣā, in distress,
cried "Where are you my lover?" as she came to consciousness.
Her girlfriends sat around her as she rose, disturbed and stunned,
exceedingly embarrassed about what she had just done.

9) Her dear friend Citralekhā confidentially inquired,
"You've just been dreaming, lovely friend. Who is it you desire?
You've never had a lover. Men have never known your touch.
Who is this unseen man you seem to hunger for so much?"

10) Said Ūṣā, "I embraced a dark blue man of mighty arms,
with yellow garments, lotus eyes and every manly charm.
He made me taste his honeyed lips and then he went away,
upsetting me and leaving me to long for him this way."

11) Said Citralekha, "I shall find this man who stole your heart—
if he is in this universe—by use of mystic art.
I know the face of every person, demigod or man,
so I shall quickly draw each one. Select him if you can."

12) The mystic Citralekhā sketched a clear and perfect face
of every male on every planet found in outer space.

No sketch appealed to Ūṣā till Pradyumna's made her blush.
Then Aniruddha's startled her. "It's him! It's him," she gushed.

13) So Citralekhā (blessed with *yogamāyā's* strength, it seems),
flew through a mystic skyway to complete her helpful scheme.
When she arrived in Dvārakā, security was tight,
so Nārada assisted her in getting in that night.

14) She sought out Aniruddha, sound asleep upon his bed.
Again, her mystic yoga powers served her in good stead.
She took the sleeping grandson of the Lord across the sea
where he awoke to find himself in Ūṣā's company.

15) When Ūṣā recognized her love, her face lit up with joy.
They slipped into the women's private rooms no man or boy
had ever even seen at any time. Alone with him at last,
she worshiped, served and pleased her man as days and weeks flew past.

16) Presenting priceless garments, scents, fine beverages and food,
the princess Ūṣā kept up Aniruddha's happy mood.
Concealed within the women's rooms, he did not seek release
for Ūṣā's love for him appeared to endlessly increase.

17, 18) In time the female guards began to notice Ūṣā's waist
expanding in a way no maiden's could, if she were chaste.
Deciding it was better to directly tell their boss,
they said to Bāna, "Somehow Ūṣā's maidenhood is lost.

We watched her very carefully and never left our posts.
How could a man corrupt her, as is clearly diagnosed?
Unless her friends, O master, played some trick we can't recall,
no man has even seen your girl within these palace walls."

19) The frantic Bāṇāsura rushed to Ūṣā's private room
and saw the Yadu family's pride, her unofficial groom.
The handsome Aniruddha sat with Ūṣā, playing dice
as if it were a normal scene you wouldn't think of twice.

20) He looked like Cupid's very son, so sweeping were his charms,
with dark complexion, lotus eyes and formidable arms.
A fragrant jasmine garland hung on Aniruddha's chest
turned crimson by the *kuṇkum* powder gracing Ūṣā's breasts.

21) The angry Bāṇāsura, who had brought a score of guards,
directed them to tackle Aniruddha fast and hard.
Pradyumna's son stood resolute and raised his iron club,
and soon the frightened guards ran off, in pain and drenched with blood.

22) The mighty son of Balī shattered Aniruddha's hopes
by seizing him and binding him by use of mystic ropes.
When Ūṣā saw her lover's plight she crumpled up and wept,
not knowing this was Krishna's plan—and what would happen next.

Shiva Battles Lord Krishna

23) When Aniruddha vanished, all his relatives had grieved.
The monsoon season came and went; no message was received.
At last sagacious Nārada informed the family
that Balī's son held Aniruddha in captivity.

24) With Balarām and Krishna in the lead, the Yadus rushed,
surrounding Bāna's city in a mood to maul and crush.
The mighty Bāna fumed to see the siege upon his home
and came out with an equally large army of his own.

25) Lord Śiva led the countercharge, his mission to protect
the city of his devotee in every respect.
His carrier, named Nandi, was a bull of awesome size;
his son, named Kārtikeya, was prepared to pulverize.

26) Pradyumna challenged Kārtikeya to a vicious fight,
and Śiva challenged Krishna with astonishing delight.
(Lord Śiva was bewildered, as Brahmā one day had been
when he made off with Krishna's friends and hid them in his den).

27) Brahmā and many other gods, their godly planes in flight,
descended from the heavens to observe this shocking fight.

They watched Lord Krishna's pointed arrows quickly drive away
the many ghosts and demons on Lord Śiva's side that day.

28) As Śiva started firing every weapon he could get,
Lord Krishna counteracted every one with great effect.
His rain attack left Śiva's fire weapon limp and drawn;
He then released a weapon that made Śiva sit and yawn.

29) With Śiva incapacitated, Krishna turned the fight
to Bāṇāsura's frightened troops, who scattered left and right.
Pradyumna poured persistent arrows down on Śiva's son
till Kārtikeya joined his fellow soldiers on the run.

30) Lord Balarām destroyed His foes. The fight became a route,
so Bāṇāsura, furious, charged Krishna with a shout.
Excited by the fighting, with his thousand arms in rows
the fearsome Bāna pulled and aimed five hundred deadly bows.

31) Lord Krishna's arrows split each bow, and Bāna's driver fell.
The demon heard Lord Krishna's conch shell bidding him farewell.
Then Bāna's mother, out of her desire to save her son,
appeared before Lord Krishna nude, her shiney hair undone.
When Krishna turned His head away (like any gracious man),
the frightened Bāna saw his chance—he quickly turned and ran.

Shiva-jvara Surrenders

32, 33) Just one remaining enemy persisted in the fight:
the Śiva-jvara, Śiva's weapon, burning left and right.
When Krishna saw this blaze personified resist defeat,
He launched his Viṣṇu-jvara to offset its deadly heat.
When Viṣṇu-jvara froze him, Śiva-jvara cried in pain.
With no escape in sight, he turned to Krishna and exclaimed,

(Meter: -|- -|- -|- -|)
34-36) "I bow before You of unlimited might,
the cause of creation, its morning and night.
You're perfectly peaceful; indeed, you imbibe
the Absolute Truth that the *Vedas* describe.

As seeds turn to plants, so the soul takes a form
to ceaselessly suffer his fate and perform
material deeds his illusions impose—
a cycle of pain only You can oppose.

Because of the demons who have no restraint,
You come to this world to watch over the saints.
Unless one finds refuge in Your lotus feet,
like me, he will suffer distress and defeat."

(iambic heptameter)
37) Lord Krishna said, "O Śiva-jvara, all you say is true.
Have no fear of My weapon; henceforth, no one shall fear you."
The Śiva-jvara bowed his head and took Lord Krishna's leave,
but Bāṇāsura wanted war and ended the reprieve.

Shiva Saves Banasura

38, 39)
His thousand arms crammed full with weapons, Bāna charged the Lord
and fired countless arrows as he furiously roared.
As Bāna hurled weapons, Krishna's *cakra,* spinning free,
began to slice off Bāna's arms like branches from a tree.
So Śiva, seeing Bāna's death was all but guaranteed,
approached the Lord to try to save his foolish devotee:

(Meter: -|- -|- -|- -|)
39-45) "O Absolute Truth, You're as pure as the sky.
The moon is Your mind and the sun is Your eye.
The seas are Your abdomen; Earth is Your stride;
Brahmā is Your wisdom and I am Your pride.

We gods all depend on Your power and grace
to care for the systems of planets in space.
Descending to Earth for the decent and just,
You benefit suffering souls such as us.

Original Person, transcendent, complete,
no one need create You; no one can compete.

Distorted by matter, our senses perceive
Your presence in various ways we conceive.

The clouds cloak the sun when observed from the ground
As matter obstructs You to souls who fall down.
You nonetheless light up this world of distress
and give what good qualities souls may possess.

'My family shall save me,' bewildered men think.
They swim in illusion and usually sink.
The pitiful human who sullies Your feet
discovers it's only himself that he cheats.

If one enjoys matter and sets You aside,
he throws away life and accepts suicide.
Brahmā, other gods, famous sages and we
surrender ourselves to You wholeheartedly.

You fashion, maintain and destroy everything.
Befriend us and free us from all suffering.
Since Bāna has pleased me, O merciful God,
save him as you did his ancestor Prahlad."

(iambic heptameter)
46, 47) Lord Krishna, gently smiling, said, "Lord Śiva, I agree.
I certainly will do whatever you have asked of Me.
Prahlad[1] received My promise his descendents would endure,
so I will spare this demon Bāṇāsura, rest assured.
[1]*Krishna, appearing as Nṛsiṁha, saved Prahlad, Balī's grandfather.*

His arms are gone, so Bāna's hefty ego will abate.
His army's gone, for it has burdened Earth with all its weight.
This Bāna, though, shall serve you well with four remaining arms
and he shall never age or die. I promise him no harm."

Aniruddha Released

48) The demon Bāṇāsura bowed to Krishna, head to ground
and ordered that the grandson of Lord Krishna be unbound.
A splendid chariot brought Aniruddha and his bride
directly up to Krishna for a festive homeward ride.

49) The party entered Dvārakā amid the sound of drums.
The royalty, the priests and common people all had come.
The welcome for Lord Krishna and his grandson was complete
with lavish arches, flags and water sprinkled in the streets.

50) Whoever rises early, well before the break of day,
and reads, recalls or speaks of the incomparable way
Lord Krishna overcame Lord Śiva, thereafter shall meet
with unremitting victory and never taste defeat.

20

King Nriga

1) While in the woods of Dvārakā, some Yadu boys one day
sought out some means to quench the thirst inflicted by their play.
On peering down a nearby well they found, to their surprise,
a huge, repulsive lizard staring back with slotted eyes.

2) The boys felt sorry for the lizard. Scurrying about,
they brought some ropes and leather thongs and tried to lift it out.
When all their efforts failed they knew exactly what to do:
they ran to Krishna, breathlessly disclosing all the news.

3) The lotus-eyed Lord Krishna went directly to the well.
As He reached down to lift the beast it seemed to break a spell.
At Krishna's touch the lizard shed its cold, reptilian skin
and, rising, took the golden form of heaven's denizens.

4) Though Krishna understood the situation, He inquired,
"Dear sir, are you a god? What sin could possibly require
an elevated soul like you to take a lizard's form?
If you are up to telling us, we'd like to be informed."

5-17) Requested by the limitless Lord Krishna to explain,
the god bowed low and spoke of how he came to be restrained.
"Though You know everything, my Lord, I'll tell my tale. You see,
I was the king named Nṛga, famed for giving charity.

I gave the *brāhmans* lovely cows in limitless supply—
as many cows as grains of sand or planets in the sky.
Each cow was youthful, well-behaved and full of luscious milk,
with gilded horns and hooves and dressed in ornamental silks.

With sacrifice to augment my philanthropic pursuits,
I gave these cows and other gifts to *brāhmans* of repute.
Each one received an elephant, a chariot, a house,
plus silver, gold and gems in quantities to please his spouse.

Amid these generous offerings, a solitary cow
belonging to a *brāhman* wandered in my herd somehow.
Not knowing this had happened, I decided to present
that very cow to someone else—and that caused my descent.

The *brāhman* who possessed the cow protested, 'She is mine!'
The *brāhman* now receiving her was equally inclined
to keep the cow himself. 'The King gave her to me,' he said.
They brought this hot dispute to me when it came to a head.

'You just gave me this cow!' the second *brāhman* priest began.
'But you stole her from me,' the first replied in reprimand.
The fearsome situation then became quite clear to me,
so I presented both these honored *brāhmans* with this plea:

'If you'll return this cow which brings disaster on my head,
I'll give you each one hundred thousand cows right now instead.
My fault was unintentional; I only meant you well,
but if I don't correct it now, I'll surely go to hell.'

Alas, both *brāhmans* wouldn't budge, and I could not conclude
the conflict with more charity. In very angry moods,
they left the palace feeling cheated. I now held the sin
of giving gifts to *brāhmans* and then claiming them again.

The agents of King Yamarāj took me, when I expired,
before their fearsome master, who observed me and inquired,
'Your pious deeds are many, yet you also have been cursed.
Your good results or bad results: which one do you want first?'

I said, 'My lord, I'll take my sinful *karma* first of all.'
At once the mighty Yamarāj commanded, 'Let him fall!'
And as I fell I saw my human body fade away
and turn into the lizard form you came across today.

My dear Lord Krishna, I had been a charitable king,
devoted to the *brāhmans* and supplying everything.
Recalling these past incidents is possible to do
because I also coveted an audience with You.

O Lord, I must be seeing You by special circumstance,
for only *yogīs*, finished with this world, receive this chance.
Govinda, God of gods, O Lord of all, be pleased with me!
Allow me to recall Your lotus feet incessantly.

All souls originate in You, the goal of every path.
You never change, although You act on everyone's behalf.
To see You makes me blessed, for my distress is now relieved.
Accept my deep respects, dear Lord, before I take Your leave."

18) King Nṛga walked around the Lord and, falling to the ground,
he touched Lord Krishna's lotus feet with his resplendent crown.
A fine celestial airplane then appeared as all looked on.
With Krishna's nod this new-born god climbed on it and was gone.

19) Because King Nṛga boasted of his generosity,
his pure devotion to the Lord was in its infancy.
His meeting with the Lord was premature to some extent,
but Krishna, for a higher cause, explained the whole event.

To Steal From Brahmans

20-26) "To take a *brāhman*'s property, however it's procured,
amounts to taking poison for which no one has a cure.
Why, even mystic *yogīs*, who can do most anything,
cannot enjoy such property—and what of worldly kings!

When ordinary fire burns, mere water puts it out.
However, if one takes a thing possessed by the devout,
he starts a different kind of blaze so dreadful and acute,
it burns the thief's entire family right down to the root.

To steal a *brāhmans*' property will send one straight to hell
along with all his children and his grandchildren as well.
And taking help to do so from the government is worse;
for that, ten generations back and forward shall be cursed.

A member of the royal order, blinded by his wealth,
sometimes usurps a *brāhman*'s assets, ruining himself.
Such royal sinners and their loved ones cook in hell for years
as numerous as specks of dust made wet by *brāhmans*' tears.

Yes, even taking back a gift will violate this rule
and makes the thief live sixty thousand years as worms in stool.
I therefore do not covet *brāhmans*' wealth. That grave mistake
will cost a king his kingdom and then turn him to a snake.

Dear friends, although he hits you or does something incorrect,
be sure to always treat a learned *brāhman* with respect.
And even if he curses you and seems to be unkind,
do not respond with harsh behavior, even in your mind.

As I respect the *brāhmans*, so must all of you as well.
If anyone refuses, I shall punish him myself.
Unknowingly, King Nṛga brought himself a lizard's fate."
Concluding with this statement, Krishna left for His estate.

21

Balaram

A Visit To Vrindavan

1) In Dvārakā one day, Lord Balarām grew keen to see
the many friends He'd known so well throughout His infancy.
He called a royal chariot and mounted it, alone,
to journey to Vṛndāvan, His beloved childhood home.

2) The residents of Dvārakā were thoroughly aware
the residents of Vraj loved Krishna far beyond compare.
They thought, "If Krishna stays and Balarām sees them instead,
both we and they may live—if they are not already dead."

3) Indeed, the pain of separation plagued the cowherd folk,
and when Lord Balarām arrived, His joyful parents spoke:
"O Master of creation, as Your foster dad and mother,
may we be kept from harm by You, and by Your younger brother."

4) Lord Balarām gave deep respects to all the senior men,
and took respects presented by His junior friends and kin.
With handshakes, folded palms, embraces, nods, sweet words and smiles,
Lord Balarām met everyone in tasteful, fitting style.

5) Lord Balarām refreshed Himself, returned and, sitting down,
accepted many questions from the cowherds gathered round.
Their voices shaking out of love, they asked about the health
of Krishna and the Yadus and of Balarām Himself:

6) "By fortune Kaṁsa died along with other enemies,
and Krishna built our relatives a fortress in the sea.
Dear Balarām, are all the Yadus doing well again?
Do some of you discuss and think about us now and then?"

7-9) The *gopīs* asked Lord Balarām, with suitable respect,
"Is Krishna happy with the city girls, as we suspect?
Does He recall His father and His mother? Will He come?
Does He recall us *gopīs* and the service we have done?

For Krishna we abandoned every person we held dear.
And how does He reciprocate? He simply disappears.
How do these learned city women give Him so much trust?
No doubt His words enchant them and His smiles arouse their lust.

Why don't we change the subject? Please do not bring up His name.
If He can live without us, let us simply do the same."
Remembering His laughter, His embraces and His eyes,
the *gopīs* thought of Krishna and gave in to mournful cries.

10) An expert in conciliation, Balarām replied,
"I have some confidential news for you that Krishna has supplied."
As Balarām repeated all His brother's secret words,
the *gopīs* felt relief and comfort, pleased with what they heard.

11) As weeks went by, the people of Vṛndāvan felt restored.
Lord Balarām went out at night, as Krishna had before.
He danced with certain *gopīs* who, at that time were too young
to come for Krishna's *rāsa* dance and join the moonlit fun.

12) Caressed by fragrant breezes, with His girlfriends left and right,
Lord Balarām enjoyed the Yamunā those pleasant nights.
The god Varuṇa sent a drink that flowed from honeyed trees,
a heavenly, intoxicating brew called Varunī.

13) That aromatic beverage perfumed the nighttime sky,
attracting Balarām and His companions to imbibe.
Gandarvas sang, and Balarām appeared to be the great
Airāvata, the elephant, surrounded by his mates.

14) The gods played kettledrums and showered flowers in their glee.
The sages praised Lord Balarām's divine, heroic deeds.
As Balarām and many girlfriends took their forest stroll,
the Varunī appeared to make His eyes begin to roll.

15) Intoxicated with delight, adorned with forest leis,
Lord Balarām felt beads of sweat like snowflakes on His face.
He called the Yamunā to come and cool His entourage
but Yamunā, who thought Him drunk, refused to even budge.

16) Enraged, Lord Balarām brought forth His famous, fearsome plow
and said, "If you don't come, I'll redirect you here right now!
You disregard My order and move only at your whim.
My plow shall make a hundred streams of you. Shall I begin!"

17, 18) The frightened river-goddess who appeared and bowed her head
was simply an expansion of the one that Krishna wed.
With trembling voice the Yamunā said, "Rām, please hear me first.
I didn't understand that you sustain the universe!

Release me from your mighty plow, O greatest of the great.
Not knowing Your position, I did not cooperate.
I come before You humbled. Now accept me, if You please,
as one of Your surrendered and committed devotees."

19) Releasing Yamunā, with all His *gopī* friends in tow,
the elephant-like Balarām stepped in her crystal flow.
He splashed His girlfriends; they splashed back. And when their play was through,
the goddess Lakṣmī gave Him gems and silks of ocean blue.

20) Adorned with silks and jewelry and fragrant sandal paste,
resplendent Balarām observed the channels He had placed
in Yamunā when He refused to let her keep away.
A visitor can see those channels to this very day.

21) For sixty evenings Balarām enjoyed Vṛndāvan's mood,
as well as the exquisite charm the *gopīs* all exude,
Their constant fun together filled His mind with great delight.
To Balarām, those sixty evenings passed as if one night.

Paundraka

22) While Balarām enjoyed His trip, a certain foolish king
named Pauṇḍraka declared himself the lord of everything.
The flattery of childish men had swelled his empty head.
He thus dispatched to Dvārakā a messenger who said:

23, 24) "O Krishna, Pauṇḍraka, my king, has sent me here. It seems
that you have failed to understand that he is the Supreme.
He is in fact Lord Vāsudev, the one and only God,
and he has come to show his grace. You must stop Your facade.

He orders You to bow to him. You must also desist
from using his four symbols: conch shell, lotus, club and disc.
Do not ignore his warning, for he told me to convey
He'll crush You if You don't stop imitating him today."

25) King Ugrasen and other members of the Yadu court
could not refrain from laughing at this ludicrous report.
Lord Krishna sat, enjoying all the laughter. By and by,
He called waiting envoy and dictated this reply:

26) "Yes, I'll release these symbols, as you impudently said,
especially my disc, which shall remove your foolish head.
Then you can grace the vultures, hawks and dogs that gather round
to worship and adore you as they eat you on the ground."

27) To Pauṇḍraka, the messenger relayed these taunting words.
As Pauṇḍraka considered them, the unforeseen occurred:
his friend, the King of Kāśī, and Pauṇḍraka (then his guest),
were shocked to see Lord Krishna and His army, battle-dressed.

28) The mighty warrior Pauṇḍraka attacked with two divisions;
the King of Kāśī brought three more to hold the rear position.

King Pauṇḍraka wore Krishna's crown, insignia and dress.
He flew Lord Krishna's flag and showed His mark upon his chest.

29) Lord Krishna laughed and laughed to see this duplicate appear
who looked just like an actor dressed in someone else's gear.
When Pauṇḍraka's militia hurled weapons in attack,
Lord Krishna neutralized them all and drove the soldiers back.

30) Dismembered soldiers, camels, steeds and elephants all fell.
It looked as if Lord Śiva danced and bid the Earth farewell.[1]
Across the blood-soaked battlefield, his enemy disgraced,
Lord Krishna turned to Pauṇḍraka and told him, face to face:

[1]*When the universe ends, Lord Śiva performs a dance of destruction.*

31) "Dear Pauṇḍraka, did your announcement not include a list
of symbols I am to relinquish, starting with this disc?
I now renounce My disc, O fool, by sharing it with you.
Now you renounce My name, which you so stupidly assumed."

32) As mountain peaks go soaring off from Indra's thunderbolts,
The head of Pauṇḍraka flew off, concluding his revolt.
The King of Kāśī, who had vowed to cut off Krishna's head,
confronted Krishna next and had his own removed instead.

33) By imitating Krishna, this Pauṇḍraka grew absorbed
in contemplating all the lovely features of the Lord.
Pauṇḍraka was thus purified and gained his liberation,
while Krishna traveled homeward to a blissful celebration.

34) Lord Krishna's arrows, having plucked the head of Kāśī's King
had flown it back to Kāśī as if it had sprouted wings.
The citizens of Kāśī gathered round it in a throng
and asked, "What is this object, and to whom does it belong?"

35) They saw it had some earrings and assumed it was a head.
They thought it must be Krishna, whom their king had wanted dead.
On recognizing what it really was, they knealt and cried,
"Oh, who will give us shelter now? Our mighty king has died!"

Sudakshina

36) The King of Kāśī's eldest son, Sudakṣiṇa by name,
performed his father's funeral and, in his mind, proclaimed,
"I must track down his killer and avenge my dear deceased!"
Sudakṣiṇa then worshipped Śiva, aided by his priests.

37) The powerful Lord Śiva, in a pleased, commanding voice,
presented Sudakṣiṇa with a blessing of his choice.
The prince requested Śiva to endow him with the means
to kill his father's killer so his name could be redeemed.

38) Lord Śiva said, "There is a sacred ritual designed
to vanquish all the foes of the brahminically inclined.
The sacrificial fire will itself destroy such men."
Sudakṣiṇa, on hearing this, was eager to begin.

39) The sacrificial fire, as the priests performed the rite,
rose up and took a human form—a most horrific sight.
The fearsome, naked creature had a beard of molten ore,
a flaming trident, furrowed brow and fangs designed to gore.

40) On legs as long as royal palms, the monster ran away.
Accompanied by ghosts, he scorched the country all the way
to Dvārakā, his destination. There, the people saw
a hellish beast approaching as they watched with fear and awe.

41) Distraught, the people cried to Krishna, "Save us from this fire!
That flaming beast will turn our lovely city to a pyre."
Lord Krishna, who was playing dice (as monarchs sometimes do)
just laughed at their alarm and said, "I'll surely rescue you."

42) Almighty Krishna understood the giant, fiery beast
had come from Śiva's sacrificial rite. He thus released
Sudarshana, His firey disc, which blazed like countless suns.
Its heat at once turned back the beast and put it on the run.

43) The fiery beast, defeated by Lord Krishna, had no choice;
when curses are reversed, they fall on him who used his voice

to speak them in the first place. Thus, empowered to destroy,
the demon turned on them who had put him in their employ.

44) Sudakṣiṇa was shocked at the arrival of the beast,
who quickly burned his boss to death, along with all his priests.
Thus men who challenge God in a demoniac crusade
end up annihilated by the weapons they have made.

45) The disc burned the entire town of Kāśī down as well,
converting all its buildings to infernos out of hell.
Sudarshana departed from that smoldering disaster,
returning to the side of his eternal, graceful master.

46) A person who recounts this gallant pastime of the Lord
or hears it with attention will attain a great reward:
release from many lifetimes of accumulated sin,
and freedom from the punishment of taking birth again.

Dvivida

47) "Dear Śukadev," said Viṣṇurāta, "is there more to hear
of Balarām's achievements in Vṛndāvan's atmosphere?
I crave that wondrous taste with which His pastimes are imbued.
As God, His actions have no limit. What else did He do?"

48) A servant of Lord Rāmacandra, Dvivida by name,
fell in with Bhaumasura and was thoroughly defamed.
This hairy ape, upset by Bhauma's death, ransacked the land,
destroying homes and villages completely out of hand.

49) He tore up mountains, using them to slaughter peaceful towns.
He churned the sea so mightily that coastal people drowned.
He spoiled sacred rites when he passed urine, gas and stool,
and shut up helpless people in dark caves—he was that cruel.

50) One day Dvivida, primed for rape and other violent ills,
heard sweet, attractive singing in the Raivataka Hills.
He came upon Lord Balarām, absorbed in luscious play
with lovely *gopīs*, drinking Varunī from pots of clay.

51) Lord Balarām wore lotuses on every handsome limb,
with drinks and songs and rolling eyes and *gopīs* circling Him.
The mischievous Dvivida scrambled up a nearby tree
and sounded out "keelaa-keelaa" in vulgar mockery.

52) The *gopīs* started giggling at the impudent display,
for, as young girls, they tended to behave in silly ways.
Without regard for Balarām, the ape displayed his teeth.
He then turned round, bent over and displayed his underneath.

53) Disgusted, Balarām picked up a rock and let it fly.
The crafty ape avoided it and, in a rude reply,
picked up the pot of Varunī and smashed it to the ground.
He pulled the *gopīs*' clothing and produced offensive sounds.

54) Lord Balarām despised these acts. He also understood
dispatching of this wicked ape would do the planet good.
But as the Lord picked up his club, Dvivida broke a tree
and brought it down on Balarām with great dexterity.

55) Lord Balarām stood motionless despite the heavy blow
and struck Dvivida's skull so hard that blood began to flow.
Dvivida snapped another tree and stripped it with his arms
but Balarām just splintered it, again avoiding harm.

56) This scene went on again and yet again till all around
the forest had grown treeless—so they fought on naked ground.
The angry ape released a rain of rocks on Balarām,
who smashed each one to pebbles with His club, remaining calm.

57) The furious Dvivida chose to foolishly persist
by beating Balarām directly with his primate fists.
Disposing of His club, Lord Balarām employed His hand
to strike a single, crushing blow the ape could not withstand.

58) Dvivida crumpled to a heap and bid his life farewell.
An earthquake wobbled Raivataka Mountain as he fell.
Lord Balarām returned to home as people sang with love.
The Earth rejoiced, as did the sages, saints and gods above.

Lakshmana and Samba

59) When Lakṣmanā, the daughter of Duryodhana, became
of age to marry, many famous kings and princes came
to take part in her *svayaṁvara* ritual, for she
would choose her husband then, and she was lovely as could be.

60) Now Samba, son of Krishna, always carried in his mind
the urge to marry Lakṣmanā, but she was not inclined.
So Samba chose to kidnap her, a custom of the day.
Before she could select her man, he carried her away.

61, 62) The kinsmen of Duryodhana, the Kuru clan, exclaimed,
"The rogue has stolen Lakṣmanā. He must be put to shame.
Arrest him. What will Krishna and his Yadu family do?
They rule their kingdom just because we still allow them to.

When we detain their precious Samba, all the Yadu men
will understand our power and be humbled once again.
As *yogīs* curb their senses by the power of the soul,
to catch this prince will bring the Yadus under our control."

63) The elder Kurus, led by Bhīṣma, authorized this plan.
Though Lakṣmanā, now touched, could not wed any other man,
the Kurus chose to show their rage and exercise their will
by holding Samba captive, though they didn't want him killed.

64) Duryodhana and many other warriors rushed the prince.
The valiant Samba bravely strung his bow; he didn't wince.
Despite the unjust nature of Duryodhana's attack,
with lion-like ferocity, young Samba battled back.

65) Heroic Samba struck the mighty Karna and six friends.
Disabling their chariots, he put them on defense.
The Yadu prince was strong, the Kuru men had to admit;
they praised his faultless archery as they were being hit.

66) A horde of Kurus next forced Samba's chariot to slow;
one warrior struck his driver and another broke his bow.

The Kurus captured Samba and, with effort, tied him down.
With Lakṣmanā, they went back home, their quarry tightly bound.

67) When Nārada reported this, the Yadus were abhorred.
King Ugrasen commanded, "We must arm ourselves for war!"
Lord Balarām, however, cooled their anger as He said,
"Instead of fighting, let us try diplomacy instead."

68) Accompanied by Yadu priests and elders, Balarām
appeared to be the moon among the stars, serene and calm.
When they made camp near Hastināpur, Balarām resolved
that Uddhava should first attempt to get the problem solved.

69) So Uddhava went in the Kuru court and paid respects
to Dhṛtarāṣṭra, Bhīṣma, Duryodhana and the rest.
When they learned Balarām was waiting in a nearby place,
the Kurus, bearing gifts, went out to greet Him face to face.

70) The Kurus worshipped Balarām with gifts of cows and scents,
and those who knew his strength bowed down, avoiding an offense.
They asked about each other's health and relatives, and then
Lord Balarām forthrightly got to business. He began,

71) "King Ugrasen, our ruler, sent instructions here with me.
These words are for your benefit; now listen carefully:
'A gang of you attacked our solitary, blameless prince.
Since we're related, I have tolerated your offense.'"

72, 73) The Kurus heard these potent words and all that they implied.
Infuriated, they conferred and angrily replied,
"Amazing as it is, it seems a shoe has left the ground
and tried to set itself on top, above the royal crown.

Because these Yadus married in our royal dynasty,
we granted them their throne, their wealth and other property.
We shared our royal symbols, such as conchshells, throne and fans.
Like serpents fed with milk, they dare to issue us commands!
Would even Indra dare usurp a fig from Kuru hands?
Why, that would be a lion's kill surrendered to a lamb!"

74) The self-important Kurus, their position clearly shown,
then turned their backs on Balarām and strutted to their homes.
Lord Balarām's expression grew as hot as scorching flame.
He laughed a laugh that terrified, then forcefully proclaimed,

75-79) "These puffed-up, passion-laden rogues have no desire for peace.
They'll only come to reason if they're punished like a beast.
Lord Krishna and the Yadus held their rage, though it was hard,
but these dull-headed rascals show Me utter disregard.

King Ugrasen commands the gods! Lord Krishna carried home
celestial *pārijāta* trees—He's fit for any throne!
Why, Lakṣmī worships Krishna's feet; do they imagine He
does not deserve accouterments reserved for royalty?

The gods pursue the dust from Krishna's feet to grace their crowns.
Brahmā and Śiva, Lakṣmī, Me, and others of renown
are simply parts of Krishna's all-inclusive state of being.
How dare these fools say He's unfit to be a mortal king!

The Kurus brag that they have granted us the land we use?
They think they are the social head and we the social shoes?
Their opulence intoxicates their foolish, swollen heads.
What genuine authority would stomach what they've said?

Why should these wretched Kurus burden Earth another day?"
With plow in hand, He stood as if to set the world ablaze.
As Balarām's expansive plow began to strike the ground,
the tremors rocked the city and caused panic all around.

80) The town itself was broken from the earth without delay.
Lord Balarām then pierced the ground and dragged the town away.
The Kurus saw the Ganges, which was flowing to the south,
about to swallow their entire city in her mouth.

81-83) In terror they brought Lakṣmanā and Samba to the Lord
and bowed to him to consummate their hasty new accord.
"O Balarām," they cried, "the whole creation rests on You.
In ignorance we made offense. Please tell us what to do.

We understand that You create, maintain, and end us all.
You move the stars and planets as if you were playing ball.
As one of countless pastimes, you keep Earth upon your head,
wind up the whole creation, and take rest upon your bed.

Resentment doesn't spark your anger; rather, you engage
in showing anger just to purify us rascals with your rage.
As our creator, helper and the soul of all we do,
O wielder of all potencies, we bow our heads to You."

84) Propitiated by the trembling Kurus, Balarām
withdrew his fearsome anger and grew generous and calm.
Relieved, the Kuru prince, Duryodhana, at once arranged
a dowry for his daughter, Lakṣmanā. The gift contained:

85) Twelve hundred full-grown elephants, each aged some sixty years;
six thousand golden chariots with skilled charioteers;
one hundred twenty thousand horses, each with full effects;
and maidservants—a thousand, graced with jewels on their necks.

86) Lord Balarām accepted this. The Kurus pacified,
his party went to Dvārakā with Samba and his bride.
His loved ones there heard every word their hero had to say,
and Hastināpur's southern side is higher—to this day.

22

Narada

The Many Krishnas

1) When Nārada, the mystic, heard that Krishna had been wed
so many times, an inspiration filled his saintly head:
"I must observe how Krishna, in a single body, gives
sufficient time to sixteen thousand wives. How does He live?"

2) When Nārada reached Dvārakā, the sounds of birds and bees
filled up the parks and greens of that municipality.
As swans and cranes sang out refrains on lotus-covered lakes,
the sage found temples, streets and houses, built without mistakes.

3) A web of spotless boulevards traversed the smooth terrain.
Festoons and trees lined arteries and kept out sun and rain.
Nine hundred thousand palaces lined brilliant avenues,
each marble mansion trimmed in silver set with rows of jewels.

4) A certain lovely area of Dvārakā stood out.
The sage saw this was Krishna's own domain, without a doubt.
As Viśvakarmā's masterpiece, where gods were often seen,
its sixteen thousand palaces were home to Krishna's queens.

5) The palaces had coral pillars set with gems that shone.
The walls were decked with sapphires, pearls and other precious stones.
The sage walked in a palace and saw serving maids who wore
expensive jeweled lockets as they floated through their chores.

6) The well-dressed palace guards allowed the sage to freely roam.
He noticed that the ornate palace rooftops were the home
of dancing, joyous peacocks who were pleased and cried aloud
as they mistook the palace incense smoke for thunderclouds.

7) When Nārada saw Krishna, Krishna's wife, with yak-tail fan,
was fanning Him, despite the thousand maids at her command.
Lord Krishna, seeing Nārada, arose and touched his feet.
With folded palms He bowed and offered Nārada His seat.

8) Delighted with His guest, Lord Krishna bathed his holy feet
and put the water on his head. Although He is complete
within Himself, Lord Krishna showed how one receives a saint.
Aware of Krishna's purpose, Nārada made no complaint.

9) When all the proper rituals of welcome were complete,
Lord Krishna spoke to Nārada in phrases nectar sweet:
"O master, are there any goods or deeds we may provide?"
Saint Nārada was smiling as he thoughtfully replied,

10) "Almighty Lord, you rule the worlds. You're everybody's friend,
yet you subdue the rogues and thieves who constantly offend.
I only ask Your blessings and the power to recall
Your lotus feet forever. I want nothing else at all."

11) The saintly guest excused himself and went outside to see
still further demonstrations of Lord Krishna's potency.
Inside the next large palace he saw Krishna playing dice
with Uddhava. Surprised to see him, Krishna said, "How nice!"

12) The Lord continued, "When did you arrive? I'm very pleased
to have an unexpected guest with saintly qualities."
The Lord seemed unaware of their encounter just before.
Surprised, the sage said nothing, took his leave and went next door.

13) In this abode he found the Lord in warm parental mood.
In others He was bathing, saying prayers and serving food.
In others He was holding morning sacrifice, and yet
in others He behaved as if the sun already set.

14) The Lord engaged in sword practice in one palatial home
while elsewhere riding elephants and elsewhere, near His throne,
at rest while nearby poets sang His praise. The sage observed
the Lord consulting, eating, playing sports and being served.

15) The Lord was, somewhere, giving cows to elevated priests,
and elsewhere he was listening to Vedic histories.
In one abode, the Lord engaged in joking with his wife
while elsewhere holding rituals enriching family life.

16) In one abode, Lord Krishna meditated on himself.
(Since He is God, how could He meditate on someone else?)
He served his elders elsewhere; somewhere else He planned for war
while planning pious peacemaking with Balarām next door.

17) Sage Nārada saw Krishna make arrangements for his sons
and daughters to wed brides and grooms approved by everyone.
He saw the Lord send out some couples; others He brought back
for festive celebrations with the crowds they would attract.

18) Sometimes Lord Krishna worshipped gods, while sometimes He'd erect
fine gardens, wells and temples that the public would respect.
He'd mount a handsome Sindhi horse and ride off to pursue
the fearsome forest animals as kings would sometimes do.

19) The sage observed the Lord don clothes of ordinary kind
and walk the streets to understand the common person's mind.
All-knowing Krishna, incognito? Kings may be required
to do such things, but not the Lord! So Nārada inquired,

20) "By studying your countless mystic potencies first hand,
it's clear to me you far exceed what I can understand.
Would you be kind and bless me with an everlasting tour
to loudly sing the glories that are so distinctly yours?"

21, 22) Lord Krishna said, "Dear Nārada, I sense that you're disturbed.
My actions simply show how one should live within this world.
You saw me worship gods, and when you came, I worshipped you.
I did all this to demonstrate what mankind needs to do.

Because I bathed your lotus feet, you're feeling some distress.
Although I'm God and you're my son, was that erroneous?
For sons to touch their fathers with their feet shows disrespect,
but if his son climbs in the father's lap, will he object?"

23) In every palace, Nārada saw Krishna's matching form
engaged in every duty pious householders perform.
This vision was a special gift to Nārada that day,
and as the sage departed, he was thoroughly amazed.

24) While keeping sixteen thousand queens romantically inclined,
Lord Krishna mimicked human life and helped improve mankind.
If someone chants or hears about Lord Krishna's daily deeds
his quest for love of God is surely destined to succeed.

Lord Krishna's Daily Life

25) Queen Rukminī would greet the rooster's crowing with a curse.
Each dawn it broke the Lord's embrace, in which she was immersed.
The fragrant breeze and buzzing bees would rouse the sleeping birds
who woke the Lord with songs as sweet as fine poetic words.

26) Despite that most auspicious hour, Rukminī felt grief.
For her, the night at Krishna's side was always much too brief.
The Lord would rise for daily chores. For her, that was a shame,
and all His sixteen thousand other wives felt just the same.

27) The Lord got up before the dawn, touched water and began
to meditate upon the Lord, like any pious man.
To contemplate the self-illumined, absolute Supreme
dispels the painful woes of this illusory regime.

28) The Lord then bathed and dressed Himself and, in the Vedic way,
held ritual oblations to receive the coming day.

He said the sacred *gāyatrī* and hailed the rising sun;
He prayed to gods, His ancestors, and sages, one by one.

29) The self-contained Lord Krishna worshipped *brāhmans* every day
with herds of decorated cows and words of thoughtful praise.
Each cow had silver-plated hooves and horns adorned with gold
and ample milk to feed her calf, each less than one year old.

30) Lord Krishna dressed in articles identified with Him:
His yellow silks, His garlands and His famed Kaustubha gem.
He saw and touched auspicious things and then, the histories tell,
gave gifts to all His ministers and citizens as well.

31) He passed out garlands, sandal paste and *pān*[1] to everyone,
including wives, advisors, priests and friends. When that was done,
He'd take some for Himself and then await His charioteer,
who, guiding steeds and chariot, would punctually appear.

[1]*A mildly intoxicating bean commonly chewed in India.*

32) Both Sātyaki and Uddhava would join Him for the drive.
The palace women watched Him leave with bashful, loving eyes.
To let Lord Krishna leave was hard, His many wives would find.
As He drove off, His loving smile entranced the women's minds.

33) As sixteen thousand Krishnas bid their loving wives goodbye,
each Krishna could be only seen by those who lived nearby.
Converging at Sudharmā, the celestial meeting hall,
a single Krishna entered from the confluence of all.

34) This meeting hall gave anyone who entered quick relief
from hunger, thirst, illusion, aging, death and every grief.
As Krishna sat upon His throne, His own effulgent light
illumined all around Him like the moonshine fills the night.

35) A host of entertainment instantaneously ensued.
First, jesters pleased the Lord with an array of comic moods.
Performers sang and danced with zest as fine musicians played,
then poets and historians recited Krishna's praise.

Jailed Kings Plea for Help

36) One day, as certain priests intoned the sacred Vedic hymns
and others told the stories of renowned, religious men,
a messenger arrived. The sentries brought this special guest
to Krishna's court with this report and staggering request:

37) "My Lord, with folded palms I come, dispatched by many kings
who lost their rightful kingdoms and are greatly suffering.
Jarasāndha imprisoned twenty thousand who refused
to aid his evil conquests. They have sent me with this news:

(Brahmā Samhita meter: -| -| -|-| --| -|-)
38-42) 'O endless Krishna, who destroys Your disciple's terrors,
we selfish kings are scared and beg for Your holy shelter.
As worldly people, we did not heed Your good instructions,
so You have come as Time and humbled us with destruction.

O Lord of all, who has descended to save the pious,
we must confess that there is something that mystifies us:
Jarasāndha has broken all Vedic regulations,
yet he's been able to put us in such tribulation.

Our happy, royal lives were simply a grand illusion.
We clutched our problems and threw out their ideal solution:
devotion to Your lotus feet, made without condition.
And now our bodies are but corpses with big positions.

Since You remove the grief of those who bow down before you,
release us from our chains of agony, we implore you.
Jarasāndha has captured us like a herd of cattle
but You defeated him in seventeen famous battles.

You then allowed him to defeat You, for Your own purpose,
but that filled him with so much pride that he freely hurts us.
Because we are Your devotees he chose us to step on.
Please rectify our plight with Your deadly *cakra* weapon.'"

(iambic heptameter)
43) The messenger continued, "These incarcerated kings
aspire for Your presence and the freedom that it brings.
They sent me with this message and submit to Your control,
so kindly show Your mercy to these troubled royal souls."

Narada's Advice

44) At this time, unexpectedly, saint Nārada appeared,
his face aglow and head adorned with tresses long unsheared.
Delighted, Krishna stood, prepared a seat and bowed His head.
Completing proper greetings, Krishna welcomed him and said,

45) "This great soul who can travel through the universe at will
today has blessed our city. We are strengthened and fulfilled.
Dear Nārada, since everything is surely known to you,
please tell us what the Pāndavas, our friends, intend to do."

(Meter: -|- -|- -|- -|)
46-50) The saintly sage said, "Your illusory might
bewilders Brahmā and has made him contrite.
My Lord, I am therefore not slightly surprised
You ask this of me and maintain Your disguise.

Creator of all, no one knows, except You,
what future may come and what others may do.
Because we're caught up in this death and rebirth,
You kindly descend to enlighten the Earth.

You know everything, yet because You have asked,
I'll tell You King Yudhiṣṭhir plans a great task:
To please You he'll hold, at incredible price,
the Rājasūya, the supreme sacrifice.

Great monarchs and gods will attend this event,
all eager to see You, if You should consent
to build the participant's spiritual wealth
and bless the occasion by coming Yourself.

Your presence is needed; it's well understood
that You represent the auspicious and good.
With You as one's shelter, success is assured;
You even make pure Ganges water more pure."

(iambic heptameter)
51) When Nārada was finished, a debate at once ensued.
The name 'Jarasāndha' put many in a fighting mood,
though Yudhiṣṭhir insisted Krishna's presence was required.
Lord Krishna saw Uddhava there and smilingly inquired,

52) "You are indeed our closest friend and farthest-seeing guide.
We trust your expert counsel and shall do as you decide."
Uddhava, seeing Krishna thus pretend to be confused,
accepted his instruction and suggested what to do.

The Pandavas

Uddhava's Answer

1-7) Evaluating both the kings' and Nārada's requests,
Uddhava said, "My Lord, as saintly Nārada suggests,
You must assist the Pāndavas by going there Yourself.
Yet You must also save the kings beseeching You for help.

To hold the special sacrifice the Pāndavas desire,
A monarch must defeat all foes. It's utterly required.
Jarasāndha stands in the way of that prerequisite,
and thus You cannot help the Pāndavas, at least not yet.

Jarasāndha is powerful and tricky to defeat.
He far exceeds ten thousand giant elephants in strength.
Since Bhīma is the only man equivalent in might,
he could destroy this scoundrel—if we stage the proper fight.

Jarasāndha will lose if he is battled hand to hand,
but not if he brings forth the mighty army he commands.
If Bhīma goes in *brāhman*'s clothes and begs for charity,
Jarasāndha will grant his wish, whatever it may be.

In charity, Jarasāndha can't bear to be outdone,
so Bhīma simply needs to beg to fight him one-on-one.
He then can kill Jarasāndha. And now, my Lord, for You,
I must say all these warriors, kings and gods are just Your tools.

The wives of these imprisoned kings keep faith in You and pray
when their young children ask them why their fathers went away.
Like they, and we, the *gopīs* see Your great ability,
for You saved Sītā and Your parents from captivity.

Not only will Jarasāndha's demise make all inspired;
the Pāndavas can hold the sacrifice that they desire."
Though younger Yadu princes would have issued war commands,
both Krishna and the Yadu elders backed Uddhava's plan.

8) Sage Nārada was pleased with this and promptly took his leave,
and Krishna told the messenger the kings would be relieved.
He sent the man to tell the kings about His rescue plan
so they could wait and tolerate the misery at hand.

Greeting Krishna

9) Lord Krishna then took sanction from His father to proceed.
His servants made arrangements for His wives' and children's needs,
for they were keen to be a part of Krishna's entourage
and see the city of the sons of Pāndu Maharāj.

10) Lord Krishna's golden chariot displayed Garuḍa's sign.
His soldiers marched around Him, and His family behind.
As music played and men paraded, other burley men
conveyed His wives and children on their golden palanquins.

11) Alongside were the serving maids, on camels, carts and steeds,
with blankets, tents and other things the travelers would need.
The soldier's swords and armor shone. In all, the great display
appeared to be an ocean full of undulating waves.

12) Lord Krishna's party traveled over rivers, fields and hills.
On nearing Indraprastha, which the gods had helped to build,

the Lord observed a multitude of ministers and priests
surrounding Yudhiṣṭhir, who was appearing very pleased.

13) While music played and *brāhmans* chanted hymns, King Yudhiṣṭhir
received the person whom his thoughts had constantly revered.
As senses gain awareness when a sleeping man revives,
the Pāndaṿas felt Krishna had restored their very lives.

14) King Yudhiṣṭhir embraced the Lord again and yet again,
forgetting, in his ecstasy, this planet of chagrin.
Then Bhīma, laughing as he cried, embraced his dearest Lord.
Arjuna and the twins were next; their teardrops also poured.

15) The Lord bowed down before the priests and elders of the clan
as singers, dancers, jesters and narrators all began
to glorify Lord Krishna with their own respective skills.
As peals of music sounded, everyone was pleased and thrilled.

16) Surrounded by His well-wishers and relatives, the Lord
came in to Indraprastha, where his name was much adored.
The city roads, adorned with flags and sprinkled with perfume,
were lined by homes with welcome lamps that shone in every room.

17) Each building had a golden dome atop a silver base.
The citizens were finely dressed and blessed with sandal paste.
As Krishna savored Indraprastha, women rushed to see,
abandoning their homes and mates with great alacrity.

18) The royal road was crowded, so the women, clothes askew,
ascended to the rooftops to see what the Lord would do.
As heartfelt, broadly smiling glances crossed each lovely face,
they showered flowers on Him and, within, felt His embrace.

19) Observing Krishna's wives, who looked like stars around the moon,
the women cried, "What have they done to win the matchless boon
of Krishna's generous smiles and loving, playful sidelong glance?"
Lord Krishna, meanwhile, took in many gifts as He advanced.

20) The royal household members rushed to their beloved guest
and brought Him to the palace to fulfill the Queen's request.
Queen Kuntī rose and hugged the Lord. King Yudhiṣṭhir, her son,
forgot, in all his bliss, how rites of greeting should be done.

21) Lord Krishna bowed before Queen Kuntī and the many wives
of other family elders who had loved him all their lives.
His younger sister Subhadrā, and Draupadī bowed down
to Krishna and His escorts, several wives of great renown.

22) As Draupadī received the wives with garlands, gems and clothes,
King Yudhiṣṭhir arranged for royal dining and repose.
Lord Krishna's massive entourage enjoyed, with each new day,
some method of reception in a fresh and different way.

Talks with Yudhishdhir

23) The Pāndavas found Krishna so addictive and sublime
they soon convinced the Lord to stay among them for some time.
So after sharing talks of quests in joyful fellowship,
Lord Krishna and the King discussed the reason for His trip.

24) One day in the assembly hall, surrounded by a group
of sages, business magnates, priests and military troops,
King Yudhiṣṭhir addressed the Lord, as brothers, gurus, friends
and elder family members all sat down and listened in.

(Brahmā-samhita meter: -|-| -|-| |-| -|-*)*
25) "Although we have no need for property, gold or mansions,
I long to worship Your auspicious divine expansions—
the gods themselves—to show the world they depend upon You.
Bless us, my Lord, that our endeavor may have some value.

26) Your devotees who have consistently sung Your praises
escape this mortal life and all of its painful phases.
Still, they achieve enough material satisfaction
to far surpass the godless souls in the mode of passion.

27) So let the world observe the power of pure devotion
and see the emptiness of tedious self-promotion.
You have no favorites, for all souls are Your dependents,
yet You prefer Your devotees in complete transcendence."

(iambic heptameter)
28-30) The Lord replied, "Your thoughts are perfect, noble and worthwhile.
You've shown divine and secular indeed can reconcile.
The sages, gods and ancestors will all be satisfied
if you perform this monumental sacrifice worldwide.

You must establish taxes and make every king enroll
until the very Earth itself is under your control.
Your brothers will assist you by collecting ample wealth
for they were born of mighty gods. O King, as for yourself,

Your self-control is so complete you've even conquered Me
by using all your senses in my service constantly.
No person lacking sense control, be he a god or king,
can conquer My devotee with his riches, fame or strength."

The Generous Jarasandha

31) On hearing this King Yudhiṣṭhir felt thoroughly empowered.
His face lit up as if it were a blooming lotus flower.
To eastern lands he ordered Bhīma; then, the King sent forth
Nakula west, Sahadev south, and Dhanañjaya[1] north.
[1]*Arjuna, the winner of wealth.*

32) The brothers told the kings they met of Yudhiṣṭhir's intent
to hold the Rājasūya sacrifice, which clearly meant
the kings would either pay a tax or fight with Yudhiṣṭhir.
So every king paid taxes out of love, respect or fear.

33) Jarasāndha alone refused King Yudhiṣṭhir's demand,
so Krishna told the King about Uddhava's clever plan.
Thus Krishna, Bhīma and Arjuna, veiled in *brāhman*'s dress,
approached Jarasāndha's domain and tendered this request:

34, 35) "Great King, you're famed for giving needy guests what they require.
We wish all good upon you; kindly give what we desire.
When begging from the generous, fulfillment is assured,
for nothing is so precious that its loss can't be endured.

A great soul has no enemy; he sees all as the same.
He overcomes all selfishness and wins eternal fame.
For instance, Balī gave the universe in charity,
and Śibi gave his very flesh to set a pigeon free."

36) Jarasāndha took notice that the voices of these guests
were more like those that grant, not those that issue, such requests.
He saw their muscled arms showed marks of bowstrings. And, what's more,
he had a hazy feeling he had seen them all before.

37) Jarasāndha thought, "Surely these are *kṣatriyas* disguised
as *brāhman* beggars. Still, a great man makes no alibis.
I too shall gain King Balī's fame by giving of myself
to satisfy these *brāhmans*, though they're clearly someone else."

38) Decisively, Jarasāndha observed his guests and said,
"I'll give you what you ask for, even if it's my own head."
Lord Krishna, Bhīma and Arjuna, very satisfied,
acknowledged his munificence. Lord Krishna then replied,

39) "We ask you for a duel. We are princes; let us fight.
That's all we ask. Here's Bhīma, with Arjuna on his right.
And I am their maternal cousin Krishna. We have met
a few times on the battlefield before. Did you forget?"

40) Jarasāndha laughed loudly and replied, "All right, you fools!
You could have had my head; now, you've gained nothing by this ruse.
But Krishna, you have run from me. No second chance for you.
And Arjuna, you're weak. But Bhīma—yes, I think you'll do."

Bhima Battles Jarasandha

41) With this, Jarasāndha presented Bhīma with a mace
and went off with his rival to a distant rural place.
The two began to strike each other. Thoroughly enraged,
they circled left and right as actors dance upon a stage.

42) Like tusks of dueling elephants, their maces would collide.
It sounded like a thunderstorm refusing to subside.
So strong were both combatants that, as blow by blow was thrown,
they smashed their wooden clubs to bits against the other's bones.

43) Their clubs thus ruined, Bhīma and Jarasāndha began
to pound each other with their fists and battle hand-to-hand.
The two were matched in stamina, in training and in might,
and thus for twenty-seven days they carried on the fight.

44) Jarasāndha had secrets in his past that Krishna knew.
It seems that he was stillborn, with his body split in two.
An evil witch procured the pieces, joined them into one
and raised him as her powerful but evil-hearted son.

45) Since Bhīma wasn't winning, Krishna showed him what to do
by picking up a supple branch and ripping it in two.
So Bhīma tripped Jarasāndha and, standing on his calf,
pulled strongly on his other leg and ripped him right in half.

46) Jarasāndha's companions saw his two halves had been breached,
with half a torso, throat and face; one leg and one arm each.
They cried in lamentation as Lord Krishna tightly hugged
the mighty warrior Bhīma, who had finally killed the thug.

47) The Lord then crowned Jarasāndha's respected elder son
as ruler of his father's land. The coronation done,
Lord Krishna freed the twenty thousand long-imprisoned kings,
just as he kindly liberates conditioned living beings.

Krishna Frees the Kings

48) The kings emerged from prison looking soiled and poorly dressed.
Their bodies looked emaciated, pale and greatly stressed.
They saw the Lord in yellow silks and skin of monsoon blue,
His smiling face adorned with lotus eyes of pinkish hue.

49) The Lord displayed His four-armed form, and in His lotus hands,
a conch shell, lotus, disc and club awaited His command.
His gorgeous gems and flowers made the Lord appear so sweet
the kings forgot their senses as they bowed and touched His feet.

50) To see the Lord was ecstasy. The kings at once forgot
the weariness of prison, having gained what they had sought.
The master of the senses stood before them, then and there.
They joined their palms, stood up as one, and thankfully declared,

51-54) "O Lord, this ghastly world has made us thoroughly depressed.
We bow to You who crushes a submissive soul's distress.
We do not blame Jarasāndha; our torment was Your grace
to rid us of illusions that attach us to this place.

As childish men seek water from mirages in the sand,
a fool reveres illusions that keep slipping through his hand.
Forgetting You and chasing wealth, we fought without regard
for anybody else. Dear Lord, Your lesson has been hard.

Mirages such as kingdoms shall no longer swindle us
to prostitute our bodies as they dwindle into dust.
We'll not hear heaven's tantalizing song, however sweet.
Our pride is gone; we only long to touch Your lotus feet.

Please tell us how to think of You as we endure our fate
of death and birth upon this Earth we can't evacuate.
O son of Vasudev, we bow to You repeatedly,
for You destroy the pain of Your surrendered devotee."

55-57) When all the kings had finished praising Krishna, He replied,
"I promise, my dear kings, you shall be always satisfied

by serving me unswervingly, as each of you aspires,
and shedding the psychosis of material desires.

Enamored with materialism, monarchs of the past—
Haihaya, Vena, Rāvaṇa, and others of their caste—
were ruined. Friends, your bodies and their trimmings start and end.
As rulers, simply worship Me, as scriptures recommend.

So live your lives, have children, feel your pleasure and distress
while keeping Me the focus of your inner consciousness.
Detached from things material, self-satisfied and firm,
eventually, you'll reach My kingdom, never to return."

58) Completing His instructions, Krishna sent a retinue
of servants who could help the scruffy kings become renewed.
Jarasāndha's successor, as the Vedic texts insist,
revered the kings with garlands, gems and many other gifts.

59) Lord Krishna then arranged to feed the kings a dazzling feast
including first-class betel nuts and other royal treats.
Thus honored by Lord Krishna, all the kings were purified
and glowed like brilliant stars and moons when monsoons cleanse the sky.

60) The Lord then called for chariots adorned with jewels and gold
and sent the kings back home to the domains they used to hold.
The grateful kings, recalling how Lord Krishna saved their lives,
exalted Him and acted on His words when they arrived.

The Rajasuya Sacrifice

61) The Lord took worship from Jarasāndha's respectful son
and rode off with His friends, their work for Yudhiṣṭhir all done.
When they reached Indraprashta, they blew conch shells to announce
their friends had been established and their enemies denounced.

62) The residents adored that sound, as did King Yudhiṣṭhir
who listened as his brothers and the Lord assuaged his fear.

When he learned that the kings were free and all that had occurred,
King Yudhiṣṭhir shed tears of love and couldn't say a word.

63, 64) At last the King addressed his Lord, with obvious delight:
"Your precious orders grace the heads of all who are upright,
including gurus of this world and heaven's every god.
Yet You accept my orders as a part of Your facade.

Just as the sun is constant, though it seems to rise and fall,
Your role-play doesn't alter Your supremacy at all.
Your attitude of service also graces devotees,
who, unlike brutes and animals, assist humanity."

65) His gratitude expressed, the King prepared the sacrifice
by waiting for the proper time and seeking the advice
of famous Vedic priests and sages. Soon he felt informed
on how the Rājasūya sacrifice should be performed.

66) These sages were invited, as were Dhṛtarāṣṭra's clan,
Duryodhana, Vidura and the kings of many lands.
The *vaiśyas* and the *śūdras* joined the *kṣatriyas* and priests,
each bringing to the sacrifice a certain expertise.

67) According to the principles the Vedic texts espouse,
the *brāhmans* tilled the sacrificial ground with golden plows.
Utensils for the sacrifice were also made of gold.
Among the guests, the gods, well-dressed, flew in to join the fold.

68) Lords Indra, Śiva and Brahmā were thoroughly aware—
as were celestial beings, who arrived from everywhere—
that devotees of Krishna like King Yudhiṣṭhir are blessed
with opulence akin to what the gods themselves possess.

69) The gods, who once performed the Rājasūya sacrifice,
observed King Yudhiṣṭhir's performance, perfect and precise.
The priests were like the gods themselves, and Yudhiṣṭhir began
to worship them according to the sacrificial plan.

Sishupal Speaks

70) After that, all present were to chose among the guests
the person most deserving to be honored as the best.
So many great, exalted sages, gods and saints were there,
the choice was hard. At last, Sahadev stood up and declared,

71-73) "Lord Krishna is the person this assembly should select.
He is the sacrifice itself, in each and all respects.
The gods, this sacred place and all these opulent supplies
come only from Lord Krishna. Does this come as a surprise?

Relying solely on Himself, Lord Krishna manifests
the whole cosmic creation. Then, He puts it all to rest.
All kinds of yoga, sacrifice and other Vedic rites
aim only for His pleasure. Therefore, choosing Him is right.

He generates the duties of this world, so by His grace,
religion, business, pleasure and release are taking place.
By honoring Lord Krishna first, we're honoring ourselves,
for He, the soul of all, views nothing separate from Himself."

74) The saintly persons present cried out, "Excellent, indeed!"
King Yudhiṣṭhir took notice and wholeheartedly agreed.
He lovingly bathed Krishna's feet, as ritual decrees,
and sprinkled all with foot-wash, making all but one feel pleased.

75) That water purifies the world. The King, in ecstasy,
gave Krishna gifts of gems and silk. He couldn't even see,
for tears of love for Krishna filled the monarch's royal eyes.
The congregation bowed as flowers showered from the sky.

76-79) Amid this scene of bliss stood Śiśupāl, enraged and red.
He thrashed his arms to gain attention, turned and boldly said,
"It seems the devastating force of time is on display
when elders let a simple child influence them this way.

O leaders of this sacrifice, you surely know who's best
for being honored. Why accept what Sahadev suggests?

Will you neglect the great exalted sages that I see
in favor of a cowherd who disgraced his family?

Why should this quirky, cunning person, suited for no caste,
be given *any* adulation, be it first or last?
It seems as if a crow has wandered in this sacrifice
to eat the holy sacrificial cakes of *ghee* and rice.

The Yadus left the holy lands to live within the sea,
degrading and manipulating others constantly.
These relatives of Krishna have been ostracized and cursed.
How can this great assembly choose to worship Krishna first?"

80) Just as a mighty lion might ignore a jackal's cries,
Lord Krishna waited silently as Śiśupāl spoke lies.
The insults, though, offended the most learned and devout,
who covered up their ears, stood up and angrily walked out.

81) By listening complacently while Krishna is defamed,
a person loses all religious merit he has gained.
So some departed when they heard what Śiśupāl had said,
while others, like the Pāndavas, prepared to smash his head.

82) Undaunted, Śiśupāl pulled out his vaunted shield and sword,
deriding the devoted souls who sided with the Lord.
As Śiśupāl was trying to despoil the sacrifice,
Lord Krishna's razor-disc removed his head in one clean slice.

83) With this great feat, the crowed released a huge, unprompted roar
while Śiśupāl's supporters deftly tiptoed out the door.
A self-effulgent light rose out of Śiśupāl just then
and entered Krishna, much as Earth-bound meteors descend.

84) For three successive lifetimes, Śiśupāl despised the Lord;
because of his obsession, he at last gained this reward.
He once had guarded Viṣṇu's gates, but later took a curse
and had to bear three evil births before it was reversed.

85) King Yudhiṣṭhir completed the momentous sacrifice
by giving gifts and bathing in accord with Vedic rites.
The King knew well that Krishna was the cause of his success,
and Krishna stayed there with the King, obeying his request.

86) The King appeared like Indra as his inner luster blazed.
The honored gods and sages left him, singing Krishna's praise.
At last the hour came for Krishna also to take leave,
and Yudhiṣṭhir permitted it, though most reluctantly.

87) Except for Duryodhan, the sinner, everyone was pleased.
He couldn't bear the happiness of Krishna's devotees.
If you, however, speak about the death of Śiśupāl,
effects of sins that cause chagrin will end, for once and all.

The Concluding Bath

88) *He'd listened now for days, but Viṣṇurāta wasn't tired.*
When Śukadev's last statement puzzled him, the King inquired,
"If people loved this sacrifice, O sage, as I just heard,
then why was Duryodhan upset? Did something else occur?"

89) *The patient Śukadev replied,* "His subjects all admired
your grandfather, King Yudhiṣṭhir, and did what he desired.
As Bhīma ran the kitchen, Sahadev was there to greet
the venerated guests. And then, Lord Krishna washed their feet.

90) The treasurer was Duryodhan; Nakula bought supplies.
The elders went to Arjuna, and Karna supervised
delivery of gifts. Queen Draupadī served out the meals,
and everyone contributed. The mood was quite ideal.

91) The sacrifice was finished, with assistance from the staff,
except for Yudhiṣṭhir's conclusive sacrificial bath.
As drums were pounded, horns resounded. Flutes and cymbals played,
delighting gods above as lovely dancers turned and swayed.

92) The kings, adorned in gold, felt bold, their armies right behind,
proceeding to the Ganga, where the waters are divine.

With infantry and cavalry and elephants as well,
the many massive armies seemed to shake the Earth itself.

93) The ritual's officials, joined by other learned priests,
recited Vedic mantras with delightful expertise.
The residents of heaven, gods and sages, looking on,
rained flowers on the gathering below and sang along.

94) The well-dressed men and women, wearing garlands, silks and gems,
began to sprinkle liquids on each other as a whim.
The men soaked lovely courtesans with yogurt, oil and scents;
the courtesans, with glee, drenched several men in self-defense.

95) Attracted by the fun, the queens of Yudhiṣṭhir came out
and found themselves as targets in the friendly liquid bout.
As Krishna, Bhīma, Arjuna and others splashed the queens,
their shyly smiling faces bloomed, embellishing the scene.

96) The queens had large syringes to squirt fluids at the men,
so yellow-tinted liquids flew, again and yet again.
As dripping, clinging saris showed the forms of thighs and busts,
the lesser men observing felt their minds inflamed with lust.

97) King Yudhiṣṭhir, resplendent in the presence of his queens,
was like the sacrifice itself among its small routines.
Queen Draupadī joined Yudhiṣṭhir to hold the final rites;
they bathed in Ganges water, to the demigods' delight.

98) The citizens bathed also, for the Ganges waters cleanse
effects of endless lifetimes full of countless dreadful sins.
The King put on new garments and then honored all his guests
by giving them fine jewelry and new, expensive dress.

99) The men wore turbans, waistcoats, gems and all things debonair;
the women sported earrings, golden belts and perfect hair.
The sages, gods and other guests, both famous and unknown,
were honored by King Yudhiṣṭhir and went back to their homes.

100) As ordinary men cannot stop drinking something sweet,
the guests could not stop praising Yudhiṣṭhir's amazing feat.
The King himself felt separation's fierce, impending pain,
so he convinced Lord Krishna and some others to remain.

101) Lord Krishna sent some leaders back to Dvārakā and stayed.
King Yudhiṣṭhir thus finished his remarkable crusade
to hold the Rājasūya sacrifice, a daunting task,
and show how Krishna helps His devotees each time they ask.

Duryodhana Embarrassed

102) King Yudhiṣṭhir's success and riches rankled Duryodhan.
His palace, for example, was resplendent far beyond
the palace Duryodhan enjoyed. And Draupadī, as well,
unsettled Duryodhan, who'd failed to win her for himself.

103) Lord Krishna's many queens stayed on, at Draupadī's request.
Their charming gait and slender waists and *kuṅkum*-dusted breasts
enhanced their lovely faces, which were framed in flowing hair.
They beautified the palace as they wandered here and there.

104) One day, as Yudhiṣṭhir held court with Krishna at his side,
he seemed as rich as Indra, but without a trace of pride.
Then Duryodhan, with royal crown, burst in his cousin's court,
admonishing the doorkeepers with insolent retorts.

105) The palace's designer, Maya Danava, had placed
protective built-in features that intruders couldn't trace.
Bewildered by these mystic hoaxes, Duryodhan mistook
a pool to be a solid floor, for that was how it looked.

106) When Duryodhan fell in the water, Bhīma laughed aloud,
along with all the women, kings and others in the crowd.
King Yudhiṣṭhir attempted to restrain this mockery,
but Krishna smiled along and gave a nod approvingly.

107) Disgraced and angry, Duryodhan got out and, looking down,
stormed out of Indraprastha without uttering a sound.
King Yudhiṣṭhir and other saints regretted all the mirth,
but Krishna simply saw a burden rising from the Earth.

24

Salva

The Mystic Airship

1) O King, that is the answer to your question as to why
the jealous, angry Duryodhan could not be satisfied.
Now hear about another wondrous deed the Lord performed
as He appeared among us in His transcendental form.

2) A friend of Śiśupāl's named Śālva watched Lord Krishna free
Queen Rukminī from wedding Śiśupāl unwillingly.
In the ensuing battle with the Yadus, Śālva lost.
He pledged, "I will destroy this Yadu clan at any cost."

3) On making this misguided vow, the foolish Śālva swore
to daily fill his hand with dust, eat that and nothing more.
He begged Lord Śiva to reward his masochistic fast
and fairly soon this Śālva got the boon for which he'd asked.

4) Lord Śiva gave, reluctantly, an airship that could fly
throughout the Earth and heavens to destroy and terrify.
The iron plane was like a town and could not be destroyed
by any curse or weapon, demon, man or god deployed.

5) So Śālva sent his army to seize Dvārakā below
as he flew overhead with every weapon he could throw.
While tree trunks, hailstones, snakes and deadly thunderbolts rained down,
a whirlwind fiercely threw up dust, eclipsing all around.

6) The citizens of Dvārakā were frightened and harassed.
Pradyumna, Queen Rukminī's son, assured them, "This will pass."
Assembling great, heroic Yadu warriors and guards,
he struck the mighty Śālva, who continued to bombard.

7) The armies clashed, their weapons crashed and witnesses were stunned.
As if he was the darkness, and Pradyumna was the sun,
the wicked Śālva quickly found Pradyumna's golden shafts
had punctured him and all his men. He energized his craft.

8) The plane transformed to many airplanes flying everywhere,
then it was one—and then it simply vanished in the air.
Although Pradyumna's prowess pleased both friend and foe alike,
the airship's mystic powers made it difficult to strike.

9) At one point Śālva's airship seemed to nestle to the ground;
then it appeared in water, on a hill or flying round.
The airship whirled and blistered like a fiery baton
and yet the Yadu army stood its ground and battled on.

Pradyumna Struck Down

10) Wherever Śālva showed his airship, Yadu arrows rained.
Their burning, poisoned shafts left Śālva's soldiers hurt or slain.
Dyumān, the chief of Śālva's forces, snatched his club of steel,
fought off his foes and struck a blow that made Pradyumna reel.

11) Pradyumna's driver thought the blow had smashed his master's chest.
Concerned for his security, the driver thought it best
to take Pradyumna from the field until he'd cleared his head.
Pradyumna, soon recovering, was furious and said,

12) "Except for me, no Yadu warrior ever left a fight.
This eunuch driver spoiled my reputation with a blight.
What will I say to Rām and Krishna to excuse myself?
My brothers' wives will mockingly say, 'Did you mend your health?'

13) Pradyumna's driver answered, "Master, all that I have done
is proper for a driver who has seen his master stunned.
A driver saves his master, and a master does the same.
I fled the battle lines with this in mind. Why feel ashamed?"

14) Pradyumna drank some water, set his armor, took his bow
and said, "Wherever this Dyumān has gone, I want to go."
Dyumān had crushed Pradyumna's army while he was away.
Pradyumna, smiling, found Dyumān and drew him from the fray.

15) Pradyumna wrecked the chariot Dyumān so proudly rode
then struck him with a deadly shaft that made his head explode.
The Yadu archers rallied and, with great proficiency
made Śālva's soldiers tumble from the airship to the sea.

Krishna Returns

16) The battle thus went back and forth for twenty-seven days.
Lord Krishna, still in Indraprastha on extended stay,
saw inauspicious omens caused by dangers still unknown.
With blessings from his loved ones, Krishna quickly went back home.

17) Lord Krishna thought, "While I am here with My beloved brother,
our capital could be attacked by one fool or another."
He soon found Dvārakā besieged. Augmenting its defense,
he warned his driver, "Śālva's magic baffles common sense."

18) His driver shook his reins and took Lord Krishna to the place
where Śālva stood, and Krishna could confront him face to face.
The crest of Garuḍa adorned the flag Lord Krishna flew,
an emblem known to Krishna's men—and his opponents, too.

19) As soon as Śālva saw the Lord he hurled a fearsome spear
across the field of battle at Lord Krishna's charioteer.
As if it were a comet, Śālva's spear lit up the sky
but Krishna's arrows splintered it in forceful, swift reply.

20) Lord Krishna then pierced Śālva with a host of deadly shafts
and filled the sky with arrows raining on his darting craft.
Lord Krishna, like the sun, emitted sharp, pervasive rays
till Śālva's arrow struck His arm and knocked His bow away.

21) On seeing this, devotees wept as Śālva roared and yelled,
"You fool! If you don't run right now, I'll send you straight to hell.
You took your cousin Śiśupāla's fiance, Rukminī,
and when he wasn't looking, you destroyed him ruthlessly."

22) The Lord replied, "Because you're dull and boast the way you do,
you fail to see that death itself stands straight in front of you.
A true, authentic hero rarely has too much to say;
he simply puts heroic deeds on obvious display."

23, 24) With this, Lord Krishna furiously swung His mighty club
on Śālva's collarbone. The demon groaned and threw up blood.
Then Śālva simply disappeared as, simultaneously,
a man in tears approached and sobbed, "I've come from Devakī.

O Krishna, Krishna, mighty-armed one! You're extremely kind
You love Your dearest parents, who are always on your mind.
This Śālva somehow seized your father Vasudev today.
He bound him like an animal and dragged him far away."

25) On hearing that His father had been taken by this thief,
the Lord, who deeply loved His father, showed concern and grief.
In this world, Krishna often acts like any mortal man,
so speaking like an ordinary person, He began,

26) "My brother Balarām protects the city very well.
He's never lost to any foe, from heaven, Earth or hell.
How could a speck like Śālva kidnap Father from his hands?
Almighty fate, indeed, has made a farce of all our plans."

27) As soon as Krishna finished, Śālva once again appeared,
this time with Vasudev in tow. With wicked eyes he sneered,
"You love your father most of all, and here your father stands.
I'll murder him before your eyes. Protect him if you can!"

28) He sliced the throat of Vausdev and flew off with his head
directly to his mystic plane, which hovered overhead.
Then, for a moment, Krishna, though aware of Śālva's scam,
became absorbed in sorrow like an ordinary man.

(Meter: -|- -|- -|- -|)
29-33) Recalling the magic that Śālva displayed,
Lord Krishna knew well it was all a charade.
With Vasudev's corpse and the messenger gone,
Lord Krishna saw through it and quickly fought on.

This version, at least, is recounted by some
who think that Lord Krishna could really succumb
to such lamentation. They somehow forget
the times that they've thought, "God cannot be upset."

How can lamentation, affection or fear,
all born out of ignorance, ever appear
in He whose perception, good judgment and might
has no limitation of length, width or height?

Brahmā kidnapped Lord Krishna's friends long ago,
while Krishna pretended that He didn't know.
As part of His loving exchanges of bliss,
He relishes spiritual pastimes like this.

If spiritual knowledge, made better with sweet
devotional service to His lotus feet,
destroys such delusions as "body is self,"
how could they appear in Lord Krishna Himself?

The Death of Salva

(iambic heptameter)

34) As Śālva hurled weapons, Krishna shot him with His bow
and used His club to smash the mystic airplane with one blow.
The plane crashed in the water. Śālva, jumping to the land,
ran madly up to Krishna with a bludgeon in his hand.

35) A single dart from Krishna cut off Śālva's arm and club.
And then, just as a mountain holds the morning sun above,
Lord Krishna raised his shining disc and cut off Śālva's head.
As head and crown rolled on the ground, the demons cried in dread.

36) While gods above played kettledrums to celebrate the scene,
another demon, Dantavakra, dared to intervene.
His partners Śiśupāl and Śālva both met their demise,
yet he attacked Lord Krishna, fury shooting from his eyes.

37) The evil Dantavakra dashed toward Krishna, club in hand.
The Earth itself shook sharply as the mighty devil ran.
The Lord jumped from His chariot and, sparring expertly,
drove Dantavakra backwards as the shore holds back the sea.

38, 39) The reckless demon said, "What luck to see you here today!
O foolish cousin, killer of my friends, you're mine to slay."
(Indeed, the two were relatives, and just two lives before,
this Dantavakra was a keeper of Vaikuṇṭha's doors).

"A relative like you is nothing more than a disease.
By killing you my debt is paid. My friends will all be pleased."
As one might poke an elephant, with all that he had said
first Dantavakra goaded Krishna, then he struck His head.

40) Though struck by Dantavakra's club, Lord Krishna stood His ground.
His own club met the demon's chest and made a crunching sound.
The blow split Dantavakra's heart. He fell and dropped his club
and, sprawling, left his body with a final heave of blood.

41) A subtle, wondrous spark of light ascended from the corpse,
for Dantavakra's sentence as a fiend had run its course.
The floating spirit merged with Krishna, seen by one and all,
exactly as had happened at the death of Śiśupāl.

42) Then Dandavakra's brother, Vidurath, snatched up his sword
and, breathing very heavily, swung fiercely at the Lord.
Lord Krishna deftly dodged him and invoked His razor disc,
decaptitating Vidurath with one flick of His wrist.

43) Since Śālva, Dantavakra and his brother all were such
extremely gifted warriors whom no one else could touch,
the residents of heaven praised Lord Krishna on and on
as He returned to Dvārakā amid festoons and song.

44) And thus, Lord Krishna, master of all mystic potencies,
turns dismal situations into splendid victories.
And only one whose consciousness resembles that of beasts
thinks someone else could better Krishna—or, indeed, compete.

Balaram's Pilgrimmage

The Pround Romaharshana

1, 2) Lord Krishna vanquished every brute who put the Earth in pain,
except for some Lord Balarām was destined to contain.
At this time, though, Lord Balarām was touring holy sites,
for Yudhiṣṭhir and Duryodhan, His friends, were set to fight,

Instead of taking sides when His two cousins were at odds,
Lord Balarām held rites to honor ancestors and gods.
He went to holy *tirthas*, rivers, temples and, at last,
Naimiṣāraṇya forest, where the sages had amassed.

3) The sages recognized the Lord and stopped their sacrifice
to stand and bow—a greeting that is proper and concise.
However, Romaharṣaṇa, infected with conceit,
ignored the Lord, remaining in his elevated seat.

4) Lord Balarām was outraged. Romaharṣaṇa, you see,
possessed, of all assembled, the most common pedigree.
Not only was he scornful by remaining in his seat;
his sitting place was higher than the sages, saints and priests.

5, 6) Lord Balarām said, "Due to lower birth and swollen head
this fool dishonors others. Such a leader should be dead.
He may read many scriptures, but his character is such
that all he's learned is in his head; his heart remains untouched.

My mission is relieving Earth of sinful hypocrites
pretending to be pious while refusing to submit
to *brāhmans*, God or any other person, great or small.
A cheater such as this is the most sinful fool of all."

7) Despite the fact that Balarām was finished taking lives,
the time for Romaharṣaṇa's demise had now arrived.
So Balarām just touched him with a single blade of grass
and Romaharṣaṇa fell down in terminal collapse.

8, 9) The sages cried, "Alas, alas! O Balarām, our Lord,
Your killing of this person is exceedingly untoward.
We honored Romaharṣaṇa by giving him this seat
and promised him protection till our *yajña* was complete!

Unknowingly You killed the *brāhman* we chose to anoint.
Though we fault You for nothing, Lord, please hear our simple point.
No scripture binds You; You are God Himself. We understand.
And yet, if You atoned for this, You'd help the common man."

10) Lord Balarām replied, "Of course, I'll gladly make amends.
Prescribe for Me whatever rite the scripture recommends.
Just say the word and you'll see Romaharṣaṇa revive,
fulfilling your assurances that he would live and thrive."

11) The sages spoke among themselves and answered as if one:
"O Lord, your acts should stay intact. Let nothing be undone."
The Lord replied, "The *Vedas* teach that one takes birth again
as one's own son. So let this *brāhman's* son fill in for him."

12) The son, Suta Goswami, was at once installed to sit
and lead the sacrifice, with all his father's benefits.
But Balarām requested, "Sages, tell me your desire.
It still appears atonement of some kind should be required."

Balvala Slain

13) The sages said, “A demon named Balvala is so cruel
he spoils our sacrifice by throwing urine, pus and stool.
Please kill that sinful demon. Then, throughout the coming year,
remain on pilgrimage. Thus, Your renown shall persevere.”

14) Before too long a wind arose, infused with noxious smells.
Balvala showered pus and stool by use of mystic spells.
He then appeared in person with a trident in his hand,
intent on driving holy sacrifices from the land.

15) Balvala looked exactly like a hill of carbon black.
His molten copper beard and topknot glowed as he attacked.
Lord Balarām observed his horrid fangs and furrowed brow
and called at once his fearsome club and demon-crushing plow.

16) His plow-tip snagged Balvala as he flew across the sky.
Lord Balarām then smashed his club between the demon’s eyes.
His forehead cracked and gushing blood, Balvala looked just like
a crimson mountain crashing down, assailed by lightning strikes.

An Attempt At Diplomacy

17) The sages blessed Lord Balarām and praised his strength and skill.
They bathed Him as the gods bathed Indra when Vṛtra was killed.
They next presented garlands of unfading blooms and leaves,
as well as first rate silken clothing set with jewelry.

18) The sages then gave Balarām permission to depart.
His pilgrimage, begun without the aid of horse or cart,
took Him by foot to India’s most sacred holy sites.
At every stop the Lord took bath and honored every rite.

19) He traveled so extensively that months and months went past.
Concluding His atonement, Balarām was told, at last,
that nearly every soldier in the Kuru’s civil war
had died in Kurukṣetra and would burden Earth no more.

20) Since Duryodhan, who Balarām supported, had survived,
the Lord went on to Kurukṣetra, bent on saving lives.
He found the sons of Pāndu had, as well, survived the war.
They offered Him obeisances but then said nothing more.

21) At that time Duryodhan and Bhīma, fighting with their clubs,
were settling the conflict with each others' flesh and blood.
Though Balarām trained Duryodhan, He wanted neither dead.
Attempting to break up this closing fight, He stood and said,

22) "You two are nearly equals in your bludgeon-fighting skill.
Since one has strength and one technique, why get each other killed?
I do not see how either of you stand to win this test,
so why not put your clubs down now and stop at My request?"

23) When Duryodhan and Bhīma couldn't set aside their hate,
Lord Balarām saw Krishna had some reason for their fate.
Since neither was agreeable to let the other live,
the Lord went on to Dvārakā to visit relatives.

24) Returning to Naimiṣāraṇya, Balarām declared
to all the saints and sages holding sacrifices there
that He would join their sacrifice. "What's more," He told His friends,
"My long career of warfare has at last come to an end."

25) Lord Balarām blessed everyone assembled in that place
with spiritual perception that transcended time and space.
They saw Lord Balarām pervading everything, and then
they saw Lord Balarām holding the universe within.

26) According to the Vedic rites, Lord Balarām took part
in rituals a common man would use to cleanse his heart.
Encircled by His family and closest friends that day,
He looked as splendid as the moon surrounded by its rays.

27) Lord Balarām's deluding powers make the common man
think He is common, too—and this exactly suits His plan.
Yet one who simply hears of Balarām's divine pursuits
becomes adored by Krishna, whose response is absolute.

26

Sudama

A Humble Wife's Request

1, 2) Said Viṣṇurāta, "Master, please, continue telling me
heroic pastimes of the greatest personality.
Could anyone who knows life's essence set aside such themes
to gratify the senses in a futile, phony dream?

True words describing God are, for true ears, the greatest wealth.
True hands work just for Him; true minds consider nothing else.
True eyes see only Krishna, and true heads bow to His feet.
True limbs regard the water that has bathed Him as most sweet."

3) Delighted, Śukadev said this: When Krishna was in school,
He had a friend, Sudāma, who became a perfect jewel.
This learned, self-controlled young priest enjoyed a simple life,
although he lived so plainly, he could not maintain his wife.

4-5) The chaste wife of this underprivileged *brāhman* felt distressed
because she could not feed him, so she made this meek request:
"Lord Krishna is so kind and rich. My dear, don't you enjoy
a friendship with Him dating back to when you both were boys?

Lord Krishna loves the *brāhmans*, and I'm sure He'll gladly give
some charity to you, His childhood friend, so you can live.
He rules a lavish kingdom; surely Krishna shares His wealth.
If someone loves Him, so I've heard, He'll even give Himself."

6) Sudāma thought, "My wife keeps asking, and the time is right.
To visit empty-handed, though, would be so impolite."
And so he said, "My dear, I'll see my friend, just as you've asked me to.
However, I have nothing to bring Krishna, dear. Do you?"

7) Sudāma's wife went begging, filled her palms four times with rice,
enclosed it in a clean, torn cloth and tied it once or twice.
This very modest gift in hand, Sudāma started out.
He thought, "Will Krishna's soldiers let me in? I have my doubts."

A Joyous Reception

8) In Dvārakā, Sudāma joined some local learned priests
and walked unchallenged past the homes of Krishna's devotees.
Approaching Krishna's palace (one he shared with Rukminī),
Sudāma felt he'd traded his distress for ecstasy.

9) Lord Krishna sat upon Rukminī's bed when He observed
Sudāma near the palace. Then, without a single word,
He went out to embrace His dear old friend, so pure and wise.
As ecstasy shot through Him, teardrops filled Lord Krishna's eyes.

10) Lord Krishna brought Sudāma in and sat him on the bed.
He washed the *brāhman's* feet and sprinkled footwash on His head.
The Lord worshipped Sudāma with a lamp made bright with *ghee*,
along with incense, sandal paste and all accessories.

11) As Krishna offered gifts and pleasant words, Queen Rukminī
began to fan the honored guest as etiquette decrees.
Sudāma looked so gaunt and wore such ragged, shabby dress
the residents throughout the palace all began to guess,

12) "What pious acts has this unkempt, impoverished *brāhman* done?
Though others would consider him a beggar to be shunned,

the guru of the universe, abandoning His wife,
embraces and reveres him like He's known him all his life."

13-20) While holding one another's hands, Sudāma and the Lord
discussed their days at Sāndīpani's schoolhouse years before.
The Lord observed, "You're moral, and you lead a godly life;
since you are not in saffron dress then you must have a wife.

Though you're involved in household duties, you remain aloof
from sense desire and money-making. Most folks spend their youth
pursuing such enjoyments, but your values have stayed high.
You've taught the common people by example, as have I.

Our school days were devoted, you recall, to the pursuit
of learning from our guru higher, spiritual truth.
A father is a guru and a priest is one as well
but one who gives transcendence is as good as God Himself.

Such gurus represent Me. They say only what I say.
By following such gurus one can vanquish all dismay.
To simply serve a valid guru pleases Me much more
than all the rites and penances the *brāhmans* so adore.

Do you recall the day when we were living at our school
and Sāndīpani Muni's wife sent us to gather fuel?
As we walked in the forest to find firewood, there arose
an out-of-season thunderstorm that drenched us head to toe.

The forest was so flooded that we couldn't even tell
the high ground from the low ground. Then the sun went down as well.
Unable to determine whether home was left or right,
we wandered through incessant wind and rain throughout that night.

Our guru understood our plight and went out with the dawn.
He searched the woods until, at last, he found where we had gone.
Compassionate at our distress, he said, "My dearest sons,
the body is most dear to every soul. Look what you've done!

For my sake you have undergone such suffering and stress.
A true disciple does what you have done and nothing less.
You boys are first-class *brāhmans*. May you both be fully blessed.
May all the Vedic mantras you have learned stay ever-fresh."

21) Lord Krishna went on reminiscing in this joyous way.
"We had such great adventures through our gurukula days.
A soul who takes a guru and then somehow make him pleased
fulfills the goal of human life and gains eternal peace."

22) Sudāma said, "O Lord, what goal could I have not achieved
when I lived in the ashram of our guru and received
the fortune of Your company? Your form is truth itself.
You demonstrate a righteous life by living it Yourself."

Hidden Treasure

23) Conversing with his childhood friend, Lord Krishna was quite pleased,
for He adores the *brāhmans*, chiefly when they're devotees.
He also understood Sudāma hid within his clothes
a bundle with some rice that he was too ashamed to show.

24) The Lord inquired, "Have you brought a gift from home for Me?
I greatly value any gift from saintly devotees.
A cup of water makes Me smile, though I could drink an ocean.
A fruit or flower pleases Me, when offered in devotion."

25) Despite this clear encouragement, Sudāma was ashamed
to give his gift to Krishna in this opulent domain.
Lord Krishna knew Sudāma's pure affection had no price,
so He reached in Sudāma's cape and snatched the hidden rice.

26) The Lord exclaimed, "My friend, what are you hiding? It's a gift!
This rice will please not only Me but all souls that exist."
When one has pleased Lord Krishna all creation can advance,
as watering the root will nourish every leaf and branch.

27) Lord Krishna ate a palmful of the rice and reached for more,
but Queen Rukminī stopped His hand and quietly implored,

"How will I share this treasure if You eat it all Yourself?
Besides, You're pleased already, which assures Sudāma's wealth."

Homecoming

28) Sudāma then took food and drink and rested for the night,
convinced that he had left this mortal world from sheer delight.
The next day, with much honor from his friend, he left for home,
too bashful to have even asked for something of his own.

29-31) Sudāma thought, "Lord Krishna loves the *brāhmans*, that is clear.
He held me to his chest, although my sins are quite severe.
I am the poorest beggar, while my friend is God Himself,
replete with strength, detachment, wisdom, beauty, fame and wealth.

He loved me like a brother. There I was, upon His bed,
while Krishna bathed my feet and Queen Rukminī fanned my head.
Though Krishna is the person all the gods and *brāhmans* praise,
as if I were a god, He worshipped me in many ways.

In heaven, hell, this planet, or in liberated states,
the worship of Lord Krishna opens wide perfection's gates.
Perceiving that if I were rich I might grow proud and fall,
Lord Krishna kindly didn't give me anything at all."

32) Sudāma reached his homesite. but he could not understand
how several soaring palaces now filled his patch of land,
complete with gardens, courtyards, ponds with flocks of cooing birds
and well-dressed male and female servants waiting for his word.

33) The palace servants welcomed him with musical reception.
On learning he was back, his wife, ecstatic with affection,
came dashing from the palace dressed like Goddess Śrī herself
emerging from a domicile of unimagined wealth.

34) Sudāma's chaste and loyal wife, her tears about to start,
bowed low before her husband and embraced him in her heart.
Though he looked just the same, and she at once saw it was him,
he barely recognized his wife, adorned with precious gems.

35) They walked in awe 'midst diamond-studded pillars in their home,
which boasted ivory bedsteads, golden couches, chairs and thrones.
The crystal walls had jeweled lamps and pearls strung overhead.
Sudāma calmly saw all this, and to himself he said,

(Meter: -|- -|- -|- -|)
36-38) "A person of my destitute circumstance
could only grow wealthy by Lord Krishna's glance.
Since I didn't ask, He kept this from my sight
as clouds gently water the fields overnight.

The Lord magnifies what His devotees bring
and thinks of His blessings as trivial things.
Though I only brought Him a handful of rice,
He transformed my hut to a god's paradise.

The Lord doesn't make all his servants this rich.
If one is a novice, he could grow bewitched,
so Krishna is cautious when giving rewards.
I'll never forsake my compassionate Lord."

(iambic heptameter)
39) Sudāma, fixed in wisdom, kept his vows and didn't fall.
He never let his opulence bewilder him at all.
Such saintly, gentle *brāhmans* are the Lord's own deities.
What person could be higher than such perfect devotees?

40) Though no one else can conquer Him, Lord Krishna's servants do.
Observing this, Sudāma's heart was thoroughly subdued.
He soon attained the Lord's domain and bid this world farewell.
If you can grasp Lord Krishna's kindness, you'll go there as well.

27

In Kurukshetra

Reunion

1) O King, let us continue with an incident before
the Rājasūya sacrifice and Kurukṣetra war.
Lord Krishna's priests in Dvārakā advised a royal trip
to holy Kurukṣetra for an imminent eclipse.

2) The mighty sage Paraśurām once dug five sacred lakes
and held the rites to sanctify that famous holy place.
The sun's eclipse gave people far and wide a welcome chance
to go there on a pilgrimage and spiritually advance.

3) Lord Krishna's entourage went there with pomp and majesty.
The chariots His soldiers rode seemed almost heavenly.
Their elephants were huge as clouds; their horses' rhythmic gait
made Krishna and His well-dressed clan appear to levitate.

4) The saintly Yadus reached the lakes, took baths and kept a fast.
They next gave gifts to *brāhmans* till the proper time elapsed.
Observing Vedic rites, they bathed again and fed their priests
while praying for devotion to Lord Krishna's lotus feet.

5) The Yadus broke their fast with Krishna's personal consent
and sat beneath some cooling shade trees, tranquil and content.
By now a thousand kings had come, both friends and enemies.
(Somewhere among them, Nanda led the cowherd families).

6) Soon countless glad reunions made all hearts and faces bloom,
for most men relished friendships they were eager to resume.
The smiling groups of women, breasts adorned with saffron paste,
pressed hard against each other as they tearfully embraced.

7) The young bowed to the elders and the elders blessed the young.
Formalities completed, talks of Krishna danced on tongues.
When Kuntī met her brother Vasudev, her sorrow fled.
Addressing him and many other relatives, she said,

8) "My dear, respected brother, through my long calamities,
I feel I've been forgotten by my loving family.
You're one of many Yadu saints—I see that on your face,
yet everyone abandons those devoid of heaven's grace."

9) Said Vasudev, "Dear sister, we are ordinary men.
Dispersed by Kaṁsa's terrors, we've at last come home again.
Regardless if one's free or ruled by despotic demands,
he's nothing but a plaything in the Lord's almighty hands."

10) The Yadus honored all the kings attending the event
who turned their eyes to Krishna and at once became content.
Though different views among the different monarchs was the norm,
they all became enchanted with Lord Krishna's lovely form.

11, 12) Once Balarām and Krishna had received the kings with praise,
the kings began to glorify the Yadus in these ways:
"You all are more illustrious than anybody else;
you daily see what *yogīs* rarely find—the Lord Himself.

His fame, His words, the water that has washed His sacred feet
have purified the universe and made our lives complete.
As His exalted relatives, you speak and walk and eat
with He who makes our goal of life in heaven obsolete."

13) When Nanda learned the Yadus and Lord Krishna had arrived,
he went at once to see them with his carts and friends and wives.
Like lifeless bodies coming back to life, they all appeared
delighted to embrace each other after many years.

14) When Vasudev embraced King Nanda, joyful as he was,
he couldn't help recalling all the grief that Kaṁsa caused.
Then Balarām and Krishna, whom he'd left in Nanda's care,
embraced their foster father and choked up in tearful prayer.

15) As Yaśodā and Nanda held their foster sons again,
they felt the pain of separation vanishing within.
The men went elsewhere, leaving Rohiṇī and Devakī
to say these words to Yaśodā, who listened joyfully:

16) "You've shown us both more friendship than we ever could forget.
With all the wealth of Indra, we could not repay our debt.
You gave our sons security, your love and all supplies,
protecting them in childhood as the eyelids shield the eyes."

17) The *gopīs*, who condemned their eyelids, now enjoyed the chance
to drink the sight of Krishna to the threshold of a trance.
More focused than a *yogī*, they stood still and stared ahead.
Lord Krishna, laughing, came to them, embraced each one and said,

18-20) "My dear, beloved girlfriends, do you still remember Me?
I've been off killing demons to protect My family.
Do you think I'm ungrateful and resent Me in your hearts?
Why, God alone unites us all and takes us far apart.

As winds assemble cloudbanks, shreds of grass and grains of dust
then scatter them again, so God has dealt with all of us.
And should you think that changeable, erratic God is Me,
because of your devotion, I've become your property.

How could we be apart if I pervade all living beings
as elements like earth and air pervade all mortal things?
And since you know yourselves as spirit souls eternally,
you surely see both matter *and* the soul exist in Me."

21) Displeased with theoretical connections with their Lord,
the *gopīs* said, "Your words of wisdom certainly afford
the shelter of Your lotus feet for mystics and the wise.
But how can we mere village girls attain that matchless prize?"

22) The gentle Guru of the cowherd girls, for whom they lived,
went on to visit Yudhiṣṭhir and other relatives.
When Krishna asked these relatives for news about their lives,
they all felt very purified and happily replied,

23) "The nectar saints dispense when they describe Your lotus feet
intoxicates us when it fills our ears. Yes, it's that sweet.
Resplendent in Your human form, You teach us and dispel
the miseries of life. As such, how could we not be well?"

Krishna's Queens Speak

24-41) As Yudhiṣṭhir and others praised Lord Krishna's qualities,
Lord Krishna's wives spoke with the Pandava's Queen Draupadī.
She asked them, "How did Krishna make you all His loving brides
when He portrayed a common man?" Each wife, in turn, replied:

Rukminī:
"When many kings had come to see me marry Śiśupāl,
Lord Krishna kidnapped me and proved Himself the best of all.
He seemed to be a lion chasing goats to get his prey.
May I forever worship He who carried me away."

Satyabhāmā:
"Satrājit, my dear father, owned the Syamantaka jewel.
Distraught about his brother's death, he acted like a fool
and tried to blame Lord Krishna, who exposed his great offense.
My father then betrothed me to the Lord to make amends."

Jāmbavatī:
"Not recognizing Krishna as Lord Rām, his Deity,
my father, Jāmbavān, fought Krishna quite exhaustively.
When he could not defeat the Lord, he realized who He was
and offered me as recompense for troubles he had caused."

Kālindī:
"Lord Krishna understood that I performed austerity
in hopes I'd gain a grain of dust from underneath His feet.
As man and wife we now live in His palace, and what's more
He kindly lets me serve Him as the sweeper of His floor."

Mitravindā:
"My *svayaṁvara yajña* brought in kings from many lands,
but Krishna crushed them all and, like a lion, won my hand.
My foolish brothers cursed at Him, yet I became His wife.
Today I pray to wash His lotus feet, life after life."

Satyā:
"My father had arranged for seven deadly bulls to test
the kings who asked to marry me, and thus find out the best.
Lord Krishna made me happy when He effortlessly tied
those fearsome bulls who devasted many heroes' pride."

Bhadrā:
"Aware I had reposed my heart in Krishna long before,
my father gave me to Him as His bride. And he gave more:
a military guard of many thousand men of worth.
I pray to serve Lord Krishna anywhere I may take birth."

Lakṣmanā:
"By hearing sages speak of Krishna, I became attached.
My father, understanding this, arranged a royal match
in which the archer had to string a superhuman bow
and pierce a target on the palace ceiling from below.

This target was quite hard to hit and only could be shot
by using the reflection in a single waterpot.
To string the bow was hard enough. A thousand monarchs tried,
but only seven managed as the rest were all denied.

The great Arjuna strung the bow and fired a well-aimed shot.
Although his was the closest try, he merely grazed the spot.
When all the humbled kings gave up, Lord Krishna strung the bow,
glanced in the pot and shot his arrow right where it should go.

The gods in heaven showered flowers. Everybody cheered
except some unsuccessful kings whose shame was too severe.
Adorned in garlands, earrings and fresh silk, my heart rejoiced.
I placed a necklace on Lord Krishna, settling my choice.

As drums resounded, conchshells blew, and men and women danced.
The singers sang, delighted by this joyous circumstance.
Some kings, however, fumed with lust, their royal egos bruised.
The rest of us praised Krishna, but they stubbornly refused.

He placed me on his chariot, protecting me from harm,
put on His armor, drew His bow and showed two extra arms.
Like village dogs who chase a lion, some kings gave pursuit.
How quickly they'd forgotten how precisely Krishna shoots.

When many kings were killed or wounded, all the others fled.
Our party rode to Dvārakā with Krishna at the head.
He looked just like the sun-god going home with a parade.
My father gave us thrones and jewels, weapons, gaurds and maids."

(As Lakṣmanā then realized she'd spoken quite a while
she promptly praised her co-wives with a shy, embarrassed smile).
"By taking up austerities and giving up all else,
we're blessed to be the maidservants who serve the Lord himself."

Rohiṇī:
"As soon as He killed Bhauma, Krishna found me and the rest
of sixteen thousand princesses, imprisoned and distressed.
Because we'd always thought of Him, though He has no desire
He married us and made us all His queens as we aspired.

O saintly Draupadī, we do not wish to rule the Earth.
We do not aim for heaven, nor to end our death and birth.
Like all Vṛndāvan's residents, we simply want instead
the fragrant dust from Krishna's lotus feet upon our heads."

42) As other Yadu ladies and the *gopīs* came to see
how Krishna's wives had married Him in loving ecstasty

and how they served him faithfully so many different ways
their eyes swelled up with teardrops and their hearts became amazed.

Conversing with the Sages

43) As men and women gathered in respective groups and spoke,
the greatest sages of the universe all came, provoked
by eagerness to see Lord Krishna and Lord Balarām.
The men bowed to the sages and stood up with folded palms.

44) Lord Krishna and Lord Balarām and all the other kings
poured water on the sages' feet and brought such offerings
as drinking water, cozy seats, fine scents and sandal paste.
As Krishna rose to speak, respectful silence filled the space.

45) "You've made our lives a great success! Today we all have gained
the audience of sages such as gods cannot attain.
We common men see God just in our temples, nowhere else.
How are we blessed to see and hear such sages as yourselves?

46) A holy lake or river, like a temple deity
will only cleanse the heart if they are seen repeatedly.
And worshipping the demigods will never make one clean.
A saint, however, purifies as soon as he is seen.

47) A man who thinks himself a bag of mucus, bile and air
assumes his wife and loved ones will protect him from despair.
He worships his hometown while using holy sites for baths,
ignoring saintly persons like a foolish cow or ass."

48) The sages sat in silence, quite confused by what they heard.
For Krishna to defer Himself to them seemed so absurd.
Concluding He behaved that way to teach the common man,
they knew just how to answer Krishna. Smiling, they began:

49-52) "Remarkable! Lord Krishna, You've bewildered all our minds.
You act just like a human being, perfectly refined,
yet it is You who manifests and ends the universe
as earth transforms to rocks and dirt—the simple grown diverse.

When You descend, the pious thrive, the wicked are undone
and You establish Vedic truth by simply having fun.
The *Vedas* are Your spotless heart, the gateway to the truth,
and thus You honor learned priests, though You are Absolute.

You cover Your magnificence by mystic energy,
confusing both the atheists and Your own family.
Illusioned by Your power, they live on, forgetting You,
as sleepers dream of other realms, forgetting what is true.

The holy, cleansing Ganges water all springs from Your feet,
which *yogīs* contemplate, though their attempt is incomplete.
You only come to those who serve those feet wholeheartedly.
We thus request this blessing: may we be Your devotees."

53) The sages, having spoken, were preparing to go home
when Vasudev approached them with a question of his own.
"O saints, if work makes karma, to which we are all subject,
can further work release us from this damaging effect?"

54, 55) Śrī Nārada said to the sages, "Is it a surprise
that Vasudev inquires from us? Lord Krishna, in his eyes,
is just a boy. He dwells upon the holy Ganges banks
yet goes away on pilgrimage to bathe in distant tanks.

The Lord's complete awareness is consistent and sublime.
Creation nor destruction of the universe, nor time
nor any other change can make it falter, shift or slip—
yet Krishna keeps it covered, like the sun by an eclipse."

56-59) The sages said to Vasudev, as others listened in,
"Yes, work can counteract effects that other work begins.
Authorities have shown that Vedic sacrifices will,
by pleasing God and man, bring the effects of work to nil.

The wise give up their urge for wealth by Vedic sacrifice,
their urge to reproduce by undergoing family life,
their urge for heaven through a whiff of instability,
and all else, leaving home to undertake austerity.

You've satisfied your forefathers by bearing progeny
and satisfied the saints by scriptural acuity.
You've paid two debts, but one remains; consider our advice,
and satisfy the gods by holding Vedic sacrifice.

We've now addressed your question in the ordinary way
by saying what a saintly person always has to say.
O Vasudev, in fact we know how much you must have done
in other lives to realize Lord Krishna as your son."

Vasudev Performs Yajna

60) The gracious Vasudev paid his respects on hands and knees
and asked the sages, "Please stay on as sacrificial priests."
The sages, all agreeable, arranged the articles
according to the strictest set of Vedic principles.

61) Then Vasudev and all the kings and queens went off to bathe.
They dressed in fine new clothing, garlands, gems and sandal paste.
The queens brought in auspicious things as Vedic dancers danced,
musicians played, reciters prayed, and singers sang, entranced.

62) The priests anointed Vasudev with butter. Very soon,
surrounded by his eighteen wives, he shone just like the moon
encircled by a host of stars. The sages blessed them all
by sprinkling them with water based on Vedic protocol.

63) Though Vasudev wore deerskin, all his wives wore silks and gold.
The priests were also nicely dressed, and everybody glowed
as if they were in Indra's world of endless opulence.
Lord Krishna and Lord Balarām looked on, embued with bliss.

64) The priests directed Vasudev to keep the fires alight
and honor his transcendent son with all the proper rites.
When everything was finished, Vasudev gave all the priests
donations such as land and cows and served a royal feast.

65) Each diner, king or dog, ate well and greatly pleased himself.
As Vasudev and all his wives distributed their wealth,

the time arrived for all the kings and sages to depart.
They went home slowly, pained by separation in their hearts.

66) King Nanda of Vṛndāvan, though, did not leave right away.
The Yadus, Balarām and Krishna honored him all day.
Then Vausdev, quite satisfied, took Nanda by the hand
and spoke to him in front of the assembled cowherd clan:

67, 68) "My brother, God has bound us all with knots of human love.
Though mystics meditate and heroes struggle, push and shove,
they cannot stop affection. I am sure love is divine,
for saints like you stay faithful to ungrateful hearts like mine.

When Kaṁsa dispatched demons to assail you with abuse
I languished in his jail. Since then, I have no good excuse.
I've blindly grown intoxicated by prosperity,
and, in my greed, ignored the needs of friends and family."

69) Remembering the unrenlenting friendship Nanda kept,
the self-effacing Vasudev choked up and and loudly wept.
For his part, Nanda felt so much affection he would say
"Tomorrow I must go!" for the ensuing ninety days.

70) King Nanda and the cowherds were reluctant, it appears,
for Krishna had preoccupied their minds for many years.
At last, their wagons loaded down with precious Yadu gifts,
they headed for Mathurā, though their pace was hardly swift.

71) Their relatives departed and the monsoons on the way,
the Yadus went back home to Dvārakā that very day,
ecstatic that their pilgrimage allowed them to attend
the sacrifice of Vasudev and see their long-lost friends.

Vasudeva and his Sons

72) Days later, Balarām and Krishna bowed to Vasudev.
Recalling what the sages said and how his sons behaved,
their father was at last convinced of their divinity.
He thus addressed them both by name and told them lovingly,

73-83) "O Krishna, Krishna, best of *yogīs*! Ceaseless Sankarshan!
I know You have created the material *pradhān,*[1]
the universal elements of heaven, Earth and hell,
though matter doesn't touch You when you manifest Yourselves.

[1]*The raw material elements of creation.*

Since You have fathered nature, everything that comes to be,
in any shape or fashion, is Your private property.
Whatever piece of nature that appears before my view
is for You, by You, from You, of You and within You, too.

And after making matter you make everything compelled
to move and grow and change and die by entering Yourself
within each atom as the Supersoul, the life of all.
The universe exists and breathes because you're thus installed.

Both life and matter, varied as they are, arise from You,
as does the brilliance of the sun, the glowing of the moon,
the lightning's flash, the twinkling of a million stars at night,
the permanence of mountains and the Earth's sustaining might.

In water You're refreshment, taste and sustenance combined.
In air, You're warmth and vigor of the body and the mind.
You're down and up, You're left and right, within and all around.
In all-pervading ether, You're the element of sound.

You energize the senses and allow them to perform.
You're speech, allowing sounds to gain the power to inform.
You're reason, memory and ego, and all that they bring.
You're one unchanging substance in a world of changing things.

Imprisoned in this world of ceaseless change, the foolish soul
neglects to understand You, his sublime, transcendent goal.
Though blessed with healthy human life, without You he's bereft
and wastes his chance to exit from the chains of birth and death.

You keep such souls bound up with ropes of love, life after life.
'My body is myself,' they think. 'I own my kids and wife.'

My wife and I believed You were our children taking birth,
when You were just arriving to relieve the troubled Earth.

(Brahmā Samhita meter: -| -| -|-| --| -|-)
O kindly Lord, I touch your feet for divine protection—
the very feet that end the pain of sustained connection
with birth and death. I am exhausted with all pretenses.
Enough! Enough! with all my cravings to please my senses.

When we were trapped in Kaṁsa's prison like beasts in cages,
You said You'd been our son before in some former ages.
You come and go like summer clouds. Throughout human history,
no one can fathom Your appearance and all its mystery."

(iambic heptameter)
83) Lord Krishna thought, 'My father's role eludes Brahmā, and yet
the sages' words remind him of what I made him forget.
I relish his paternal love.' With that, He bowed his head.
Replying in a gentle, smiling voice, Lord Krishna said,

84, 85) "Dear father, everything you've said describes creation well,
referring, as examples, to My brother and Myself.
Yet you and all the Yadu dynasty exemplify
the oneness of existence, Father, not just he and I.

Although He looks as different as every living being,
the bright, eternal Supersoul is one in everything.
As water may appear or disapper in many shapes,
the Supersoul appears diverse in all that He creates."

Rescuing Devaki's Sons

86) Imbibing the impression that the Lord was someone else,
Lord Krishna's father felt paternal love consume himself.
Lord Krishna's mother Devakī, however, was distressed.
She turned to her two sons, looked down, and tearfully expressed,

87-89) "O Krishna, Rāma, masters of all mystics, Lords of all!
As I see You before me I cannot help but recall
the fact that, as your mother, it appears I gave You birth
when You, in truth, descend yourselves to liberate the Earth.
A fraction of a fraction of Yourselves is all it takes
to build, maintain, and end the planets, stars and outer space.
Because success escorts whatever You decide to do,
today, my Lords, please contemplate what I now ask of You.

When all Your childhood studies at the *gurukul* were done,
I learned that You both rescued Sāndīpani Muni's son
directly from the realm of death. You surely know the fact
that I lost my six sons to Kaṁsa. Could You bring them back?"

90) As Devakī requested, Balarām and Krishna used
their mystic strength to find the boys that Kaṁsa had abused.
Arriving in the nether regions, home to the deceased,
they met the famous Balī Maharāj, his friends and priests.

91) The demon Balī, long ago, usurped Lord Indra's throne,
yet later freely gave to Krishna everything he owned.
On seeing his beloved Krishna, Balī Maharāj
stood up and bowed, along with his entire entourage.

92) He seated Krishna and His brother in his finest chairs,
and bathed their feet, dispensing sacred footwash everywhere.
He then presented clothing, jewels, food and all his wealth.
And then, as he had done before, he gave his very self.
While grasping Krishna's lotus feet upon his chest and head,
King Balī swooned in ecstasy. Then, tearfully, he said,

93-98) "Lord Krishna and Lord Balarām, I bow my head to You,
the persons whom great *yogīs* and philosophers pursue.
We living beings rarely get to see You in this way
unless You choose to show Yourselves as You have done today.

When You appear, however, even demons such as me
can set aside their pride to take the opportunity.

Some demons grow adverse to You because they are misled
while others shun the truth, preferring ignorance instead.

And others simply hate You, while still other fiends like me
associate with You to build their own prosperity.
Your mystifying energy covers up our eyes.
Indeed, the greatest *yogīs* cannot see through Your disguise.

Please take me to Your lotus feet where even I can find
necessities from generous trees and saints of loving minds.
But have I been too bold, my Lord, presenting my desire?
Have You come with a purpose? Is there something You require?
To serve You supercedes all Vedic rites and cleanses sin.
Please tell us what to do, my Lord; we're eager to begin."

98-99) Lord Krishna said, "Marīci, a great sage, once had six sons
who laughed at Lord Brahmā because of something he had done.
They thus took birth as children of Hiraṇyakaśipu
and then as sons of Devakī. They now live here with you.

King Kaṁsa killed all six of them, and Devakī laments.
We wish to stop this series of unfortunate events
by ending all their suffering—and Devakī's as well—
and sending them to heaven now that they have lived in hell."

100) As monarch of the lower planets, Balī easily
located and returned the six young sons of Devakī.
Again he worshipped Balarām and Krishna, who then left
for Dvārakā, where Devakī had so long felt bereft.

101) When she saw her lost children, Devakī became possessed
with such maternal love that milk cascaded from her breasts.
She let the babies drink that milk, which Krishna once enjoyed.
Then, tenderly, she sniffed the head of each beloved boy.

102) Entranced by Krishna's powers of illusion, Devakī
saw each young baby reassume his past identity.
The six became the gods they'd been before they misbehaved.
and bowed before Lord Krishna, Devakī and Vasudev.

The saintly Devakī was struck with wonder and deduced
she'd just seen an illusion that Lord Krishna had produced.

103, 104) Amazing as it was for Him to save His mother's sons,
Lord Krishna showed us countless marvels. This was merely one.
This pastime of Lord Krishna sanctifies the universe.
A devotee will decorate his ears with every verse.
If one repeats or hears about this wonder Krishna showed,
his mind will dwell on Krishna, and he'll gain the Lord's abode.

28

In Mithila

Arjuna Weds Subhadra

1) *Said Viṣṇurāta, "Teacher, may I raise another theme?*
My father, Abhimanyu, who was killed in his late teens,
was born to Krishna's sister, Subhadrā. I'd like to know—
how did she marry Arjuna so many years ago?"

2) When Arjuna, on pilgrimage, heard Balarām had said
that Subhadrā would marry Duryodhan, he shook his head.
"I can't agree that she should marry someone so despised."
So Arjuna decided to go see her in disguise.

3) He dressed as a renunciant. Lord Krishna, quite involved,
said nothing to His relatives and watched the scene evolve.
Lord Balarām and other family members didn't see
that Arjuna, the soldier, was their saintly company.

4) One day when Balarām invited Arjuna to dine,
Subhadrā also came. At once, Arjuna lost his mind.
He cautiously examined her with camouflaged delight.
When Subhadrā saw Arjuna, she loved him at first sight.

5) The handsome Arjuna, despite his saffron-tinted[1] robes,
attracted Subhadrā, who then intuitively chose
to shyly smile and glance at him. Within herself she knew
this holy man would be her husband. No one else would do.
[1]*Saffron robes indicate a celibate renunciate.*

6) As Arjuna's desire grew more passionate each day,
he made a plan to capture Subhadrā and get away.
At Rathayātrā[2] Arjuna arranged a final move
that Krishna and Subhadrā's parents secretly approved.
[2]*A festival featuring a large chariot (ratha) with a Deity of Viṣṇu.*

7) As she rode past amidst the joyful, colorful parade,
the fearless Arjuna sped by and carried her away.
He fought off many guards and foiled the weapons they released
exactly as a lion snatches prey from lesser beasts.

8) On hearing this, Lord Balarām grew angry as the sea
beneath a full moon pulling with its fiercest gravity.
But Krishna touched His brother's feet and, with His relatives,
convinced Him Subhadrā was pleased and begged Him to forgive.

9) The gracious Balarām calmed down and, later on, supplied
a host of precious wedding gifts to please the groom and bride.
The gifts were servants, elephants and prancing thoroughbreds.
And this was how your grandparents, O King, came to be wed.

Srutadev and Bahulasva

10) Now listen to another case of Krishna's sympathy.
A learned priest named Śrutadev, whose heart was fully free
of any needless sense desires, captured Krishna's eye.
This *brāhman* served Lord Krishna and remained quite satisfied.

11) In Mithilā, his native city, Śrutadev maintained
a simple, pious home by any alms he might obtain.
By Krishna's will, each day he somehow got enough to live,
fulfill religious duties and support his relatives.

12) The king of Mithilā was yet another pious man,
the monarch Bahulāśva. So, to see these two firsthand,
Lord Krishna filled His chariot with many saintly guests
who usually would walk but joined the Lord at His request.

13) The guests included Nārada, Vyās, Bṛhaspati,
Paraśurām, Maitreya and some others—even me.
In every town and village we drove through, a crowd would come,
for all those saints with Krishna looked like planets with the sun.

14) The citizens of many kingdoms drank the pleasing sight
of Krishna's smiling face as He threw glances left and right.
Each glance freed all who saw it from material distress,
bestowing knowledge of the truth and utter fearlessness.

15) The residents of Mithilā, each woman, child and man,
came forth to greet the party with a present in each hand.
They'd heard about Lord Krishna and this famous company,
but seeing them in person filled their hearts with ecstasy.

16) King Bahulāśva, rich and wise, came quickly on the scene
along with Śrutadev, the humble soul of modest means.
They both bowed down to Krishna's feet, believing He was there
to show His great compassion by responding to their prayers.

17) They both invited Krishna to their residence to stay,
along with all the sages in His entourage that day.
By mystic duplication, Krishna honored both requests
by going to both places at the same time—*with* His guests.

18) If you recall, Lord Krishna showed this same ability
when all His cowherd friends fell in Brahmā's captivity.
He also manifested it with sixteen thousand queens
who daily felt themselves the center of the Lord's routine.

19) King Bahulāśva saw the Lord arrive with all His friends.
He seated them on thrones, washed all their lotus feet and cleansed
the sins of all his relatives by sprinkling their heads.
"I can't believe my luck! Give them the finest gifts," he said.

20) The King received his guests with incense, silks, and many cows.
They feasted to contentment. Then, the Lord kindly allowed
the king to take His feet upon his lap for a massage.
Then, speaking gently, Bahulāśva told the entourage,

21-24) "Almighty Lord, You are the soul of all created beings.
As such, You know all hearts—including one imprudent king's
who meditates upon You day and night. You've kindly come,
responding to whatever little service he has done.

You say Brahmā or Lakṣmī or Ananta[3] are less dear
than your sincere disciples. That is surely why You're here.
What person could abandon You for any sort of wealth
when You love devotees so much You give your very self?

[3]*Ananta Śeṣa, the divine serpent upon whom Lord Viṣnu rests.*

Your deeds inspire the Yadus, where You've chosen to appear.
Discussion of Your pastimes conquers death for all who hear.
As Nara and Nārāyaṇ stay and purify their land,
please peacefully remain with us, forever if You can.

If You can't stay indefinitely, won't You kindly stay
within our humble kingdom for another several days?
My palace is more simple than Your palace; nonetheless,
please sanctify our home with all Your honored friends and guests."

25) Lord Krishna and the sages then consented to remain
to bless the citizens of Bahulāśva's fine domain.
At that time, Śrutadev was, like the king, extremely eager
to welcome Krishna's party, though his dwelling was quite meager.

26) That blissful *brāhman* bowed before Lord Krishna and His guests.
He stood and danced and waved his shawl, awash in happiness.
He borrowed mats of straw so every guest could have a seat
and, with his wife, excitedly bathed every pair of feet.

27) The joyous Śrutadev then sprinkled footwash all around
his home and on his family member's heads as they bowed down.

He then presented flowers, fruits and other simple gifts
and fed his guests with foods prepared to nourish and uplift.

28) The *brāhman* wondered, "How is it that I, a common man,
am able to see Krishna and these saintly souls firsthand?
These sages carry Krishna in their hearts; of that I'm sure.
Their footsteps carry dust that make the holy places pure."

29) His guests well fed and comfortable, Śrutadev sat down.
His children, wife and relatives sat near him on the ground.
Approaching Krishna modestly, the *brāhman* bowed his head.
He then massaged Lord Krishna's lotus feet and gently said,

30-33) "It's not that we have seen You just today, my Lord. In fact,
since You alone create and keep the universe intact,
we living beings constantly associate with You.
And yet, despite Your majesty, You walk among us, too.

As sleeping people dream entire worlds of fantasy
and see themselves within such worlds in nightime reverie,
You enter Your creation in Your chosen time and place,
untouched by the illusions that the rest of us embrace.

You stay concealed to people who pursue illusion's spells.
Though You reside in ev'ry heart, You only show yourself
to those of wholesome consciousness who always chant Your name
and hear and speak of You with other souls who do the same.

Illusion is excruciating; Krishna, You're sublime.
I much prefer to bow to You than to Your form of time
that leaves the dreaming, foolish soul defeated and subdued.
Reliever of all misery, I pray: may I serve You?"

The Glorious Brahmans

34-38) On hearing Śrutadev's address, Lord Krishna took his hand,
smiled broadly with compassion and replied, "Please understand:
these sages have come here to bless you. They remain with Me
to purify the planets that they walk on constantly.

A person slowly cleans his heart when he adorns or sees
the lovely transcendental forms of temple deities
or bathes in sacred waters in a famous holy *dham*.
How quickly, though, does one grow pure when sages come along.

Among the residents of Earth, a *brāhman* is the best,
especially when he is learned, grave and self-posessed.
A *brāhman* with devotion, though, so far exceeds the norm
that he is just as dear to Me as My own four-armed form[4].

[4]*Referring to His avatar of Lord Viṣṇu.*

As all the gods in heaven can be found within Myself,
within the hearts of learned *brāhmans*, every scripture dwells.
A fool offends the *brāhman* yet adores My deity,
not knowing he's a guru and, as such, as good as Me.

These realized *brāhmans* see Me everywhere in everything.
To worship them delights Me more than any offering.
Please serve them just as you serve Me, for doing so conveys
your faith in Me more tellingly than any other way."

39) Instructed by Lord Krishna, with attentive, focused minds,
both Śrutadev and Bahulāśva thoroughly entwined
devotion to the Lord with love for Krishna's devotees.
In Mithilā, Lord Krishna offered lessons such as these.

29

The Personified Vedas

The Absolute in Sound?

*1) At this point Viṣṇurāta asked, "Can any sort of sound—
including spoken words or even Vedic texts—propound
to properly describe the Absolute? Some men believe
that words depict dull matter well, but not divinity."*

2) *The learned Śukadev replied,* Lord Krishna gives the means
for spirit souls to function in their physical machines.
If He makes mankind able to sense ordinary sound,
can He not make them able to sense something more profound?

3) Descriptions of Lord Krishna can attract the human mind
and when one starts to serve Him, He reciprocates in kind.
Though words may be material and, therefore, circumscribed,
can God not let them make the indescribable described?

4) In any circumstances, any time or any place,
if people concentrate upon this principle with faith,
their lives will be relieved of all attachment and distress
and death, in time, will bring them to the ultimate success.

5) On various occasions, many sages in the past
replied as I shall now when others asked what you have asked.
The great sage Sanandana said as much, and then
Nārāyan Rsi said the same to Nārada again.

The Vedas Answer

6) When Sanandana heard your question from his saintly friends,
he told them of an ancient recitation that began
when Vedic texts personified, who never make mistakes,
said this to Mahā-Viṣṇu when His time came to awake:

(Meter: | - - - - - - - | - - | - | - |)
7-24) Victory to You, Lord Mahā-Viṣṇu, who can't be overcome.
Please defeat the power of illusion that troubles everyone.
Maker of the worlds, who stirs the life force within all living things,
we can sometimes see You as You sport like an incognito king.

Potters transform clay into a cup or some kind of pottery.
Ultimately, though, the cup again becomes clay by destiny.
Equally, Your energies appear, stay, and then go back inside.
Sages thus see only You, as feet touch the Earth with every stride.

Diving in the ocean of Your pastimes and great activities,
saintly persons purify their hearts and discard their miseries.
When we follow You with faith we savor the taste of ecstasy;
otherwise we sleepwalk through our lives, taking breaths unconsciously.

Yogīs seek to find You in the heart, so they sit and meditate.
Others seek You as the changeless one among those who fluctuate.
Some, however, fascinated by Your sublime activities,
leave aside their cozy homes and seek You among Your devotees.

Common people disregard the kindness and help that You provide.
Following illusion, they abandon their souls to suicide.
Certainly it's difficult for us, undergoing deaths and births,
to conceive of He who spawns the gods and creates the universe.

Even vicious demons who approach You in animosity,
due to thinking of You, gain the fruit of religiosity.
Similarly, we, who tend to see You in all-pervasiveness
someday will enjoy the love Your consorts and You exchange in bliss.

All of this is lost to so-called leaders who sit and speculate, that
matter is the cause of the creation, which You alone create.
Taking help from other fools whose teachings they tend to overrate,
they assume the soul and flesh are one and will both disintegrate.

Goodness, passion, ignorance; these three modes impose their sovereignty
on the soul, as man or beast or insect. And yet, concurrently,
sages know that its creator gives concrete value to this Earth.
Anything comprised of gold is gold, which has fundamental worth.

Therefore devotees within this world find their strength in You instead.
Loving you, they're purified and trample on death's relentless head.
Others remain captured, like a beast, by Your mundane energies,
in spite of how erudite and cultured they may appear to be.

Even sense attachment thrives because You have made it possible.
You sustain our mundane senses, though Yours are fully spiritual.
As the district rulers gather taxes to give to royalty,
gods themselves present to You the offerings of their devotees.

If we were God too, we souls would not need to be obedient.
How long can a thing defy the sole source of its ingredients?
Bodies come and go like ocean foam, but all souls eventually
join You in a way that suits their own individuality.

Those who understand all this serve You, Lord, in transcendental love.
In this world of death, Your servants have nothing to be frightened of.
They take help from gurus, though the mind is inclined to act alone,
for what good is a boat without a captain to guide it safely home?

When You share eternal loving bliss with authentic devotees,
they lose their attachment to their finances, sex and families.
Focused on Your service and residing in sites of pilgrimage,
faultless devotees uplift mankind as they find the highest stage.

Others say that, since it comes from you, everything is permanent.
Sometimes, though, a cause and its effect are completely different.
Something that is true can conjure something that is illusory;
something that is fleeting can be born out of vast eternity.

Fools imagine something that can't last will amass them happiness,
thinking their ideas, so awry, justify their ignorance.
We have found our happiness in you, Lord, for on the face of it,
nothing we enjoy came to exist until You created it.

Māyā stumps the soul and then embodies him with her qualities, but
You avoid her power, as a snake sheds its withered skin with ease.
Yogīs who are still attached, yet outwardly not declaring it,
have the jewel of You on their necks, but don't know they're wearing it.

Knowing You means one will not disdain some mundane catastrophe.
He will neither choose the upper class, lower class, nor bourgeoisie.
Such a person simply fills his ears with the famous dialogues
spoken about You by noted sages and leading demigods.

Nobody, however, man or god, can know You entirely.
Even You cannot describe Your glories in their entirety.
How can we, the Vedic scriptures, claim to attain describing You, when
universes, numerous as dust specks, reside inside of You?"

(iambic heptameter)
25) The saintly Sanandana's recitation reached its end,
delighting the assembly of his relatives and friends.
Nārāyaṇ Rsi taught all this to Nārada in turn,
who taught it to my father. Now, from him, we all have learned.

26) You asked how God exists as sound, and now I have replied.
You've heard His endless qualities; I hope you're satisfied.
Surrendering to Krishna, you'll forget *māyā*'s embrace
as dreamers leave their flesh behind and find a better place.

30

Vishnu

Shiva's Devotees Wealthier?

1) Said Viṣṇurāta"Why are Krishna's devotees so poor?
Lord Śiva's devotees, in general, seem to own much more.
Since Krishna is much wealthier than Śiva, I suspect,
this fact seems just the opposite of what one would expect."

2) Lord Śiva interacts with matter; that is his domain.
Appeasing Śiva makes objectives easy to obtain.
Lord Krishna, on the other hand, transcends the mundane realm;
His devotees, like Him, are pure and never overwhelmed.
Your grandfather, King Yudhiṣṭhir, once raised this paradox
directly to Lord Krishna, who responded with these thoughts:

3, 4) "When someone truly pleases me, I pilfer all his wealth.
His relatives and friends then leave this beggar to himself.
Abandoned, sad and thwarted, he befriends My devotees
and quickly gains My mercy in exceptional degrees.

Although I give enlightenment and freedom from distress,
conditioned souls, in general, want to keep what they possess.

So they appeal to gods who are much easier to please—
though when they thrive, they sometimes try to kill their deities."

5) Lord Śiva, Lord Brahmā and the supreme Lord Viṣṇu all
can elevate a person or create a person's fall.
Unlike Lord Viṣṇu, Śiva and Brahmā are quickly pleased,
as wicked Vṛka once confirmed by his activities.

The Story of Vrika

6) The demon Vṛka met the saintly Nārada one day
and asked which god would fill his wish the most efficient way.
Said Nārada, "If you ask nicely, Śiva won't take long,
but he gets angry instantly if you do something wrong."

7) So Vṛka worshipped Śiva with a sick, bizarre device:
he cut his flesh and burned it in the fire of sacrifice.
A week went by. Impatient, Vṛka dropped that plan; instead,
he washed his hair and bared his ax, prepared to cut his head.

8) As Vṛka poised to lop his head directly in the fire,
Lord Śiva swiftly grabbed his arm and mercifully inquired,
"What is it that you want, my friend? Here, let me mend your wounds.
Why give your head? A cup of water's fine! I'll grant your boon."

9) The crooked Vṛka cackled as he gave this sick reply:
"When I touch someone's head, I wish that he at once shall die."
Lord Śiva showed consent and gave his head a little shake,
although he feared that he was giving nectar to a snake.

10) To test Lord Śiva's blessing, Vṛka raised his hand and said,
"I'd like, my Lord, to see if this will work upon *your* head."
Lord Śiva turned, and, terrified, fled swiftly into space.
The mystic Vṛka ran behind and managed to keep pace.

11) Since no one counteracts the boon that Śiva has bestowed,
the gods could only stare as Śiva ran through their abode.
At last he reached the sea of milk, that luminous domain
inhabited by Viṣṇu, that the greatest souls attain.

12) Lord Viṣṇu knew that Śiva had been threatened with demise
and stepped in to protect him by assuming a disguise.
Appearing five or six years old, with beads and deerskin dress,
Lord Viṣṇu summoned Vṛka, smiled, and pleasantly expressed:

13) "My dear, respected sir, you've come so far. You must be tired.
Please stop and rest your body, for your body is required
for any great pursuit. That's good, relax. Now, if I'm fit,
please tell me of your mission. I would love to hear of it."

14, 15) Lord Viṣṇu's words pleased Vṛka, and the demon gladly stayed,
explaining, in complete detail, his clever escapade.
The youthful student listened well, then shook his head in doubt.
"In this case," said the student, "we have something to find out.

This Śiva, cursed by Dakṣa, gobbles flesh in ghostly haunts.
He gives his fellow ghosts and goblins anything they want.
His blessing must be useless. Quickly, touch your head and see,
for if he lied, you must reply and end his treachery."

16) Enchanted and bewildered by the student's artful words,
the foolish Vṛka touched his head. A piercing blast was heard
as Vṛka's head exploded. Then, their voices joined as one,
the gods cried out in admiration, "Victory! Well done!"

17) As denizens of heaven showered flowers on the scene,
Lord Viṣṇu said, "Lord Śiva, Vṛka's deeds were so obscene,
he met a violent destiny. What else could he expect,
offending you, a kindly guru, wise in all respects?"

18) Lord Krishna, Viṣṇu's origin, directly manifests
the energies of matter, spirit, truth, and all the rest.
A soul who hears or tells how Śiva's problem was dispelled
shall overcome his enemies—and birth and death as well.

Brghu's Quest

19) To show how Viṣṇu differs from Brahmā and all the rest,
I'll tell you of some *brāhmans* who performed a certain test.
They sent the learned Bṛghu Muni to research and see:
was Viṣṇu, Śiva or Brahmā the foremost deity?

20) "I'll see who is most tolerant," thought Bṛghu. To inspect,
he went to Lord Brahmā's abode but failed to genuflect.
Brahmā became quite angry, but before he came undone
he managed to control himself, for Bṛghu was his son.

21) To Mount Kailās went Bṛghu, where Lord Śiva domiciles.
The sage was Śiva's brother; they'd not met in quite a while.
When Śiva came to hug him, Bṛghu turned away and said,
"You're nothing but a deviant." His brother's eyes burned red.

22) Lord Śiva raised his trident and was set to make a kill
when Pārvati, his wife, stepped in with diplomatic skill.
Escaping to Vaikuṇṭha, where Lord Viṣṇu lay at rest,
the daring Bṛghu marched to Him and kicked Him in the chest.

23) Arising from his bedstead with his lovely consort, Śrī,
Lord Viṣṇu bowed and said profoundly, "Kindly pardon Me.
Your tender, sacred foot has made Me purified and blessed;
from now on, Śrī, the queen of weath, shall live upon My chest."

24) This solemn speech left Bṛghu stunned; he couldn't say a word.
Reactions to his first two tests were nothing like the third.
His heart full of devotion for Lord Viṣṇu, he returned
and told his fellow *brāhmans* what he positively learned:

25) "Dear friends, there are offenses of the body, speech and mind.
I tested these three Lords with a transgression of each kind.
Lord Viṣṇu was so gracious he accepted my offense
as if it were an offering; the others were incensed."

26) Amazed and swayed, the *brāhmans* prayed, "Lord Viṣṇu is the source
of courage, peace, religion, wisdom, truth and mystic force.

Those saints of keen intelligence adore Him selflessly
without a secret motive to enjoy His energies."

Though Viṣṇu pardoned Bṛghu and the *brāhmans*, ever since
the *brāhmans* gain but poverty from Śrī for their offense.

The Brahman's Sons Saved

27) Another time, Lord Krishna and Arjuna went to see
Lord Viṣṇu in His own abode. Now, listen carefully,
for walking on this worldly path reduces us to tears
unless the fragrant nectar of Lord Krishna fills our ears.

28) In Dvārakā, a brahaman's wife once bore a baby son
who died before he touched the Earth. The father, deeply stunned,
laid out the corpse upon King Ugrasen's palatial stairs.
Lamenting and distraught, the *brāhman* said, in great despair:

29) "This greedy, lying king has ruled his kingdom with such fault
my blameless newborn son has passed away as a result.
The subjects of this violent, self-indulgent monarchy
are doomed to suffer poverty and constant misery."

30) The *brāhman* lost his second son, and then, again, his third.
He laid the blame on Ugrasen each time this occurred.
The ninth time, Krishna and Arjuna, nearby, overheard.
Distressed, Arjuna then addressed the father with these words:

31) "Will not one single royal warrior stand and guard your door?
Why do your so-called rulers leave you wretched and ignored?
A kingdom in which *brāhmans* lose their children, wealth or wives
is ruled by mere imposters leading sedentary lives.
Dear *brāhman*, I won't tolerate a loss so grim and dire.
I vow to save your children, or—I swear, I'll enter fire!"

32) The *brāhman* said, "What Balarām and Krishna couldn't do
is far beyond your powers. Why on Earth should I trust you?"

33) Arjuna, grave, said firmly, “You are partially correct;
I’m neither Balarām nor Krishna; still, I will protect
your future children from their brothers’ strange fatalities.
You’ll come to know my powers. Even Śiva has been pleased.”

34) The *brāhman* became reassured and went home satisfied.
Returning to Arjuna when the next child came, he cried,
“Please, save my child from death!” Arjuna, fast as he could go,
said prayers to Śiva, chanted hymns and strung his famous bow.

35) Arjuna rushed directly to the cottage of the sage,
surrounding it with mystic arrows structured as a cage.
The *brāhman*’s wife delivered a fine boy who cooed and cried.
Yet after a few minutes, he just vanished in the sky.

36) The *brāhman* wept and told Arjuna, “I was so unwise
to trust a bragging eunuch in a warrior’s disguise.
God damn your lies Arjuna, and your weapons and your fame.
You said this child would stay, but now his fate is just the same!”

37) Arjuna didn’t hear these words, for he was occupied
traversing to the planet where the Lord of death resides.
The infant wasn’t there, nor up in heaven, nor in hell.
Arjuna, with the case unsolved, resolved to kill himself.

38) Arjuna, planning suicide, stopped short when Krishna said,
“I’ll take you to those boys; it’s not your fault that they are dead.
These men who criticize you now will shortly sing your praise.
Now join Me on my chariot.” With that, they rode away.

39) They traveled through the universe and then its outer shell.
When all turned dark, the horses balked, for they could not see well.
The master of all kinds of mystics, Krishna, tossed his disc,
which lit the scene around the team with perfect vividness.

40) Like one of Rāmacandra’s arrows, Krishna’s disc shot through
the inky ignorance with which this cosmos is imbued.
Beyond that realm of darkness lay the spiritual sky;
its shining outskirts made Arjuna blind. He shut his eyes.

41) Beyond that bright effulgent light, Arjuna saw a sea
endowed with giant windswept waves that churned resplendently.
A gorgeous palace rose above the waves, its charm enhanced
by countless jeweled pillars. How Arjuna was entranced!

42) The mammoth serpant Śeṣa lay upon his back within,
his thousands of enormous hoods lit up by shining gems.
His massive body, whiter than a mountain clad with snow,
set off his necks and hissing tongues of blue and indigo.

43) Lord Mahā-Viṣṇu lay upon the serpant's underside,
attended by His many energies personified.
A brilliant yellow robe adorned His skin of raincloud-blue;
His hair reflected radiance that graced His crown and jewels.
Of all His gems, Kaustubha, midst his garlands, was the best;
the famous mark, *śrīvatsa,* showed quite clearly on His chest.

44) Lord Krishna bowed His head to this expansion of Himself.
Arjuna, quite astonished at the sight, bowed down as well.
Lord Mahā-Viṣṇu, our Creator, smiled majestically
and stated in a solemn voice of great authority:

45) "I brought the *brāhman*'s sons here to induce you both to come.
Though you are Nara and Nārāyaṇ, lately you've become
engaged in killing demons. By your work, the Earth is free.
Continue your religious deeds; they're most exemplary."

46) Though Mahā-Viṣṇu always stays in Krishna's full control,
He gave commands to Krishna as an actor plays a role.
Because Arjuna thought Lord Viṣṇu senior to His friend,
the Lords spoke so Arjuna could directly comprehend.

47) Instructed by Lord Viṣṇu, Krishna and Arjuna bowed
and took the ten still-infant sons past oceans, space and clouds
back to their joyful parents. Still, Arjuna, quite amazed,
thought, "Why would Mahā-Viṣṇu call for Krishna in this way?"

31

Krishna

Krishna's Family

1) In Dvārakā, Lord Krishna and His sixteen thousand wives
enjoyed, with all the citizens, divinely lavish lives.
While calvalry, bedecked in gold, patrolled attractive streets,
the cuckoos, bees, and larks used landscaped parks as their retreats.

2) Parading giant elephants enjoyed a jubilee.
Each one of Krishna's wives saw Him as private property.
In sixteen thousand palace grounds, they frolicked in clear ponds,
embracing amid lotus flowers, cooing birds and swans.

3) While singers sang and drummers drummed and bards recited verse,
the Lord's wives filled syringes and pushed out incessant squirts.
They doused the Lord, and He doused them in blissful spousal sport,
while laughing and enjoying life like gods in Indra's court.

4) Their saris drenched, their royal breasts and thighs shown in relief,
the queens brushed back their slackened braids and, swift as any thief,
would try to steal the Lord's syringe with clever thrusts and fakes
yet always, somehow, wound up smiling in His warm embrace.

5) Lord Krishna so enjoyed this play. Hair scattered on His head,
He pressed His garland to His spouses' breasts and turned it red.
Repeatedly He sprayed his wives and they sprayed Him in turn
like elephants might play in jungle lakes without concern.

6) When all this fun was over, they went in to change their dress
and brought their moistened silks and precious gems to give their guests.
In this way Krishna spent his days and played the husband's part.
With glances, smiles and laughter, He enthralled His consorts' hearts.
Lord Krishna's queens, unstable in their bliss with Him, appeared
to go insane. In ecstasty, they spoke like this. Please hear:

The Queens' Ecstasy

(Brahmā Samhita meter: -| -| -|-| --| -|-)
7-13) Dear cranes and ospreys, it is night but instead of sleeping
you're wide awake. Is it because in your heart you're keeping
Lord Krishna's smiling, playful glance? There is no denying;
like us, you're hankering for Krishna; we hear you crying.

Dear ocean, are you also sleepless? We hear you roaring.
Are you the sea of milk, and hopeless of now restoring
the famed Kaustubha gem and Lakṣmī, of blessed endeavor,
whom Krishna took from you and keeps on His chest forever?

Dear moon, you're dim. Are you diseased, or, like us, forgetful
of promises that Krishna gave you when you were fretful?
Dear breeze, are you displeased? We feel how your touch enhances
our lusty hearts, already struck by Govinda's glances.

Dear cloud, we see that you love Krishna, for you protect Him
from scorching sunlight and the sunburn that might affect Him.
Like us, you crave Him, as your teardrops are now expressing.
Associating with this Krishna is so depressing!

Dear cuckoo, how your song reminds us of Krishna's speaking.
We wish to serve you, friend. Is there anything you're seeking?
Dear silent mountain peaks, like us, do you wish to be blessed
by Krishna's footprints falling softly upon your raised breasts?

Dear rivers, you have grown so dry. What has made you shrivel?
Have you become attached to Krishna, who's so uncivil
He now withholds those loving looks that you found endearing?
No wonder all your lotus flowers are disappearing.

Dear swan, please sit and drink some milk. We know Krishna sent you.
Did He forget what He told us—or does He pretend to?
Tell Him to come to us and show some reciprocation
and leave behind the queen of fortune for this occasion."

(iambic heptameter)
14) The simple act of speaking these ecstatic, loving thoughts
allowed Lord Krishna's wives to thus revive their love of God.
If hearing of Lord Krishna can make someone feel this way
imagine how His wives loved Him—they saw Him every day.

Lord Krishna's Family

15) Lord Krishna, as a householder, performed the proper rites
to show the perfect mix of wealth, religion and delight.
Not only did He show us how to lead religious lives;
He did so after gathering some sixteen thousand wives!

16) The absolute Lord Krishna, whose endeavor never fails,
begot, in every single wife, one female and ten males.
Lord Krishna's kindred thus expanded exponentially.
The leading son, Pradyumna, was His child by Rukminī.

17) Pradyumna's son was Aniruddha, who would sire, in time,
a son named Vajra who, in turn, preserved the family line.
The countless Yadu offspring never suffered from ill health,
distaste for being spiritual, or lack of sons or wealth.

18) King Ugrasen brought countless teachers in to educate
and servants, too, in quantities too large to calculate.
As demons born as humans sullied Earth with their demands,
Lord Krishna stopped them with the help of gods born in His clan.

19) The Yadus gave Lord Krishna their unbounded loyalty.
His closest friends especially enjoyed prosperity.
While having talks or taking walks or sitting to refresh,
they thought of Krishna always, undistracted by their flesh.

Blessings

(Meter: | - - - | - - - | - - | - | -)
20, 21) As we now are coming to the end of this long narration,
let me offer Krishna my respectful appreciation.
Formerly, the Ganges was the first place of veneration;
now it is the Yadu dynasty, Krishna's own relations.
Enemy or friend, to see Lord Krishna provides salvation;
Lakṣmī stays with Him, although she's mankind's infatuation.
Every truth has Krishna as its source and its sole foundation,
for simply saying, "Krishna" will destroy one's contamination.
Wielding as He does the disc of time with its sharp gyrations,
only Krishna rescues Mother Earth in her desperation.
That He is the son of Devakī is no limitation;
Krishna dwells in every living being throughout creation.
Krishna's very presence brings all sin to annihilation.
Krishna's smile imbues the *gopīs*' hearts with anticipation.
Krishna conquers others, too, in various incarnations.
May you ever hear of Krishna's deeds as your meditation.
May He ever stay with you in glorious jubilation!

(iambic heptameter)
22) By hearing and repeating and reflecting on my words—
the matchless deeds of Krishna, stated just as they occurred—
you'll surely grow more fascinated, faithful and sincere,
and soon move on to Krishna's world, where death invokes no fear.
For Krishna, many souls, both rich and poor, like you and me,
have overthrown the lives they'd known to dance in ecstasy.

– End of the Tenth Canto of the *Bhagavat Purana* –

Epilogue

(Excerpts from Cantos Eleven and Twelve of the *Bhagavat Purana*)

Krishna Departs

Śukadev told Viṣṇurāta that after Krishna relieved the Earth's burden by killing many demons and annihilating the world's armies at the battle of Kurukṣetra, He considered that His own dynasty, the powerful Yadus, remained a burden.

"No outside force could kill the Yadus," Krishna thought, "but if I arrange a quarrel they will destroy themselves. They will kill each other just as a bamboo grove burns to the ground, ignited by friction created by the wind agitating the stalks."

So Krishna arranged for a number of esteemed *brāhmans* to curse His family.

Viṣṇurāta was confused. "How could *brāhmans*, who always respect the Lord, curse His family? And how could a quarrel arise among the Yadus, who all shared the same goal in life?"

Śukadev explained that, one day an assembly of sages, having completed religious rites in the house of Krishna's father, retired to a nearby holy place. Samba, a young son of Krishna, dressed as a pregnant woman and approached the sages with some of his playmates. Pointing at Samba, the playmates said, "Dear sages, you can see the future. Please tell us if this woman will give birth to a male or female child."

The sages, angered by this mockery, replied, "She will give birth to a club that will destroy your family."

The boys drew their breath, stunned by the sages' unusually sharp tone. They removed the covering from Samba's abdomen. There, to their horror, was an iron club. "What have we done," they wailed. "Is our family doomed?"

The terrified boys ran to Ugrasen, the Yadu king, and confessed. After hearing the whole story, King Ugrasen reassured them. Without consulting Lord Krishna, Ugrasen had the iron club ground into slivers. Only a single lump remained intact. King Ugrasen then had all of this tossed into the sea and considered the matter resolved.

The sea carried the iron slivers to the shore at Prabhāsa, where they grew into a grove of reeds that were in fact sharp iron rods. A large fish swallowed the remaining lump of iron.

In time, a fisherman caught this same fish, and a hunter named Jarā purchased it. On slicing open the fish's stomach, Jarā was pleasantly surprised to find the iron lump. He fashioned the pure metal into a sharp arrowhead, attached it to a shaft and put it in his quiver.

Sometime later, the Yadu men gathered at the beach at Prabhāsa to perform a religious ritual. After the ceremony, in a buoyant mood, they began drinking a mild wine brewed from rice.

The Yadus were not used to drinking any sort of alcohol, and soon they were drunk. Impelled by the *brāhmans*' curse, they began to chide each other in good humor. Someone took offense, and suddenly the mood turned ugly.

The powerful Yadus began shouting at each other. Their angry words led to blows, and when fists weren't enough, the pulled nearby reeds to use as weapons. Much to their surprise, the reeds were like sharp iron rods in their hands, ideal weapons for continuing the pitched fight. Thus armed, the mighty Yadu warriors, whom no one else could kill, began killing each other.

Krishna and Balarām soon arrived and tried to make peace amid the carnage. Too enraged to listen, the wild-eyed Yadus turned their wrath on the brothers, their ultimate leaders. While defending themselves from their maddened relatives, Krishna and Balarām quickly dispatched the survivors.

"Now," Krishna thought, "the last needless military force on Earth is finished."

Balarām, through with His earthly pastimes, promptly left. He sat in meditation under a nearby tree and then returned to the spiritual world.

Krishna went to a nearby *pippala* tree and sat down in the shade.

Nearby, the hunter Jarā spotted the pinkish sole of Krishna's lotus foot as He sat. Mistaking it for a deer, he shot the arrow tipped with the fated iron arrowhead. It merely grazed Krishna's foot.

Dashing on the scene in search of his prey, Jarā was shocked to find his arrow next to Krishna's wounded foot. He fell before Lord Krishna and begged to be punished.

In a past life, Jarā had been the inquisitive Bṛghu Muni who once kicked Lord Viṣṇu in the chest. As a result of that offense, Bṛghu was forced to take birth as a low-born hunter and play a role in Krishna's pastimes that would fill him with regret. Seeing Jarā had completed this role, Krishna sent him back to the spiritual world.

Krishna's eternal body can never be injured. Still, to satisfy atheists, He manifested a material body and left it as a cadaver, all the while remaining self-satisfied in His eternally blissful form. He too then left this world for His eternal abode.

Prophecies For Kali-Yuga

Krishna had departed Earth, as had the Pāndavas, King Viṣṇurāta's relatives. Viṣṇurāta, too, was about to die and had asked for direction from Śukadev. Śukadev reminded the King that the goal of everyone, especially one who sees death's ever-present hand, is to think, hear and speak about Krishna. The King understood that attending to Krishna awakens joy in this world and leads to His company in the next.

Śukadev then gave a chronology of what was to come after the King's departure.

For the next 4200 years (roughly through the 12th century, AD), a series of kings would rule India and other parts of the Earth. Each monarch would be more evil and greedy than the last. Their subjects would imitate their behavior, leading the entire world to increasingly sad and degraded conditions.

Bad rulers and social conditions indicate Kali, the age of degradation. To give the King a taste of Kali's coming influence, Śukadev recited these prophetic descriptions:

In Kali-yuga, a man's behavior and qualities will be evaluated by his wealth. The ability to deceive will determine success in business. Audacity will be mistaken for honesty.

Low-class people who manipulate through greed and fear will gain power. Such leaders will use their office to extort property and exile honest citizens, who will in turn suffer all kinds of discomforts. Law and justice will be applied only according to one's power.

Men and women will live together for sex without benefit of marriage. Family ties, if they exist at all, will rarely extend beyond the immediate family. A male-supported nuclear family will become increasingly rare.

People will take the role of religious leaders by simply donning robes. One who can cleverly juggle words will become known as a great scholar. The path of the *Vedas* will be lost, and whatever passes as religion will be mostly materialistic and godless.

Man or woman, one's beauty will be judged by one's hairstyle. The maximum human life span will be fifty years.[1] Human bodies, as well as crops and trees, will become smaller and weaker.

Concluding his prophecies, Śukadev said, "By the end of the Kali age, honest, religious people will have been hunted to near extinction. Crude, animalistic men dressed as kings will dominate the Earth. At that time Krishna will appear as Kalki, the son of Viṣṇuyashā, in the village of Śambhala. He will destroy these imposter kings and their followers. The survivors will repopulate the Earth. Kalki heralds the end of the Kali age and the beginning of a fresh age of goodness."

"The *Bhāgavat Purana* has described everything about Krishna," said Śukadev. His kindly eyes narrowed as he gazed at the King. "Now, let's discuss your situation."

Pausing for a moment, Śukadev continued in a clear, firm tone, "Give up the animalistic mentality of thinking, 'I am going to die.' Your body has taken birth, but you have not. There has never been a time in the past when you didn't exist, and you are not going to be destroyed now.

"Think about this logically. In a dream you may see your own head being cut off. Then you can understand that your actual self is standing apart from the dream. Otherwise, how could you see it? Similarly, when you're spiritually awake, you can see your body made of matter. Therefore you, the eternal soul, are distinct from this body you are observing. When you break a pot, the portion of space within the pot remains. In the same way, when your material body dies, you, the soul, remain. Remember this and you will easily resume your spiritual identity."

"Now," Śukadev concluded, "is there anything else you wish to hear?"

King Viṣṇurāta bowed and said, "It's not surprising that people like you, with minds absorbed in Krishna, are kind to foolish people like me, tormented as we are by material problems. With your help,

1 Modern medical advances have extended the average life span, unless we consider abortions. In that case, the average life span of a human being conceived in the modern world is in fact diminishing.

now that I have absorbed myself in Krishna, I have no fear of death. Please give me your permission to think of Krishna and leave this world."

Śukadev raised his hand in a blessing. The king and all the many sages offered their respects to Śukadev.

Then, as suddenly as he had come, Śukadev got up and left.

King Viṣṇurāta walked to the bank of the Ganges and sat down. With perfect concentration he thought of Krishna in his heart and forgot everything else.

At that moment, Takṣaka, a venomous snake-bird, was flying swiftly toward the King. Seeing his opportunity, the mystic creature assumed the guise of a sage and stepped easily through the assembly toward the meditating Viṣṇurāta. Changing back to his original form, the vicious Takṣaka abruptly bit Viṣṇurāta. The intense poison of his venom ignited the King's body, reducing it to ashes in an instant.

Everyone sat in stunned silence. Then a great cry of anguish arose amongst the sages. In their grief they cried out, "Who will protect us now?"

Within a moment, their wails were drowned out by the sounds of kettledrums and sweet words of praise descending from above. The shocked sages looked skyward. There, in heaven, the gods and saints had begun a celebration.

A great soul had just gone back to Krishna.

Conclusion

Where do I go from here?

Though materialists take the *Bhāgavat Purana* to be mythology, thoughtful people recognize its urgent relevance. As our bodies move closer to death every day, materialistic teachers, leaders and advertisers advise, "Forget about dealing with it. Distract yourself with this activity or cause or product instead."

To make matters worse, we're in the age of Kali. In this age, nearly all people believe they are their bodies. Actual knowledge of the soul is all but extinct.

Although Krishna departed just before Kali began, the *Bhāgavat Purana*'s Eleventh Canto predicts Krishna will return as a special *avatār* for the Kali age:

In the age of Kali, intelligent persons perform congregational chanting to worship the incarnation of Godhead who constantly sings the names of Krishna. Although His complexion is not blackish, He is Krishna Himself. He is accompanied by His associates, servants, spiritual weapons and confidential companions. (BP. 11.5.32).

As prophesized thousands of years earlier, five hundred years ago the renowned Śrī Caitanya appeared in Bengal. There he organized a *sankīrtan* movement that spread throughout India and eventually the entire world. *Sankīrtan* refers to the congregational chanting of God's names without sectarianism, obligation or price.

According to the foremost authorities on Krishna, Srī Caitanya was Krishna Himself, assuming the role of a devotee in order to taste ecstatic love of God. Encouraging all to chant the names of Krishna, He taught, "There are no hard and fast rules for chanting the names of God."

One can begin chanting anywhere and anytime without changing anything else. Chanting increases the ability to hear Krishna sitting in one's heart. With help internally from Krishna in the heart and externally from new friends whom Krishna sends, one breaks attachments and extracts oneself from materialism.

Today, millions around the world enjoy Śrī Caitanya's teachings and chant the *mahāmantra*: Hare Krishna, Hare Krishna, Krishna

Krishna, Hare Hare, Hare Rāma, Hare Rāma, Rāma Rāma, Hare Hare. This simple appeal means, 'My dear Lord Krishna, please allow me to serve You.' Lord Caitanya left this sublime and easy meditation especially for people feeling trapped in the dark materialistic age of Kali.

By chanting Krishna's names, as well as reading and grasping this book, you will gain a basic understanding of Krishna and, perhaps, a taste for learning more. If you do want more, there is no shortage. You can explore Śrīla Prabhupāda's full, definitive editions of *Bhagavad-gītā* and *Bhāgavat Purana,* books that for the first time have brought a transformative understanding of Krishna outside of India. You can further explore other translated Sanskrit classics about Krishna such as the *Mahabharata,* the *Brahmā-samhita* and the *Bhakti-Rāsāmrta sindhu* (translated by Śrīla Prabhupāda as the *Nectar of Devotion*). All of these books and more are available at Krishna.com.

Great peace of mind awaits one whose happiness no longer depends on a fragile, doomed material body. And peace of mind is just the beginning. A sweet, natural and empowering relationship with Krishna grows in the heart as one practices *bhakti yoga* by chanting Krishna's names, hearing about and serving Him.

One who practices these simple methods of *bhakti* yoga very soon dances with Krishna.

Acknowledgements

Heartfelt thanks to these individuals who helped bring this book to print.

Śrīla Prabhupāda, my spiritual father, who lovingly and skillfully gave the science of Krishna to the world and turned on the lights in so many dark lives.

Jita, my loving and supportive wife

Nitai Ram Poddar, who critiqued the prose sections of this book.

Krishna-kṛpa Prabhu, who critiqued the poetry sections.

Dr. Howard Resnick and Dr. Kiyokazu Okita for technical help and guidance.

Caitanyacarana, Devadatta, Dina Bandhu, Nimāi Pandit and Keshihanta Prabhus who edited, proofread and offered valuable editorial advice.

Dr. Frank Orlando for his pre-publication review.

Alister Taylor, of the founder and director of Torchlight Press.

Jahnudvip and Manideep Prabhus who did the cover design and layout.

The artists of the Bhaktivedanta Book Trust for the wonderful paintings of Krishna.

My beloved friends, teachers and students who encourage me to write.

My gracious friends who contributed the printing costs and chose to do so anonymously (gupta dhan). May Lord Krishna always bless you.

Appendix

Subsections of this version of the *Bhagavat Purana*, Tenth Canto